Dismembering the

Men's Bodies, Britain and the Great War

PICTURING HISTORY

Series editors
Peter Burke
Sander L. Gilman
Ludmilla Jordanova

Dismembering the Male
Men's Bodies, Britain and the Great War

Joanna Bourke

E M U.

REAKTION BOOKS

Published by Reaktion Books Ltd
33 Great Sutton Street,
London, EC1V 0DX, UK

www.reaktionbooks.co.uk

First published 1996
First published in paperback 1999
Transferred to digital printing 2009

Designed by Humphrey Stone
Jacket design by Ron Costley
Photoset by Wilmaset Ltd, Birkenhead, Wirral
Printed and bound in Great Britain by
CPI Antony Rowe, Chippenham and Eastbourne

British Library Cataloguing in Publication Data

Bourke, Joanna.
    Dismembering the male: men's bodies, Britain & the Great War.
    – (Picturing history) 1. Body, human – Social aspects – Great Britain
    2. Men – Great Britain – History – 20th century 3. World War, 1914–1918
    4. Great Britain – History – George V, 1910–1936
    I. Title II. Series
    941´.083

ISBN 978 1 86189 035 1

Contents

Acknowledgements

The research for this book has been made pleasurable by the companionship of many people. Jay M. Winter's thoughtful counsel changed the course of the book. Avner Offer reminded me of the humanity as much as the inhumanity of war. The inspiration given to me by David Fitzpatrick cannot be adequately acknowledged. Thank you.

I am fortunate to be working within an extremely supportive and stimulating department at Birkbeck College. My students have frequently found themselves sitting through early versions of the book. I thank them for their patience. My colleagues at Birkbeck are some of my closest friends. In particular, I want to thank Emma Dench, Costas Douzinas, Marianne Elliott, Richard Evans, David Feldman, Marybeth Hamilton, Vanessa Harding, Michael Hunter, Emma Mason, Dorothy Porter, Hilary Sapire, Michael Slater, Ros Tatham and Paula Woodley. Michael R. Leaman and Harry Gilonis of Reaktion Books provided me with much useful criticism and support. Susan Haskins was an exemplary copy editor. Within an increasingly competitive academic environment, the generous advice of colleagues is particularly valuable. It is impossible to mention all the people who commented on parts of the book during seminars and conferences and who encouraged me in the process of writing it. However, thanks must go to my family, Vincent Brome, Nicholas Brown, Peter Burke, Martin Chalk, Hera Cook, Roger Cooter, Peter Dolan, Dominick Dumbar, Peter Edwards, Michele Field, William Foot, Roy Foster, Mark Harrison, Robin Haines, Cecilia Ishmael, Ken Inglis, Marie-Lou Legg, Peter Londey, Alistair Lunn, Iain McCalman, Oliver MacDonagh, Bert Massie, George Mosse, Jim Obelkevich, Anna Pierre, Roy Porter, Robin Prior, John Remy, Peter Rickard, Juanita Roche, Edward Sands, Jonathan Schofield, Barry Smith, Peter Stanley, Kosmas Tsokhas, Trevor Wilson and (most especially) C. Kaye.

This book could not have been completed without financial help from the Birkbeck College Research Fund and the British Academy. I hope they will consider their money well invested. Many people kindly gave me permission to quote from letters, diaries and unpublished manuscripts found in various archives: there are too many to name, but my work could not have been contemplated without their donations to archives and generous agreement to allow me to use their material. The staff at the following archives and libraries kindly searched dusty shelves for some of their more obscure collections: Belfast Central Library, Birmingham City Library, Bristol Record Office, the British Library, the British Library of Political and Economic Science, Cambridge Central Library, Cambridge University Library, the Contemporary Medical Archives Centre at the Wellcome Institute for the the History of Medicine, the Costume and Fashion Research Centre, the Imperial War Museum, the Kings' Regiment Collection at the National Museums and Galleries on Merseyside, the Labour History Archive, the Lancashire Record Office, the Liddell Hart Centre for Military Archives, the Liddle Collection of First World War Archive Material, Liverpool Local History and Records Office, Liverpool University Archives, Manchester City Council Local Studies Unit, the Modern Records Centre, the Public Record Office, the Public Record Office of Northern Ireland, Queen's University Library, the Royal Association for Disability and Rehabilitation, University of Birmingham Library, University of Bristol Library and the Wigan Archives Service. In addition, many archives and libraries granted me permission to use some of their pictures in my book. Particular thanks must go to the staff at the Imperial War Museum: their friendliness and practical suggestions were greatly appreciated. In addition, copyright permission has been granted by the Bath Museums Service, Birmingham Central Library, the British Library, the Liddell Hart Centre of Military Archives and the Photograph Library of the Bibliothèque de Documentation Internationale Contemporaine, Paris.

Abbreviations

CMAC: Contemporary Medical Archives Centre
(Wellcome Institute for the History of Medicine)

IWM: Imperial War Museum

MDRP: Men's Dress Reform Party

MRC: Modern Records Centre, Coventry

NAS: National Association of Schoolmasters

NUT: National Union of Teachers

PRO: Public Record Office (London)

RADAR: Royal Association for Disability and Rehabilitation

RAMC: Royal Army Medical Corps

Introduction Embodiment

This book is an exploration into the impact of the First World War on the male body. The body was the subject of both imagination and experience. Men could be able-bodied: fortified, forceful, vigorous. Yet, their bodies could also be mangled, freshly torn from the war and competing for economic and emotional resources with civilians. Although men might possess useful bodies capable of performing their allotted civic and military functions efficiently, they might choose instead to malinger by refusing to acknowledge their duties in the workplace and in the armed forces. For some, theirs was the beautiful physique, adored by other men and cultivated by masculine fraternities – yet commonly offered to women. They expressed their freedom through their bodies, but were besieged on all sides by military, medical and educational disciplines which were governed by different aesthetics, economic objectives and moral economies. The corporeal male would eventually become a corpse on some battlefield or mortuary slab, inviting reconstruction through the memories of loved ones. All men's bodies were endowed with signs and declarations of age, generation, class and ethnicity. It was within this socially constructed 'frame' that bodies lived, were imagined and died.

There is no clear distinction between the study of men's bodies and masculinity. In 1975, Gayle Rubin defined a distinction between 'sex' and 'gender' whereby sex referred to anatomical differences and gender referred to the social construction of these differences.[1] The idea that the biological body is itself subjected to construction has been adopted by most historians examining relationships between men and women.[2] There is no inevitable association between the male body and masculinity. Historical representations and individual embodiment often become confused. Anatomy may not be destiny, but the belief that it is moulds most lives.

This interest in the relationship between biology and culture has generated an extensive historiography. It has, however, been slow to incorporate analysis of the social construction of masculinity (as opposed to femininity) into its purview. In the past decade, this has been changing. Some of the pioneering work on masculinity looked at institutions such as the public school and boys' organizations.[3] Historians have also examined maleness in the context of literature,[4] the empire,[5] liberalism,[6] religion,[7] sexuality[8] and domesticity.[9] The male body, however, remains (in the words of Roy Porter) 'pitiably ignored'.[10] Furthermore, despite frequent assumptions about the link between male virility and war, very few British historians have tackled this theme directly.[11] This is a surprising omission. The historiography either focuses on Victorian and Edwardian manliness or on post-war masculinity. When the war is broached, the analysis tends to be speculative. It is difficult to understand the lack of analysis of masculinity and war within the British historiography tradition. In part, the explanation lies in the way the Great War has developed as a specialist area of study within the discipline. Leaving aside the more conventional 'military history' approach, people who research on the war tend to fall into two clearly defined groups: literary scholars and economic historians. Exceptions are rare.

What we do know about men's bodies in the nineteenth and early twentieth centuries remains sketchy. The ragged bodies of the poor enlisting for military services in the empire are contrasted with the heroic frames of miners, dockers and boxers which, in turn, draw attention to the effete gestures of the aristocracy. That working-class boys were lighter, leaner and in poorer health than their middle-class contemporaries is well known: that they were less liable to be circumcized also comes as no surprise. Although the empassioned attempts of élite groups within society to mould the bodies of their successors have been extensively studied through analysis of public schools, hunting expeditions and sporting events, we know remarkably little about the gestures, play and carriage of the mass of boys and men.

This neglect is not due to any sense amongst historians that the way men experienced and imagined their masculinity was in any way unproblematical. The period prior to the war has been portrayed as one in which men struggled to assert their 'reason' over the disruptions and disturbances of the Industrial Revolution and related social and spatial upheavals. Men gained power within the public sphere, but they lost some of their domestic influence as they crowned women 'angels in the home' and as a series of legislative reforms conferred certain legal rights on wives and mothers. By the 1870s, the ideologies of separate spheres had firmly placed men and women within secure enclaves in which their roles were clearly acknowledged. The womanly woman was gentle, domesticated and virginal: the manly man was athletic, stoical and courageous.

Given that the historiography of pre-war masculinity tends to focus on élite masculinity, it is not surprising that the public school is considered to be the site within which the manly virtues were inculcated. Most famously, 'muscular Christianity', with its stress on aggressive spirituality and physical prowess, was a powerful agency inside public schools. The extent to which these traits were stimulated within grammar and state schools is a matter for debate. It is clear, however, that for the mass of boys, a closer examination is needed of the state school system and its environment. In 1870, an Education Act was passed which attempted to give a minimum level of education to everyone. School attendance over the entire country was made compulsory in 1880, and fees were abolished in 1891. The state explicitly used the education system to teach boys (and girls) what they considered to be appropriate gender roles. The debates from the late nineteenth century about the provision of playing fields for state schools may have been concerned with enabling poorer boys to adopt the masculine traits implicit in 'muscular Christianity'. The introduction in the late nineteenth century of classes in cooking, childcare and general housewifery for girls is well known, but less has been said about the education of boys in manual training. These classes began in 1862 and became a compulsory part of the curriculum for secondary school boys in 1904 and for elementary school boys in 1909. The classes had two aims: to prepare boys for manual trades and for masculine domestic duties. The employment aspect of manual training declined in importance from the turn of the century and, as we shall show later in this book, the war raised the importance in the eyes of both legislators and men themselves of ensuring that boys were suitably equipped to fulfil their domestic responsibilities.

This study focuses on the First World War since it provoked a major crisis in the lives of the great majority of men in Britain. The South African War (1899–1902) had been, in contrast, a much less catastrophic event, although politically it had resulted in a similar 'crisis' of masculinity as men's weakening virility was thought to be threatening British imperial prowess and national efficiency. Of the 20,000 volunteers for the Boer War, only 14,000 were considered 'fit' to join. In particular urban areas men's bodies were found to be notoriously inadequate as, for example, in the case of Manchester where out of 11,000 volunteers, 8,000 were rejected outright and only 1,200 were accepted as fit in all respects. State intervention aimed to mould men's bodies into more appropriate shapes: the report of the Interdepartmental Committee on Physical Deterioration was cited as the rationale for legislation as diverse as the school medical inspections, school meals, factory acts and the extension of education.

The period following the Great War is portrayed as the end of Victorian certainties. Society was less secure. World-wide economic depression and labour unrest undermined men's roles as bread-winners. The gains they made in the political sphere were offset by those made by women. Indeed, feminism came to be regarded by many men as a direct hit below their belts. As will be shown later, the new masculinities of the inter-war years have been seen as a response to the perceived need to reassert manliness in a society undergoing rapid change.[12]

Within this literature, there is considerable ambiguity about what constitutes 'masculinity'. For many writers, 'masculine' is what men 'are': it is what differentiates men from women, or the feminine. How men came to be 'manly' is sometimes regarded as unproblematical (it is part of men's 'nature'), or as the product of socialization. On the other hand, Foucault's attempt to demonstrate how human interactions are constructed through particular genealogies and systems of knowledge has been highly stimulating. Those knowledges produce networks of power. Voluntaristic individuals are replaced by socially constructed subjects. Feminists have integrated the politics of power into their scholarship: 'patriarchy' is one term that has dominated their discussions of gender, but is not a term used in this study. By drawing attention to male oppression of women, it ignores the way in which power structures also oppress men. As Lynne Segal and Victor Seidler have argued, 'masculinity' is as much about the power of certain men over other men as it is about the power of men over women.[13] Michael Roper and John Tosh agree, pointing out that the concept of patriarchy portrays men as 'having a natural and undifferentiated proclivity for domination, because their subjective experiences are left unexplored'.[14] The emphasis on the subjectivity of masculinities is deconstructed in psychoanalytical approaches to 'masculinity'. In the context of the themes in this book, Graham Dawson's Kleinian analysis of masculine heroes from the Victorian period to the modern world is the most convincing. Dawson reminds historians that external social roles are only powerful because of men's psychic desires and pleasures.[15] While not adopting the psychoanalytical approach in Dawson's book, readers may be aware of the sub-text of desire and fantasy.

Sympathy with the psychoanalytical approach has meant that subjective experiences and imaginings have been prioritized in the present work. Within the 'constructionist' tradition, this book explores the period from the late nineteenth century to the 1930s, but its chief concern lies with the Great War. It focuses on servicemen although evidence is drawn from the letters and diaries of people within civilian contexts as well as within the military services. The vast majority of these texts has been ignored by historians in the past, and it is hoped that this study will encourage greater use to be made of them. Throughout, letters and diaries have been cited as they were written: frequently without punctuation, containing many spelling errors and often using imaginative forms of abbreviations. These sources have the advantage of providing us with a much broader range of men than those studies that have used published material only. In addition, memoirs and oral histories are used extensively and, despite the fact that we must be cautious with such sources (Ian Beckett has described them as 'arguably . . . most susceptible to conscious (or unconscious) manipulation by their authors'), they provide an invaluable guide to the construction of gender identities.[16] Undeniably, many men whose lives are chronicled here regarded themselves as having been transformed by their encounter with warfare: many echoed the words of a Dublin soldier at Passchendaele when he affirmed, 'if I get out of here, I'll be a changed man'.[17] In Britain, more than 5 million men – or 22 per cent of the male population – were active participants in military services between 1914 and 1918. Although war was a 'relative experience', around 7 per cent of all men between 15 and 49 years of age were killed in battle: these men experienced warfare 'absolutely'.[18] Furthermore, most of those who fought in this war were not professional servicemen. When war was first declared, they had been mainly enthusiastic, middle-class volunteers, eager to 'do their bit' while they had the chance. From 1916, they were conscripted men, often ambivalent about their newly assumed roles and generally unprepared for the realities of modern, mechanized warfare.

The decisive impact of the Great War on men's bodies can be seen most clearly by looking at the war-maimed. Irrevocably re-moulded by their experiences, these men struggled to create new lives that challenged their status as physically disabled. They occupy the first chapter of the book. For men who were spared disfigurement, military life enabled them to experiment with different masculine aesthetics. Some of these will be examined in later chapters but, to give one example, these corporeal alterations could be closely related to socio-economic class. Thus, in a diary entry in October 1918, Ralph Scott marvelled over the way the war had altered the appearance of his hands: 'I looked at my great murderous maulers and wondered idly how they had evolved from the sensitive manicured fingers that used to pen theses on "Colloidal Fuel" and "The Theory of Heat Distribution in Cylinder Walls". And I found the comparison good."[19] The war did not only change the bodies of soldiers, sailors and airmen. The return of war-mutilated servicemen radically transformed the lives of all disabled people in Britain. Within the non-disabled civilian population, masculine images and ideals were also modified. The wartime aesthetics of the male body (and the disciplines applied to it by military and medical authorities) spread into civilian society after the war. The male body was no more than the sum of its various parts and the dismembered man became Everyman.

This book, therefore, contributes to a well-known historiographical debate: how decisive was the First World War in changing British society? During and immediately after the war, few people questioned its revolutionary impact. John M. Connor expressed it passionately in his diary for 21 November 1914: 'seeing your pals blown into bits, it makes a new man fellow in spirit, moral & character . . . it will make many changed man [I] tell you, better men in every respect this war will.'[20] Similarly, in 1919, the historian J. L. Hammond (who served during the war) maintained that the returning serviceman had 'broken through the strongest force in our nature, the customary standard, the habit of accepting the world as he [found] it . . . This is a new moral force in our society: the presence of a great mass of men, conscious of sacrifices and services, who look on the world with new eyes.'[21] For spiritualists, the returning ex-servicemen could be messianic. Thus in one session of 'automatic writing', a spiritualist medium wrote of a dead soldier (named Cooper) who had been judged to be 'special' by the higher authorities in the spiritual world and was, therefore, to be returned to earth. Cooper would 'take up his old life on earth, and his mother [would] have her son. But he [would] not be the same. None of those who [went] back [would] be the same. Angels, dressed in stained and faded khaki, [would] walk the familiar streets.' The recipient of the letter was advised to 'Listen to them.'[22]

Historians have not always agreed that the war transformed men and society. Systematic analysis about the impact of war was first undertaken by Arthur Marwick, and the resilience of the debate is due in part to his persuasive contention that wartime experiences are crucial if historians are to understand British society and culture between 1918 and 1939.[23] The debate has tended to focus around four topics. The first of these is the effect of war on population trends and social policy. Jay Winter has led the way in the analysis of the demographic legacy of the war, showing how the lives of civilians (especially those who had been worse off prior to the war) improved between 1914 and 1919 directly as a result of economic changes which had been promoted by the hostilities.[24] In addition, new psychological disciplines stimulated by wartime economies contributed to a new kind of intervention into the lives of children.[25] Reflecting on the war of 1914–18, Sara Josephine Baker remarked that when 'father had been torn apart by shrapnel or smothered by poison gas, his small sons and daughters, the parents of the future, took the spotlight as the hope of the nation'.[26] A related argument examines the relationship between war and scientific and social policy.[27] Alisdair Reid champions the idea that the war was crucial in advancing government policies beneficial to the working class. In his analysis, the bargaining position of British workers improved as employers competed with each other for scarce labour and as low unemployment and high earnings strengthened the power of trade unions. Consequently, the state and capitalists were encouraged to engage in consultation with employees and their representatives.[28] In addition, the management of the war led Whitehall to take over many areas of the economy that had previously been in private hands. After the war, these institutions and policies could not be entirely dismantled, in part due to the need to fulfil commitments made during the war (for example, the provision of war pensions) and the fact that people had become accustomed to a higher level of taxation. The war also abolished many pre-war restrictions on government intervention into the economy and society.[29]

Secondly, much attention has focused on how the war affected social cohesion, political values and the relationship between the government and the populace.[30] For example, government propaganda came into its own. Before the war, the manipulation of public opinion was regarded as the province of the church, the press, political parties, philanthropists and non-governmental organizations, but with the declaration of war, this changed as the government mobilized its resources in an attempt to counter German propaganda. Thus, a new weapon of war was invented.[31] Thirdly, a lively debate flourishes concerning the impact of war on women. Historians such as James F. McMillan suggest that the war had no lasting effect on the position of women, while Sarah M. Gilbert and Susan Gubar contend that the war radically altered the whole sex struggle by 'offering revolution in economic expectations, a release of passionate energies, a reunion of previously fragmented sisters, and a revision of social and aesthetic dreams'.[32] Arthur Marwick also contributes to this debate, observing that the war encouraged divorce and 'spread promiscuity upwards and birth-control downwards'.[33] One part of this argument concerns the influence of the war on female employment, with most commentators concluding that the gains have been exaggerated and were temporary.[34]

This book will touch on some of the issues brought up by the historians mentioned above. For instance, some scholars of women's history contend that femininity was 'disrupted, constructed, and reconstructed' during the war: this prompts the question as to whether this was true of masculinity.[35] The impact of the war on social policy is also a central theme of this study. Chapter Two examines the way in which the application of new psychological techniques to discipline war malingerers provided a framework for dealing with their industrial counterparts after the war. We will see in Chapter Four how the wartime economy legitimated and extended surveillance of the male body. Policies of physical education in schools were directly affected by the status of the War Office within government and educational circles and by wartime contradictions between the need for military manpower and the demand for male teachers who would mould a new generation of boys into 'masculine men'.

However, the main point at which this book intersects with the debate on the impact of the Great War on British society concerns cultural ideas and discourse. Historiographically, the persuasiveness and potency of the argument that war fundamentally changed British culture owes a great deal to the analysis of literature by Paul Fussell in his study entitled *The Great War and Modern Memory*.[36] Fussell argues that this war stimulated a literary revolution, in which the adoption of an ironic mode of writing dominated. Leaving aside for a moment the heavily contested notion of modern literature, Fussell located the stimulus for change in the widespread despair felt by servicemen. Others have taken up the theme. Disillusionment is at the heart of Eric J. Leed's psychological study entitled *No Man's Land*.[37] Leed contends that the war altered traditional sources of identity, and he concludes that it was, therefore, a 'modernizing experience'.[38] Similarly, although Samuel Hynes stresses the continued strength of traditional literatures, he also sees the war as heralding in a period of radical change.[39] In his stimulating *A War Imagined*, he argues that the war created a set of 'abrupt disjunctions – between generations, between fighting soldiers and those who controlled their lives, between the present and the past – which can be reduced to two terse propositions: the old betray the young: the past is remote and useless'.[40] John Cruikshank sees it as heralding in the 'modern age', dominated by cynicism, relativism and despair.[41] Modris Eksteins writes that the conflict led to the birth of a 'modern consciousness'.[42] Peter Buitenhuis stresses the way in which military experiences opened an unbridgeable abyss between the 'schoolboy version of war, the imagery of knights and angels, and the reality of Flanders'. According to him, the post-war world was characterized by a 'widely shared sense of loss of decency and the diminution of civilized values'.[43]

More recently, these writers have been challenged by historians who remind their readers of the continuities between the late nineteenth century and the mid-twentieth century. We are warned against exaggerating the impact of war.[44] For example, although the war may have been crucial in the political history of Ireland, its impact on Irish arts and literature was negligible.[45] It has often been noted that the disillusionment thesis rests too heavily on a small number of writers and artists such as Siegfried Sassoon, Wilfred Owen, Edmund Blunden, Robert Graves, Wyndham Lewis and Paul Nash.[46] These were self-proclaimed truth-tellers who may or may not be regarded as representative.[47] It is further pointed out that the heroic (and therefore anti-modernist) tradition in literature and the arts remained vibrant after the war.[48] Ted Bogacz draws attention to the persistence of the tradition of 'high diction', despite widespread knowledge about the facts of the war.[49] Jay Winter's work is even more ambitious. Examining a disarmingly broad range of social and cultural experiences, he has argued that people responded to the war by looking backwards rather than forwards in time. This was particularly true for the bereaved who turned to a traditional vocabulary (mediated by classical, romantic and religious languages and rites) in an attempt to cope with their sorrow.[50]

This book applies the debate to the study of manliness. Although the war was crucial in disrupting former expectations and expressions of masculinity, men drew on their understanding of the past to re-assemble their lives after the war. As Leed argues, the Armistice did not signal the end of the war experience but 'the beginning of a process in which that experience was framed, institutionalized, given ideological content, and relived in political action as well as in fiction'.[51] Furthermore, the war not only affected men who fought: the lives of civilians whose positions were analogous to servicemen were transformed and a generation of men who had been too young to be actively engaged in military services grew up in a world in which certain aspects of 'being a man' were believed to be threatened, and their aesthetics of the body reflected this perception.

Emphasizing that wartime experiences subtly shifted concepts of masculinity does not require adherence to the disillusionment thesis. Indeed, the idea that the war induced widespread feelings of betrayal and alienation is not sustained in the present study. Self-proclaimed truth-tellers may be regarded as an aberrant group. The men focused on here were not the 'generation of innocent men, their heads full of high abstractions like Honour, Glory and England'.[52] Very few had imbibed the public school ethos. They were more likely to view their surprising survival as a lucky and joyous opportunity to create a sphere of comfortable domesticity than as a chance to reflect on their social alienation and despair. This is not to go too far in the opposite direction. When Harry Siepmann was demobilized at the age of thirty, he felt that his life had practically passed him by. He wrote,

I remember shocking my youngest brother around this time [early 1920s] by saying, 'There is not one of my friends whom I would mind seeing having his teeth pulled out one by one.' What I really meant to convey by this remark was the bitterness that the war had left inside me: all my youthful good intentions had given way to cynicism. As for friends, I no longer dared make any: I had known too much the grief of seeing them hacked down.[53]

However, bitterness was only *one* response to wartime experiences: and it was a response that few could afford to maintain for long periods, or were willing to maintain in the face of renewed hope for happiness.

In addition, to argue that the war altered perceptions of the male body is not to insist that men's responses were wholly, consistently or even particularly novel. Sometimes they were. Many of the war-disabled searched for new ways of interpreting the devastation wrought upon their flesh (Chapter One). In this quest, they failed: although initially they won special status, the broader public to whom they appealed eventually reverted to pre-war ways of thinking about disabled bodies. It will be seen that a distinction needs to be made between attitudes and material provisions. Although medically and technologically the experience of all disabled people was fundamentally changed by the war, within a short time public assumptions about the war-maimed came to be identical to those of the wider population of disabled men, women and children prior to 1914. In the case of men suspected of evading their duties (Chapter Two), a similar argument will be made. Malingering was not a product of the war, but the wartime crises concerning the extent of such behaviour resulted in a dramatic increase in the techniques used to expose, punish and treat suspects in industry as much as in the military. Again, there was a divergence between the attitudes of officials and those of certain other groups within society.

As this study will attempt to show, there are also cases where older forms of interpretation remained paramount. Thus, the debates about malingering men also kindled arguments about the relationship between body and mind and the extent to which some men classified as malingerers might actually be harbouring mental illnesses such as neurasthenia (or 'shell shock'). In wartime, neurologists tussled with psychologists for power over the male body. In this instance, however, there was more continuity with pre-war treatments: although psychology and (in particular) psychoanalysis did gain some prestige as a result of wartime treatments, there was only a slight shift of opinion in their favour.[54]

In the chapter entitled 'Bonding', the site of conflict was within that haven of tradition: the home. The dislocations of wartime experiences made men yearn for the comfort and security of conventional domesticity. The gulf between civilians and servicemen was not as wide as historians have sometimes portrayed it, despite the fact that much information about life in the front lines was suppressed. The most obvious example of silence in wartime discourse concerns the ugliness of the military death (Chapter Five) – even the customary truthfulness of Graham Wallace faltered when cornered in his hospital bed by the widow of a friend who had died at Suvla Bay. He described how 'she sat quite dry eyed while I made up fairy tales of how painlessly poor old Howard had died. I hoped I lied well for the poor old fellow had died in horrible agony.'[55] Despite such horrors, civilians anxiously sought information about the war and did their best to keep in touch with what was happening to their menfolk. One indication of this is the circulation of newspapers which soared during the war. The sales of the *Daily Mirror*, for instance, totalled 850,000 copies a day in 1914, compared with 1,580,000 two years later. In total, well over 6 million copies of newspapers were sold each day. At times of particular crisis, even greater numbers were sold, as in the case when, at the start of the Battle of the Somme, the *Sunday Pictorial* alone sold nearly 2.5 million copies.[56]

Of course, the press was a propagandist organ: as Douglas Haig (British commander-in-chief on the Western Front) boasted to his wife in November 1916, 'the correspondents have played up splendidly'.[57] They suppressed news that might lower morale, they invented atrocity stories and they generally submitted to the rules laid down by the War Office. Consequently, personal correspondence between servicemen and their families and friends was much more important than public rhetoric. At the start of the war, the army postal force numbered 300: by the end of March 1915, it had increased five-fold. Although much of this was due to the employment of army censors, it also reflected a vast increase in correspondence. In October 1914, the army postal service handled 650,000 letters and 58,000 parcels a week. Within five months, this had shot up to 3 million letters and 230,000 parcels, and by 1916, correspondence for troops had reached a weekly average of 11 million letters and 875,000 parcels.[58] Furthermore, most of these letters would be read by more than one person.[59] Of course, letters were rigorously censored both by the military authorities and by servicemen themselves.[60] The regulations forbade mention of where letters were written (Boulogne was excluded), military plans, defensive works, the organization and number of troops, amount and type of armament, the morale and physical condition of the troops, casualties and any criticism of operations.[61] This did not negate what both senders and recipients saw as the principal purposes of these letters. The first function was for servicemen to 'set the record straight' about their feelings. Thus, in a letter to Miss D. Williams in 1917, 'Jack' raged about how it made him 'wild when people [wrote] out & [said] what a lovely time, you [were] having & lovely sights we [were] seeing in this so called Holy Land if only they were out here & crossed the desert as we did & saw the battle field'.[62] In spite of censorship, servicemen regularly sent horrifying stories back to family and friends at home.[63]

The second function was for those left behind to keep the serviceman informed about home. It is often asserted that for 'men at the front the only reality was their dangerous, exhausting and inhuman existence in the trenches, a hell-on-earth'.[64] Yet, leaving aside the fact that servicemen (even in France) did not spend most of their time in the trenches, it is clear that, on the whole, 'reality' remained firmly located back in 'dear old Blighty' and men continued to be engrossed in the day-to-day lives of their family and friends.[65] Most soldiers were not living 'for a seemingly endless period of time beyond civilian social categories'.[66] Contrary to the work of Klaus Theweleit, wartime experiences did not inevitably brutalize these men.[67] Scrawled inside an autograph book, which had been handed around a convalescent home in 1915, an unknown corporal wrote the following: 'I have been asked to write an account of my experiences in France and Belgium. To tell the truth, I would rather not, as they to me are best forgotten. I can only describe modern warfare as horrible in the extreme and I'm sure all will agree, that such incidents as are daily witnessed in the line should be forgotten as quickly as possible.'[68] The urge to forget was the dominant urge and, despite the stress placed in Chapter Two on man's inability to 'will' forgetfulness, the vast majority of servicemen did not need recourse to professionals to fulfil this aim: the comfort of their kin and companions was sufficient. As shall be seen in Chapter Three, ex-servicemen were not 'liminal figures formed on the boundaries of domestic life'.[69] Throughout the present work, private correspondence will serve to counter the idea of separation: the war did *not* frame the real world for many men. For most, home remained the touchstone for all their actions. Related to this point is the tendency of historians to assign descriptions of the love felt by servicemen for women into a trichotomy consisting of whore, nurse and madonna.[70] The deployment of such categories is misleading as the vast majority of men did not think in these terms. The more usual yearnings involved the desire to share fond love with one person. Rather than fleeing domesticity and femininity, the servicemen who will appear in this book pursued these two ideals in an attempt to regain their sense of honour and a taste of contentment.

This is not to deny that there was some friction between men and women arising out of the war. Sarah M. Gilbert and Susan Gubar have contended that 'as young men became increasingly alienated from their pre-war selves, increasingly immured in the mud and blood of no man's land, increasingly abandoned by civilization of which they had ostensibly been heirs, women seemed to become, as if by some uncanny swing of history's pendulum, even more powerful . . . these formerly subservient creatures began to loom malevolently larger'.[71] It is, however, incorrect to assume that women prior to the war had been regarded as 'subservient creatures'. More fundamentally, the wartime economy did not challenge the relative position of the two sexes as dramatically as these authors imply. There were important exceptions. Certain groups of men believed themselves to have been particularly affected by the changes that had taken place 'behind their backs' while they were at war. In Chapter Four we shall examine two of these groups: schoolmasters and a tiny professional élite. Both regarded the war as having fundamentally shifted the balance of power between the sexes. The schoolmasters responded by establishing a vigorous 'union for men' dedicated to stamping out women's newly gained influence over the physique of young boys. They styled themselves 'the men's movement' and were extremely popular amongst ex-servicemen and teachers of physical training. The professional equivalent was composed of a few eugenists and social commentators who formed an organization called the 'Men's Dress Reform Party'. They responded to what they regarded as war-induced feminism by advocating that men become more 'narcissistic' (their term), thus stimulating the evolution of masculine creativity and enabling them, once again, to supersede women.

However, an impassable barrier between the sexes was not erected. As many other historians have pointed out, the wartime employment market rapidly reverted to its pre-war status. The fury of ex-servicemen against flappers, who were demanding an equal right to employment – although certainly present – has been exaggerated. More generally, one reason why masculinity has been equated with disdain of women and domesticity is the concentration by historians on young, unmarried men. Boys and young men were expected to spurn femininity: it was the transition to adulthood that necessitated an adoption of manly gentleness and nurturing. Thus, it is easy to find examples of youngsters rejecting female traits, although the same cannot be said when we consider the case of older men. This point can be illustrated by examining an inter-war survey of the reaction of boys and men to tender love scenes in films. Sixteen-year-old Edward O'Neill had this to say: 'In films I see there is too much love in every picture, women change a man's mind. Instead of a man being tough he is made soft.' Eighteen-year-old Robert Whiteside agreed: 'In my opinion films have good and bad points. When the picture commences the male star generally hates the female, and yet at the end he falls for her. Why can't he go on hating them and instead of kissing her give her the best thrashing she ever had.' A completely different story is told by older men. Forty-year-old J. Parkinson asked for 'more of present-day life pictures, of home life'; forty-four-year-old Noel Charnley wanted 'films with action, some love, beautiful scenery, a little mystery, beautiful women in beautiful gowns'; and forty-five-year-old F. Pollitt pleaded for 'that little insight into the little domestic scenes which happen in our own lives. Odd spots of physical jerks from Pa in the bedroom. Little domestic squabbles etc.'[72] Both the young and the middle-aged men were expressing appropriate masculinities. Men who joined the military services aged eighteen years in 1914 returned to civilian society only too prepared for mature manliness.

Male sexuality during the Great War is another area of historiographical controversy. For many writers, there is a relationship between war and homoeroticism. To some extent this is true: Paul Fussell persuasively argues that wartime experiences stimulated 'physical tenderness, the readiness to admire openly the bodily beauty of young men, the unapologetic recognition that men may be in love with each other'.[73] Homoeroticism in the poetry of this war was legitimized by a long tradition of poetry that included Milton's 'Lycidas', Shelley's 'Adonais', and Tennyson's 'In Memoriam'.[74] Furthermore, it will be argued in Chapter Three that love between men was expressed by those outside an élite literati. Male intimacy was not primarily a legacy of the public school tradition: men who had little education drew from other pre-war traditions (such as body-building clubs and the scouts) to express similar sentiments. We must be wary of calling these homoerotic feelings 'homosexual'.[75] Despite the scandal surrounding Oscar

Wilde, it was only after the war that the 'innocence' of friendship between men came to be questioned by popular psychology. However, as will be evident from the earlier discussion, the belief that the relationships forged in war challenged the primacy of heterosexual love and caused femininity to lose its 'potency' is not borne out here.[76] Rather, it shall be argued, the female image became increasingly, and more tenderly, potent for most men as a result of their wartime experiences.

Some writers who discuss homoeroticism during the war equate masculinity with aggression. Thus, in his spirited analysis of the war poets, Adrian Caesar speaks of his attempts to understand why 'this homosexual or homoerotic love [at the Front] was predicated upon violence'. He queries the reason why 'in order to express gentleness, tenderness, loving kindness, and love for each other, men had to go to war'.[77] This present work sets out to counter such assumptions of masculine brutality. The men examined here brought with them a tradition of lovingkindness towards other men: a tradition forged not in that most exclusive of institutions, the public school, but in pubs, sports fields, gymnasia, allotments and over garden-fences in suburbia. Aggression and stoicism were regarded as characteristically masculine – but they were traits that were expressed only because of the exigencies of military existence and men longed to return to their familiar worlds where manly nurturing and emotiveness could once again flourish.

The need for emotion was never so intense as when faced with mortality. In the final chapter, the male corpse will be examined. The military services, government inspectors, poor law guardians, medical officers, funeral directors and the bereaved struggled for possession of the dead body. The war increased the relative power of the military in this fight, while simultaneously spreading the experience of youthful death and undignified burial to a wider section of society. Faced with such devastation, people could do no more than turn to the past in their search for meaning to what was almost beyond contemplation. They returned to older forms of bereavement.[78] Simultaneously, however, the novel approaches to death that were being adopted before 1914 were advanced as the rhetoric of purification (with its emphasis on personal sanitation) came to be substituted for the older public-health rhetoric of putrefaction. Chapter Five also addresses shifts in the heroic ideal. There was no modernist rejection of the man of valour. Instead, there was a shift in the definition of heroic from the 'common man' (such as 'Tommy' or the 'Unknown Warrior') to the renowned military man (such as T. E. Lawrence or Lord Kitchener).[79]

It is clearly not sufficient to identify themes such as those above and to trace pre-war, wartime, and post-war patterns. In each case, we need to distinguish the 'action of war from the action of mere time'.[80] This is a difficult, and sometimes impossible, task. Firstly, it is misleading to regard 'war' as a straightforwardly identified episode: the boundaries between war and peace were continually being crossed. Designating as 'the war period' the years between 1914 and 1918 (or 1919) is as artificial as dogmatically separating male civilians from servicemen.[81] Secondly, identifying changes as accompanying or following war does not necessarily mean that they were caused by war.[82] Arthur Marwick goes further, warning his readers against adopting the 'middle road' in these debates by ascribing everything to the 'accelerating' effect of war. As he correctly reminds us, this simply side-steps the question of why war might accelerate a pre-existing trend. An illustration of the problems arising out of these points may be seen when we look at Chapter Two. Malingerers were regarded as a problem before the war. From the end of the nineteenth century, national insurance acts had brought shirking to the attention of employers and the state. However, the wartime economy and conscription altered the nature of malingering and responses to it. Techniques used to detect, punish and discourage military malingerers were applied to civilian workers after the war. The crucial question concerns the mechanism that brought this about. In the relationship between the state, employers and workmen, it is easier to ascribe causal links; but when we attempt to understand the way malingerers themselves were affected by their military experiences, the links are less certain. The difficulties of drawing assured relationships between wartime life and shifts in masculinity can also be illustrated by turning to male sexuality (Chapter Three). In their letters, diaries and memoirs, men spoke only hesitantly about their sexual bodies. Despite the fact that sex was clearly very important to them, we are unable to apply too rigorous a test to any suspected trend. Often, no authoritative formula can be devised and the historian must simply weigh up the evidence for and against any particular cause-and-effect equation. On this matter, it is hoped that this book will serve as a contribution to a much wider debate.

Although drawing too dramatic a distinction between servicemen and civilians has to be avoided, comparisons between these two groups are important in this book. This should not be taken to imply a belief in the existence of a generation of men whose experiences as servicemen forever distinguished them from older and younger cohorts. The most quoted proponent of the belief in a war generation is Charles Edmunds Carrington who described First World War veterans as a 'secret army'.

In the 1960s, he declared that middle-aged men 'strenuously as they attempt[ed] to deny it, [were] united by a secret bond and separated from their fellows who were too old or too young to fight in the Great War. Particularly the generation of young men who were soldiers before their characters were formed, who were under twenty-five in 1914, [was] conscious of the distinction, for the war made them what they [were].'[83] Siegfried Sassoon agreed: 'the man who really endured the War at its worst was everlastingly differentiated from everyone but his fellow soldiers'.[84] Less well-known writers concurred, writing with great bitterness about their sense of distance from civilians in safe jobs who claimed to want to 'see the fun'.[85] In contrast, Chapter Three stresses the alienation of servicemen from each other: the limits of male bonding.[86] The war experience fractured along lines of personality, age, ethnicity, class, military unit and branch of the services, as well as differentiating men according to the timing of their entry into active service (for instance, there were marked differences in the experiences of men who entered active service in 1914, compared with those entering between 1915 and 1917, and those who did not join one of the armed forces until after March 1918).[87] Although I agree with Denis Winter that 'there was much more during the war to unite men than to divide them',[88] male bonding was limited and contingent on a huge range of factors. The struggle for comradeship with other men, if it was attempted, failed.

Finally, notice must be taken of the boundaries of this book. The 'body' has an infinite number of histories and we shall be dealing with only a few of the issues that dominated the diaries, letters and memoirs of servicemen. In the chapter on the dead body (Chapter Five) we look cursorily at 722,000 British corpses and ignore the rest. But, in the fifty-two months of the war, 9.5 million men of all nations were killed. Furthermore, although this book is concerned with the interaction between masculinity and the First World War, it only approaches it through the corporeal body. Thus, in Chapter Two, the focus is on malingering (that is, the deliberate use of bodily ailments to avoid designated duties) rather than the broader practice of shirking. Even within the corporeal framework, much has been set aside. Although the bodies of the maimed are examined, those of prisoners-of-war are not.[89] Eighty-six per cent of men who enlisted were from England and Wales, and their traditions dominate the analysis.[90] Men from Wales, Scotland and Ireland all speak in this book, but their separate military and medical traditions await analysis. The book omits the other combatant countries: a different story could be told if Australian or American servicemen were included and interesting comparisons could be drawn with the French and German experience.[91] Jay Winter's *Sites of Memory, Sites of Mourning. The Place of the Great War in European Cultural History* provides a European framework.[92] The experience of the Western Front is stressed since, in 1918, the British army on the Western Front numbered 1,764,000 compared with 648,000 in all other theatres of war. A large proportion of the men in Italy, the Dardanelles, Salonica, Mesopotamia, Egypt, East Africa, Afghanistan, North Russia and Vladivostok would also have served in France. Total war casualties for the Western Front were nearly 2.3 million compared with 73,000 for Gallipoli (the next largest).[93] In terms of tracing the changes in perceptions of the male body, the experiences of the Western Front also dominate. In the words of Henry Gother Courtney, who had served in both Salonica and France, comparisons between the two places were like juxtaposing 'an April shower and the Deluge'.[94] Finally, although seamen and airmen are represented in this book, soldiers predominate.[95] Of the 6.1 million men in all the services, 5.2 million were in the Regular Army and the Territorial Forces, 600,000 were in the Royal Navy, and 300,000 were in the Royal Air Force.[96] Numbers are not the only criteria. The experiences of sailors and airmen were very different from those of soldiers. The navy failed to gain decisive victories and seemed irrelevant to the 'real war' in Flanders.[97] The cult of the airman developed during the war as an heroic counter to the squalid and anonymous war in the trenches. It contained three features: a belief in the dynamic power of flying, an illusion of the airman as a hero and a militarist recognition of the potentially offensive use of the aeroplane.[98] These very different traditions are not dealt with in the present work.

There are three other important omissions. Firstly, we shall not be looking at the professional-medical constructions of the male body during the war.[99] The second is concerned with the relationship between war and developments in film and art. These have been ignored largely because they have been analysed by other historians.[100] The third omission is the absence of any discussion of the great icons of masculinity. Their exclusion is due to a lack of evidence as the servicemen whose diaries or letters are discussed here did not refer to such icons. John M. MacKenzie, Brian Holden Reid and Graham Dawson have established the importance of T. E. Lawrence in British popular culture. Although he was unknown during the war – indeed, his exploits of 'derring-do' remained secret – by the early 1920s Lawrence had been firmly placed within a tradition of heroic imperialists that included David Livingstone. In the words of his greatest propagandist, the journalist Lowell Thomas, Lawrence was 'one of the most picturesque personalities of modern times, a man who will be blazoned on the romantic pages of history with Raleigh, Drake, Clive and Gordon'.[101] Immediately after the war, he represented all that the men from the trenches were not: he was clean, serene and vigorous. He was almost like a boy scout in his approach to warfare. In the 1930s, he was the masterful man who (it was hoped) might be able to pull the country out of the sluggish quagmire into which it had slipped. Lowell Thomas's film and lecture on Lawrence was heard by over 4 million people.[102] Thomas's book *With Lawrence in Arabia* sold 200,000 copies in its first year.[103] Yet, I searched in vain for mention of T. E. Lawrence in the personal papers of servicemen. To study men's bodies through such icons requires the use of different sources from those studied in the writing of this book.

As mentioned at the beginning of this introduction, the topics have been shaped by my choice of sources. The major texts of such writers as Siegfried Sassoon, T. S. Eliot and Virginia Woolf have not been discussed as others have done this.[104] Instead, servicemen's correspondence, diaries and memoirs form the basis of the present study. As will become evident, concentrating on these texts alters perceptions of what is important about men's bodies. For instance, the absence of the image of the body as a machine may surprise some, especially those readers influenced by Eric J. Leed's argument that the war exposed the brutal alliance between industrial disciplines in civilian life and alienation in the trenches.[105] Although the horror of mechanical efficiency in war can be seen in the jottings of the war poets and in the fragmented images in Futurist art,[106] those whose written words and crude sketches are examined here rarely used such metaphors. Another example of the way the sources have influenced the argument refers to the shape of the male body. In art, there are three distinctive traditions of representation: the adolescent softness of Narcissus, the firm gracefulness of Apollo and the muscularity of Heracles. However, when the shape of the male body is discussed here, such language is absent precisely because it is not the tradition in which men tended to describe their own bodies and the bodies of their friends. Certainly, we can find these traditions mentioned in some of the popular manuals for boys (such as *Health and Strength*), but once attention has been drawn to the other languages used to describe men's bodies (the more homely representations), one is alerted to the *comparative* rarity of artistic and literary traditions.

The wartime constructions of the male body had diverse origins. They moved in fits and starts, drawing inspiration from the distant past, near past and imagination. During the First World War, military interference disturbed the relative importance of aesthetics and economics in governing the male body. Contending authorities waged war over it. The resurgence of traditionalist rhetoric could not eradicate the recollection of ambiguities and uncertainties that wartime experiences had conferred upon it. Even if the outcome of that conflict was a reversion to a more traditional language, those experiences still fundamentally affected not only the shape and texture of the male body, but also the values ascribed to the body and the disciplines applied to masculinity.

One Mutilating

Between 1914 and 1918, more and more bodies of young, healthy men were at risk of frighteningly new ordeals of mutilation. All were forced to face their fears of physical destruction. The night before joining the army, Wilfred Willett held his weeping wife in bed and wondered, 'Should I ever sleep with her again? Or should I be limbless or faceless next time? I would meet her in heaven but in what state?'[1] This chapter examines the predicament of such men as Willett who, by fighting in the war, made themselves liable to disfigurement. Given the extent of devastation wrought upon the male body in this period, it is appropriate that a history of men's bodies should start not with ideal types but with the everyday experience of imperfection. The war magnified the experience of deformity, and the broader reality of disablement in twentieth-century Britain changed dramatically as a result. In this way, the war did not simply affect the population 'at risk' (that is, servicemen), but it altered the lives of people physically disabled from birth or by accident as well. The war-maimed competed for limited economic and emotional resources with disabled civilians: in the end, there were no winners in this struggle. By the late 1920s, the respect that had initially been given to the fragmented bodies of war-mutilated men had ended.

War and Everyday Disablement

The most important point to be made about the male body during the Great War is that it was *intended* to be mutilated.[2] The cowering, agonized expressions on the faces of soldiers struggling back from the front lines (illus. 1) suggests recognition of their inability to struggle against the forces determined to wreak havoc on their bodies. Stripped of their uniforms, bloody and unable to fully escape the terrifying barrage of death and dismemberment, military attempts to sustain high morale were reduced to insignificance. Irrespective of such horrors, over 6 million British and Irish men were to risk their limbs and lives

1 Fortunic Matantia, 'Battered but Victorious', pencil hatching on grey wash. From *The Sphere*, September 1918.

between 1914 and 1918. The risk was not shared equally but varied by region and branch of military service and rank. In France there were 5 casualties for every 9 men sent out, compared with 2 casualties for every 9 in the Dardanelles and only 1 to every 12 in Salonica and East Africa.[3] Furthermore, 31 per cent of those who served in the army were wounded, compared with only 3 or 4 per cent of those in the navy and the air force.[4] In the first year of war, 24 per cent of officers and 17 per cent of soldiers in the Other Ranks were wounded. Between October 1915 and September 1918, 12 to 17 per cent of soldiers of Other Ranks were wounded each year. The severity of these mutilations was unprecedented: nothing in British history (neither nineteenth-century wars nor in the grim injuries perpetrated upon the human body in factories or mines) was adequate preparation for the physical devastation of the First World War. All parts of the body were at risk: head, shoulder, arm, chest, intestines, buttock, penis, leg, foot. Over 41,000 men had their limbs amputated during the war – of these, 69 per cent lost one leg, 28 per cent lost one arm, and nearly 3 per cent lost both legs or arms.[5] Another 272,000 suffered injuries in the arms or legs that did not require amputation. Sixty thousand, five hundred were wounded in the head or eyes. Eighty-nine thousand sustained other serious damage to their bodies.[6] In 1920, pensions were still being paid to 31,500 men as compensation for having an arm or leg amputated. Just before the Second World War, 222,000 officers and over 419,000 servicemen in other ranks were still being paid disability pensions.[7] In the middle of the 1970s, there were nearly 3,000 limbless survivors of the Great War living in the United Kingdom.[8]

This chapter focuses on men who survived mutilation in their extremities. The First World War led to amputations on a scale never seen before, or since.[9] One-quarter of battle casualties arriving in military hospitals were orthopaedic cases.[10] Some doctors were thrilled in 'anticipation of cutting off legs and arms upon the stricken field, amidst a hail of shrapnel and machine gun bullets'.[11] Indeed, in the early years of the war, surgeons may have been showing more enthusiasm for amputation than was strictly necessary. As Dr Doyan of the French Army Medical Services reported in 1915, military surgeons were amputating limbs 'in a haphazard kind of way . . . in some places amputations multiplied to a rather dangerous extent'.[12] However, the more typical reaction was probably that of 'F.A.V.' at a casualty clearing station when he moaned about 'amputation after amputation. The surgeons were tired of cutting off legs and arms – it was "so monotonous and uninteresting".'[13]

The unusually high proportion of amputations was due to the fact that mutilations in this war tended to be more severe than they had been in previous wars. This was partially due to the use of more effective instruments of dismemberment, such as artillery fire, hand grenades and small firearms. As Edward Devine dryly noted in 1919,

Shrapnel and bombs and pointed bullets cause extensive lacerations of the soft tissues and multiple fracture of bones and joints. The intense force of the bullets – and occasionally of other projectiles – has disproved the classic belief of the days of slower missiles, that the fibres of nerve cords merely separate and let the ball pass through and cannot be injured by firearms. Now nerves are actually shattered like bones.[14]

Furthermore, the geography of this war favoured complications. In a period before penicillin and other germ-killing drugs, cleanliness was difficult. Experienced military doctors frequently compared the 'pure air, bright sunlight, and uncontaminated sandy soil' of South Africa during the war of 1899–1902, with Flanders where wounds quickly became infected.[15] The mud and lice of the trenches were conducive to trench-foot which sometimes necessitated amputation. Almost continuous fighting placed the burden of reaching dressing stations more firmly on the backs of the injured: consequently, medical help was commonly delayed for many hours. The irregular fragments of high explosive shells, used for the first time during this war, were particularly dangerous because they carried soil and pieces of clothing (especially woollens) into the tissues. Front-line surgeons, working in dimly lit dug-out dressing stations where dust, dirt and mud could not be avoided, became acutely sensitive to the 'sweet', 'mouse-like' smell that characterized gas gangrene.[16] This was a sinister smell: 6 per cent of soldiers who had their limbs amputated at the Front died – but when infection was present, this jumped to 28 per cent.[17] Not surprisingly, many doctors despaired: within three days of a battle, a casualty clearing station might be swamped with 1,000 injured men and mutilated limbs sometimes had to wait days before being amputated. As one doctor confessed, they were 'very helpless': once the 'unutterably foul smell' of gas gangrene became acute, the soldier might avoid death only if the limb could be rapidly amputated or 'scarcely less mutilating incisions' be made.[18] And amputation itself significantly increased a wounded serviceman's risk of death.[19]

The horror of front-line dismemberment was beyond the imagination of many civilians in Britain. They were not, however, totally unaware of its impact on hundreds of thousands of men's bodies. The war-maimed were particularly obvious in those towns and cities where they were sent to recuperate. Brighton was one of these places, as Caroline Playne described it in 1917: 'the sight of hundreds of men on crutches going about in groups, many having lost one leg, many others both legs, caused sickness and horror. The maiming of masses of strong, young men thus brought home was appalling.'[20] Throughout Britain – in every town and on every street – someone was affected. Thus, the son of a costermonger recalled that in his street 'there was a Mr Jordan who'd lost his right arm, my old man who'd been gassed, and the man at the top of the street who was so badly shell-shocked he couldn't walk without help. And there were always lots of one-armed and one-legged old sweats begging in the streets.'[21] Mass-mutilation was there for all to see.

Despite the shocking suddenness of wartime disfigurement, these men were not unique: they joined a wider population of disabled men, women and children. Even without war, physical disabilities were not rare in many communities. Indeed, as is indicated in the hasty sketch from an autograph album (illus. 2), in some areas (notably London), up to 2 per cent of men attempting to enlist in the military services during the war had one or more amputated limbs. Reliable statistics about the extent of disability within civilian communities do not exist.[22] A study in 1919 concluded that over 3 per cent of the civilian population required orthopaedic treatment.[23] In 1926, it was alleged that every year around 10,000 children became crippled.[24] In 1930, it was estimated that there were 200,000 people in England and Wales who were physically disabled. Half of this number were children under the age of sixteen years.[25] Disabilities were the result of rickets in 14 per cent of the cases, but diseases such as tuberculosis, infant paralysis and spastic paralysis also played their part.[26]

Civilian disablement was not solely a product of disease. It was also a common part of urban life and employment. In the late 1930s, over 50,000 people were seriously injured in road accidents and three times this number were slightly injured.[27] Rugby led to contusions, twists and wrenches: soccer resulted in injuries to the viscera.[28] In *The Indian Army ABC*, published in the early 1920s, football injuries were regarded as equivalent to the 'blood-thirsty strife' of warfare (illus. 3). Not for these men the gentlemanly rules taught in public schools: instead, the game of football reproduced the disorders and brutality of front-line service. Indeed, the connection between sporting and war injuries might be extremely close. On the eve of the Battle of the Somme, the commanding officer of the 13th Battalion of the Rifle Brigade 'got a Blighty' (or a wound) during a game of rugger.[29] Boxing was a frightening sport, less because of the physical pain than because of the fear of ending up with the occupation's stigmata – a cauliflower ear.[30] The deliberate injuring of another man was part of growing up. It

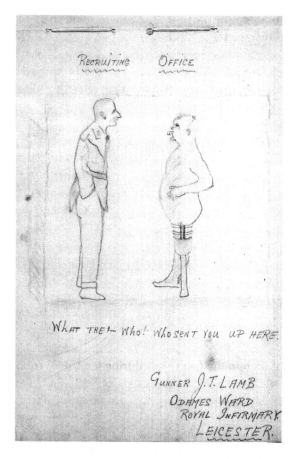

2 Gunner J. T. Lamb, 'Recruiting Office', cartoon of 1917 in the autograph book of E. Drathall, a nurse at the Royal Infirmary, Leicester. [CAMC RAMC 2002]

3 'F is for FOOTBALL', cartoon from 'Myauk', *The Indian Army ABC*, London, c.1920.

was part of the tradition of working out male hierarchies within a street or village.[31] To be 'decorated' or 'well-painted' with blood was a manly accomplishment.[32] It trained men for war, and could sometimes be as damaging to the male body.[33] Employment also contained risks. Certain jobs were more dangerous than others.[34] Mining and building injured thousands of men each year. Indeed, the problem was so serious that a special investigatory parliamentary committee was established in 1907 to report on the unacceptably high level of accidents in the building trade.[35] Men's work became more dangerous in times of high unemployment when competition was more fierce and the materials used were of lower quality.[36] The language of warfare was applied to these men: they were 'Wounded While Working' or, as industrial efficiency experts were wont to remind people, 'Peace as well as War has its Toll of Life and Limb' (illus. 4).[37]

Although the war-maimed were regarded as part of this wider constituency of disabled people, no one could fail to notice their distinguishing features. As already mentioned, the injuries received on battlefields tended to be more severe than those experienced by civilians. In addition, the war spread the experience of disability to a wider section of the population. This was due, most obviously, to the fact that the number of men in the front lines during the First World War was in the millions rather than tens of thousands. However, there was also a change in the characteristics of disfigured men. Prior to 1914, limblessness was confined largely to the children of the poor, adult factory and dock labourers and professional soldiers. In contrast, amputees during this war were fit men, many were conscripts rather than professional or volunteer soldiers, and they generally survived their ordeals. Seventy per cent of the amputees were less than thirty years of age: 10 per cent were officers.[38] They were also different from those who followed. During the Second World War, civilians were at risk of limblessness. Since then, amputees were increasingly elderly people suffering from degenerative diseases of the vascular system. They were generally in poor physical condition, with reduced mental and physical resilience and adaptability and their statistical life expectancy was quite short.[39]

Given the fact that the war created a new constituency of disabled people, it is not surprising that it fundamentally altered the *whole* experience of disability. For instance, the distinction between the active and the passive sufferer was blurred. In the case of people disabled from birth, the chief metaphor was passivity, and this childlike, 'innate' detachment was encouraged in institutions caring for them.[40] In war, however, the injured man was not disabled but

GLORIOUS BRITISH HISTORY.

THE FLAG. ALBUERA

PEACE as well as WAR
has its
TOLL of LIFE and LIMB.

4 'Glorious British history', poster reproduced in the *Journal of Industrial Welfare*,
September 1925.

mutilated. He was the fit man, the potent man *rendered* impotent. He
was mutilated and mutilator in one. This was true in two senses. A
small proportion of servicemen were self-mutilators. In an analysis of
over one million casualties in the war, less than one per cent of men
came into this category.[41] More usual was the man who mutilated other
men's bodies, and – in turn – had his body mutilated. While in
hospital suffering a wound, one soldier in the Machine Gun Corps
illustrated his wartime fantasies (illus. 5). In a tidy hand next to the
crude drawing of a rugged, square-jawed soldier bayonetting another

5 'He who hesitates is lost', cartoon in a Machine Gun Corps notebook, that of Private A. Forman, 1918. [IWM Misc. 73 Item 1097]

soldier, the gunner has written, 'HE WHO HESITATES IS LOST'. Underneath, in an untidy scrawl, he has penned, 'SEE THE Point. I – well sure Gerry sees it.' Similarly, a soldier who had a bayonet wound below his left groin boasted having 'fairly put the wind up' the man who wounded him: furthermore, when he had 'finished with him . . . he wasn't goin' to do any more bayonetting; and he wasn't goin' to shout 'kamerado' no more, same as he did before he got me. Served me right for trusting a dirty Boche. But after he stuck me I fairly cut him up. Oh, I made sure of him all right.'[42] The words 'Comrade! Kamerad!' united men in mutilation (illus. 6). This was the true 'Spirit of the Bayonet', the exchange of deformation.[43]

It was this change in the population of the disabled from passive to active sufferers that altered the entire language of disablement. This can be most clearly illustrated by considering the debates within one important organization, the Guild of the Brave Poor Things. This guild was founded by Grace Kimmins in 1894 to care for disabled children. By 1901 it had twelve branches and over 1,000 members.[44] In the early years of the century, Ada Vachell, leader of the Bristol branch, felt perfectly at ease calling her young charges 'little lame dogs' who needed to be 'helped over the stiles of difficulty lying across their paths'.[45] This language did not go entirely unquestioned. For instance, in 1905 the minutes for the City of Bristol Guild of Brave Poor Things recorded that 'many people, outsiders & strangers especially, much disliked the members being termed Poor Things'. The most popular

6 'Comrade! Kamerad!' Photograph of a scene of wounded. [CAMC L9146]

alternative names included the 'Masters of Fate', the 'Guild of Courage', the 'Cripples' Guild of Courage', and the 'Guild of the Handicapped'. However, when a vote was taken, the original name was retained.[46] The war made this conservative position untenable. In 1916, between a discussion about whitewashing the walls and obtaining the use of a piano for a fête, Vachell's proposal to change their name to the 'Guild of the Handicapped' met with general agreement.[47] It was no coincidence that this resolution was easily passed during the war: although it retained a sentimental attachment to the old name, the Guild of Brave Poor Things recorded:

> our lads and younger men are very anxious for the change. They have told us they find the name misunderstood by their friends . . . Also we look ahead to the time when fathers and sons and brothers will come back to their homes, maimed and broken after the awful War. We think some will like to join us and we already know that 'Guild of the Handicapped' makes more appeal to the wounded soldier than 'Brave Poor Things'.[48]

This movement from a language of childlike passivity to a more positive language of mutual aid was mirrored by a shift in the balance of guilt and responsibility for disablement from the individual to the collective. This occurred unevenly and was less universal. Frequently, in the case of disabled civilians, individuals continued to assume the brunt of the adverse criticism.[49] Injured workers were alleged to have been careless.[50] They were 'undesirables' whose main object was to 'trade upon their fellowmen'.[51] Despite a growing belief that the nation must bear some of the responsibility for disablement (because local and national politics allowed slums to exist), the often-repeated slogan that 'cripples [were] made not born' continued to be interpreted narrowly.[52] Time after time, the 'gross ignorance' of mothers was blamed for their children's disabilities and used as a rationale for the introduction of compulsory domestic education classes into schools.[53] Even disabled children were morally suspect: their sufferings were the 'wages of sin'.[54] In contrast, the wartime mutilated were regarded as the responsibility of the nation. In 1918, the journal *Reveille* portrayed the state's responsibility graphically (illus. 7). A young crippled ex-serviceman implores Britannia to acknowledge their sacrifice. Below the sketch are the words: 'What shall you say to us England – England our soul – Say to us young who were broken that you might be whole.' Standing on symbols of the English countryside, Britannia holds out her hands to the mutilated heroes. Unquestionably, the nation had a debt to repay. As Geoffrey Howson wrote in 1922, 'If a man has given a leg in the flesh, the least the country can do is to repay him with the best artificial one.'[55] In the Ministry of Pensions, Matthew Nathan agreed:

What shall you say to us England –
  England our soul –
Say to us young who were broken.
  That you might be whole.

THE APPEAL.
by WILL DYSON

7 Will Dyson, 'The Appeal', drawing in *Reveille*, 1918.

it was the 'duty of the State' to generously help those who had 'suffered in its service'.[56] Although military authorities remained convinced that some of the injuries could have been prevented by better training, more effective artillery, education and a more passionate display of patriotism, they had to recognize that the individual serviceman represented merely carnage. As soldier after soldier reminded them, the Great War was not 'war' but 'bloody murder'.[57] The injuries were not even usually caused by another identifiable individual, but by long-distant shells. Many servicemen never saw 'the enemy', and they longed to bring the tradition of mutilation in wartime into line with that of peacetime, that is, hand-to-hand combat.[58]

The perception that the state owed these men something was heightened by the enormous need for voluntary soldiers and, from 1916, the compulsory conscription of healthy, young men. As the assistant secretary to the Ministry of Pensions explained in 1920 to the Commission on Workmen's Compensation, the disabled war pensioner had been *compelled* to put himself at risk, and this affected not only the scale of pensions but also the conditions that could be applied.[59] Before 1915, disabled ex-servicemen had to rely on voluntary bodies such as the Prince of Wales's National Relief Fund, the Soldiers' and Sailors' Help Society, the Soldiers' and Sailors' Families Association, and the Royal Patriotic Fund. When state funds were made available by the Naval and Military War Pensions Act of 1915, public control became necessary and local war pensions committees were established under a central war pensions statutory committee. These local committees were appointed by county or town councils and had to contain representatives of the trade unions as well as of the voluntary bodies. One-third of the administrative cost was paid by the council, and the rest by the state. By the War Pensions (Administrative Provisions) Act of December 1918, the whole cost of administration was placed under state control under the Ministry of Pensions (which had been formed in 1917 to replace the War Pensions Statutory Committee). This powerful state apparatus was created as a contribution to the debt owed to disabled servicemen and, as this chapter will show, fundamentally altered the relationship between the state and the population of disabled civilians as well as servicemen.

The Battle of the Limbs

Despite the differences between disfigurement in war and peace, it was commonly assumed that the war was going to radically improve the position of disabled civilians. Grace Kimmins, founder of the Guild of the Brave Poor Things and co-founder of the Heritage Craft Schools for the disabled, wrote, 'This then is the vision: that the glorious new world shall arise from the ashes of the old, and that the lesson so terribly taught – so heroically mastered – during the Great War, shall become a "heritage" for all time to our crippled children.'[60] She was right to expect that the treatment of disabled ex-servicemen would have wider repercussions. In 1922, Ernest Muirhead Little, adviser on artificial limbs to the Ministry of Pensions, wrote that 'the battle of the limbs [was] still raging'.[61] He was concerned with technological rivalries in the provision of artificial limbs, one area in which disabled civilians might have benefited from military investment. However, contrary to the hopes of such people as Kimmins and Little, the war exacerbated the low social and economic status of disabled civilians. The rhetoric favoured the war-maimed: men rendered disabled in war were 'unnaturally abnormal' while those who had been born with physical disabilities were 'naturally abnormal'. Resources moved from the female to the male; from the young to the middle-aged; from the civilian to the ex-serviceman. There were no winners in this 'battle of the limbs', but those rendered disabled in the war experienced a brief period of favour.

At the outset it must be noted that the position of disabled civilians was poor at the time of the war. Bone-setters were accused of causing disabled children 'violent torture' and aggravating their disabilities.[62] Both the disabled child and adult relied upon charitable help, but while the young might be able to claim sympathy from benevolent middle-class philanthropists, older disabled people were socially invisible.[63] Even as late as 1931 there were only two residential training colleges for such adults in England and the first Adult Cripples' Welfare Association had only just been established.[64] Their lives were typically hard. In 1911, only twenty per cent of physically disabled men in Birmingham were employed, and their average wage was less than 12s. 7d. a week.[65] Men disabled in the course of their work were explicitly excluded from the right to a minimum wage.[66] Levels of compensation for injuries received at work were pitiable: for instance, in 1911, the average lump-sum compensation for the loss of an arm was £120: a broken back might be awarded £50.[67] Prior to the war, despite the reforming zeal of a rising generation of doctors and nurses with a particular professional interest in orthopaedics (the most prominent being Sir Robert Jones and Agnes Hunt), accommodation for the disabled remained very limited, especially in the eastern and northern counties of England and in South Wales.[68] When asked in 1906 if there were many 'defective' children who had not been reported to the council, a medical officer for the London County Council replied, 'We are not looking out for them. The accommodation is so limited that we do not want to find them.'[69] The population of disabled civilians before the war was more liable to be living at home than in institutions and it bore more than its share of poverty and dependency.

The sudden influx of disabled adult men into this realm exacerbated this situation and it resulted in a transfer of resources. The shift was most effective in economic terms, as wounded ex-servicemen were given priority over disabled children.[70] In part, there was a demographic reason why this should have happened. With the declining incidence of congenital disabilities, there were proportionately more disabled adult men than there were disabled children.[71] Furthermore, ex-servicemen were more liable to suffer from other injuries and illnesses that demanded a relatively higher capital investment. Even without these effects, the transfer of economic resources was not surprising. The disabled ex-serviceman was an indisputable part of the body-politic: he was male and enfranchized. Many were too young to have voted more than once at a pre-war election, so politicians regarded them as free-floating voters. They were educated, unlike the disabled child who – through the shortage of state and private funds – was regarded as an undependable, 'ill-educated citizen'.[72] In contrast, disabled ex-servicemen were drawn from the most dependable section of the citizenry: those who risked their flesh and bones for the nation. These servicemen were of a completely different class from their predecessors: as Major Robert Mitchell reminded the members of the Association of Technical Institutions in 1916, disabled ex-servicemen from this war were people who had 'held good positions in civil life'.[73] They were in a better position to transfer capital towards the ex-serviceman's cause that in the past would have gone to help other disabled groups. Children could not go on strike as disabled ex-servicemen could, and did.[74] The Council for the Care of Crippled Children had none of the economic resources or political influence of the ex-servicemen's Disabled Society and the Royal Legion.[75] Disabled ex-servicemen believed that they possessed a right to more resources than civilians. As Emanuel Miller wrote, 'despite the high social evaluation of the war wounds, many soldiers felt that the wound and its discomforts were worthy of greater compensation than were the injuries of peace'.[76]

The most valuable of resources was the artificial limb. These were expensive. In 1919, at a time when the average wage for a skilled craftsman was £2 a week, a wooden artificial limb for an amputation through the hip joint cost over £22. Artificial limbs for other leg amputations or for arm amputations through the shoulder or above the elbow cost anything from £15 to £18.[77] The right of the war-disabled to artificial substitutes was not disputed – the battle was primarily over the type of limb that was to be fixed. From the point of view of the limbless, there was no contest: the metal limb was lighter – and lighter was better.[78] In the words of one limbless man, 'In the old days when wearing a wooden leg weighing eight and a half pounds hung by a network of straps over the shoulder, I felt like a "trussed fowl". When I first wore a light limb I felt as if I had jumped from a "horse cab" into a

Rolls Royce car; my health improved immediately.'[79] There was, however, a problem: limbs made of alloy of aluminium were four times more expensive than wooden limbs. Desoutter's All-Metal Artificial Limb cost £80, compared with £20 for the average wooden limb. Until the early 1920s, the War Office and, later, the Ministry of Pensions, refused to authorize them. It was the politicizing of the servicemen's Disabled Society that forced the government to establish a committee of enquiry in 1922 to examine the relative benefits of metal versus wooden artificial limbs. The committee concluded that metal limbs were not, in fact, more expensive than wooden limbs since the official life of a wooden limb was four years compared with six or eight years for one in metal. In addition, repairs for metal limbs were considerably less expensive than those in wood. Taking these factors into account, every twelve years a wooden artificial limb typically cost £120 while a metal one cost £96.[80] Once the financial objections had been removed, provision of a sufficient number of limbs was on the agenda. Only a limited quantity of metal limbs could be supplied because fitting the metal bucket was extremely difficult, and a mere one or two people in Britain were said to be capable of satisfactorily manipulating the metal. In consultation with the manufacturer, Mr Desoutter, the Ministry of Pensions agreed to provide the metal limb with a wooden bucket. Guaranteed a large market, Desoutter also agreed to reduce the cost of his limb further.[81] Thus, by the mid-1920s, more than three-fifths of artificial limbs provided by the Ministry of Pensions were made of light metals.[82]

The provision of artificial limbs should not, however, be seen simply in terms of financial negotiations. Aesthetic considerations were paramount. In his introduction to a book on artificial limbs, Edward Marshall declared that the chief aim was to make these 'poor chaps . . . almost, in many instances quite, as good as new'.[83] The question was what constituted 'good as new' – an efficient unit of production or an aesthetically pleasing body shape. The two could not be achieved in the one limb, which was why the Ministry of Pensions differentiated between 'show', 'mechanical' and 'workers'' limbs.[84] Despite the fact that governmental authorities tended to favour the workers' limbs, they never discarded aesthetic considerations entirely. Thus, in 1918, Daniel Robinson argued that although such considerations should not be allowed to 'interfere unduly with the efficiency of the mechanism', the limb also had to 'restore as nearly as possible the normal appearance of the wearer'.[85] It was only in the case of men who had lost *both* arms that aesthetic considerations were to be discarded entirely for efficiency. As the Ministry of Pensions decreed, 'The man who has lost both arms and who must have substitutes will worry less about appearance than the man who has lost one arm only . . . however . . . whilst utility should not be sacrificed, appearance cannot be entirely ignored and there will be a number of men who will insist on this.'[86] Armless men often took the principle of efficiency even further than the authorities wished. For instance, the Ministry of Pensions was distressed to discover that most of these men preferred the ordinary hook to the more intricate mechanical arm.[87] They were also dismayed to find legless ex-servicemen substituting their artificial replacements for crutches because (while begging) people were more sympathetic to this display of mutilation.[88] With this exception in mind, however, when it came to legs aesthetic considerations generally dominated. Thus, the Desoutter All-Metal Artificial Limb remained the favourite choice because it corresponded (as their own advertisement declared) 'as nearly as possible to the natural one, there being no ugly gaps at the ankle or bulges at the knee'.[89]

These war-inspired changes in the provision of artificial limbs had scarcely any impact on other disabled groups. The state did not provide artificial limbs to civilians until the welfare settlement after the Second World War.[90] Until that time, unless a disabled person had access to charitable or private funds, he or she was not likely to be fitted with any artificial limb more sophisticated than a peg leg. While these limbs were considered aesthetically unacceptable (even as duplicates) to ex-servicemen, similar view-points were regarded as irrelevant in the case of children: for them, merits of cheapness were paramount.[91] In the fight to transform disabled children into 'useful and efficient citizens', the peg leg was judged adequate.[92]

Equally, working-class men injured in industrial accidents were thought not to require anything sophisticated. In 1917, a county court judge under the Workmen's Compensation Acts noted that in the hundreds of cases involving loss of limbs over which he had presided, he had never heard of a workman being offered anything more than a peg leg. According to his account, the workman did 'not appreciate or understand the advantage of an artificial limb, and, if he did, ha[d] not the means to buy one'.[93] Workers' organizations agreed that privation was the major constraint. In 1920, Frank Hall, a representative of the Miners' Federation of Great Britain, contended that the responsibility for providing artificial limbs should rest with the employer. However, employers were only willing to provide peg legs while workers preferred more sophisticated varieties. Although Hall admitted that the peg leg might be more useful at work, he reminded the committee that life did not revolve around the workplace: outside the mine, aesthetically appealing limbs were more desirable.[94] Although the evidence is uneven, it is clear that most companies made very little (if any) provision for artificial limbs. This can be seen in the evidence before the Departmental Committee on Workmen's Compensation immediately after the war.[95] Only a few employers (or their representatives) boasted that they *did* provide artificial replacements. Thus, the director of a wholesale chemical business firmly reminded the committee that his company did not 'do everything entirely from a pounds, shillings and pence point of view'.[96] More typical, however, was the evidence given by Charles Frederick Allsop, representing a large shipping firm. He said that the insurance firms that he used provided artificial limbs to men injured in the course of employment. However, when cross-examined he was forced to admit that he could not name one that did so.[97] In mining, trade unions usually provided limbs.[98] The Miners' Federation noted that they relied on donations given at concerts and football matches to get sufficient money to buy limbs for disabled workmen.[99] In Somerset, employers paid seventy-five per cent of the cost of an artificial limb: workers paid the rest.[100] Henry Eustace Mitton, giving evidence on behalf of various colliery companies, stated that employers and employees shared the cost of providing the limb, and that 'the workmen join[ed] together very enthusiastically for these things' by declaring a 'cap week' in the particular section of the pit where an injured man had worked. The employer paid half of the total cost and the miners would contribute the rest.[101] Other trade unions expressed resentment at having to make 'sympathetic appeals' to employers for what should – in their view – have been a 'right'.[102]

For the industrially maimed, provision of artificial limbs was a luxury: indeed, receiving any form of compensation was often a struggle. In the compensation court, the injured worker was customarily treated as though he were 'on trial'. Thus, the secretary of the Trades Union Congress's Social Insurance Department complained how the injured worker was callously

handed over to the tender mercies of a concern whose main purpose is to make a profit out of him and he finds himself confronted with some of the most expensive medical and legal brains in the country, not to help him but to prevent him getting a few shillings which the law says he ought to have. In fact he may not be able to get even the few shillings' so-called compensation because, whilst the law says he is to have it, it does not provide any source from which it is to come, with the result that in a great number of cases the employer is unable to meet his liabilities and the worker gets nothing.[103]

Insurance doctors tended to be hostile to workers.[104] While insurance companies employed eminent medical specialists, workmen had to rely on over-worked panel doctors.[105] It is not surprising to hear bitter comments by disabled men about their treatment. Michael McAleer was such a man. One of his legs had been amputated in 1925 (as a result of a tubercular bone disease), and his other leg was 'ankylosed at the knee'. He was angry about the limitations of National Insurance and what he saw as the inequitable treatment between disabled civilians and ex-servicemen. Although he had been paying National Insurance since 1916, he complained,

I find it very hard to go on meeting the cost of repairs to my limb (which is now fully paid for). And yet there is 1/4 stopped out of my wages every week to pay Insurance. Why is it, can you say, that an artificial limb cannot be provided for a member and kept in repair, as many of the Societies have large surpluses and we are compelled to pay Insurance?

His real bitterness, however, was directed at ex-servicemen, as his letter makes clear:

Had I been disabled (the way I am now) in the war I should not only have had artificial limbs provided but I would have had a good pension to [sic]. As it is I have neither but I have to earn my living as best I can, and if I fail to do that there is no other shelter or place for me that I know of but the workhouse infirmary. I was hoping for some improvement under a Labour Government; but things seem to go on without any sign of a change. We adult civilian cripples have no provision allowed.[106]

Although disabled civilians neither gained nor lost from improvements in the supply of artificial limbs to disabled servicemen, in certain other ways their material well-being deteriorated. The war, for example, exacerbated the shortage of accommodation for disabled civilians as the war-maimed were often sent to recuperate in the workshops and homes that had been established for civilians. Thus, as soon as war was declared it was announced in Agnes Hunt's famous home for disabled children at Baschurch (Shropshire) that 'England's need must come first and that of course the women and children must be sent to their own homes' and their beds be filled with wounded soldiers.[107] Such actions caused Sir Napier Burnett to lament at a conference on the Care of Invalid and Crippled Children in 1920 that giving priority to ex-servicemen had resulted in 'an appalling amount of suffering' amongst disabled civilians.[108]

It was not only in terms of the distribution of economic resources that the position of disabled civilians deteriorated after the war. The shift of attention towards the war-mutilated resulted in an increased militarization in the treatment of civilians. The use of military rites and the imposition of militarist values were not novel disciplines applied to disabled people. Crippled members of the Bristol Guild of the

8 Photograph of crippled Boy Scouts, n.d., from the Bristol Guild of the
Handicapped Papers in Bristol Record Office.

Handicapped wore uniforms, saluted the flag and performed military
drill (illus. 8). They were both typical representatives of urban slum-
dwellers, and pitiable objects requiring special attention. From the
establishment in 1894 of the Guild of the Brave Poor Things, they
described themselves as a 'military Religious Order'. Their rooms
were covered with military flags, members pinned badges to their
uniforms, battle hymns were sung and they represented themselves by
a sign consisting of a crutch crossed by a sword.[109] Their members
were exhorted to act as 'brave soldiers' and their leaders described
their members as a 'small battalion' that belonged to

a great army of suffering ones. They have all fallen on life's battlefield,
wounded and maimed – men, women, and children. But the spirit of the guild
has put a new courage in their hearts and a new defiance of failure; the sword is
gripped afresh by feeble hands as they realise that there is still a place for them
in life, and that they are called, even with the strongest, to 'Fight the Good
Fight'.[110]

Within a wide range of organizations, this militarist tone increased
during the war years. It is not surprising to find that the admission of
adult, high-status and politically sensitive servicemen into institutions

accustomed to dealing with children and young people should have such an impact. There was the direct adoption of techniques used for the rehabilitation of soldiers to civilians. Remedial exercises were copied directly from the War Office. While in schools, military drill was being replaced by gentler forms of reformed-Swedish drill (as shall be seen in Chapter Four), in institutions for disabled civilians, the harsher system prevailed.

Furthermore, after the war, there was increased surgical intervention into the lives of civilians.[111] The Royal Cripples' Hospital published a pamphlet entitled *You Can Help Perform this Miracle* (illus. 9). The 'miracle' referred to is depicted on the cover of the pamphlet: to the upper left stands a vacant-eyed boy in irons; in the centre, surgeons and nurses lean over an operating table; in the bottom right corner, the same boy wields a cricket bat. The message is clear: surgery transforms dependant cripples into real Englishmen. Prior to this time, homes for disabled civilians had been largely concerned with educational and/or vocational training rather than surgical intervention. The dramatic development in orthopaedic surgery during the war reversed this emphasis. A large surgical infrastructure was established to deal with the sudden increase in the number of mutilated men. This infrastructure included not only buildings and equipment, but also trained doctors, nurses and technicians. The demand for orthopaedic surgeons to perform delicate and highly skilled tasks such as suturing nerves, transplanting tendons, treating fractures and making artificial limbs (for which demand was relatively rare in peacetime), now became so overwhelming that American orthopaedic surgeons had to be imported. In addition to those belonging to the military, hospitals specializing in orthopaedics opened in Aberdeen, Edinburgh, Glasgow, Belfast, Newcastle, Leeds, Liverpool, Manchester, Bristol, Birmingham, Cardiff, Dublin and London.[112] As Roger Cooter has pointed out in his book *Surgery and Society in Peace and War*, it was not inevitable that the demands of war would have resulted in a growth of orthopaedic surgery: equally important was the opening up of a political space in medicine for this new specialism.[113] Military medical services also stressed the need for long-term treatment: discharge from hospital no longer indicated the end of the investment. Rather, orthopaedic teams, consisting of doctors, nurses and voluntary workers, were established to provide for the treatment and the aftercare of the disabled.[114] Thus, the wartime economy created an army of people whose livelihood was dependent on maintaining a supply of cripples.

Dismantling this industry was scarcely considered by the interested

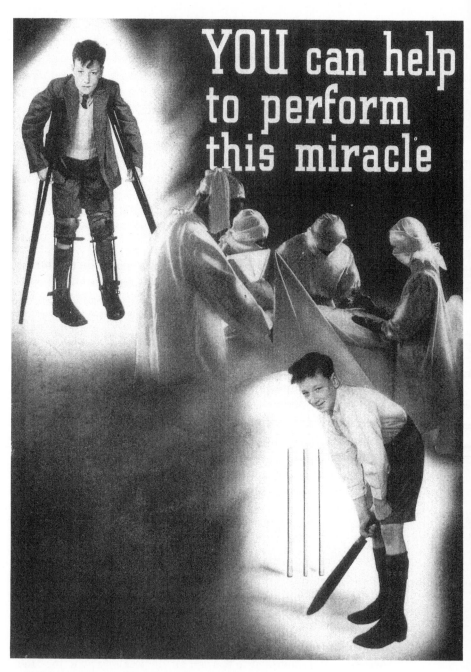

9 'YOU can help to perform this miracle', cover from a pamphlet, Royal Cripples'
Hospital, Birmingham, 1939.

parties. As Frederick Watson recalled, 'Suddenly the Armistice came, and in the rush of demobilization . . . what was to happen to the orthopaedic centres, the trained staff, the workshops, the vast store of practical experience? Were all these things to go down to the grave of discarded things? . . . The War had produced at a cost a gigantic plant not to turn out munitions but to help the disabled.' For him, the solution was obvious: the resources needed to be redirected towards disabled children.[115] The surgeon and senior medical officer of the Ministry of Health, J. Smith Whitaker, spoke on behalf of the industrially maimed. He was concerned that if decisive action were not taken, orthopaedic resources would be dissipated and the 'masseur might find this occupation gone and [might] turn to some other trade'. He advised, 'You have the organisation in existence, and you do not want to see that broken up if you can help it.'[116] Resources were redirected, and orthopaedic hospitals for disabled ex-servicemen were converted into orthopaedic hospitals for workmen.[117] Within six years of the end of the war, 120 local education authorities had made provision for the orthopaedic treatment of children, and the Board of Education had decided to target the 200 areas that had not done so.[118] In the first half of the 1920s, a number of orthopaedic hospitals were built through personal beneficence, several general hospitals were enlarged or provided with orthopaedic departments, and after-care centres were established.[119] As A. H. Wood admitted caustically in a minute to the Board of Education in 1923 when defending plans to establish an orthopaedic hospital in Yorkshire, there was no such thing as a disabled child who did not need surgery.[120]

The well-being of the physically disabled was also changed by the sudden influx of a new constituency of disabled men into the employment market. The entire responsibility for the deterioration of the welfare of disabled civilians after the war should not be laid at the door of ex-servicemen. Industrial competition was partly to blame as it intensified during these years, and the higher than normal levels of unemployment in parts of Britain in the 1920s and 1930s to some extent reduced the chances of employment for disabled people.[121] The cheery quips of the limbless men in a contemporary cartoon (illus. 10) emphasize the distance between a well-meaning, but rather stupid, woman and mutilated servicemen, while at the same time denying the bitter realities of post-war employment for the disabled. In 1937, 740,000 ex-servicemen from the First World War were said to be unemployed. Employers had no incentive to give jobs to disabled men.[122] With characteristic insensitivity towards their members, the City of Bristol Guild of the Handicapped lamented in 1920 that 'now

By Miss Urquhart.

"What will you do when you leave hospital, my poor fellow?"
"Oh! I've got a splendid job – in a brewery making 'ops, and my friend here
he's goin' in for short and!'"

10 Miss E. M. Urquhart, 'What will you do when you leave hospital, my poor fellow?', cartoon in *The Fourth: The Magazine of the 4th London General Hospital, RAMC (T.F.)*, vol. 1, September 1916.

the soldiers [were] back, the unemployed problem [was] with [them], and there seem[ed] no place for these little lame dogs'.[123] In the mining industry, increasing competition from abroad, the hindrances of the quota (which placed a limit on production) and continuing trade disputes meant that employers attempted to cut costs even further, consequently allowing 'little scope for the sympathetic treatment of disabled workmen'.[124] Employers recognized that disabled workers were a greater compensation risk since they were more liable to have accidents and, when they did, they tended to be more serious.[125] Thus employers' representatives in shipbuilding, engineering, railways, building, master printing, iron and steel manufacture and cartage refused to employ disabled ex-servicemen unless the state agreed to assume liability for compensation.[126] Many employers preferred to employ single women and foreigners – a state of affairs that some commentators found repellent.[127]

Competition between the able-bodied and the disabled, however, was probably more important in the employment prospects of the slightly disabled than the severely disabled. The high unemployment of the severely disabled between the wars was less due to the recession, since the market for their labour tended to be artificially protected from national trends, than to the over-supply of severely disabled workers.

One man, signing himself simply 'Cripple from Childhood', wrote of the difficulties involved in earning a living by selling goods in the streets:

Almost every day people asked me if I was disabled in the war. I was often tempted to tell a lie and say 'yes', for then I would have got more custom and more civility . . . Everywhere I found that disabled soldiers always got preference. When I was selling chocolates, I had often to compete with these men at the theatre queues and elsewhere. They wear their medals and have 'Disabled Ex-Service Man' notices on their caps and on the trays. A civilian cripple has no chance beside them.[128]

Although there were calls for disabled civilians to be allocated a proportion of the jobs given to maimed soldiers, in the fight for resources, it was these civilians who fell to the bottom of the heap.[129] Even able-bodied ex-servicemen received priority.

The war also changed the types of work considered appropriate for the disabled. As John Galsworthy wrote in 1919, 'Of little use of man to nation would be the mere patching up of bodies, so that, like a row of old gossips against a sunlit wall, our disabled might sit and weary out their days. If that were all we could do for them, gratitude is proven fraudulent, device bankrupt; and the future of our countries must drag with a lame foot.'[130] Rather, disabled ex-servicemen were deemed to be in need of 'curative work'. In part, this was intended to prepare them for their return to productive labour. The philosophy behind curative work stressed the interrelationship between the mind and the body. Physical disability was said to have

always been attended by certain temperamental reactions, and prolonged treatment due to an ever-advancing skill in operative technique made it essential that recovery of body should not be jeopardized by impatience or despondency of mind . . . Productive and interesting labour took the place of mechanical implements; training in handiwork, or trade suitable for future employment, brought a new routine into hospital routine.[131]

This regime had another side to it: it gave increased power to officials as opposed to parents. There is much evidence to suggest that parents resisted the pressures on them to send their disabled children to work instead of keeping them at home. The Ministry of Labour's Employment and Insurance reports in the 1920s provided many examples of such parents who challenged attempts by the wartime army of After-Care Specialists to find remunerative work for their young children. One work-seeker spoke of a mother who insisted on telling every prospective employer that her disabled son 'might drop dead at any moment'. The work-seeker protested to the Ministry of Labour that this was absolutely untrue and that the boy could be seen playing football in the streets.[132] Curative work further solidified the emphasis on vocational education, as opposed to a general education in the arts and sciences which people lobbying on behalf of disabled children had been demanding.[133]

Absence Versus Presence

Thus far, it has been argued in this chapter that a combination of wartime policies and practices which were carried into the inter-war period, and economic insecurity in the 1920s and 1930s, resulted in a shift in the allocation of economic and emotional resources away from disabled civilians. To argue that the experience of dismemberment during the war made things worse for disabled civilians is not to idealize the position of servicemen. All men in war feared being torn apart physically. Rowland Luther wrote, 'I didn't mind dying, but the fear of mutilation played havoc with our minds. I had seen much of it, and wanted to die whole.'[134] More positively (perhaps because he had just been sent away from the front lines), Lawrence Gameson confessed in his diary to his great sense of relief, 'it is very good to be here. As I look at my limbs, in the bath, I rejoice, somewhat ridiculously, that they are still whole.'[135] After the war, men who had not been so fortunate struggled with the devastation wreaked upon their bodies. Not only were disabled civilians adversely affected by the wartime excess of disabled men, but maimed ex-servicemen also rapidly lost their claim to special consideration. Indeed, the social status of disabled civilians deteriorated after the war partly because of the increased callousness and neglect towards the weak in general – *even* the heralded heroes back from the battlefields.[136]

The early sentimentalization of the war-wounded during the war and in the early 1920s is well documented.[137] 'Whole' men and women simpered over absent parts. A film on disablement in war, called *Lest We Forget*, was released all over the country in 1920, and only cinema managers in the north of England protested against its excessively sentimental representation of disablement.[138] Public rhetoric judged soldiers' mutilations to be 'badges of their courage, the hall-mark of their glorious service, their proof of patriotism'.[139] Popular myth has it that women were particularly fond of falling in love with the wounded, who were not beneath bargaining pity for love, as in a cartoon (illus. 11) where a somewhat complacent-looking archetypal Englishman murmurs to his nurse, 'Love's a fine tonic when you're wounded, what?' The parading of mutilated 'warriors' was praised for encouraging other men to enlist ('To-day some boys in blue was passin' me, and some of 'em they 'ad no legs to walk . . . And – well, I couldn't look 'em in the

11 A. C. Williams, 'Love's a fine tonic when you're wounded, what!', cartoon, dated 7 October 1916, in the autograph album of a nurse, E. Campbell, in the 15th General Hospital, Egypt, 1916–17. [IWM Misc. 93 Item 1386]

12 Limbless men. [IWM Q108161]

face, and so I'm goin', goin' to declare').[140] The disabled soldier was 'not less but more of a man'.[141] The phantom limbs of the maimed soldiers represented their loss in a way that the bodies of the congenitally deformed could not replicate.[142] These men were 'young chaps . . . broken and useless': they were 'broken warriors'.[143] A popular song during the war substituted 'doll' for 'warrior' in an effort to gain greater pathos:

> A man and maiden met a month ago
> She said, There's one thing I should like to know
> Why aren't you in khaki or navy blue
> And fighting for your country like other men do?
> The man looked up and slowly shook his head
> Dear Madam, do you know what you have said?
> For I gladly took my chance
> Now my right arm's out in France,
> I'm one of England's Broken Dolls.[144]

Poets, writing in their honour, adopted the ironic passive tone of the newly styled, modern poetry.[145] Photographers (see illus. 12) used the traditions of portraiture to stun their viewers: lined up, tidily dressed as civil servants, with calm smiles, this photograph represented the height of pathos and denial.

The absent parts of men's bodies came to exert a special patriotic power. In the struggle for status and resources, absence could be more powerful than presence. The less visible or invisible diseases that disabled many servicemen (particularly those in Mesopotamia) could not compete with limblessness (which was more prevalent amongst those being shipped back from France).[146] This was the first war fought by British men in which the number of deaths from battle casualties was higher than deaths from disease (official statistics report that there were 740,000 deaths from casualties compared with 84,000 from disease). From the first months of war, injured men were accorded greater respect than those who were ill.[147] Thus, Sir Thomas Lewis wrote to the secretary of the Disabilities Committee, pointing out that the diseased ex-serviceman was at a disadvantage when compared with the mutilated man because his body did not display the 'signs' of injury: yet, he added, 'you can never get away from the hidden flaw in the wood'.[148] Lawrence Gameson was one officer who admitted to feeling uneasy about the distinctions being made between men designated 'W' (wounded) and those designated 'S' (sick). He noted that 'once a man had been officially labelled 'W' . . . he [was] in a much better bargaining position than one marked 'S''.[149] He spoke from personal experience: when he was eventually sent back from France suffering from epidemic catarrhal jaundice, women at the quay speculated about the nature of his wounds. He wrote, 'I lay doggo, feeling an awful fraud to be only sick.'[150]

Indeed, the sympathy allocated to the ill or diseased ex-serviceman was often negligible. The War Office, Admiralty and Air Force frequently simply decreed that there was no proof that the illness had been contracted in service – or they hinted that the sick man had contracted it 'on leave'.[151] The Eugenics Education Society argued against awarding pensions to servicemen who had been invalided out of the armed forces because of illness.[152] Military medical officers were accused of betting that a recruit would be killed before his physical weakness would make him a tax on the government.[153] Royal Army Medical Corps men were (unfairly) denounced for being disinterested in anything other than wounds.[154] Nurses in France admitted that they found 'medical' work boring in comparison to 'surgical' work.[155] Even chaplains near the Front confessed that they ignored the spiritual needs of diseased soldiers on the grounds that 'the wounded work appeared always the more important'.[156]

Servicemen paid a high price for such attitudes. For instance, the assistant secretary to the Ministry of Pensions defended the more flexible system of allocating pensions to diseased ex-servicemen, when compared with the physically mutilated.[157] As he told the Committee on the Employment of Severely Disabled Men in December 1920,

the man with a physical injury is predominantly a healthier type of man originally, who, for that reason, was put in the firing line and thus exposed to injury. On the other hand, the case of disease is, in the great majority of instances, a case of disease aggravated, or claimed to be aggravated, by war service . . . But, to a very great extent, the disease case . . . is the case of a man of inferior physique or mentality in the first instance. Hence, the pension assessment of these cases, according to the evidence, rules on the low side, that is, for the most part, under fifty per cent.[158]

According to a writer to *The Times* in 1920, 'Next to the loss of life, the sacrifice of a limb is the greatest sacrifice a man can make for his country.'[159] Absent bodily parts rather than sickly ones were noticed.

The sentimentalization of the war dismembered did not, however, last. Despite emotional reminders in the *Liverpool Chronicle* of what would have happened to the value of real estate and Britain's womanhood if men had not given their limbs for freedom, residents in West Kirby successfully resisted a plan to establish a home for disabled soldiers in their area.[160] By the early 1930s, the *Tailor and Cutter* could advertise the sale of silk braces made of the ribbon of the Mons Star, the Military Cross or the Distinguished Conduct Medal for a shilling. For a smaller sum, men could buy garters made from other famous ribbons.[161] Those who remained in hospital after the war found that many of the privileges that they had enjoyed before the Armistice were removed. A navy man, crippled as a result of war service, complained,

The hospitals had many patriotic visitors and supporters during the years of the war, when the nation was in peril, but since the Armistice this band had dwindled down to just a few. Many of those people who during the war, visited the hospitals with gifts, and took the men out for long drives, and to entertainments, gave up – at the signing of the Armistice – what they were pleased to call their 'war-work'.[162]

Limblessness became normalized. As one woman noted, 'A lady I met who lived in Brighton said that at first, when the Dome was turned into a hospital and the men who had lost legs were collected there, they had all felt horrified. But now when in most parts of the town, on the front and the piers, you saw swarms of such men getting about on crutches, it had ceased to affect most people.'[163]

More importantly, the Ministry of Pensions came to see its job as primarily one of limiting state liabilities. Lawrence Gameson accused the ministry (for which he developed 'the greatest contempt') of being 'curiously inhibited' in helping disabled ex-servicemen. He agreed that it had to 'exercise restraint in its disbursement', but asserted that it was 'under no obligation automatically to regard almost every claim as suspect; which it did, summoning medical and surgical yes men to help it wriggle out of its minimal responsibilities'.[164] He accused it of being concerned only with the 'distant question of employers' liabilities: PENSIONS, that is to say'.[165] Gameson could have levelled the same charge against local pension committees as he levelled against the state. At the regional level, pension committees tended to be composed of old soldiers. Accustomed to dealing with what they considered to be malingering-prone professional soldiers before the war, they regarded it their duty to distribute funds as widely as possible. The pensioner was a 'criminal in the dock'. His statements 'were considered lies unless they [could] be proved up to the hilt; he [was] never given any benefit of doubt; and every possible snare cunningly laid by red tape and officialdom [was] used to the fullest extent to prejudice the pensioner's case'.[166] In a largely conscripted army, the petitioner's resentment at being treated as 'the worst type of pre-war sweat' was scarcely surprising.[167]

There were also administrative explanations for the long-term neglect of men disabled by warfare. As mentioned earlier, from 1915 the financial and material care of the war-mutilated was the responsibility of local committees. However, these were slow to be established. Early in 1916 only 50 out of 250 local committees had been constituted.[168] In other cases, the naïvety of committee members meant that they planned to assemble too infrequently to be effective. For instance, it was reported in March 1916 that the Carmarthen County Council was not intending to meet until May and when it did was to be 'composed mainly of farmers, a class notoriously incapable of understanding an industrial centre like this town'.[169] Conflict between the ex-servicemen and the pensioning authorities was inevitable, even after it was made compulsory to include at least one disabled ex-serviceman on each committee (it was hoped, rather optimistically, that this might not only encourage the committees to show more sympathy but would also strengthen the loyalty of ex-servicemen).[170] Some hint of the problems that the inclusion of ex-servicemen on these committees caused may be seen in the report of a deputation from the Donegal Local Committee to the Ministry of Pensions in Belfast, which protested against proposals to increase the number of disabled ex-servicemen on the committees. As the secretary of the County Donegal Local Committee reported,

I am afraid the stamp of disabled men at present residing in this county is not one that can be given a seat on a Committee. We had a case at Stranorlar where the disabled man did not agree with the finding of the Sub. Committee and instead od [*sic*] moving an amendment he walked out from the Meeting and published the whole proceedings of the Meeting in his own words to everyone in the district, with the result that members who were business men suffered loss by being boycotted. The majority of men residing in these districts are or were farm labourers and the degree of education can be put down as practically Nil.[171]

Local committees and government agencies refused to bear the entire burden of relief for disabled ex-servicemen. Charity was evoked. Ex-servicemen naturally fought this demeaning of their status. Raven Hill's sketch of a one-legged ex-serviceman with wooden limb, ragged clothes and begging hat was intended to dismay readers of *Reveille* (illus. 13). The fact that the man portrayed was obviously a soldier from an earlier conflict only served to heighten people's fears that the modern-day serviceman (conscript as well as volunteer) was not going to be accorded greater national status than the professional soldier of the past. Montague A. Bere, a popular war padre, fumed in a letter in 1918 against these 'ribbon hunting organisations'.[172] James M. Hogge of the Federation of Discharged and Demobilized Sailors and Soldiers spluttered against the YMCA's appeal for old clothes and boots for unemployed, mutilated ex-servicemen, 'Do we recollect public promises made to men who volunteered? No workhouse, no neglect, no unemployment. Instead, pensions, training, employment, priority of claim. And now a charitable organization asks the same public for old boots and old clothes!'[173] All that was allegedly demanded was the 'British idea of fair play and justice'.[174] As one disabled man reiterated, 'it is not charity I want, but what I am entitled to'.[175]

Furthermore, although the state was willing to accept some of the responsibility for male mutilation, it demanded proof of heroic status. The question of entitlement was most clearly spelt out in the 'Memorandum on Pensions for Invalided Soldiers' of 1916 where Sir Frederick Milner and others were criticized for appearing to treat all soldiers as 'Noble heroes' anxious only to fight to the death on behalf of the country. The Minister of Pensions knew better: 'I think it will be agreed that we should pension all those who are "Noble heroes", but I see no reason why we should pension those who are not.'[176] Indeed, notice was taken of the fact that many of the mutilated soldiers were pleased with their injuries: it had got them out of the war, thus saving their lives.[177] In a nurse's autograph album, an unknown soldier sketched two figures (illus. 14): to the left, a dispirited clerk stands beneath the words, 'YOUR KING AND COUNTRY NEED YOU'; to the right, the same man is shown, one-legged but joyously alive and optimistic. In the words of the soldier and dock labourer, Bert Conn,

13 Raven Hill, 'Lest We Forget', drawing in *Reveille*, 1918.

'many men would willingly have sacrificed an arm or leg to have been able to get out of it'.[178]

Debates regarding entitlement became increasingly bitter and divisive. The politics of absence was a crucial variable. What were parts of the body worth? In 1915, the Revd Andrew Clark wrote in his diary, 'One of the reasons why recruiting is slow in Dundee is the belief which the Dundee women have got that permanently wounded men

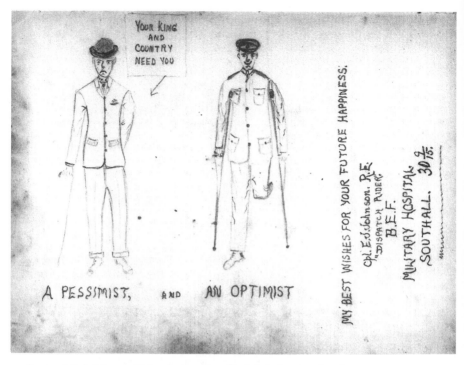

14 Corporal E. J. Johnson, 'A Pessimist and an Optimist', drawing, dated 30 September 1915, in the autograph album of a nurse, Miss E. R. Knight, 1915–18. [IWM Misc. 4 Item 62]

are to receive only 1s. a week pension. One of the women said to Miss Alice Paterson the other day "It isn't likely that I'm going to let my sons go to the front to get a leg or arm off and then come back to me with only a shilling a week." '[179] One shilling a week was not sufficient compensation – but what was? Since thousands of sons did sign up in Dundee in 1915, the question must obviously have been – the sum that was considered adequate compensation for increasing an individual's risk of disability. The evaluations made by the recruits and their families were underestimates: they were betting not only on disability but also on death, and imperfect knowledge of the odds meant that they could not make an informed decision. Furthermore, not all rationale can be reduced to economics – as many historians have noted, there were other reasons for enlisting (such as patriotism, boredom and desire to defend the women of Belgium).[180]

However, we can hazard some guesses as to the value the *state* put on various parts of the body. In the early years of war, war disablement pensions were decided according to loss of earning capacity. This followed in the tradition of legislation providing for industrial compensation. The problems with this method of evaluation were clear: it penalized the man who tried to return to work as against the man who deliberately refrained; the particular work that a man happened to have at the time of entering the armed forces did not necessarily represent the type of work he would be normally capable of performing; and it took no account of the additional risk of unemployment due to reduced capacity or of the loss of the amenities of life independent of the ability to earn a wage. In the context of disabled workers, it was possible to ignore these problems: not so for a conscripted workforce. From 1917, therefore, disability pensions for ex-servicemen were made dependent on the degree of disablement. The assistant secretary to the Ministry of Pensions pointed out that when the committee sat down to work out pension levels, the important question was: disablement for what purpose? Disability was to be judged 'in relation to a theoretically perfect physical machine'.[181] Thus, the question came to centre on whether a man was better or worse off if he had lost this, that or the other part of his body.[182] The criterion was not earning capacity. For example, an ex-serviceman who had lost an arm and who worked as a highly paid bank manager would still be entitled to a disability pension for the loss of his arm. The rationale can be seen in a series of questions and answers between Judge Stewart, chairman of the Home Office Committee on Workmen's Compensation, and Dr Stewart, principal medical officer of the Ministry of Pensions:

Chairman: In effect he gets his pension because he is disabled?
Dr Stewart: Yes.
Chairman: Qua man?
Dr Stewart: Yes.
Chairman: And not qua worker?
Dr Stewart: Yes.
Chairman: Therefore in effect it might be regarded from some points of view as a physical disfigurement. He suffers from a physical disability which is a wider term, for which he is compensated.[183]

What was being compensated was 'loss of amenity', not 'loss of working capacity'.[184] Each part of men's bodies was allocated a moral weighting based on the degree to which it incapacitated a man from 'being' a man, rather than 'acting' as one. Thus, men who had lost two or more limbs or suffered severe facial disfigurement were said to have a 100 per cent disability (worth a pension of 27s. 6d.) while men who had lost two fingers of either hand were said to have a 20 per cent disability (worth 5s. 6d.).[185]

Compensation based on disfigurement rather than loss of earnings

TABLE: WAR PENSIONS FOR PHYSICAL INJURY

Proportion Corresponding to Degree of Disablement

Specific Injury	Proportion of Pension
1. Loss of two or more limbs, loss of an arm and an eye, loss of a leg and an eye, loss of both hands or all fingers and thumbs, loss of both feet, loss of a hand or a foot, total loss of sight, total paralysis, lunacy, wounds or disease resulting in a man being permanently bedridden, wounds to internal organs or head involving total permanent disability, very severe facial disfigurement	100%
2. Amputation of right arm at shoulder joint	90%
3. Amputation of leg at hip or left arm at shoulder joint, severe facial disfigurement, total loss of speech	80%
4. Short thigh amputation of leg or of right arm above or through elbow, total deafness	70%
5. Amputation of leg above knee (other than 4) and through knee or of left arm above or through elbow, or of right arm below elbow	60%
6. Amputation of leg below knee or the left arm below elbow, loss of vision of one eye	50%
7. Loss of thumb or of four fingers of right hand	40%
8. Loss of thumb or four fingers of left hand, or of three fingers of right hand	30%
9. Loss of two fingers of either hand	20%

(Source: Ministry of Pensions leaflet, c.1920).

was an important concession, and one that the industrially maimed argued should be applied equally to them.[186] This was certainly the view of a machinist signing himself as 'T. Knight'. In 1935, a letter he had written to his trade union representative was passed on to the Social Insurance Department of the Trades Union Congress. Knight had been employed in a cabinet-machine shop, where a piece of wood thrown out by a faulty cutter had hit his face, cutting through the cartilage of his nose, and requiring him to have an operation and a fortnight in bed. In compensation, he was paid half-wages for the time he was out of work (i.e., 22*s.* in total). He wrote, 'I now have an unsightly scar on my nose and upper lip and the nose is very much out of shape . . . and it struck me that my nose was worth more than that to me and also the operation was rather a painful one. Please tell me if I am entitled to anything further than the 22/-.'[187] Unfortunately, the response was negative. Major A. C. Farquharson of the Committee on Workmen's Compensation could have been referring to a man such as Knight when he noted, 'Workmen always assess their compensation on the wrong basis. They think they have a right to compensation for pain or disfigurement or shock – not medical shock. It is very difficult to make them understand that it is merely loss of earning capacity and it seems to them unjust that, after a great deal of pain, they should get such a small amount.'[188] Such an attitude caused much concern among trade unionists. For instance, in 1920, Robert Barrie Walker of the Parliamentary Committee of the Trades Union Congress deplored the fact that under the workmen's compensation acts, the disabled man was compensated only for the loss of earning capacity and not for the disfigurement itself.[189] George W. Booth, director and secretary of a large insurance company, partly agreed, stating that compensation for loss of earnings only was appropriate in the case of temporary injury, but not in the case of permanent disablement. He added, 'we should like to see a fixed scale according to the injury similar to that set by the War Office'.[190] This battle was not won until after the Second World War.

Even in the case of war pensioners, however, the official schedule was only one side of the story. Further differentiation had initially been considered necessary. Pensions were divided into a flat rate and an alternative pension. The latter pension was paid at a higher rate and was intended to provide 'something extra' for men who had been earning over 25*s.* a week prior to the war.[191] Despite the fact that it had been decreed that the value of each part of the male body was identical irrespective of social class or military rank, it was argued that there were psychological variables that differentiated men. Those of the rank of officer and above, therefore, had to be given an additional gratuity to compensate them – not for anatomical loss, but 'for the pain and suffering [they had] experienced'.[192] Pain and suffering were not similarly compensated for among the rank and file. However, it took 'almost superhuman' effort to get the alternative pension.[193] In the year to 31 March 1919, 668,700 pensions were being paid, of which only 1,700 (or less than 0.3 per cent) were alternative pensions.[194] With the introduction of conscription, and on the grounds that it was 'grossly undemocratic' and based on a man's pre-war occupation instead of 'common service to the country', it had to be discontinued.[195]

The importance of the fact that this was a conscripted army cannot be minimized. Professional soldiers were *intended* to be mutilated – like certain classes of labourers, it was the penalty they paid for volunteering for the employment. This view was widespread, and most directly stated by H. Wolfe, responsible for the Liabilities Department of the Ministry of Labour, when giving evidence to the Committee on Pensions in 1920. Although he admitted that 'it sound[ed] harsh', his sympathy rested with the conscripted serviceman:

It is assured that when a soldier undertakes a soldier's career he undertakes it knowing the risks he would run. It is his profession, it is his life's occupation. Therefore if he is in a specially bad position – and heaven knows many of them are – that is the business of the War Office. Our business is to look after the civilian who in normal circumstances would not have been a fighter. With regard to the ex-regular soldier, that is his life.

Major MacKenzie Wood questioned Wolfe on this point, pointing out that the regular soldier was not to know that the Great War was to be different from all others and that, after the war, he would have to compete with hundreds of thousands of other disabled servicemen. Wolfe agreed but reiterated that 'putting it in its most brutal form – it [was] the risk of the soldier's life'. The ex-Regular soldier 'was on a different footing to the civilian. The man [they had] in mind had set up in life on an ordinary basis. He [was] pulled away from that life and his business [was] interrupted. He [was] shot in again and [found] his business ruined.' This was the man they helped.[196] The tension was not only between the Regular soldier and those who signed on for the duration of the war. There was another distinction and that was between the volunteer and the conscript. Politically, however, the Ministry of Pensions could not afford to distinguish between these two groups. As the ex-serviceman's MP, James M. Hogge, replied to a question from a Captain Coote about whether it was possible to provide different pensions for volunteers from those given to con-scripts, 'No: besides, it is not the kind of distinction you want to carry further forward into the public life of the country. You want to keep those things behind you, however much you may have felt about it.'[197]

It was also argued that entitlement should be limited in many other ways. State resources were only to be shared between men who could prove themselves to be 'white British': thus, despite fighting alongside British servicemen, Maltese soldiers and their widows received signifi-cantly lower pensions.[198] Accepting that the First World War was different from previous wars in that it was fought by conscripted men, the government restricted entitlement to First World War veterans – excluding, for example, men whose injuries were due to service in prior conflicts such as the Boer War.[199] Furthermore, it was not sufficient simply to have been injured between 1914 and 1918. A man also had to have sustained his injury overseas.[200] More important, he had to be adjudged to be deserving. As we shall see in the next chapter, servicemen suspected of malingering were excluded from all resources. The controversy created by these rules can be seen in an example provided in October 1917 by the medical superintendent of the County Mental Hospital in Cheddleton, Leek (Staffordshire). In his institution was a man – called Jack Frost for convenience – who was a 'ne'er-do-well, moral defective'. Frost was a 'congenital defect' with 'many convictions for minor crimes', yet because compulsory military service put him in uniform, since the war he had 'never lived so well in his life'. The superintendent compared Frost with four other men: Jack Heraty, Thomas Woolley, William Allen and Henshall Gater. Patriotism had led these men to voluntarily enlist, but 'on account of age and other like reasons for which they were not responsible', they had not served abroad. Consequently, when under stress of military service the health of Frost and the four patriotic men broke, it was the 'ne'er-do-well' who lived happily ever after.[201]

The requirement that the disabled exhibit signs of patriotism also posed problems in Ireland. A Tralee man Gerald McDonnell had lost an arm serving with the First Munster Fusiliers. In 1935, when living in Liverpool, he wrote to the Ministry of Pensions asking,

Are Discharged Soldiers in Southern Ireland whom are republican Soldiers now of De Valera entitled to draw Pensions from England which they are now doing. I know of a Discharged soldier drawing 2.0.0. per week and is a republic soldier who struck Gerald O'Duffy with a hammer on the head when he was making a speech in Tralee last year. Here is another case of a 100 p.c. Pensioner who is living in one of Earl Haigh's homes in Tralee and is an officer in the republic Army. The same man has a son who is also training Republic Soldiers and living on John Bull's money which his father draws as a Pension. Well, Sir, I could give you dozens of men who are drawing Pensions from the British Government and are Traitors to our King and Country; there are hundreds and thousands of Ex-service men who fought for England and who are still loyal to King and Country: my blood freezes in my body to think England paid pensions to traitors of this country.[202]

The Ministry of Pensions was certainly not happy with this situation.

Furthermore, the disabled ex-servicemen in Ireland found themselves living in a country that was not prepared to acknowledge owing anything to men disabled in the war. In a report from Dublin in 1936, the Ministry of Pensions was reminded that the Irish Free State refused to regard itself as having participated as a nation in the First World War and had repudiated any responsibility for men disabled during military service.[203] Ex-servicemen found that employers (especially in rural areas) were reluctant to give them jobs once they discovered that they had fought in the war. According to W. G. Fallon, secretary of the City of Dublin War Pensions Committee,

A reaction took place in Dublin in this sense that these men went off amidst applause and God-speeds, but in the intervening period things happened in Ireland, and when these men came back disabled and broken down in some cases they found that their own relatives had changed their views on public affairs and matters were extremely uncomfortable for the unfortunate man . . . the public in its resentment is inclined to threaten the disabled man.[204]

Irish ex-servicemen were fugitives in their own country. An ex-serviceman working as a tram conductor in Dublin related how a Christmas card for the 5th Division was all he had left: 'they won't even let me wear my medals or ribbons. I spent the twelve happiest years of my life in an Irish regiment. I am a Dublin man, but had I known what Ireland was like now I would never have left the army.[205]

Glorious Fragmentation

The question arises as to why ex-servicemen lost the sympathy of the public and politicians. There are a number of obvious answers to this, amongst which was a widely felt desire to forget the war and its effects. Harold Mellersh wrote of the reaction of people when he returned wounded from the Battle of the Somme, of the widespread kindness he experienced, which he described as a 'kind of shocked pride'. It was as though 'A soldier back from France [had given] the people at home a chance to show their concern, their pity, if it were needed, and their admiration.'[206] This was in 1916 – in less than a year, everything had changed. Shocked pride was replaced by horror and disgust and the attempts by people at home to square the balance of sacrifice with kindly words and actions was obviously a hopeless task: too many servicemen had sacrificed too much. This feeling was exacerbated after the war when a few months – perhaps years – of sympathy were discharged before more realistic goals were returned to. The ex-serviceman was subjected to a similar form of forgetfulness as the disabled child; that is, when young and novel, he was lavished with gifts, but when old and unastonishing, he went unnoticed.[207]

Furthermore, it is easy to assume that the disabled ex-serviceman was unhappy and disillusioned about his treatment. In 1917, an anonymous civil servant in the National Service Department regretted that mutilated soldiers were being dismissed from military hospitals before being sufficiently helped. It was his belief that the average soldier was unconscious of any grievance: 'Quite probably he treats as a matter for entire satisfaction this finish of his therapeutic, as well as his active military career.'[208] Although it was estimated that between 50 and 60 per cent of the war-disabled would benefit from retraining courses, only about 15 per cent proved willing to attend them.[209] This was not solely due to apathy – the fear of losing one's pension and the high wages paid for unskilled labour immediately after the war played some part in the reluctance of disabled ex-servicemen to attend retraining classes. However, even after their pension rights had been assured, and a bonus granted to men while in training, the increasing rates of unemployment by the mid-1920s still failed to drive disabled, unemployed ex-servicemen into training schemes.[210] In part, some of the schemes were obviously impractical: as one observer noted, '[was] it likely that a Cockney car conductor [could] be trained into a successful farmer?'[211] More important was the distaste felt by many ex-servicemen about returning to institutional life – especially one bearing a militarist taint.[212] They were 'fed up with discipline, sick of the sight of khaki, and doctors, and their first idea was to get away and hide themselves'.[213] According to Amy Baker, 'The one craving of each broken hero, after all he ha[d] gone through, was "to go back home to the wife or children" or to the "old mother" if not married. No institution, however comfortable, will keep him for long.'[214] This was echoed by Major Mitchell, the director of training for the Ministry of Pensions: 'They want to be back at their old homes, near their relations and their wives' relations, to sing in the choir of the old church or chapel, to drink in the snug corner of the old public house, to be employed about the old works, or to take such advantage as they still can of the high wages now going in the old town.'[215]

In addition, the disabled could not put up a united front. Organizations representing their interests proliferated and much energy was spent competing with each other.[216] Disabled ex-servicemen could not even count on the comradeship of their fellow soldiers.[217] Most mutilated ex-servicemen preferred suffering in silence to joining the various fraternities.[218] Socialist federations fought right-wing associations. Limbless ex-service organizations competed with groups concerned with both healthy and disabled ex-servicemen. Regional loyalties divided men. Scotland claimed a need for greater resources on the grounds that Scottish regiments ('being thoroughly to be trusted') had been sent to the most dangerous fronts in the war and had therefore suffered disproportionately.[219] The North Western Region pension authorities defended their higher pension costs on the grounds that the poor physical inheritance of soldiers from their industrial cities was more liable to sustain double disabilities – illnesses such as chest complaints and rheumatism in addition to mutilation.[220] Disabled men in Bradford refused to attend workshops in Leeds.[221] Those in Glasgow said that they preferred to be treated in London than in Edinburgh: 'all Scottish soldiers are not Edinburgh men . . . a Glasgow or Dundee soldier would feel as much at home in Regents' Park as in Blacket Avenue . . . After all, London is but little less Scottish than Edinburgh.'[222]

However, broader explanations need to be considered. From the mid-1920s, economic depression had increased the pool of the needy, while simultaneously limiting the supply of capital. The Board of Education reduced staff in 'special schools' and disabled organizations retrenched (cutting their work with disabled adults first).[223] The Central Council for the Care of Cripples described these years as the 'Lean Years'.[224] Short of funds, Poor Law Unions began to resent the implication that they still owed something to disabled ex-servicemen. In 1929, the West Ham Union complained that 'too often the pensioner, instead of regarding his allowance as compensation for his disability and loss of earning power, consider[ed] it a reason why he should in addition receive assistance from the rates . . . the idea that the disability pension entitle[d] him to be kept by the rates ha[d] to be dispelled'.[225] Ex-servicemen came into competition with other needy groups, some of which were seen as *more* needy. The most important was the unemployed – especially the married unemployed man. Not surprisingly, this demeaning of their status was resented by ex-servicemen. W. H. Baker of Tunbridge Wells wrote to the War Pensions Department on 1 June 1937,

Excuse me taking up your valuable time, I am writing to you through comrades & myself, now the State are allowing £6,000 a year to a child while the parents are allso [sic] being allowed £410,000 a year & M. P.s having a rise in salary dont you think Sir that in your Capacity as Minstry [sic] of Pensions it is a time us 100% War Maimed men received a little extra on our £2 per week . . . , so we could have a little more of the necessitys [sic] of life & so that we could feel more like citizens than the position we are placed in now paupers, while other people living on the State are living like millionaries that includs foriegns [sic].[226]

According to many disabled ex-servicemen, the unemployed were in more enviable positions than they themselves were. In 1938, approximately half of disabled ex-servicemen were receiving less than the minimum award of 17s. given to single, young unemployed men without dependants.[227] Sir Frederick Milner pointed out that while an unemployed, able-bodied man and his family were said to be unable to subsist on £4 a week, a man who had 'three ribs and a lung blown away by a shell and who has to be fed through a hole in his teeth as his jaw is locked fast' was entitled to only 12s. 6d. a week.[228] This view was not widely accepted. Trade unions opposed employing disabled ex-servicemen at full wages, arguing that this discriminated against their members (i.e., their able-bodied members only) and led to a general undercutting of wages.[229] Even in the mid-1930s, the situation of disabled ex-servicemen was plaguing the Trades Union Congress, causing Dame Georgiana Buller of the Council for the Care of Cripples to apologize to the TUC for the fact that the employment schemes after the war had been 'very, very badly handled' and reassure them that, in the future, disabled ex-servicemen would only be taught to perform unskilled jobs.[230]

In addition, between the wars, there was a new imperative for adult men to retreat into the home. Male domesticity was regarded as out of the question for those disabled from birth: although not regarded as sexless (indeed, the problem was precisely that it was feared that they might possess too much sexuality), the idea of marriage for them was wholly repugnant to many able-bodied commentators. In contrast, the war-mutilated were regarded as 'real men'. Many had been married before the war and it was assumed that they would make their way back to their wives and families. Of course, no one – least of all the maimed – believed that returning home would be easy. The fear of returning home mutilated was present for all servicemen, and was poignantly expressed by Wilfred Willett in the quotation at the start of this chapter. Willett and his beloved wife were only imagining it. Lieutenant Arthur E. Kaye was one of hundreds of thousands of servicemen who lived through the horror. We have a second-hand account of his suffering in a letter written by the nursing sister, J. Badger, to Kaye's mother. On behalf of the injured soldier, Badger wrote,

Your son Lieut Kay [sic] asked me to write to you & tell you the worst – poor boy he had his left Eye knocked out – & his right leg Amputated, he is very ill indeed, besides the Eye & leg his jaw was fractured, so you see how very ill he must be. he [sic] wished me to write & tell you all, because he said he could not do it. he [sic] says he cannot come back to his Wife like that, but I tell him you will be glad to see him anyhow . . . he worries so much about things.[231]

Such fears and embarrassments were common. The advice and practical help of officials could do little to ease what must have been a difficult transition for wounded men. As the Heritage School at

15 Armless man and boys painting with their toes at the Heritage School, Chailey.
[IWM Q30552]

Chailey recognized, crippled soldiers had to be 'made' into men again, often being reduced to the level of children and expected to gradually redevelop into adults (illus. 15). 'Curative work' was not only intended to teach the disabled how to become productive workers, but also to become 'men', shrugging off what was regarded as the feminizing tendencies of disability. Thus, there was a progression of labour in many homes for the disabled: from stitching bags, to work with machinery.

For single men, marriage was rarely mentioned. Indeed, it was suggested to the 1919 Select Committee on Pensions that a disabled man who married was rather 'improvident', despite the fact that it was 'in his own personal interest that he should, if he want[ed] someone to look after him'.[232] On a popular level, however, prejudice flourished.[233] It was still believed by some people that the children of maimed ex-servicemen would be born minus a limb.[234] There was little place for disabled ex-servicemen in the new ideal of male domesticity. By failing to assert a masculine role through bringing in an adequate wage-packet, the disabled man could only be further feminized by the performance of male domestic labour.[235]

Public identification of the disabled civilian with the war-mutilated had a negative long-term effect for both groups of men. By the Second World War, the lives of all disabled people had deteriorated as the increased military, governmental and medical intervention into their lives coincided with a growing attention to the beautiful, moulded male physique (as we shall see in Chapter Four). Although this chapter has concentrated on the impact of the war-disabled on other groups, for the war-maimed, the link between themselves and disabled children eventually removed their claim to a special status. By the mid-1920s, they too had become identified with passivity – the helplessness of children who needed to be looked after for the rest of their lives.[236] With the distaste for soldiering after the war, their heroic potency on the field of battle came to be held in great disfavour. Even the increased militarization of society from the mid-1930s failed to revive their status as warriors – rather, it further emphasized their uselessness: their crippled bodies were exempted from warfare, their technical understanding of the art of fighting was outdated, and they were prematurely old.[237] In the words of Harry Smith, a character in a play entitled *The Unknown Warrior* (1923) who had been given a job making toys, 'I'm fed up with making silly toys. It's not work for a man – but we're not men now, with half our insides and half our limbs gone; it's a good enough job for us, I suppose.'[238]

Two Malingering

Showers of lead flying about & big big shells its an unearthy sight to see them drop in amongst human beings. The cries are terrible, I escaped being hit but got caught in Barbe-wire & had blood poisoning & got buried once that caused me to have fits . . . & trip to France is nice but not when the murderers are killing anyone children included, & destroys Churches May the Lord put an unholy curse on them for ever & ever The sights cannot cannot be explained in writing. Writing is not in my line. No fighting either For they that wants to let them fight Because I will never like it no no never.[1]

Language and reason failed when faced with the threat of physical devastation. Stripped of these safeguards, men used their bodies to evade perilous situations. In the last chapter, we examined the aesthetics of mutilation in wartime and exposed the contradictions within the wider population of disabled people after the war. In the present chapter, the debate is also concerned with tensions between the male body as aesthetic object and the body as an instrument of production. By feigning illness or incapacity, some men attempted to avoid exposure to the horrific physical risks discussed in the last chapter. Malingering was not confined to times of greatest risk – such as war – but was part of a broader response to the miseries of a world not of one's own making. Although the wartime experience was similar to that in peacetime, the war malingerer was more estranged from other sufferers and he paid a higher price for being caught. In addition, prior to the war, the policing of malingerers was primarily the responsibility of employers. The war saw a dramatic expansion in the state's concern with civil as well as military malingering. Belief during the war in the effectiveness of techniques developed to suppress men's urge to evade fulfilling their civic obligations resulted in an increased discipline of potential and suspected malingerers after the war.

Before pursuing the malingering male, a slight detour is necessary. We need to acknowledge that malingering (and shirking) were not the only responses to physical threats associated with doing one's duty. In war, alternative responses might be divided into three broad categories:

men who enthusiastically adopted the risk of blood sacrifice; those who clothed themselves in a mantle of stoicism; and those who gave up the fight and took the ultimate revenge on their own bodies. Enthusiastic adoption of the risk was understandably more common in propaganda than in reality, but some men lied about the state of their bodies in an attempt to get into the armed forces.[2] In many cases, they did so because of an incorrect evaluation of the dangers and an exaggerated assessment of the likely subsequent gratitude of the nation on their return. Few men could maintain this zest for warfare for long periods in active service. More typically, the threat of physical devastation could only be endured by stoicism, shortening perceptions of time, and resolutely ignoring the threatening environment. William Clarke summarized this attitude when he wrote,

You became hardened in the trenches, you got fed up with being frightened and hungry, cold, wet and miserable and often you just didn't care whether you survived. Seeing so many corpses became just another sight. Often when you moved in the trenches you trod and slipped on rotting flesh. Your feelings only came to the fore when it was a special mate who had been killed or wounded and then it would go quickly away. Because what you really wanted to do was to go to sleep, get warm, get clean and have a good hot meal.[3]

'Fate' was deemed responsible: every shell was inscribed with a particular man's name.[4] Men unable to maintain such a philosophy often took a more dramatic route to oblivion. Although suicide was rare, it was an important option for a minority.[5] Of course, none of these responses was mutually exclusive. The unfit man who bribed his way into the navy might very rapidly become fatalistic, and suicidal impulses could seize anyone unawares. All these reactions were as compatible with a patriotic temperament as with a malingering state of mind.

Malingering, therefore, was simply another response to the public responsibilities of masculinity. The price for male citizenship was paid on the industrial site and on the field of war. The bodies of women, children, the elderly and the ill could be maltreated or ignored, but they were spared indiscriminate exposure to peril merely as a consequence of their gender, age and physical condition. Furthermore, as shown in Chapter One, there was no limit to the danger to which the male body could be subjected. Machines twisted limbs and burned faces. Gunfire cut bodies in half. At the centre of ideologies of masculinity was an acknowledgement that the male body could be rendered unsightly. Men who refused to, or were incapable of, fighting were not deemed to be worthy of active membership in the wider body-politic. Civilian and martial employment were related. As two young men were informed by their employer when rejected as medically unfit for the army, 'you cant fight, so you cant work'.[6] During the war, conscientious objectors were disenfranchized and some men even thought that soldiers who had not seen overseas service should also have their right to vote taken from them for up to twenty years. Retired officers campaigned to give men in the Territorial forces additional citizenship rights: as Lieutenant-Colonel Frank Garrett suggested, 'every youth who [became] an efficient Territorial of whatever Service should be entitled to full citizenship and obtain his Parliamentary vote forthwith, and moreover that he should be entitled to some marked privilege in securing early access to an Old Age Pension, in that he ha[d] made himself efficient, and therefore a valuable asset in his country.'[7] Men who refused to enlist could be denied Poor Law relief.[8] If they did enlist, they ran the risk of not living to apply to the Poor Law Guardians again. As Major Valentine Fleming commented in a letter of 6 December 1914, 'it may be bloody in Britain but it's positively *fucking* in France'.[9] A stiff penalty was exacted for male citizenship.

Shirking and Malingering

In attempting to gain industrial or military compensations, the threatened body became blameworthy. In peace and war, malingering was regarded as an evasion of man's duty to the state and to other men. It was the physical manifestation of a more general phenomenon: shirking. The two must be seen within a similar context. In peacetime, shirking included a range of activities aimed at avoiding particular duties. Thus, miners on their way to the pit might yield to the superior attractions of the bar, the football field or the billiards saloon.[10] Many workmen slowed down after producing an agreed amount.[11] Even when the nation was in greatest peril, workers went on strike.[12] The famous proponent of scientific management, Frederick Taylor, described these types of industrial malingering as 'soldiering'.

In the military sphere, these industrial manifestations of shirking were replicated. At the level of military propaganda, shirking included the failure of men to enlist in the 'fight for freedom' (illus. 16). At the Front, however, the most dangerous form of shirking was desertion: a man could turn and run, or, when expected to 'go over the top', he could simply not move. Thus, Bert Rudge described having to get drunk before 'zero hour' because he was frightened that he would be one of the men who had to be forced out. As he put it, 'If they didn't go, they was shot. They used to count down (to zero) and then "Over the top" and then the Military Police would come along and see that they

16 'Who said they'd deserted us?', poster. [IWM Q79995]

17 'D is your DUTY', cartoon from 'Myauk', *The Indian Army ABC*, London, *c.* 1920.

had all gone over. Some was coughing, some was spewing, some was singing, some was shouting – ah, it was terrible.'[13] Hiram Sturdy's first attempt to shirk occurred in a house rather than in a trench. Although he eventually learnt the art of stoicism, Sturdy recalled his first battle; 'I bolted, yes, bolted, thought of nothing only jump all those stairs at once . . . Was that running away cowardice, if it was it wasn't me it was my legs, they bolted and I had to go with them.'[14] Such forms of desertion went uncounted, but official levels averaged out at around 10 soldiers per 10,000 a year, although the figures varied considerably year to year.[15] In the twelve months after October 1914, 40,000 soldiers deserted from the army – that is, 21 soldiers deserted out of every 10,000. The rate fluctuated around 6 and 9 for the rest of the war.[16] Less dramatic ways of shirking were more common. Forging signatures to ensure that they were miles away at zero-hour, getting another man to answer their names at roll call, dodging parades and slipping out of camp were habitual activities for many servicemen.[17] Robert Johnston recalled that Regular soldiers of the 81st Infantry Brigade studied the Manual of Military Law to calculate precisely how far they could transgress without risking the most fearful punishments.[18] A sketch from *The Indian Army ABC* (illus. 17) shows a soldier reclining on a chaise-longue in dressing-gown and slippers with a cigarette and drink and a speech bubble issuing from his mouth reads, 'It is better, *far*, to incur a slight reprimand than to perform an onerous duty.' The officer's hysterical reaction further justifies the complacency of the Other Ranks. Furthermore, rather than being a shameful private vice, shirking was a companionable activity. Men slipped away in groups, they swapped advice and information and they attentively cared for other shirkers.[19]

Malingering was a particular form of shirking. The malingerer's weapon was his body. Although the shirker who withdrew his labour from a particular task by definition withdrew his body from the workplace, the removal of his body was incidental. The demand for the improvement of wages or conditions obviously affected the body, but the demand was not expressed through that body. In contrast, the malingerer's protest *centred* on his body: often, it was the last remaining thing he could claim as his own. In some aspects, peacetime malingering differed from that in war. For instance, harsher regimes of discipline for servicemen during the war probably resulted in a growth in the proportion of malingerers relative to shirkers. During the war, monetary gain was a less important motive than the evasion of risk or duty. The war malingerer might be less certain of his comrades' sympathy, particularly in the early years of the conflict. He had less time to be coached in the ways of malingering; he could not change his doctor; nor did he have a right of appeal to any authority outside his military employers.[20] While the industrial malingerer was more anxious to win concessions or compensation within his chosen employment, the war malingerer might simply desire to be dismissed. Thus, although both the serviceman and the worker might be punished by dismissal, only the soldier malingered *in order* to be punished in this way.[21] There were also differences in the degree of illness feigned or wound deliberately inflicted. War malingerers were more liable to be found at both extremes. It was unlikely that a factory worker would purposefully amputate his fingers to be sent on holiday. However, in feigning illness, the war malingerer also might not have to claim as much as the factory worker. While the industrial malingerer might declare that he had been almost blinded by an industrial accident, the man attempting to be invalided out of the armed forces had only to claim that his eyesight was below a particular standard.[22]

War malingering may be divided into three categories: actions aimed at avoiding the armed forces altogether, those aimed at prolonging incapacity and those aimed at being sent back from active service. The first category of men tended to suffer less. Men imbibed drugs such as

18 John Hassall, 'Bones broken while you wait', cartoon in Walter Emmanuel and John Hassall, *Keep Smiling: More News by Liarless for German Homes*, London, *c*.1914–18.

BONES BROKEN WHILE YOU WAIT.

digitalis, belladonna and thyroid extract to produce circulatory disturbances. They pricked their tonsils in order to cough up blood.[23] Epistaxis was provoked by self-induced injuries to the nose. Albuminuria was feigned by the addition of egg-albumen to urine – indeed, the ingestion of the albumen of six raw eggs before providing a specimen to a doctor would have a similar effect (it did not work if the eggs were cooked).[24] Inhaling pipe smoke before the examination might result in palpitations of the heart that would disqualify a man for active service.[25] A deliberately fractured arm would delay mobilization. The caption below the cartoon shown above reads, 'Almost the only persons making a respectable income in London now are the bone-breakers. Young men are flocking in their thousands to doctors who make a speciality of breaking a leg, or an arm or even a neck, in order to make them of no use to the press gang.' It cynically shows the lengths to which businessmen and 'toffs' would go to avoid service. In the background lurks the gloating doctor, eagerly making money at the expense of the 'man at the Front' (illus. 18).[26]

Hazel Thompson Clements' diaries provide us with an account of the ways soldiers successfully evaded prolonged military service by feigning incapacity. Injured while serving in France, he had been sent to a convalescent camp in Brighton. Since his health was – according to his own admission – 'A1', he was constantly being threatened with being sent back to the Front. Therefore, on 23 August 1916, he informed the medical officer that he was experiencing headaches, dizziness and sleeplessness. On 2 September he wrote in his diary that friends had advised him that the best way to malinger was to visit the doctor frequently. Taking the advice seriously, two days later he returned to his doctor and was told to continue taking the medicine for a further week. Meanwhile, however, he was frightened by reports that men who went sick too frequently were being sent back to the Front. On 17 September 1916, he again had the 'wind up', but boasted that he had discovered a new way to malinger. His diary note of three days later explains that while awaiting the examination, he had begun smoking, which made him dizzy. On 5 October, 30 November and 10 December, he tried similar 'wheezes'. Meanwhile, he was constantly leaving camp with the aid of faked passes. On 2 January 1917, he was caught and was confined to barracks for fourteen days. This did not concern him greatly since during this period he pretended that he was on fatigue-duty until four o'clock, thus avoiding both the drills which started at 1.15 p.m. and the drill starting at 4.00 p.m. Such forms of malingering and shirking continued for the rest of the war. On 20 July 1918, he recorded that he had discovered that everyone (of all ranks) was malingering. His final attempt was to claim that he had suffered from rheumatic fever when young. Again, he was crossed off the draft.[27]

Clements was lucky in that an original wound provided him with an excuse for prolonging his rest. Malingering was a more desperate business on the field of war. John William Rowarth was a typical front-line malingerer. Although he had frequently been punished for being absent without leave, he came to recognize that more drastic action had to be countenanced: 'I started to scheme, how the hell can I work my ticket and get out of this bloody war . . . I admit I am a coward. a bloody, bleeding coward, and I want to be a live Coward than a dead blasted Hero.' He faked madness and, when he suspected that the doctors distrusted him, he stepped in front of a truck, crushing his foot.[28] Other forms of self-mutilation could be restored to – and often were just prior to a major attack.[29] Illustration 19 speaks for itself, showing the hands of a man who had shot himself in an attempt to return to Britain. F. P. Roe, of the 6th Battalion of Gloucesters, told of a man who had axed off the fingers of his right hand with the shout, 'Bugger this bloody war!'[30] A bomber could decimate his own legs.[31] The most insidious form of malingering was gunshot wounds. Com-

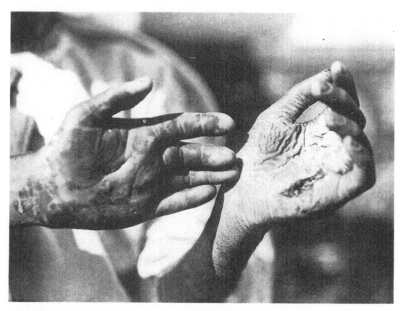

19 Photograph of self-inflicted wounds from the collection of Lt-Col. G. J. S. Archer, RAMC. [CMAC RAMC 738/11]

rades could make pacts to shoot each other in the hand,[32] or they could do it themselves.[33] W. A. Quinton recalled watching a man standing on his hands on the firing step with his legs exposed above the trench, hoping the enemy would shoot at him.[34] Gunshot wounds 'honourably got' could be soaked in stinking ponds of water before being reported.[35] Such cases posed serious problems for military doctors: according to Sir John Collie (president of the Special Pension Board on Neurasthenics), 'it [was] not necessary for a man to blow his own fingers off. By holding his hand up he [could] get the enemy to do it for him. This form of self-inflicted injury [could] only be detected and suppressed by observation on the spot.'[36] The 'red caps', or military police, were kept busy throughout the war.

Diseases could also be simulated. Appendicitis could be feigned.[37] When a doctor was discovered to be particularly sympathetic towards sufferers of lumbago (he himself was tormented by aches), an epidemic of such pains ensued.[38] For a fee, an orderly would prepare a long needle, drag it through some caustic black powder and then pass it through the joint cavity of the knee, resulting in a painful, oozing inflammation.[39] Around barracks, a man could recruit the services of an 'unscrupulous chemist or other person' to induce an abscess by injecting an irritant (such as paraffin or turpentine) under the skin.[40] Royal Army Medical Corps men – including those holding the rank of captain – could easily infect their own abscesses.[41] They could also drink petrol.[42] Soldiers hawked specimens of saliva containing tuberculous bacilli to their mates. A series of cases of jaundice was found to have been caused by taking pucric acid. Indian soldiers were accused of being particularly adept at feigning eye diseases,[43] and tobacco and pepper were found as efficacious in inducing conjunctivitis. One man tied up his arm in a sling until it atrophied.[44] In Mesopotamia, the skull of a dead jackal was used to start a rabies scare that had men evacuated to hospital.[45] In another case, a man managed to vomit after every meal for eleven months.[46] It was also discovered that a high temperature and symptoms of an erratic heart condition could be induced by chewing a stick of cordite, extracted from a .303 rifle cartridge.[47] Scurvy – with its symptoms of fetid breath, spongy and ulcerated gums and effusions of blood under the skin – could be simulated with the help of horse dung rubbed into the gums, avoiding teeth cleaning and passing a sewing needle through the vein behind the knee.[48] Obliging orderlies caused epidemics of dysentry by giving enemas of saturated solution of alum followed by the introduction into the anus of pledgets of cotton.[49] Men bruised their penises. They deliberately sought out prostitutes infected with venereal disease or, if these exertions came to naught, they faked venereal discharge by injecting condensed milk into the urethra.[50]

The extent of war malingering is impossible to determine with any accuracy. Certainly, by increasing the number of men serving unwillingly in the armed forces, conscription magnified its prevalence. This inflation may be represented in Sir John Collie's book on *Malingering and Feigning Sickness*, first published in 1913. When a revised edition was released during the war, the book was nearly twice the size: most sections had been extended and new chapters had been added on self-inflicted injuries and neurasthenia (or shell-shock). Medical statistics provide a conservative estimate of the extent of malingering in wartime. Of nearly 2,000 cases examined by Alan Sichel at the No. 58 Ophthalmic Centre Military Hospital, 5 per cent of soldiers claiming that their eyesight did not fit them for military service could be shown to be lying. When Sichel instituted a more ingenious test, the percentage of dissemblers increased to eleven.[51] At the Front, the main statistics refer to the small proportion of malingerers who were caught and prosecuted. Between August 1914 and demobilization, courts-martial dealt with over 300,000 offences of which 90 per cent resulted in convictions.[52] Most of these cases involved shirking rather than malingering. The only form of malingering represented in the evidence of courts-martial was self-mutilation, which according to the statistics, was negligible. Despite the claim by Major-General Sir Wyndham

Childs that self-maiming was 'a very prevalent crime', only 1 per cent of offences brought before a court-martial came under this category.[53] However, these figures severely underestimate the amount of self-mutilation. Examination of the lists of injured soldiers belonging to the 55th (West Lancashire) Division shows that between February and July 1916, of all injuries or casualties due to causes other than enemy action in this division, 26 per cent were self-inflicted (i.e., there were 96 self-inflicted wounds). The remainder was thought to be the result of accidents.[54]

Self-mutilation was only the most dramatic form of malingering. Much qualitative evidence suggests that lesser forms of malingering were ubiquitous. The chronic malingerer Hazel Thompson Clements firmly believed that everyone was 'swinging the lead' and his diaries provide ample evidence that many assuredly were.[55] As we will be seeing later, the widespread refusal to inform on malingerers suggests not only that it was acceptable practice to many men in the rank and file but also that it was common, and one that was celebrated in popular songs. Thus, W. A. Roger jotted down the following song in his notebook:

1. When the M.O. goes around, to see if you are sound,
   And fit for the firing line, Oh dear boys that's the time,
   To start and swing the lead, pretending to be half dead,
   Then he makes blighty instead, but just you keep your head.

CHORUS
   While swinging, swinging, swinging the lead
      some funny ideas you get
   When you pack your kit to take that trip,
      of submarines you've got no dread.
   Don't you start to wink your eye,
      when the doctor says goodbye.
   Just smile sickly, get it over quickly,
      don't start to dance the highland fling.
   But when you're on the boat
      and you're sailing far away
   Just give three cheers and say goodbye to old Salonica.

2. When the doctor strives, to soothe that awful pain,
   And all his efforts fail, you spin the same old tale,
   Till he marks you for the boat and to long to be afloat,
   But sailing homeward bound, be careful you're not found.[56]

From this point of view, malingering was part of the game of war, enabling ex-servicemen to recall the war not in terms of bloody conflict but within the context of 'playing crown and anchor, and swinging the lead, and putting one over on the sergeants'.[57]

How did such wartime practices compare with those in peacetime? From the start of the war, officials anxious to reduce levels of shamming equated the war malingerer with his industrial counterpart.[58] The detection of both types was dealt with in the same textbooks.[59] For both, a distinction was drawn between conscious and unconscious varieties.[60] In civilian life, malingering was also thought to be commonplace. In the nineteenth century, the first English physician to write on malingering was Hector Gavin, whose work *On Feigned and Factitious Diseases* (1843) was the main textbook until the second decade of the twentieth century when Sir John Collie and Archibald McKendrick infused a new panic into the subject. In 1917, A. Bassett Jones and Llewellyn J. Llewellyn declared, 'In all ages, in all epochs, and in all ranks of society, malingering has never lacked its votaries; the monarch, the mendicant, the slave, the warrior, the statesman, the minister of religion, likewise the condemned malefactor, the seeker after compensation, and the child who would evade school.'[61] By this time, however, politicians, employers, doctors and civil servants were all agreeing that the problem had reached epidemic proportions.

In civilian life, concern about the 'crisis of malingering' had become urgent with the establishment of the Employers' Liability Act of 1880, the Workmen's Compensation Acts of 1897, 1901 and 1906, and the National Health Insurance Act of 1911.[62] This legislation made particular employers liable for industrial injuries to their employees, if the worker's incapacity lasted a stipulated number of days.[63] These Acts were thought to change the relationship between the worker and the state because they destroyed the workman's 'sense of equity, of the moral obligations essential to the well-being of every well-organized society'. Instead, the worker felt himself to be a 'mere unit' pitted against the state or insurance company, and it was further explained that 'in this conflict of personal and *corporate* interests, the person's sense of justice [became] attenuated, perverted, or wholly lost . . . he [was] apt to develop a very distorted idea of his relationship to the State or any public body with which he [was] brought into conflict, and but too readily [forgot] that the interests of the individual [should] not run counter to, or be allowed to supersede, the requirements of justice and equity'.[64] State funds had become a 'store of hoarded wealth to which they ha[d] contributed and from which, moreover, they mean[t] to draw their share by fair, or if need be by unfair, means'.[65] It was such paranoia that led to sarcastic comment from trade unionists that, if carried to its logical conclusion, the hysteria generated by debates about malingering would lead to calls to repeal all legislation providing for industrial compensation because then malingering was discouraged 'in the best possible way'.[66] More than ever, simulation was a 'matter of National import' and the typical malingering workman was portrayed as loafing about street corners 'with a bottle of physic in one pocket, and a copy of the Workmen's Compensation Act, 1906, in the other'.[67]

Just as the extent and nature of war malingering varied according to the relationship between punishment and the exposure to physical risk, so too the extent of industrial malingering was thought to fluctuate according to the relationship between levels of compensation and wages. In occupations with high levels of insecurity, workmen could not afford to malinger.[68] During periods of high wages, the returns to malingering were proportionately less. Thus, it was believed that the wages paid during the war had resulted in a decline of industrial malingering. For instance, in 1920, Herbert K. Beale, a solicitor for the Midland Railway Company, argued that increased wages during the war and the comparatively small increase in levels of compensation had led to a reduction in malingering. In his view, accidents were a proxy for malingering. Between 1912 and 1914 the percentage of accidents for which the Midland Railway Company paid compensation was around 4.3. In 1915 and 1916, this increased slightly to 4.5 per cent. In 1917, however, when wages soared, it fell to 3.8 per cent. By 1919 it was 3.2 per cent. This declining incidence of accidents occurred despite the fact that in the later years older and unskilled men were being employed to replace younger workers who had entered the armed forces.[69] Indeed, during the war period, it was not only less common for workmen to malinger, but it was much more common for men to return to work before injuries had healed in order to reap the benefits of high wages.[70] In wartime, heightened concern about industrial malingering was not due to increased incidence, but to the perceived needs of the wartime economy.

In the longer term, employers and state officials continued to believe that legislation providing compensation encouraged the prolongation of disabilities and was leading to a dramatic increase in the number of so-called accidents requiring medical attention. For instance, Dr Dickson of Lochgelly, a doctor of twenty years' standing in the kingdom of Fife, found that the average time it took a miner to recover from a fracture below the knee was three months before the act of 1906 and six months after it.[71] In all insured industries between 1908 and 1913, despite a similar number of employees, the number of accidents increased by 44 per cent and the amount paid in compensation for these accidents increased by 62 per cent. A worsening of conditions could not be blamed: the number of *fatal* accidents remained stable during these years (with the exception of 1911, due to an exceptionally large number of colliery and shipping disasters).[72] One method used by employers of estimating the number of industrial malingerers was to examine the results of those who appealed to the Ministry of Health against the decision made by the Approving Society in arbitration under the National Health Insurance Act. In the annual report of the chief medical officer of the Ministry of Health, 186,116 cases of doubtful incapacity to work were referred to the regional medical officers. Only 102,576 of these workers bothered to attend the examination and, of these, over one-quarter was found to be capable of employment.[73] Of course, none of these statistics can be taken at face value, and the caution with which they must be regarded may be illustrated by considering the estimates of Sir John Collie. In his study of 3,667 industrial accidents in 1916, Collie reckoned that eight per cent of the accident cases were feigned.[74] A year later, however, this same researcher had decided that the problem was even more severe. In 1917, he concluded that one in every four injured workmen was fit for work.[75] Although more cautious commentators remembered that the increase in accidents might equally be due to the growth in the size of the industrial workforce in high-risk occupations, the 'speeding-up' of modern industrial processes and expanded and improved diagnostic techniques, few people questioned the belief that malingering was widespread.[76] Doctors specializing in the malingering workman had an interest in stimulating panic about levels of malingering and, in times of labour shortages, in refusing suspect men compensation in order to accelerate their return to civic duties.

Doctors as Detectives

Exposing malingerers was an important business: indeed, as one army surgeon responded when asked if he was a doctor, 'No . . . I am a detective.'[77] This metaphor was widespread, as attested by Dr Henry Cohen's admission that it was 'tempting to compare the methods of diagnosis with those of crime detection'.[78] This was particularly true during war. Indeed, the War Office explicitly argued that one of the most important tasks of medical officers was to police the behaviour of servicemen.[79] But this was not merely due to wartime needs: civilian doctors had a duty to employers, and similarly tended to agree with the War Office. According to Archibald McKendrick in 1912, simulation was endemic: although 'all men [were] not malingerers', all were 'tempted to make the most of any injury received while at work'. He

20 YMCA stall at St. Jean supplying hot drinks to New Zealand walking wounded after the battle of Broodseinde, October 1917. [IWM Q2973]

had learned to 'look with more than usual scrutiny into any case of accidental injury to a workman'.[80] Suspicion prevailed precisely because malingering was believed to be ubiquitous, particularly amongst the 'walking wounded' staggering to safety behind the lines (illus. 20). Even a soldier known as 'a good 'un' could deliberately shoot off his trigger finger.[81]

The medical profession, therefore, invented signs by which the malingerer could be distinguished. It did this in two ways. Firstly, by identifying groups of men who were to be regarded as least trustworthy. This took many forms – from the ludicrous claim that colliery managers should regard men wearing earrings with misgiving,[82] to the sweeping assertion that certain ethnic groups were untrustworthy. Thus, James Henson of the National Sailors' and Firemen's Union noted that industrial malingerers were easy to detect because they came from 'the lower class of labourers and foreigners'.[83] Martial vigour was said to be determined racially. Suspicion fell most heavily on the Chinese and the Irish, followed closely by Lowland Scots.

English servicemen were thought to be least susceptible to the vice. However, there was no necessary contradiction between the most courageous ethnic groups and those most prone to malinger. Thus, Irish servicemen were renowned both for their martial valour and their poor discipline. Similarly, although Lowland Scots were considered to be highly likely to malinger, they were also praised for being as courageous as Londoners.[84]

Secondly, doctors were taught how to identify malingerers by certain physical signs, such as a look of 'open-eyed candour' or 'cunning'; the 'tendency to overact'; the vagueness and diffuseness of their symptoms; their 'florid, rude health'.[85] Cases of pretended insanity were easy to detect: 'if [a claimant could] be induced to throw a fit at the time of the examination, he will probably give a most convincing demonstration of the true character of his condition'.[86] The physical nature of mutilations required careful study. The medical officer Donald Norris instructed military doctors to examine the situation and character of all lesions: whether they were within easy reach of the right hand; if the lesions were in sets of four, whether they might have been caused by fingernails or forks; were there signs that acid had been deliberately used to burn the skin ('betrayed by a streak of inflammation set up by a drop of the liquid running down from the site of application')? In cases where it was suspected that the healing of a wound was being deliberately delayed, Norris provided practical advice: the doctor simply had to conceal a sheet of tinfoil inside a dressing. This would reveal if a patient were pricking his wound through his bandages. Once detected, plaster of Paris could be applied to a wound to 'secure healing of a troublesome lesion'.[87]

As the above advice would suggest, detecting malingering itself required cunning. Doctors were advised to feign interest and sympathy: 'the "sucking dove" mood, with at the same time an eye for every casual and apparently trivial occurrence, [would] trap the most case-hardened sinner,' declared army doctor William Wallace.[88] Elaborate eye tests which would trick any malingerer were developed.[89] It was best to catch the malingerer *in flagrante delicto* but, if that did not work, doctors could 'wring it out of them'.[90] They should encourage patients to claim more and more symptoms until they caught themselves in contradictions.[91] Surprise was useful, as was shame, ridicule and satire ('strange to say, as a rule they resent with more bitterness scorn cast upon their *abilities* than upon their fraudulent practices').[92] Doctors were advised to frighten patients out of minor illnesses by asserting some deadly disease such as cancer.[93] They were encouraged to lie to patients – assuring them that, if they recovered, a 'cushy' job behind the lines would be given to them.[94] No amount of trickery on the doctor's part was considered excessive.

In civilian society, such techniques for exposing malingerers were justified on the grounds that doctors had a duty to protect the state, approved societies and employers 'from the unjust and improper demands' that were being made upon them, and to 'help the state to count amongst her citizens the maximum number of units capable of working'.[95] The justification for such techniques in wartime was even more obvious. Unlike most forms of industrial malingering, war malingering endangered other men. This fear was summarized by an unnamed medical officer in his diary of 17 October 1917. Although his anger was directed towards shirkers who were not being punished as harshly as he thought they deserved, his argument applied with equal force to malingerers. He fumed, 'To gratify a mawkish humanitarianism two or three score mean fellows are encouraged to slip away every time there is a risk to their skins, so more and more average men learn to shirk with impunity; attacks fail, and losses run into untold thousands, because the most dutiful of our men are not backed up.'[96] Captain J. C. Dunn agreed, reporting that his medical orderly had taught him one important thing, 'that the first duty of a battalion medical officer in War [was] to discourage the evasion of duty'. This had 'to be done not seldom against one's better feeling, sometimes to the temporary hurt of the individual, but justice to all other men as well as discipline demand[ed] it'.[97] Given such sentiments (and as concern with military morale reached hysterical levels), it is not surprising that doctors tended to regard every soldier who reported sick of being a 'scrimshanker'.[98] Phil J. Fisher light-heartedly commented on this in his *Figures and Phases of the War 1916–1919*. According to him, medical officers treated everyone with the same No. 9 pill, a cure-all for the malingerer as much as the 'really ill' (illus. 21). As an anonymous diarist suffering severe dysentery in Mesopotamia complained in his diary of 18 May 1916,

I am still hanging on, very weak, but unless you have a temperature of about 150 [degrees], or half your head blown off the *Dear* Doctor says there is nothing the matter with you and you are loafing. Our doctor is sick himself. I hope he doesn't die, that would be too easy. I only hope he is ill about a year, so we don't see him again and so he will have time to think of the way he has treated sick men here. I heard him tell a youngster who said he was run down and could not do his duty: 'Oh, I've nothing to give you. A lot of you have got to die yet.'[99]

Although it would be wrong to portray all military doctors as unsympathetic detectives, even kindly physicians found the pressures

PHASES OF THE WAR:—4.   Our Doc. at Work.

21 'PHASES OF THE WAR:– 4. Our Doc. at work', cartoon signed 'Ypres', n.d., from Phil J. Fisher, *Figures and Phases of the War 1916–1919*, London, 1919.

on them to police malingering too great. James Henry Dible was one such man. Disliking his job as medical officer to the 3rd Battalion North Lancashire Regiment, he claimed that his colleagues were obsessed with 'the debasing idea' that 'the men [went] "sick" to escape duty'. He continued, 'I absolutely refuse to co-operate in schemes for catching scrimshanks, because in the event of a mistake such shocking miscarriage of justice would occur, and because it is almost impossible to exclude the risk of a mistake; and that is a risk I won't take.'[100] However, despite 'doing [his] utmost', he was unable to have himself transferred and was forced to do his duty. Lieutenant G. N. Kirkwood was another kindly medical officer. In July 1915, he became the scapegoat at a court of enquiry concerning allegations of cowardice and disobedience. On 9 July, a party of 11th Border Regiment 97th Infantry Battalion had refused to carry out a raid, on the grounds that they were suffering from 'shell-shock', mental distress and physical exhaustion. As medical officer, Kirkwood agreed. He noted that the men had been living under constant shell-fire for too long, had suffered under immense stress (they had lost all their officers and half their men on 1 July), and 'had not recovered their mental equilibrium'. Their state was made worse by the fact that their few days' 'rest' behind the lines had been spent sorting out the kits of the killed comrades and burying the dead. The military authorities, however, relieved Kirkwood from his position, accusing him of showing 'undue sympathy with the men'. According to the commander of the 32nd Division, 'Sympathy for sick and wounded men under his treatment is a good attribute for a doctor but it is not for an M.O. [medical officer] to inform a C.O. [commanding officer] that his men are not in a fit state to carry out a military operation. The men being in the front line should be proof that they are fit for any duty called for.'[101] Like it or not, the doctor as detective was under War Office authority and had to act unsympathetically.

Prevention and Punishment

The Major: 'You're in France now, Starrett [his batman] and must watch out. Here you are shot at dawn for disobedience!'
Starrett: 'Obedient or disobedient, Sir, there's always the chance of being shot here.'[102]

The malingerer had to be punished and treated, and the rise of a new generation of scrimshanks prevented. In this section, there are two arguments: firstly, that there were differences between the punishment and treatment of malingerers in times of peace and war, but that, secondly, these differences narrowed after the war as the techniques developed within a military context were transferred into the civilian world. Prior to 1914, attempts by civilian authorities to reduce malingering focused on punishment, although these punishments were much less severe when compared with the penalties of wartime. However, during the war, it was clear that coercive measures were ineffectual and new disciplines based on perceptions evolved within psychology came to play a larger role in the policing and prevention of malingering.

The military exacted the harshest penalties for both shirking and malingering. Although a distinction has been made in this chapter between these two activities, when examining the punishments, the distinction becomes hard to maintain. Thus, a serviceman who ran away from the fighting was shirking and subject to punishment under the category of cowardice. However, as we shall see later, men exhibiting the physical symptoms of 'shell-shock' were regarded as malingerers and were also liable to be shot for cowardice. In the records, therefore, it is the impossible to distinguish these two forms of cowardice.

Ironically, the harshness of the penalties for various forms of shirking increased the relative importance of malingering. This was particularly true with regard to desertion. Soldiers who turned and ran during battle might be shot by those in reserve.[103] If they were arrested, they could be shot at a later date. In the British forces, 3,080 death sentences were passed during the war, of which eleven per cent were

22 Execution of a French soldier, print dated 1913/1917. [BDIC No 895 Box 15]

carried out. Although men were executed for murder, cowardice, quitting post, striking or violence, disobedience, mutiny, sleeping on post and casting away arms, desertion was the most common crime. A contemporary print shows the execution of a French soldier, a scene in which the attempts to maintain some type of military dignity have failed (illus. 22). The use of the death penalty was vigorously defended by military authorities as a deterrent: one death prevented 'hundreds of others from committing that particular offence'.[104] Brigadier-General James Lochhead Jack believed that without the 'sickeningly terrible end' of disobedient soldiers, the army would become 'a rabble'.[105] Captain David W. J. Andrews boasted that he did not need to execute a soldier for being drunk because mere hinting at this ultimate punishment was effective. He wrote, 'Mental punishment is a most excellent thing.'[106]

As a punishment, however, the death penalty was less successful than these officers suggested. It may have deterred the dead from committing further acts of cowardice, but men whose death sentences had been commuted often committed their offence again. Indeed, one soldier was sentenced to death on three separate occasions before he was made to suffer the penalty.[107] Furthermore, the existence of the death penalty made soldiers reluctant to inform on military shirkers and malingerers. As John Francis Jones recalled, 'it was not for us to take sides with the authorities against mere privates; the scales of military justice were too heavily weighed on the one side to begin with. So we gave them [deserters] our rations and wished them luck.'[108] This lack of confidence in military justice was often vindicated. A young and inexperienced officer, Guy Chapman, recalled his first time as a member of a court-martial early in the war when an elderly pioneer sergeant was brought before him having been found drunk in the trenches. Thinking he had to 'go by the book', Chapman duly passed the death sentence. It was only through the advocacy of a more sympathetic major that the sentence was reduced to demotion.[109] In a similar vein, Major Reginald S. Cockburn argued that a knowledge of a civil law was actually a hindrance when leading courts-martial: 'one had to be careful to avoid squibbles' since 'leniency on the part of the court was . . . visited by malediction'.[110]

Concern about the appropriateness of the death sentence increased as the war progressed. Chapman described a group of 'ignorant and frightened' young boys who joined his regiment near the end of the war:

the next morning, one was found missing. A month later he was picked up by the military police twenty miles behind the lines. It was, according to the manual, desertion in the face of the enemy: and yet – we had lost our rigour of 1915. The charge could not be slipped on one side. The F.G.C.M. [Field General Courts Martial] took place. But somehow the prosecutor . . . was nothing better than prisoner's friend. The sentence was trifling.[111]

Sympathy towards frightened servicemen who shirked or malingered was widespread. Hiram Sturdy described how deeply disturbed his platoon had been when a soldier dubbed 'Duck' was sentenced to death. Duck had gone 'absent without leave' after seeing his comrade's arm shattered by a bullet. He had returned after a week, was arrested and sentenced to death. Sturdy was shocked, exclaiming, 'Duck sentenced to death, as good a man as we had, the biggest comic, only fond of drink. We did'nt [sic] know much about court-martials, or any martials, but if these were the kind of men that got sentenced to death, we thought justice was a bit off the mark.' Shortly afterwards, Duck's sentence was commuted to two years' punishment in the front lines. Although better than death, this did not reassure the rest of the platoon: 'We think quite a lot about this business. First, death sentences seem to be given if the superior officer is not feeling too well at the trial, and second, if the front line is to remain for two years, [sic] theres. [sic] more than Duck has got the death sentence.'[112] As one soldier commented, 'it [had to] stand to reason that a man who [could] go to sleep *standing up* while his life [was] in danger [had to] be in a pretty bad way'.[113] It was widely felt that executions had been carried out without any reason, save as an example.[114] After witnessing the execution of a soldier shot for cowardice, an unnamed diarist in 1915 commented that although he agreed that discipline was crucial, the executed man's bravery prior to execution demanded respect: 'he mate [*sic*] have been a coward but he marched to his death with a Soldiers heart'.[115] As a member of a firing squad recalled, 'it was some time before we could dismiss the happenings of that morning from our minds'.[116]

Not all officers disagreed. Colonel Walter Norris Nicholson had a particular reason for disliking the death penalty: it was not 'sporting'. He explained,

Once we had a deserter who was tried, condemned and shot. To make all arrangements, guard, firing party, burial part, chaplain and doctor, was quite horrible. It was felt by those concerned far more deeply than the many deaths that occurred every day in action. It seemed a coldblooded murder, and all were horribly depressed at the thought of the fellow waiting in his barn for a cold dawn and death. Our casualty list included many deaths; but they all had a sporting chance, which this fellow did not.[117]

Although Nicholson's sympathy more closely resembled that of the rank and file, his assumption that men 'going over the top' had a 'sporting chance' was ridiculed by them. War was murder: if the bullet had your name on it, nothing could be done. For these soldiers, execution was simply one more way to die: probably equally random to 'going over the top', but particularly horrifying because of the way it stripped the individual and the regiment of their heroic status. Thus, Alex Knight, of the 12th (Service) Battalion, Highland Light Infantry, confessed that his entire battalion had been relieved when one of their men who was court-martialled for cowardice was imprisoned for two years (with hard labour) instead of being executed: 'had the death penalty been exacted, it would have appeared in Army Orders & been blazoned all over the Army that a 17th man had been shot for cowardice'.[118] To protect the reputation of a regiment, evidence of serious forms of shirking or malingering had to be suppressed.[119] 'Private X' was the first (and only) soldier in another regiment to be executed. In response, the soldiers developed a great hatred for 'Sergeant-Major Y' for passing the sentence. They were mortified not because a fellow soldier had lost his life, but because of 'the imputation of cowardice' to someone in their ranks. They further 'swore a sort of oath of comradeship to redeem their name at the next battle. They would fight on, no matter at what cost, and never surrender themselves, and take no prisoners.' In their next battle, half of the company were killed, earning them the title of the 'Immortal Eighty'.[120]

Execution was the punishment for serious forms of shirking. There was less certainty and uniformity in the punishment of malingerers. Indeed, some commentators were particularly naïve about appropriate punishments. Dr Hugh Wansey Bayly imagined that ejection from the 'honoured ranks' was sufficient, writing, 'The man who evades service in the field in time of war must be accepted and recognized as an inferior creature: one deserving of some contempt as not fitted or worthy of admission to the ranks of the happy warriors.'[121] For minor infringements, the preferred response of officers was persuasion. All that indecisive malingerers needed was some rum and a 'good talking to'.[122] More coercive measures included denying separation allowances to the widows, wives and mothers of deviants. Pay was forfeited by men in hospitals accused of inflicting their own injuries and, in serious cases, they were removed from military service without pensions.[123] In the South African Army Corps, public floggings were meted out.[124] In other fields of war, culprits were forced to parade at night as a punishment for not conducting themselves with sufficient valour.[125] The most common form of punishment for minor types of malingering was 'jankers' or confinement to barracks for a few days and being made to perform the most odious jobs (such as emptying urinal tubs). More lengthy terms of imprisonment could be imposed, and were supported by the Army Suspension of Services Act that enabled military authorities to suspend sentences until after the war. Thus, a soldier sentenced to ten years' penal servitude for malingering could be sent back to the Front, with the sentence hanging over his head. The act also provided for the remission of the sentence as a reward for good conduct or any act of gallantry.

Military authorities had a problem deciding on appropriate punishments for malingerers. According to General Douglas Haig (general officer commanding-in-chief of the British Armies on the Western Front) punishment had to be composed of two elements – the infliction of physical discomfort and the stimulation of a sense of shame. Imprisonment was inappropriate in wartime because it removed men from the front line and because it was 'difficult to make the prospect of future discomfort in prison compare unfavourably with present discomfort in the trenches'. Furthermore, it was not desirable to inflict the stigma of imprisonment on men whose offences were largely military and whose characters were not sufficiently bad to render it necessary. The two other most common punishments – extra work and the forfeiture of pay – were equally unsatisfactory since servicemen were already working to the limits of their endurance and they had few opportunities for spending money.[126]

The most controversial military response to malingering was Field Punishment No. 1. This consisted of lashing a man to a gun-wheel by his wrists and ankles for an hour at a time in the morning and in the evening. The soldier could not be subjected to this punishment for more than three out of any four consecutive days, nor for more than twenty-one days in all. The War Office decreed that the discipline must not cause physical injury or leave any permanent mark.[127] Not surprisingly, the military establishment approved of this castigation. Major-General Sir Wyndham Childs defended Field Punishment No. 1 on the grounds that 'war [was] a beastly, brutal and abnormal state of affairs and ha[d] to be handled as such'.[128] The War Office feared the consequences of its abolition. General Haig was acutely aware of the need to impose discipline: soldiers had to recognize that they were not 'free agents'. Further, 'the surest way to undermine discipline [was] to impose a series of small penalties which [were] not of sufficient significance to the offender'. He warned that the consequences of abolishing Field Punishment No. 1 would be to undermine the 'moral fibre' of a large percentage of men who required 'the daily fear of adequate punishment' to keep them as effective units of production.[129] There was a general concern that its abolition would increase the need to resort to the death penalty.[130]

In addition, the military hierarchy believed that it was an effective form of punishment. There is some evidence to support this. When John William Rowarth was sentenced to five days' Field Punishment No. 1, he was surprised to discover how terrible the punishment actually was. He wrote, 'I said to my self, thats better than the front. as [sic] usual I was wrong again.'[131] Rowland Luther was present when a soldier in his battalion was sentenced to this punishment for falling asleep on duty. He admitted, 'it certainly made us more alert on sentry after witnessing this punishment'.[132] Only a small proportion who underwent Field Punishment No. 1 ever re-offended.[133] To support this point, C. D. Morris of the Suffolk Regiment was interviewed by the War Office officials. The précis read, 'Has been at the front a considerable time. Started his service by bad behaviour, states F. P. No. 1. cured him, and promotion followed.'[134] The humiliation of the errant soldier was thought to be particularly efficacious. According to Lieutenant-General George F. Milne, it was effective not because it caused physical pain, but because it made servicemen 'look and feel foolish and [was] monotonous'. He continued, 'the mere fact that the men feel foolish acts as a powerful deterrent . . . I am averse to tying up a full grown man, but I am equally convinced that it is essential in the interests of the army as a whole.'[135]

Non-military personnel disagreed. Parents, trade unions, humanitarian societies and organizations concerned with human rights protested vigorously.[136] In 1916, their protests were taken up by the editor of the *Clarion*, Robert Blatchford, when he publicized the case of a Liverpool boy of the Pals' Battalion who died while undergoing what was described as 'crucifixion'.[137] According to all these people, Field Punishment No. 1 represented what was most feared in German militarism. This view was summed up in a letter to the Home Office from Miss Fanny C. Grieve on 8 January 1917, who wrote, 'Why should our brave men who are laying down their lives for others be subjected to such a wrong and wicked punishment? We are trying to fight Militarism in Germany and are in danger ourselves of the same evil. How can people endure that their loved ones should not only be in danger of death, or maiming by the enemy, but also be in danger of suffering such cruel wrong from the hands of their own fellow countrymen?'[138] F. Hardy of Forest Hill echoed her sentiments in a letter to Lloyd George of 19 November 1916: 'We should then at least be satisfied that the militarism which we so heartily despise in Germany has no abiding place in the heart of liberty-loving England.' Field Punishment No. 1 was a degrading and inhuman form of torture.[139] The anonymous author 'Mark VII' described the corrective procedure in the following words,

There is a boy from D company during Field Punishment No. 1 down by the road this afternoon. His outstretched arms are tied to the wheel of a travelling field-kitchen. The regimental-sergeant-major has just told me that the boy is there for falling out on the march. He defended himself before the C.O. by saying that he had splinters of glass in his feet; but the M.O. decided against him. Quite possibly the boy is a liar, but wouldn't the army do well to avoid punishments which remind men of the Crucifixion?[140]

Moreover, it was inappropriate for a volunteer and conscript army.[141] Field Punishment No. 1, one soldier wrote, 'turned our minds against the British Army, as we had not enlisted for our own benefit, we were all civilians, who had never entertained the idea of being soldiers before the war started, and to see men strapped to the wheels for an hour was nothing more or less than cruelty, and to be on view of all passer by's [*sic*] was not pleasant'.[142] It was argued that the crimes that servicemen had committed did not merit degradation. Roy Horniman (of Kensington), considered Field Punishment No. 1 to be evil because 'the degradation of the soul [was] far greater than the degradation of body.

Men ha[d] left this ordeal broken, and they ha[d] been the best who ha[d] thus suffered.' On less strong grounds, he further asserted that 'it [was] wiser, more economic to shoot a man than to send him forth poisoned in mind'.[143] It was said to destroy morale, especially in racially mixed units. A provost sergeant who had served in the East argued strongly for its abolition on the grounds that when inflicted against white soldiers, it lowered their prestige in the eyes of the natives.[144] The real criminals were 'stupid officers' who, by their incapacity to inspire respect and obedience from the soldiers, made punishment necessary.[145]

Finally, although (as has already been mentioned) it is possible to argue that the punishment was effective, opponents of the punishment could counter with an equal amount of contrary evidence. Gunner G. Butterworth of the RFA who had spent three years in the Special Reserve and had seen four and a half years' service at the Front, argued for the substitution of pack drill or some similar severe physical exercise on the grounds that Field Punishment No. 1 did 'not do any good, men [got] accustomed to it, and it [did] not act as a deterrent. Majority of men really [thought] nothing of it. Men [felt] loss of pay more.'[146] Some men did not even seem to be much concerned by it.[147] In contrast, however, Field Punishment No. 1 led to 'murmurs of unrest in the camp' at Suvla Bay.[148] Soldiers cut loose the men suffering this punishment.[149] They secretly brought the punished man food and water.[150] The punishment was widely regarded as being used to set an example, with little regard for justice.[151]

Statements concerning Field Punishment No. 1 reflected the attitudes of servicemen towards *all* coercive forms of punishment. T. A. Silver spent much of his time in the navy and army being punished for various forms of malingering – but was never deterred.[152] Even two severe birchings during his brief period in the navy did not make him more obedient. He noted, 'I hardly felt as my behind was numbed after the first stroke and that was why I was not afraid of the next six strokes.'[153] Conscripted servicemen considered that they had rights over and above the petty demands of military discipline – and were not fearful to exert these rights, irrespective of the disapproval of their superiors. Thus, Hazel Thompson Clements reported that soldiers in his convalescent camp considered it their right to sneak away over the weekend. When they were informed on 22 October 1915 that anyone who did so would be treated as a deserter, Clements blandly jotted down in his diary that desertion levels were ready to soar.[154] The triviality of the offences militated against strict obedience: as one soldier hinted, it was impossible to take seriously the sensibilities of an officer who sentenced a soldier to seven days' 'confined to barracks' for refusing to stop singing, 'Pack up your troubles in your old kit bag and Smile, Smile, Smile.'[155] Punished men were often resentful as they did not consider that they deserved such fates.[156] Furthermore, it was generally felt amongst the soldiers that everyone was at risk of punishment: after days of fighting, there was nothing to differentiate the man who fell asleep for a minute while on duty from any other soldier on duty.[157] Men were frequently too tired to be intimidated by threats of courts-martial and firing squads.[158] The malingerer was often treated sympathetically by other servicemen, and men being punished were given presents of tobacco to cheer them up.[159] When R. Campbell Begg came upon an Royal Army Medical Corps captain infecting his own sores, he noticed that the captain was not at all embarrassed: 'He made no bones about his feelings; he had stuck out the front areas for a fortnight, was quite sure he wouldn't survive there much longer, and was determined to get out of it. He relied on me not to give him away. I readily promised this; I suppose I was accessory to a serious military crime, but who was to accuse me? We had a cup of tea together.'[160] More than one blind eye was cast in their direction.[161] Men turning up at casualty clearing stations with feigned wounds or diseases might be gently advised to return to their units.[162] Sentences would be passed, but soldiers might simply be informed that charges would be placed on the conduct sheet and need not be endured.[163] Successful malingering required skill – and it was a skill that was appreciated and admired.[164] Amongst soldiers, war could be a game played as much against military superiors as against the Germans.[165] Authorities might punish with brutality, but malingering servicemen might be assured of sympathy from their comrades.

In comparison to war malingerers who were caught, industrial malingerers seemed to get off lightly. Only two per cent of claims for compensation had to be settled in court around the time of the war.[166] However, of the cases that came to court, there was an increasing chance that the decision would be in favour of the employer.[167] If an employer decided to prosecute, the industrial malingerer found the scales of justice weighed against him. As the *Bath and Wilts Chronicle and Herald* on 16 May 1927 noted, if an accused employee brought forward the evidence of one doctor, his employer would call two.[168] Attempts to police industrial malingerers increased after the war. Upon demobilization, many medical officers who had specialized in detection during the war offered their skills to employers. For these specialists in dissimulation, the chief problem was that employees (unlike servicemen) had little to lose, except their jobs. The most that employers could do was to punish the entire family of the malingerer by not employing any family member. Although these experts agreed that the only real cure for industrial malingerers was a 'hard-labour sentence', in reality very little could be done.[169]

After the war, therefore, the medical specialists in malingering turned their attention away from punishment and towards prevention. The key question became the reason for workers malingering. It was a question that had been asked during the war with blame being directed at recruiting boards for passing into the army all willing recruits and inadequate development of *esprit de corps*.[170] Pressured to pass as many as 200 recruits a day, military selection boards were hurried and medical examinations were often perfunctory.[171] Similarly, it was alleged that employers were failing to ensure that proper recruitment processes were in operation in their factories.[172] The presence of 'inefficient, slow, lazy' workers were indications of poor selection procedures.[173] Efficient personnel departments were crucial in preventing 'the evils of high labour turnover with its accompaniment of bad work, expense of replacements and training, and a general lack of *esprit de corps*'.[174] Selection had to become scientific: employers needed to apply the 'exact measurement of the presence or absence of the various mental and physical abilities required for efficient work'.[175]

Crucially, the tool used to answer the question as to why employees malingered was psychology. Wartime needs for increased production had led to an interest in the 'human side' of industry, if only because of the failure of the government's campaign to increase production by lengthening the hours of employment of munitions workers.[176] Thus, industrial malingering came to the attention of a new set of professionals with an interest in human psychology. Not surprisingly, Charles S. Myers, a leading expert on malingering in war, was a founder member of the Industrial Fatigue Research Board and founder of the National Institute of Industrial Psychology. In 1918, when the Health of Munition Workers' Committee released its final report on low productivity and the increase in accidents and absenteeism, the Industrial Fatigue Research Board was set up under the auspices of the Department of Scientific and Industrial Research and the Medical Research Committee. Three years later, the commercially orientated National Institute of Industrial Psychology was established. For both, the body was to be understood as bipolar, or as consisting of both a physical and a psychological 'pole' that needed to be balanced.[177] This balancing required the comprehensive reorganization of industry. Thus, the National Institute of Industrial Psychology aimed, as Myers wrote, to

discover the best possible human conditions in occupational work, whether they relate to the best choice of a vocation, the selection of the most suitable workers, the most effective means of avoiding fatigue and boredom, the study and provision of the most valuable incentives to work, the causes and remedies for irritation, discontent and unrest, the best method for work and training, the reduction of needless effort and strain due to bad movements and postures, inadequate illumination, ventilation and temperature, ill-considered arrangements of materials, or defective routing, layout, or organization.[178]

The conventional carrot-and-stick approach of many employers was rejected.[179] Instead, management was advised to analyse working conditions scientifically and to pay attention to the psychology of workers.[180] Malingering and shirking could be eradicated by the better 'handling of men'.[181] As Herbert N. Casson wrote, 'when workers [were] not well managed, then outside leaders spr[a]ng up and [taught] the workers to demand all sorts of absurd and injurious things'.[182] While American industrialists were adopting Taylorist principles (or the application of efficiency practices such as time-management to industry), British employers were attracted by 'human factor' psychology.[183] Ease of work, rather than speed, was also regarded as more conducive to the stronger tradition of trade unionism in Britain.[184]

This psychological approach to preventing malingering encouraged improvements to staff facilities and systems of communication.[185] Management was instructed to intervene in the lives of employees, even to the extent of showing an interest in their sex lives.[186] Increasing the sociability of the workplace, instituting frequent rest pauses and regular changes in tasks were all promoted as reducing monotony and thus doing away with the urge to malinger.[187] Concentration could be stimulated by making work a 'direct objective' (like scoring a goal), by connecting each task with a strong sentiment (such as self-respect or ambition); or by inciting feelings of rivalry and competition.[188] In the words of that writer on wartime neurasthenia, Charles S. Myers, 'if all causes of mental friction – irritability, annoyance, anxiety, and the like – are reduced, the worker will be all the happier, even if he has to work as hard as before'.[189]

There was one further lesson learnt during the war that was adopted in peacetime – the importance of *esprit de corps*.[190] As we shall see in Chapter Four, army physical instructors had discovered the importance of sport in binding men together, and employers took the hint.[191] Peacetime employers concerned with reducing levels of malingering had an advantage over their military counterparts: they could give the workers a stake in the firm. This was not an option for the War Office, forced to deal with conscripted servicemen who wished nothing less than to have a long-term stake in the army. Radical industrialists could, however, adopt this solution to the problem of malingering. Thus, T. B. Miles argued that industrial unrest would disappear (or at least decline) if industry was owned by the workers.[192] For proof that it was effective, supporters pointed to the South Metropolitan Gas Company. Despite opposition from the Gas Workers' Union, a profit-sharing scheme was introduced in 1897, giving workers a share in the property of the company and a voice in the management. All accidents were referred to a jury of workmen. As a result, the accident rate dropped dramatically. At the turn of the century, 8 per cent of employees sustained injuries annually: in 1913 this had dropped to 3 per cent. Fewer men were absent from work, and morale was high.[193] Such an obvious way to reduce malingering was not, however, popular amongst employers who were anxious to squeeze profit out of workmen but not at such a high cost to their power.

A slight detour is required at this stage. As we have seen, although in the policing of malingering workers there was a transfer of discipline between the military and civilian worlds, the malingering man in war was treated more harshly than the civilian malingerer. This caused great resentment amongst rank and file servicemen, in part because *their* definition of malingering and shirking differed from that of the state, employers and the medical profession examined in this chapter. In their view, very different groups were shirkers – the businessmen who remained in Britain and made money out of war industries, the conscientious objectors, the sportsmen who continued to play football, workers who went on strike during the war.[194] A postcard (illus. 23) refers to a specific incident early in 1915 when the shortage of both men and munitions reached crisis point. After 1915, the War Office and the Ministry of Munitions competed for manpower. Although the creation of a ministry for National Service did help in the co-ordination of manpower planning, the need for both servicemen and skilled munitions workers continued to cause problems. For servicemen, it seemed that the government and civil servants were bickering over superficial details while they were risking their lives and limbs by being left short of ammunition and reinforcements. Harold Clegg wrote bitterly, 'while men were being churned up by shell-fire until there was nothing left of them but pieces of flesh adhering to the revetting on the trench, Army Contractors and Munition Makers at home had been waxing fat and greeted those returning from the Wars with a gross display of opulence . . . money that had been reaped from the bodies

23 'Oh yes – there is a war in Flanders!', cartoon postcard, signed 'Toy'.

24 'Soldiers all', cartoon, initialled 'B.P.', in *Punch*, 10 March 1915.

of the dead'.[195] Most despised were conscientious objectors, the 'white-livered' section of the population who were accused of murdering soldiers.[196] The irreverent trench paper, *The New Church Times*, claimed that it made them 'nauseau' to hear about the peace meetings in Trafalgar Square.[197] 'F.A.V.' recalled the words of a wounded soldier at a casualty clearing station:

They won't catch me volunteerin' for the next war, not this child, no bloody faer! Look at the way they treat yer – like bleedin' pigs. There ain't no justice anywhere. There's strong an' 'ealthy fellers at the Base just enjoyin' theirselves. Then there's the 'eads what 'as servants to wait on 'em – d'yer think French or Duggie 'Aig ever 'as shells burstin' round 'em? Then there's the Conchies what 'as a easy time in clink – if I ever see a Conchie in civvy life, I'd knock 'is bloody 'ead orf, struth I will. And the civvies – garblimy – when I was 'ome on leave they kep' on arstin' me, 'Ain't yer wounded yet?' and 'When are yer goin' back?' But d'yer think they care a damn – Not they, you bet yer life on it! *They* don't want the war to stop – they're earnin' good money an' go to dances and cinemas.[198]

The most serious split, however, was between servicemen and strikers.[199] A cartoon from *Punch* (illus. 24) shows a handsome, but wounded, soldier reminding a slinking striker of the results of his actions. As the soldier draws the worker's attention to the sacrifices being made in Flanders, the guilty expression in the workman's eyes accepts the rebuke. In 1918, F. A. Mackenzie complained that politicians and generals had confused their priorities:

The soldier thinks a lot about the contrast between his life and the life of the man who has not put on khaki. He feels that there is something rotten in the state of affairs which treats the man in uniform with great severity for some offence which in the workman, engaged on vital state work, is met by a small fine. A young soldier goes into battle. He is appalled by his experiences, half buried in mud, his nerves shattered by the sight of comrades killed and smashed up around him, and worn out with long hours and exertion, and with the cold and mud. A second battle comes on a day or two afterwards. The young soldier lingers behind, whereupon he is shot for cowardice in the field. A workman in a Clydeside yard . . . absents himself for days [and] . . . probably receives . . . a few rough words from his foreman.[200]

It is not surprising that wounded soldiers in hospital amused themselves by discussing whether the strikers should be shot.[201]

Shell-Shocking

Thus far, we have compared industrial and war malingerers. However, one important theme has been excluded, the debate around what came to be popularly known as 'shell-shock' or neurasthenia. This deserves a

25 'Private E', suffering from a war neurosis, from Arthur F. Hirst, *Medical Diseases of the War*, London, 1918.

separate discussion for a number of reasons. Firstly, it does not fit into the overly neat distinctions made in this chapter between the real and the feigned. Secondly, it draws attention to the ambiguities inherent in the word 'malingering'. Finally, and most crucially, it highlights the debate surrounding organic versus psychological interpretations of ill-health and thereby identifies competing interests within the medical profession for authority over the male body. As this chapter has already implied, throughout the period it was customary to divide patients into two distinctive groups – the organically ill and the imaginary ill. For doctors, the chief interest in this latter group – labelled malingerers – lay in the way organic diseases were mimicked.[202] Although from the late nineteenth century these tidy distinctions were being questioned by a number of specialists (particularly those interested in hysteria), it was the wartime experience of what came to be called shell-shock that irrevocably blurred the rigid distinction made between the body and the mind. Although this insight was primarily applied to men's emotional and physical reactions under shell-fire, attempts were made by medical officers back from the war to apply this lesson to a much broader range of industrial and social processes. In the end, it will be argued, they failed in their mission. In the longer term, men whose bodies were tortured by their minds gained little – if anything – from the furious debates surrounding shell-shock. The look of terror on the face of the man in Illustration 25 would never leave him. Private E's war neurosis was described thus: severe hyperadrenalism and hyper-thyroidism with exophthalmas (protrusion of the eyeball), resulting from prolonged terror. The war left these servicemen stranded in no-man's-land, isolated from both the sane and the insane.

Shell-shock was primarily a phenomenon of the First World War. For the first time, the technology of war included high velocity, explosive shells employed in frightening and seemingly endless bombardments. As instruments of terror and death, these shells were hells apart from cannonballs. Given the levels of physical and psychological fear engendered in front-line warfare, any estimate of mental conflict must err on the low side. The only statistics we have refer to men who were admitted to hospitals or receiving pensions for neurasthenia. In a report early in the war, it was noted that between 7 and 10 per cent of all officers and 3 to 4 per cent of all men from other ranks admitted to hospitals in Boulogne were sent home suffering from 'nervous shock'.[203] In the crisis year of 1916, neurasthenia accounted for 40 per cent of casualties in combat zones.[204] If we exclude men sent home with wounds, neurasthenia was responsible for one-third of all discharges from the army.[205] In 1917, when Sir John Collie analysed 10,000 discharge certificates, 20 per cent were on the grounds of some form of neurosis.[206] By the end of the war, 80,000 cases of war neuroses had passed through the army hospitals.[207] The problem was so serious that in 1920 the War Office established a committee of enquiry into neurasthenia, chaired by Lord Southborough.[208] Furthermore, the numbers of men suffering did not end with the Armistice. In 1921, there were still 65,000 men receiving pensions for neurasthenic disablement.[209] In the early 1930s, 36 per cent of ex-servicemen receiving disability pensions were listed as 'psychiatric casualties'.[210]

Concern about such high levels of psychological ill-health were related to fears about malingering. In the early years of the war, most medical officers believed that men suffering from nervous shock were feigning it. As we have already seen, men desiring to malinger could choose from a wide range of methods: one option was to fake madness.[211] Thus, 'Ex-Private X' befriended a young soldier who had been 'combed out' of a government office and sent to the Front: 'he used to whimper to me and ask me if I thought it was any use for him to sham madness. I think he had tried every other complaint on the M.O. except leprosy and womb trouble.'[212] Similarly, the veteran malingerer John William Rowarth was so desperate to return to Britain that he pretended to be shell-shocked and was hypnotized. He described the experience: 'The Doctor who put me to sleep, examined me again. I had to tell hime [sic] every thing I remembered before the barrage. Talking and telling him lies while he wrote every word I spoke, in a book, telling me my complaint of shattered nerves was becoming very prevalent.'[213] It was said that there were two types of sufferers. On one side was the serviceman whose 'higher ethical conceptions' meant that he could not run away: he simply 'cracked'.[214] On the other side was the serviceman with a 'feeble will': he decided 'in cold blood' to malinger.[215] These distinctions enabled A. Jack Abraham to say of a man suffering from neurasthenia that he was a 'genuine case . . . and not just a coward'.[216]

Part of the problem faced by these medical men was that they believed that all that separated the neurotic from the malingerer was intention. This distinction between conscious and unconscious malingering had been adopted in the industrial sphere even before the war. Archibald MacKendrick insisted that unconscious malingerers were extremely common in civilian life. In his view, such a man was 'more frightened than hurt':

He craves for sympathy, and in his quest goes from one medical man to another, and eventually finds his way to the electrical department of a hospital where his daily attendance gives him the official stamp of an invalid. If he is not discovered by the medical officer in charge, and discharged within a few weeks, he becomes a victim to introspection, and gradually drifts into a hopeless neurasthenic state. His symptoms may be founded on fact, but they are mostly imaginary. The more he thinks about them, the worse they appear and the more firmly he believes in them.[217]

Similarly, in the military sphere, Thomas W. Salmon argued, 'the cardinal point of difference is that the *malingerer simulates a disease or a symptom which he has not in order to deceive others* . . . he lies and *knows that he lies. The hysteric deceives himself by a mechanism of which he is unaware and which is beyond his power consciously to control.* He is usually not aware of the precise purpose which his illness serves.'[218] In other words, 'in both, a disease or symptom [was] simulated . . . The hysteric [was] a malingerer who [did] not lie.'[219] In a textbook on malingering, another expert drew a distinction between malingerers who made a 'conscious effort to deceive others only' and 'hysterics' who indulged in 'subconscious malingering' that 'always commence[d] with self-deception'. In both cases, deception was present, but while the hysteric revelled in examination, the malingerer did not like it: 'The hysteric by his conduct shows that he is in great measure, unconscious of the unreality of his symptoms: the malingerer, on the other hand, conscious of the unreality of his symptoms, is suspicious and ill at ease.'[220]

These definitions, however, were not particularly helpful. Most doctors also recognized that a malingerer might sincerely believe himself to be ill: 'a man who pretend[ed] to be paralyzed for a sufficiently long period [might] well end up by genuinely believing he [was] paralyzed'. Similarly, 'the German people [had] repeated the official lies as to the cause of war so frequently that many now doubtless believe[d] in the truth of what they originally knew to be untrue'.[221] All ill-health was 'more subjective than objective'.[222] In his diary on neurasthenia during the war, Charles S. Myers noted that 'pure' malingering was 'comparatively rare', but that 'many cases [arose] from the combination with the effects of conscious or unconscious sugges-tion, or from a voluntary or involuntary surrender by the soldier of his control over his emotions; they [were] then largely of the nature of self-inflicted (mental) wounds'.[223] Even Thomas W. Salmon conceded this point when he reminded his readers that 'like criminals in civil life', neurasthenic soldiers were often 'neuropathetic individuals'.[224] Doctors were said to have a very serious duty to perform when distinguishing between men who 'consciously feign[ed] and those who unconsciously dissemble[d]'.[225] In war, the consequence of an incor-rent diagnosis was grave: Salmon believed that 'not a few' soldiers suffering from war neuroses were executed by firing squads as malingerers, and he also knew of hysterics committing sucide because of the shame of being 'falsely accused' of malingering.[226]

By 1917, however, the dominant medical view in military hospitals was that most cases of neurasthenia involved men who could not be accused of malingering. George Rutherford Jeffrey made his argument most strongly, pointing out that the most serious cases of neurasthenia occurred in men who could be shown to be of 'steady and fearless character' both before and during the war; the same symptoms were apparent in both seasoned soldiers and raw conscripts; in a large number of cases, these men pleaded to be sent back to the front line; and many did return to the battlefield, only to collapse again.[227]

The increased willingness of military authorities to label neurasthe-nic men 'sick' rather than malingerers was fortunate: it certainly reduced their risk of being shot.[228] However, there were much more pragmatic reasons for this shift in terminology. It was very difficult for the War Office to claim that so many servicemen were malingerers, particularly since the wartime neurasthenic was typically an experi-enced soldier, having spent eighteen months in the army, ten of which would have been spent abroad.[229] Some had won medals for valiant behaviour under fire.[230] They proved themselves keen to return to the fighting.[231] If these men were to be labelled cowards, they would have to be punished as such, but executing so many servicemen was impossible, as it would permanently wreck morale.[232] Manpower shortages made the War Office keen to get these men back to the front lines.

A more important explanation for the willingness of military authorities to adopt pathological or psychological explanations for shell-shock was political. Many of the shell-shocked men were of a high social class. In the year ending 30 April 1917, while the ratio of officers to men at the Front was 1:30 and of wounded officers to men 1:24, the ratio of officers to men in hospitals for war neurasthenics was 1:6.[233] It would have been politically difficult to accuse these men of cowardice. This class dimension to the rhetoric concerning what was sickness and what was malingering is most clearly seen in the distinctions made *between* different types of neurasthenic servicemen. Thus, most sympathy was reserved to those suffering anxiety neuroses (the form predominantly experienced by officers) as opposed to hysteria (the form predominantly reserved for privates). Certain sections of the medical profession provided a socio-cultural explanation for these distinctions. According to them, privates experienced hysteria because of the conflict between two primal instincts: self-preservation and the esteem of the herd. This conflict was settled by the occurrence of some disability – paralysis, mutism, contraction, anaesthesia – that incapacitated them from further participation in the conflict, thus removing the clash between instinct and duty. It was alleged that the more highly educated officers were less able to be convinced by this crude solution. Public school training and military discipline taught them to suppress their instinct of fear. Therefore, they experienced anxiety neuroses. As Major-General Sir W. P. MacPherson and his team summarized it: 'Any soldier above the rank of corporal seemed possessed of too much dignity to become hysterical.'[234] For military authorities, hysteria was more likely to conceal cowardice.

Despite the repudiation of the simple equation 'neurasthenia equals malingering', the connection continued to be made at the professional, public and popular levels. Thus, Millais Culpin, lecturer in psycho-neuroses at the London Hospital, could point out that neurasthenic men shared many characteristics with those suffering from self-inflicted wounds.[235] Medical officers admitted that the distinction was often confusing. In an article on how to detect malingerers through eye tests, one doctor declared that he had come across 'some undoubted cases of neurasthenia, many borderline cases, and a goodly proportion of hysterias', as though 'hysterias' were malingerers.[236] In giving evidence before the War Office's Committee of Enquiry into Shell-Shock, Dr William Brown admitted that doctors were 'struck by the fact that men from certain regiments came up again and again . . .

where there was more "shell-shock" there was more "scrim-shank-ing" ... it seem[ed] as if a panic rose and they all came down together'.[237] For the doctors, there was little to differentiate the soldier who began screaming in the trenches in an attempt to be moved behind the front lines from the shell-shocked man wandering dazed further and further behind the line.

The confusion continued after the war. In 1920, Arthur Henry Leech, the general manager of the Northern Employers' Mutual Indemnity Company in Wigan, informed the Committee on Work-men's Compensation that in his opinion 'malingering [was] a neuras-thenic condition very often'.[238] Many others agreed. For instance, the longtime secretary of the Shipping Federation, Michael Brett, giving evidence at the same commission, declared it was well known that neurasthenia was 'a very common form of disablement following accident', adding, 'I think the opinion of most medical men is that it is very difficult to diagnose a genuine case of neurasthenia, and a certain proportion of the men who are paid compensation, and alleged to be suffering from this affection, are malingerers. We have a great number of those.'[239] Such beliefs were not the prerogative of employers. George Baker was a member of the National Executive Committee of the Miners' Federation of Great Britain. He defined malingerers as men who continued to claim compensation even after they had recovered from illness or injury. When questioned about this defini-tion, he pronounced that the man who 'brood[ed] over his injuries and, without any ill intention, [did] not make the best of himself and [did] not get back to work when it [was] to his interest that he should get back to work' was not a malingerer but was 'suffering from neurasthenia'.[240] Also referring to industrial production, Edward Mansfield Brockbank believed (in 1926) that 'traumatic neurasthenia in any station of life [might] sometimes cause an obsession or fixed idea that a disability exist[ed] where there [was] none, without there necessarily being a conscious attempt at malingering. The fact that legal proceedings [were] at issue often help[ed] the idea.'[241] Fear was thought to be at the heart of industrial malingering. Thus, in 1931, the industrial psychol-ogist Leonard P. Lockhart commented upon the dramatic increase in the numbers of incapacitated workers between 1920 and 1929. He wrote that the

vast machine of modern life is at times a terrifying thing. It even looms larger to many than did the old idea of a wrathful and avenging Deity . . . In the face of such forces as unemployment; mechanical displacement of labour; the competition of girls with men and the success of the former in handling machines and in executing small repetitive processes at lower cost; the economic difficulties of the home and the resulting problems of sexual adjustment, there a tendency for many, and males especially, to develop a feeling of inadequacy to life which is liable to be rationalized in consciousness as illness rather than to be acknowledged frankly for what it really is – namely, a fear of the unknown and the intangible.[242]

The relationship between sufferers of war neuroses and more conventional types of malingering was reiterated in many legal and medical textbooks. In 1926, to help doctors involved in industrial arbitration under the National Insurance Act, Brockbank listed (alphabetically) the most common causes of disablement. Under 'malingering', he referred doctors to 'neurasthenia'.[243] Whether at war or in industry, neurasthenic men were thus defined as unconscious malingerers.

However, the wartime afflicted received different treatment from their civilian counterparts. Whether they were viewed as 'unconscious malingerers' or 'genuinely ill', war neurasthenics generally received a more sympathetic response. The rhetoric of the war stressed that everyone was at risk – not simply (as in the case of industrial malingerers) one section of society. Thus, in his diary of 26 September 1916, the Revd Victor Tanner described the aftermath of a battle:

worst of all were the shell-shock cases which came in. One big powerful Highlander was absolutely demented – shouting at the top of his voice the most utter nonsense and waving his arms and legs. One man who was quite obviously too old to see active service, hung about all day in the doorway trembling from head to foot, we [sic] could not persuade him to go down the Line, try as hard as we could. Two others, quite young boys were shaking from head to foot and cowering down every time a shell came over.[244]

Although the medical profession was anxious to establish who were most susceptible to war neuroses, in the field no one doubted that *all* could fall victim: the young, old, strong, feeble. Furthermore, debates about the relationship between the body and the mind encouraged people to hesitate before condemning servicemen who had 'broken' under stress of shelling: they had at least acknowledged that they owed something to the state. They had fulfilled some of the duties of citizenship. Furthermore, no one could deny that the war was horrible. Everyone sympathized with Daniel Sweeney who confessed in a letter to his fiancée that after the Battle of the Somme he had 'sat down in the mud and cried'; he continued, 'I do not think I have cried like I did that night since I was a child.'[245] That more men did not go mad surprised some. In contrast, industrial workers suspected of feigning madness in order to gain some little concession found it difficult to impress upon outsiders that their lives were blighted by low wages and poor conditions. Everything paled beside the conditions at the Front.

To what extent, however, did wartime experiences alter treatment towards the mentally ill after the war? We have already seen that attitudes about the extent to which neurotic civilians were malingering scarcely changed as a result of the increased sympathy given to men who 'cracked' during war. A similar story will now be told as we turn to treatment regimes. Again, medical officers during the war significantly changed the way they attempted to cure neurasthenic servicemen, but the lessons learnt were rapidly forgotten.

For servicemen described as neurasthenic, the balance between treatment and punishment shifted during the war, largely as a result of changes in the explanations given for war neuroses. As already mentioned, in the early years of the war, shell-shock was believed to be an organic illness caused by the violent concussion of a nearby exploding shell that paralysed the *nervi nervorum*.[246] The bursting of a large shell in a closed space such as a trench led to 'commotional shock' as the sudden rise of atmospheric pressure produced minute haemorrhages in the brain.[247] Burial in the debris of an exploding shell was also a causal factor.[248]

However, by the middle of the war, psychological arguments had gained sway. Charles S. Myers was at the forefront of this shift, arguing that emotional disturbance was sufficient cause for neurasthenia.[249] Medical officers were reminded that many cases of shell-shock occurred in men who had never been near a shell. In 1919, O. P. Napier Pearn's investigation of 200 neurotic soldiers found that 20 per cent had never been under fire.[250] By 1922, Sir Frederick W. Mott (a leading organicist in the early years of the war) was arguing that only 5 per cent of shell-shock cases were due to 'commotional disturbance produced by proximity to the explosion of a large shell'.[251] There were many varieties of psychological explanations. Some maintained that, like all neuroses, neurasthenia was a 'reactive' disorder. By this, they meant that it was the consequence of a failure of psychological adaptation. All servicemen found that military life caused mental conflict. Those who failed to adapt were not necessarily mentally inferior: they could be 'too individualistic' and thus unable to merge with the 'herd'.[252] Other medical officers more attuned to psychoanalytical theories stressed suppression. According to E. Fryer Ballard in 1917, servicemen who were (quite naturally) terrified under shell-fire, 'suppress[ed] it to the subconscious'. However, the time came when the censor failed. As a result, Fryer Ballard wrote, 'the fear-complex [arose] reinforced in symptoms of fear, [and the subject would] develop neurasthenia or anxiety neuroses. If he struggle[d] to re-suppress and fail[ed], he [might] have fits.'[253] Ernest Jones, the president of the

British Psycho-Analytic Association, agreed. In his view, war neuroses confirmed Freud's contention that the mind contained beneath the surface 'a body of imperfectly controlled and explosive forces' that were in conflict with civilization. War was, Jones continued,

an official abrogation of civilized standards. The manhood of a nation is in war not only allowed, but encouraged and ordered to indulge in behaviour of a kind that is throughout abhorrent to the civilized mind, to commit deeds and witness sights that are profoundly revolting to our aesthetic and moral disposition. All sorts of previously forbidden and buried impulses, cruel, sadistic, murderous and so on, are stirred to greater activity, and the old intrapsychical conflicts which, according to Freud, are the essential cause of all neurotic disorders, and which had been dealt with before by means of 'repression' of one side of the conflict are now reinforced, and the person is compelled to deal with them afresh under totally different circumstances.[254]

These debates had important implications for the treatment of neurasthenic men. If neurasthenia was a 'paralysis of the nerves regulating nutrition or a disorder of metabolism', then massage, rest and dietary regimes had to be invoked. Thus, hysterical men needed a vigorous (even painful) massage, while neurasthenic men required a gentle massage because their nerves were 'hypersensitive, overtired, or irritable'.[255] For these doctors, it made sense to apply what was described as 'the most powerful agent we have for stimulating the nerves to activity' – that is, electricity.[256] 'F. S.', an inmate of Southall Auxiliary Military Hospital, was unable to walk until 'the stimulus of an electric battery . . . was applied very vigorously. He then brought his flexes into strong action.'[257] Doctors who favoured this treatment were more liable than most medical men to view the sufferer as a malingerer. As a consequence, electric treatment contained a strong element of torture. One of Lewis Yealland's patients was mute even after he had been strapped down for up to twenty minutes at a time while strong electricity was applied to his neck and throat, lighted cigarette ends to the tip of his tongue and hot plates to the back of his mouth. In Yealland's opinion, such treatment had been too haphazard: he eventually cured the young soldier by locking him in a darkened room and giving him electrical shocks for one hour, then another hour, then raising the voltage for another half-hour, after which the boy spoke.[258] This technique was said to be 'almost infallible': the malingerer might stand one or two applications, but 'quickly recovered under the prospect of daily repetition'.[259]

Medical officers who favoured psychological explanations were much more eclectic in their favoured cures. Psychotherapeutic treatments included persuasion and re-education.[260] Hypnosis could also

26 'Room of Recovery', drawing from Frederick W. Mott, *War Neuroses and Shell Shock*, London, 1919.

be effective.[261] One of the most important of the psychological cures was suggestive psychotherapy where an 'atmosphere of cure' was created in a ward and patients were provided with simple explanations for their incapacities, together with easy remedies.[262] 'Rooms of Recovery' required that men regained hope and trust. The slumped gait of the ill man before treatment would be replaced by a proud, military stance afterwards, as in the sign hanging on the door of the special treatment room in the Pathology Department of the Maudsley Hospital (illus. 26). These doctors also recommended rest and quiet surroundings (for the mildly afflicted) and work (for others).[263] By removing a 'sensitive nervous system as far as possible from the ordinary worrying', a man might be cured.[264] For mildly neurotic men, Charles S. Myers prescribed a few days' rest in bed, with careful attention paid to sleep, diet and the evacuation of the bowels. The seriously afflicted needed to have their thoughts directed away from the body and back into the peacetime world of employment.

In this way, under the discipline of psychology, neurasthenia came to be treated as though it were a disease of the 'will', rather than of 'nerve force'. This had important ramifications for the mentally ill as it made men increasingly blameworthy for their own illnesses. Conventional cures stressing the need for rest were jettisoned on the grounds that they could encourage laziness – ultimately destructive of manliness. As Dr H. Crichton put it, neurasthenia was an infantile condition and 'rest in bed and simple encouragment was not enough to educate a child'.[265] The medical superintendent for the Poor Law infirmaries for the mentally ill in Bristol agreed, arguing that the worst treatment for neurasthenic men was rest: the sufferers 'remain[ed] in hospital, attended to by sympathetic nurses, until all inclination for work [had] disappeared from their minds . . . All initiation [*sic*] [was] lost, and they gradually drift[ed] to a low ebb, [were] easily led, and [became] the associates of a low class of scoundrels, who use[d] them as tools for a variety of evil deeds.'[266] It was, therefore, important that these men were encouraged to work. A popular booklet entitled *Daily Drill for the Voice. A Book of Exercises Composed to Help Men Whose Speech Has Been Affected by Shell-Shock or Other Cases*, published in 1917, accepted the idea that neurasthenia could only be cured by re-activating the power of the will. It instructed men to 'use self-control' and exercise 'will power' to put 'worries and thoughts resolutely from [them]'. Such men should always keep their hands busy.[267] Brooding over the war had to be avoided, at all costs.[268]

There were two other ways in which the shift from organicist to psychological explanations was seen to worsen the status of neurasthenic men. Firstly, a physical cause was more reassuring than explanations that carried with them the taint of insanity or cowardice. Consequently, the organic explanation was preferred by servicemen, as in the case of Albert Andrews who described his experience in his diary when a 'coal box' or shell dropped in front of him and his four friends, three of whom were wounded or killed. Andrews himself 'went skating with the concussion' and remembered nothing further until he awoke to find himself walking.[269] He firmly adhered to an organic explanation. Similarly, the consulting physician to the forces overseas, Major-General Sir W. P. Herringham, noted that some men suffering from neurasthenia repeatedly insisted that they 'had not been in the least afraid, but that the condition was due to some physical cause which they could not explain'.[270]

Secondly, for servicemen, organic explanations had one major compensation. As we saw in Chapter One, wounds (as opposed to illnesses) were granted a high prestige during the war. The organicist explanation for shell-shock enabled neurasthenic servicemen to be regarded as wounded – a much higher status than ill and infinitely better than insane.[271] When the condition was considered to be organic, soldiers were 'allowed to reckon the condition as a wound, and even to wear a wound stripe'. However, the increased popularity of psychological explanations stopped this practice for all except the most severe forms of neurasthenia.[272]

The more sympathetic response to neurasthenic servicemen and the acknowledgement that they were 'genuinely ill' (rather than cowards and malingerers) did not last. After the war, social commentators once again began to slip between use of the terms 'malingering' and 'neurasthenic'. Thus, during the Second World War, General G. S. Patton could declare, 'Any man who says he has battle fatigue is avoiding danger and forcing on those who have more hardihood than himself the obligation of meeting it. If soldiers would make fun of those who begin to show battle fatigue, they would prevent its spread, and also save the man who allows himself to malinger by this means from an after-life of humiliation and regret.'[273] In the words of Lord Moran in 1945, the term 'shell-shock' gave 'fear a respectable name'.[274]

Furthermore, in the popular press it was argued that neurasthenic men were malingerers who had been born with debased bodies. This case was put forward vigorously by T. W. Standwell in *Health and Strength* in 1920, who stated that most cases of neurasthenia were 'precipitated collapses'. Such men were 'degenerates', and the war simply accelerated the process of mental decline. He quoted from the *Evening Standard*, which drew a connection between the increase of crime and neurasthenic men, saying that 'scenes of war, which [left] only a momentary impression on normal persons, excite[d] the animal propensities of the feeble-minded'. He continued, 'The lure of lust or the irresistible love of publicity takes the mentally defective over the abyss, his powers of inhibition being, at most, but small.'[275] Doctors provided statistics to support such arguments. In 1919, Frederick W. Mott compared 100 men suffering from war neuroses with 100 men who had war wounds and found that seventy-four per cent of the psychoneurotic patients had been born in 'neuropathic or psychopathic soil'.[276] He concluded that it was 'perfectly certain that among the general population there [were] a large number of men who [were] constitutional neuropaths or psychopaths'. These men, with their 'predisposition of emotivity', found themselves involved in a war that converted this 'latent tendency' into a 'pronounced functional disability'.[277] In his study of 200 neurotic war soldiers, O. P. Napier Pearn decided that heredity was a causative factor in ten per cent of the cases.[278] From his work in France, William Robinson argued that a large proportion of soldiers who were suffering mental collapses had been 'potential psychopaths' before enlisting. Furthermore, early in the war 'it [had been] common for men to suppress factors in their family and personal history which would be liable to result in rejection on presenting themselves for enlistment. As hostilities were prolonged and more men were necessary, many who had formerly been regarded as exempt from military service [had become] eligible.'[279] In addition, as mental hospitals were turned into military hospitals, discharged patients often found their way into the army.[280] This was even admitted by some recruiting doctors. In 1916, one such doctor agreed that a man with a 'direct insane inheritance' should be excluded from the military armed forces – but, he admitted, there was a problem because the 'previous breakdown [was] unknown to companies and employers, and these look[ed] upon the man a shirker or coward, and [might] let him know their opinion'. He had seen 'several such patients who [were] becoming unstable because of the idea that people mistrusted them', and he had 'even decided to run the risk of enlisting some of these men, as . . . there [was] a real danger of their developing delusional insanity with auditory hallucinations'.[281] The price to be paid for allowing men susceptible to mental illness into the army was great: once a man was allowed to enlist, the government was obliged to accept further responsibility for him, even after demobilization.[282] Thus, the Victorian theory of hereditary degeneracy as a central explanation for psychiatric disorders may have been dented by ideas about shell-shock, but after the war such lessons were placed to one side.[283]

The lessons learnt during this war were certainly instrumental in the growth of psychiatry as a discipline.[284] One of the first clinics in Britain for outpatients requiring psychotherapy, the Tavistock Clinic, was established in 1920 as a direct result of the experiences of Hugh Crichton-Miller in treating neurasthenic servicemen.[285] Although the neurological understanding of nervous disorders continued to dominate, the war had resulted in a wider knowledge and understanding of psychological and psychoanalytic theory (albeit stripped of some of their sexual interpretations) in Britain.[286] The British Psychoanalytical Society was founded soon after the war. Furthermore, during the war it is clear that there was great hope that the insights of military medicine would be transferred to the civilian population. Thus, in September 1917, an article in the *Lancet* reported the great interest that had been created for new ways of treating men with nervous disorders:

An outcome of this revised interest is undoubtedly the expression of dissatisfaction with the risks existing in methods of handling such cases in civilian life . . . we have repeatedly drawn attention to the inferior position we occupy amongst the nations in our attitude to psychiatry. But the war is changing things. The problems of 'shell shock' and other new more mysterious illnesses, they are of the every day problems of 'nervous break-downs'.[287]

Doctors such as Charles S. Myers transferred their experience of working with shell-shocked men to industry after the war, arguing that the war had taught them that nervous disorders were essentially of 'mental origin' and therefore required treatment by men trained in psychological theories, rather than by neurologists or asylum doctors.[288]

It is, however, easy to exaggerate the extent to which these medical officers actually succeeded in transferring their wartime knowledge into the civilian world.[289] Myers may be regarded as untypical. According to Montague David Eder, the 'institutions of medicine ha[d] remained unshaken by the war'.[290] The situation of the mentally ill had deteriorated during the war as asylum medical staff volunteered and psychiatric resources were redirected towards military needs.[291] After 1918, these resources continued to be biased in favour of ex-servicemen. Although at the end of the war there were nineteen specialist neurological hospitals catering for ex-servicemen, civilians reaped few benefits. There was little long-term improvement in the services and facilities offered to civilians suffering from nervous disorders. Some provision was made for psychiatric teaching in hospitals in London, but before the Second World War there was little expansion in the number of outpatient clinics and even hospital beds remained scarce.[292] The Tavistock Clinic provided a valuable service, but other clinics were slow to be established.[293] The first psychologist to be employed in a psychiatric setting was not appointed until 1928 (at the Tavistock Clinic).[294] Hostility towards psychoanalysis continued to dominate: it may have been suitable for Germans, but not for 'virile, sport-loving, open-air people like the British'.[295] The greater knowledge of Freudian ideas after the war did not benefit mentally ill men: mental breakdown became even more shameful, vaguely associated in the public's mind with sexual deviance and moral degradation.[296] For patients, the only improvements came in 1930 with the passing of the Mental Treatment Act which allowed a patient to be voluntarily admitted to a mental institution without having to be certified insane.[297]

Even at the professional level, the wartime situation failed to improve dramatically the social standing of psychiatrists who continued to earn less than physicians and to be regarded as inferiors.[298] Although in 1922 the War Office's Committee of Enquiry into Shell-Shock recommended that Royal Army Medical Corps officers should be instructed in psychoneurosis, little was done to put his recommendation into practice. At the outbreak of the Second World War, the Royal Army Medical Corps captain, Robert H. Ahrenfeldt, could complain that the British army had made scarcely any provision for psychiatric help.[299] Similarly, in 1947 William C. Menninger indicted the psychiatric profession for permitting the military 'to forget almost all the lessons that we learnt in the last war'. As a consequence, he continued, the war was begun 'with hospital treatment forbidden, with no plan of treatment for combat troops, no unit to provide such, no plans for training, no psychiatrist in combat divisions, and not even a psychiatrist in the headquarters when war was declared'.[300] The historian Janet Oppenheim summarized the situation accurately: the 'Great War may have demonstrated beyond doubt that psychological aspects [could], by themselves, utterly disrupt the body's functions, but the lesson [had done] nothing to mitigate the certainty that nervous breakdown unmanned men'.[301]

Furthermore, servicemen who had suffered as a result of their wartime experiences soon faced a new threat: denial of their existence. Shell-shock did not end with the war. In 1929, the government granted more pensions for psychiatric illness than they had in the four years immediately following the war. Thus, the miner Rowland Luther did not suffer until long after the Armistice. As he admitted, it was only after he failed to find a job back in the pits that he 'cracked-up' and became 'just skin and bone'. His life 'had even been in despair . . . [He] picked up again, after being delirious, and re-living [his] life as a soldier'.[302] Hospitals dedicated to helping such men were kept short of money, and many sufferers were dismissed from care prematurely. A twenty-five-year-old clerk writing to Marie Stopes in 1923 described how the Ministry of Pensions was 'hopeless, useless. I had a cause [sic] of Psychoanalysis but it was of no avail.'[303] As shown in Chapter One, government resources were transferred to other groups. By the 1930s, in a review of Erich Maria Remarque's *All Quiet on the Western Front*, Arthur Kenneth Chesterton could argue that British soldiers had proved themselves to be more civilized than their German counterparts: 'The hysterical scene in the dug-out, caused by excessive fear, could scarcely have happened on our side of the line', he wrote.[304]

As has been shown, the rules and rituals governing malingering were understood by a wider group of men than simply those who malingered. In the words of a popular toast, 'Heres Sham pain to my true friends, and real pain to my sham friends.'[305] The cost of refusing the demands placed upon men for obedience to a military or civil authority was high. In the context of war, the policing of the male body was more vigilant and punishments for infringing the rules more stringent. In the next chapter, we shall look at the extent to which soldiers in the Other Ranks 'bonded' together against the almost omnipresent military authorities. As has been argued here, however, it is clear that most civilian and war malingerers were content to simply avoid their duty or alter the nature of compensation rather than attack the nature of the duty itself. The balance between shirking and malingering shifted according to the power structures being opposed: the protection afforded by co-operation between men (for instance, in unionized industries) encouraged 'go-slow' practices. In the armed forces, men were more liable to be forced to resort to individual, isolated acts of rebellion. The struggle between medical officers and psychiatrists over men suffering from neurasthenia did little to ease their suffering, or to improve the position of the mentally ill after the war. The failure of 'will' labelled these men malingerers in the eyes of many comment-ators. Despite the large numbers of men who did feign illnesses during periods of immense stress, it is still surprising that *more* men did not do so. However, as many realized, in times of economic depression or in the midst of a battle, it was sometimes a more sensible strategy to attempt to shorten their horizons and do their manly duty. As Major Valentine Fleming affirmed in a letter of 6 December 1914, 'The men have realized the fact that it's safer to sit in a trench than to get out of it and run away.'[306]

Three Bonding

The male body may be passive, simply waiting for love. The picture introducing this chapter is taken from the scouting book, *A Peace Scout*, published three years before the First World War. In the picture, a small, blond boy called Physog lies feebly against a tree. By lifting a branch from the tree, an older, more vigorous lad makes him visible, exclaiming, 'I've run you to earth at last.' It is tempting to see in this picture all the conventional features of modern romance: Physog is associated with Nature, the feminine; the older lad is Hunter, the masculine. The viewer is unsure whether the older boy is about to attack or rescue the one who is fainting. To know the answer, we have to read the book. In it, we discover that Physog is the 'Tenderfoot' of the Wolf Patrol. He is also an orphan who lives with an elderly bachelor artist and an old matronly Irish servant. A slim, fair-haired boy, his 'high white forehead', 'pink cheeks' and 'girlish features' have earned him the nickname 'Physog' from the other scouts (his real name is Rolfe). He is also the best cook in camp. One day, Physog slips out of camp to visit some newly born squirrels to which he is especially attached. He hears a woman scream and cycles off to get help for a villager who has been hit in the head during a local feud. Meanwhile, thinking that Physog is lost, the other scouts mount a search. Physog does his scout's duty – but it proves to much for him and he collapses against the tree. The older lad in the picture – who is identified as the 'lithe' scoutmaster, Geoffrey De Quincey, son of the squire of Stretton – then discovers the orphan Physog. This is how the scene depicted in the picture is described:

in a limp heap, half propped up against the trunk of a pine tree, sat the missing Tenderfoot. His eyes were closed and blue veins showed like tattoo marks on his white forehead. Beside him lay a dead squirrel. Rolfe roused himself at the familiar sound of the Scoutmaster's voice, and tried to smile. 'I'm – not – shot,' he said feebly, 'but – the – squirrel was – in his shoulder – beastly poachers – you – know – and I finished him off – out of – his misery – you know – but the sun on Pitmouth road made me sick – but I'm all right now – and I'm coming

'I've run you to earth at last.'

27 'I've run you to earth at last', illustration, initialled 'J.A.G.', from Irene Barnes,
A Peace Scout, London, 1911.

into – camp – and . . .' here Rolfe's voice failed and his eyes closed again.

Reading these words, we can be in no doubt of the role of the scoutmaster: he is a rescuer, not abuser. The son of the squire of Stretton picks up the orphan who has fainted and gently carries him back to camp.[1]

The attraction of this story lies in the way it identifies the male body as the focus of romantic adventure between men. With the exception of a couple of women (whose cluckings and whimperings rarely take up more than a few sentences) and the faithful Irish servant, there are no female figures in this novel. There is, in fact, no need for women since boys and men play all the required parts: parent, sibling, friend, lover. These are the masculine roles examined in this chapter: the young boy entranced by the older man's skill; the stronger man cradling the weaker; two men smiling at each other. In the last chapter, the man attempting to avoid the risk of mutilation or death was portrayed as being forced to fight a lonely battle against the military establishment. To what extent did men manage to forge links of deep comradeship under such difficult circumstances? Throughout this study, but especially in this chapter, it is our intention to show that masculinity is multi-dimensional: fortitude and tenderness coexisted. Total war made reconciling the tension between the man as fighter and man as lover more problematical. During wartime, men were removed from their mothers, wives and female lovers. Admired male friends were taken away. Men were provided with imperfect substitutes to domestic intimacy. Military rules and rites that had been developed to alleviate the disquiet evoked by the removal of the most intimate spheres of men's lives were antipathetic to a largely conscripted army. To some extent, there was a re-creation of the domestic sphere within an all-male environment. However, such pageantry could not contain men's need to express the 'other side' of masculinity: that is, private, domestic manliness which gave meaning to the public man.

This chapter is also about isolation and vulnerability. The alienation of men from each other is a common theme in the histories of masculinity, and wartime experiences are generally portrayed as overthrowing those male inhibitions. It is axiomatic in the history of the First World War that servicemen 'bonded' together, united by the gender-specific experiences of warfare.[2] Two brothers kiss passionately in front of their proud parents: war was regarded as legitimating such displays (illus 28). It was sufficient to be 'men': branch of service, rank and age meant little within the bond of shared military experiences. However, this chapter questions the extent of male comradeship

28 British soldier and sailor brothers greeting one another outside their home while on leave. [IWM Q31046]

during the war. We need to define what constituted male bonding, and how it differed from other forms of human interaction. In this chapter, male bonding will be taken to mean intimate, emotional interaction between men in which the individual identifies himself as an integral part of an all-male group. It implies a consciousness of masculinity as gender and although distinctions such as those based on class or ethnicity may be recognized, these distinctions are subordinated to the gender identity. Wartime experiences may have given greater potential for experimentation in intimacy between men and may have injected a new uncertainty into romantic masculinity, but these same experiences ultimately crushed such sentiments. Relationships between servicemen during the war failed to result in any true reconstruction of masculine intimacy.

Fighting Friends

Male bonding was not an inevitable, organic sentiment of war: it was in the interests of military authorities to foster in servicemen a sense of group solidarity, a merging of the individual's identity with that of the battalion.[3] The central features in the military encouragement of *esprit de corps* do not need to be rehearsed at length here. They include the use of uniforms, ritualized humiliation and rites of powerlessness.[4] Military regimens invoked manly interaction through discipline: indeed, during officers' training, the lecture devoted to *esprit de corps* was entitled 'Discipline'.[5]

These oppressive regimes, aimed at breaking down the individual in anticipation of his merging into the group, were only one side of the military code. They were also the weaker side: surrender to the group because of intimidation has none of the power of submission because of love. Alongside the negative disciplines was a series of positive reinforcements. An expedient method of binding together servicemen involved inspiring pride in the aesthetic qualities of men as a group, and was effected by the military authorities' affirmation of the male body's beauty, both in its states of dress and undress. The function of uniforms, for example, was not simply disciplinary. It was widely recognized that uniforms enhanced men's masculine appearance: a well-designed headdress made them look taller, stripes on trousers gave the illusion of length in stocky legs, epaulettes exaggerated the width of shoulders. The use of uniforms to bind men together visually was certainly not novel: it has a long history in the armed forces and, from the late nineteenth century, within a wide range of boys' organizations such as in scouting.[6] There was an irony in this positive bonding: the aesthetically binding function of uniforms could only succeed by encouraging the development of narcissism. The group could only be adored if the individual serviceman could first admire his own body. This was true throughout the military services. For instance, Reginald George Garrod was a seventeen-year-old clerk in 1913 when he set eyes upon his first hussar. He recalled, 'I saw a gorgeous figure in blue with yellow band, red hat and clinking spurs and said to myself, "That's for me", got off my stool, rushed into the street and stopping the soldier I said "Could I please be like you?" . . . That night at home, I could think of nothing else but this Hussar.'[7] Similarly, George Hewins identified enthusiastically with his volunteer unit, exclaiming, 'I had a scarlet tunic, a helmet with a spike in – oh I was pushed out! – five rows o' crowns, gold epaulettes hanging down, blue undress.'[8] Potential military recruits chose their regiments with care, based on the uniform they judged to be the most flattering for their particular body shapes. The Irish Liverpudlian Pat O'Mara noted that his cousins 'wanted very much to be seen' in the uniform of the 8th Liverpool Irish, while his Irish friend Henry Roche believed that he would look best in the plaid kilts of the Liverpool Scottish. For O'Mara and the rest of his friends, the 'Yankee suits' of the Merchant Marines were the first choice.[9] The excitement of war speeded up the transition from narcissism to group adoration.

Uniforms were only one of many techniques used to unite service-men into an obedient, efficient unit. Another positive way that the armed forces attempted to stimulate *esprit de corps* was through public nudity. The parading of naked men began as soon as a man entered the recruiting office. Again, it is too easy to assume that this was simply a technique of humiliation. Some men certainly experienced it as such. A group of naked men sits waiting for their clothes to be cleaned (illus. 29). Hands protecting genitals, legs crossed: they look very uneasy. Russell L. Venables might have been one of these men. He had decided to join the Rotherham Howitzer Brigade and turned up at the enlisting office only to be told to wait in the examining room. He soon panicked: 'I changed my mind about joining His Majesty's Forces; I did not like the idea of parading in public without clothes, so I made for the door.'[10] Unluckily, he was ordered to sit down (and he obeyed!). But other men were either not so shy, or they were already accustomed to undressing rites in other all-male contexts. Thus, the scout John Hargrave was asked to strip when he entered the Marylebone recruiting office. He relished the experience, recalling that the 'smell of human sweat was overpowering in the little ante-room. Some of the men had hearts and anchors and ships and dancing-girls tattooed in blue on their chests and arms. Some were skinny and others too fat. Very few looked fit.'[11] Hargrave was proud of his body and more than happy to flaunt it in front of others. Once in the armed forces, this exposure of the stripped body occurred on an almost daily basis.[12] Men walked about 'starkers' while their clothes were fumigated.[13] They bathed together, (illus. 30). It was a truly 'gladsome sight', Charlie May brooded, to watch hundreds of men 'stripped to the buff' digging in a trench: 'Big muscles and supple joints swelling and swinging with the

29 Interior of Undressing Room. [IWM Q58122]

30 Soldiers bathing in the pond of a farm near St Eloi, 19 June 1917. [IWM Q5500]

rhythm of the pick.'[14] Whether dressed or undressed, the aesthetics of military life could rouse men to intense feelings of *esprit de corps*.

During the war, however, these conventional attempts to stimulate group identity had to work for a largely conscripted armed force. We have to consider the extent to which volunteers and conscripts during wartime reached out in comradeship to other men. Many men may have been like Maberley S. Esler who eagerly enlisted precisely in search of that 'comradeship in arms' of which he had heard so much.[15] Certainly, wartime emotions might nurture male bonding even prior to the individual man entering into the army, navy or air force. Beloved menfolk were not difficult to name. Even the twelve-year-old boy signing himself 'Blumstead' was fluent in his affections. He begged an officer to give him a position as a drummer or bugler because, he wrote,

My greatest friend has been killed by trechery [*sic*] at the front, my brother has been discharged medically unfit from the West Kents, and my father is making shells in the Arsenal. For the first thing I want and feel I *must* avenge my friend, Secondly, I feel I must keep up my brother's honour by taking his place and thirdly I feel that I *Must* carry on the work my father has begun.[16]

All over the country, men claimed affection for other groups of men they wanted to serve alongside – whether this included the Old Boys of the Wintrington Secondary School in Lincolnshire (the 'Grimsby Chums')[17] or merely their work friends, neighbours and pals.[18] The Pals' Battalions were novel and extremely important in that they were comprised of men from the same community or workplace. Nearly forty per cent of the service and reserve battalions created between August 1914 and June 1916 were raised by bodies other than the War Office.[19] When he heard that the London Household Artillery Company was recruiting ex-public school boys, Ralph Ernest Barnwell (formerly of Rugby) immediately signed up, confessing that 'the idea of serving with the sort of people with whom one had been associated had a natural attraction'.[20] The poster 'All Together!' (illus. 31) was popular in large part because of the way it appealed to the manly traditions of romance based on fictions about 'old seafaring'. It appealed to those brought up on romantic swashbuckler adventure stories in which men fought and boozed together. Similarly, the slogan 'Join the T.A. so that you can fight with your friends' was effective in recruiting men to the Territorials.[21] Men boasted about how their fighting friends 'longed' to be joined by them.[22] They even followed their employers into the army on the grounds that they represented their ideals.[23] Other soldiers rejoiced when moved to the front line with their 'large family',[24] while one William Walls even refused promotion a number of times 'not wishing to leave [his] pals'.[25] After being

31 'All Together!'. [IWM Q31046]

wounded, servicemen worried guiltily that these friends might feel deserted.[26]

Furthermore, the actual experience of war *could* enhance male friendships and *could* enable further expression of male emotion. The possibilities of war in enhancing male bonding may be illustrated by looking at the will of Basil Liddell Hart. On 9 September 1915, he asked his parents not to wear mourning clothes in the event of his death. He wrote, 'I do not wish you to regard my death as an occasion for grief, but of one for thanksgiving, for no man could desire a nobler end than to die for his country & for the cause of civilisation.' Eight months of battle altered these noble sentiments. On 27 May 1916, Liddell Hart appended the following words to his will:

Also I wish to say that while I feel it an honour to die for England, I feel it an even greater honour to die as an officer of the British Regular Army, in which I have been associated with, as my fellow-officers & men many of the finest gentlemen whom God has sent into this world, men of the finest of whose character the world is strangely ignorant, but who nevertheless have brought added lustre to our name.[27]

The country for which Liddell Hart was preparing to die had become less important than the men next to whom he fought. Love was a word frequently used to describe this affection. John Francis Jones described a soldier (a 'man among men') from the East End of London who 'came to be loved – the word is not too strong – not only by me, but by almost all the company'.[28] The Revd C. Parry Okeden wrote to his wife about searching no-man's-land for the body of 'the gallantest fellow that ever walked – as simple as a child, quite irresistibly attractive: it just seemed as though it couldn't be true that he is gone. I loved him in an extraordinary way.'[29] Men took on a new attractiveness for each other during war.

Part of the stimulus for this development of intimate male friendships was the absence of women. Thus, Lawrence Gameson believed that the 'fellowship of active service' was the result of 'the absence of women's quite normal disrupting influence as between man and man'. As opposed to the idea that wartime intimacy between men was a substitute for the 'natural' intimacy between men and women, Gameson regarded male intimacy as normal behaviour that women 'disrupted'.[30] The absence of women had an additional component: gender roles were rendered more fluid in wartime as men were required to carry out many tasks that had formerly been the preserve of the opposite sex. They sat down together to darn their clothes.[31] They washed their dirty trousers.[32] Experienced soldiers boiled up cans of tea together with an ease that seemed 'completely fantastic' to one new recruit.[33] Another man reported incredulously that he had to cut and butter his own bread and wash his plate after use.[34] Not all men were so new to domesticity, however. One man who had prepared food for his wife and lodger at home transferred these skills to the Front when the unit's cook was injured.[35] Others begged female friends to send them cookery books.[36] With a favourite friend, they fried meat cutlets and cheese together, and washed them down with cocoa.[37] Men took over the roles of mother, sister, friend and lover. They held each other as they danced (see illus. 32). They impersonated women at concerts and dances – and sometimes in their tents afterwards.[38] The delight that many found in impersonation may be seen in a photograph of a concert: the couples in the centre appear distinctly cosy (illus. 33). One officer's servant (a 'batman') was described as 'a lady-like individual'.[39] Another batman characterized himself as 'the Colonel's Slut' who was 'always on hand to tuck [the colonel] up at night'.[40] Mothering was important. A quartermaster-sergeant in France reminded one man of 'a harassed but efficient mother of a reckless family'.[41] Men nursed their friends when ill; they wrapped blankets around each other 'as a mother would a

32 British troops dancing to a French marine band, Salonica, May 1916. [IWM Q32011]

33 A concert, probably at No. 6 Clearing Station, Flanders, from Lt.-Col. H. T. Minden Wilson's album of photographs. [CRAC RAMC 2081]

34 Men of the Duke of Wellington's Regiment after the capture of Marfaux on 23 July 1918, during the battles of the Marne. [IWM Q687]

child'.[42] In sleep, their bodies easily 'spooned' together as in the photograph above (illus. 34), showing men of the Duke of Wellington's Regiment resting in a shell-hole in July 1918. Domesticity was exemplified by two friends who would lie together in the trench's candlelight, reading books such as *Blind Love* and *The Pearl Maiden* to one another.[43] Together, they curled up and slept,[44] perhaps describing it in words similar to those used by 'Jack' in a chatty letter to Miss D. Williams on 23 November 1917: 'Hell I think I must close now as my *wife* is in bed (if you can call it so. 1 blanket on the ground not bad eh.) & wants me to keep her warm but it is only a Palestine wife. another Sussex boy. & we are both Jacks so there is nothing doing . . . I really must ring off now as my mate keep saying some nice words which I do not understand. getting cold I suppose. it is very chilly at night right now. & it is nice to have some one to keep each other warm.'

This intimacy – whether nostalgically reminiscent of the public school or scouting camp, or whether indulging for the first time – drew men together. As Henry Gervis observed,

After twenty-five years of married life it seemed passing strange to me to be living in a society of men, as if I had gone back to college again or had entered a monastery . . . Living with the same men day after day one gets to know them more thoroughly than when merely meeting for business, professional or social purposes, and one is struck by the extraordinary differences in character that such intimacy reveals.[45]

This intimacy was physical and personal. Thus, in the first eight pages of his memoirs, Lawrence Anthony Humphries was able to recall in detail the men who had fought with him between 21 March and 5 April 1918. His mates were described as 'tall thin, bright, breezy, always with a laugh typical Public school type'; had 'tensed blue eyes, facing death with an intense stare, concentrated like a martyr'; 'a fine person'; 'a most handsome blonde haired young Lieutenant'; 'a curly haired youngster'; 'a lovely chap'; 'a legal man, languid drawl. humorous eyes, very tall'; fair, blonde with blonde moustache. one of the most handsome fellows I have ever seen'.[46] A world of men was opening up, revealing the wide range of roles played by males and exposing the fluidity between masculinity and femininity.

The absence of women was only one feature that encouraged male intimacy. The very experience of war also demanded closeness. The soldier William Walls described a concert that had been arranged for the soldiers: 'It was a sight worth seeing all those big grown up men who had seen death scores & scores of times all jesting and singing in the chorus's round that fire like sand-boys.'[47] Hiram Sturdy decided that the 'fear of hell or the hope of heaven' were the two things that encouraged a 'noisey [sic] comradeship'.[48] The absolute reliance on other men for the staples of life (indeed, for life itself) required trust and affection.[49] As W. A. Quinton wrote, '*Sharing everything*, down to the last cigarette-end, the last army biscuit, the last bit of cover under an enemy bombardment, can you wonder when I say we almost loved each other. Facing hardship and death together day after day, brings out that something in a man that lies dormant in the monotonous round of everyday civilian-life.'[50] In a moving love letter to his wife in 1917, Jack W. Mudd advised her to stop worrying: 'Out here, dear, we're all pals what one hasn't got the other has, We [sic] try to share each others troubles, get each other out of danger. You wouldn't believe the Humanity between men out here . . . It's a lovely thing is friendship out here.'[51] This mutual dependence undermined male self-control. A. C. Warsop met his childhood friend just before the Battle of the Somme, and narrated his experience of 'going over the top': 'I looked at Herbert, I could see his lips move – I shouted but I couldn't hear myself at all. I wanted to tell him that we would keep together so I grabbed his hand and we went over together as we had gone to Sunday school, hand in hand.'[52] Similarly, the tough and emotionless ship's stoker who joined the army changed: 'he would always do his best for a pal, could see a joke against himself, and undoubtedly softened in his attitude towards life under the influence of Army comradeship: the spirit of fighting soldiers is evidently gentler and kindlier than that of a stokehole.'[53] Male comradeship served to make war less unbearable, and more human.[54]

Furthermore, faced with the terrifying experience of death, conventional emotional responses no longer sufficed. As one hospitalized soldier admitted, 'You may get used to seeing wounded men, but not to seeing men wounded.'[55] Or, in the words of the Revd John M. Connor, in his diary for November 1914, 'seeing your pals blown into bits, it makes a new man fellow in spirit, moral & character'.[56] Fathers appeared in visions to comfort frightened men.[57] The gunner John A. Boullier wrote of the aftermath of the battle at Mons, 'my friend saw men face each other and cry, the reason for which no one can thoroughly understand, and words cannot be found to explain. The scenes were ghastly beyond description. Only those who were there will ever know and understand.'[58] The omnipresence of death enabled emotion. The Revd Connor wrote in his diary for 22 December 1914, 'Spoke' [sic] *Pte Ernest Rawlinson*, Liverpool Scottish, Caledonia St Liverpool dang'ly wounded / abdomen (y'day) This bright eyes, frank young face; said another minister had been – suffering pain – I prayed to God for the dear lad – I said, "*I'll give you your mother' kiss*" – "Let me do it to you", & the dear lad kissed me.'[59] Dying men 'laid back' and were cradled in the arms of other men.[60] In a letter to the mother of a recently killed soldier, David H. Fenton wrote, 'I held [Jim] in my arms to the end, and when his soul departed I kissed him twice where I knew you would have kissed him – on the brow – once for his mother and once for myself.'[61] 'Inseparable companions' warranted a common grave, with no 'layer of earth' to keep them apart.[62]

The Roots of Bonding

Deliberate stimulation of male bonding was not unique to the armed forces but was part of a broader agenda within institutions focusing on the discipline and pleasure of men. One aspect of this has been dealt with by other historians, namely, the public school tradition. However, this tradition was very much a minority one, as only a tiny proportion of men would have been exposed to such an education. It was not a tradition that was known in the working classes.[63] As was suggested at the beginning of this chapter, for the majority of men male bonding had a long history within the scouts and physical training clubs. It is beyond the scope of this study to examine the full diversity of male comradeship outside the military context, but two attempts to stimulate male bonding in this period may be instructive. The first is represented by the League of Health and Strength, an organization within the narcissistic tradition that attempted to bind young men together in loyalty and masculine love through competition centred on the male physique. The second example to be examined in this chapter is very different. The Boy Scouts stressed male bonding much more overtly, but did so through emphasizing co-operation and community. Those entering the military services were more liable to be drawing on one of these two traditions of male friendship than on any public school training.

The League of Health and Strength, a highly successful muscle-building club, denotes the importance of the male body in the history of bonding. The story of the League's motto provides an insight into the principal way that it endeavoured to forge links between young men by stressing the desirability of the ideal male physique. It begins with the image of an isolated young man lying in a 'darksome vale . . . languid, feeble, suffering, yet content; content with the contentment of the brute creation, content with the contentment of despair'. The vapours from a fetid swamp have lulled him into an 'unwholesome and unholy lethargy'. Suddenly, his restlessness is disturbed by the figure of 'a man so beautiful, so Strong, so noble'. Together, these two companions undertake a pilgrimage up the 'mountain of endeavour' where they discover an entire 'City of the Strong'. In this city the young man finds the 'Spirit of the Perfect Man – *for he has found himself*'.[64] This story was intended to appeal to young men (over the age of fourteen years) concerned with 'health and Right Living'. In 1910, the League had more than 10,000 members and the circulation of its *Annual* was over 90,000 a week.[65] On the eve of war, it could boast of a membership of 23,000.[66] From 1914 on, its appeal to boys increased dramatically, so that by the mid-1930s, membership had reached 124,000. These members had to pledge themselves to help forward the cause of physical culture, to exercise daily, to encourage others to keep fit, to 'extend the right hand of fellowship to all brother P.C.s'; to adhere to the principles of temperance and chastity; and to discourage juvenile smoking 'and all other evil habits'.[67] The League's purpose was summed up by two slogans: the motto embossed on its badge was 'Sacred thy Body, even as thy Soul', but the motto by which members were advised to 'order their lives' was 'Brotherhood'.[68]

Comradeship between men was the League's central, but not sole, pursuit. It also attracted young men concerned with their own health because, for members of the League, the solution to poor physique was exercises designed to encourage muscular development. 'Health *was* strength.'[69] Thus, the labourer Jack Preston joined the League after an attack of diphtheria, Albert Parker because he was 'a mere wreck', the machine-fitter Peter C. Vigor because of his chest troubles, the policeman Cecil Hewitt because all the children in his area were 'a sickly delicate lot', and others because it promised a cure for tuberculosis.[70] The individual's health problems were easily transferred to concern about degeneracy within British society generally. Members were encouraged to think of themselves as a 'band of missionaries', responsible for serving their country 'in the most useful of all causes, namely, that of raising the standard of the race, of doing their greater or lesser share towards the provision of sane, healthy and interesting pursuits for a people which of late years, alas, ha[d] followed baser paths'.[71]

Much more important, however, than these noble considerations, was the League's concern with uniting young men through worship of the gorgeous physique. By providing a seemly language with which men could praise the manly body, the League raised male narcissism to new heights. Its rhetoric centred on the admiration of men for men, more than on the infatuation of women for men. Indeed, there are very few references to women in their publications. The male body *as male* was paramount. Their supporters declared that they aimed to inculcate in their readers' minds a 'desire and love for the Physique Beautiful'.[72] Members were reassured: *all* men – even pale, intellectual types – admired muscular bodies.[73] For many young physical culturalists, the beauty of the male form was fascinating. Albert Parker joined because he had 'always been an admirer of strong, robust men'.[74] According to 'Uncle Bob', the arms of a strong man 'captivated [the] fancy' the moment they were seen, in the 'mental vision, ready to take up his daily work'. The reason was simple: 'They impressed you with a sense of importance, usefulness and value for where [was] the man who [did] not love the strong, active man with the limbs that look[ed] ready for anything?'[75] The most virile man was the strong man.[76] It was not enough to *be* strong: the muscular man wanted to be

thought strong and thus gain the admiration of his acquaintances. Vanity does certainly enter largely unto the desire and it mostly happens that a young man takes up physical culture for the first time after witnessing some feat of strength and realizing that his present poor physical condition would prevent him from duplicating the performance.[77]

Competition between men – initially stimulated (as in the armed forces) by humiliation – was a step towards gender identification. Thus, Britain's 'Strongest Man', Edward Aston, asked,

Have you ever stood by ashamed of your weakness while strong men have been able to do the things you would have liked to have done? Perhaps you remember a time when you had to keep in the background and let others come forward to do a real man's job, not for lack of grit or courage, but because you realized that you did not possess the necessary muscle power to back that courage and you were afraid of the ridicule to which you might expose yourself?[78]

There was a distinction between strength as muscular force and strength as irresistible attractiveness: muscle building provided both.[79] Given high levels of illness and poor nutrition, strength was not something everyone possessed. Pat O'Mara ran errands for a fish merchant in the 1910s. After work, he would meet with his friends on the street corner. He noted that 'the gang minimized the phenomenal nature of my ten-bob-a-week salary. Those working in Reed's Tin Works proudly showed the calluses on their hands – and talked about "fifteen shillings with overtime", or "almost a quid on Sunday". We all compared muscles, and I fared the worst.'[80] Another example is Max Bygraves, the son of a casual dock labourer. He later recalled, 'Charles Atlas was a big influence in our boyhood days. This man with ripping muscles jumped out at you from a paperback, saying, "You too can have a body like mine!" . . . To look like this man, we scraped and saved to raise the half-a-crown to send for the course that could make us take on a Tommy Farr or Joe Lewis, if we wanted.'[81] The strong male was the young man's identikit.

The League of Health and Strength was only one of many organizations providing boys and young men with a rationale to unite in admiration of the male physique. It was an individualistic movement and the form of male bonding it encouraged was more concerned with comradeship between two young men, or a small gang of boys, than between a large group. Community-orientated boys' movements drew much more from the traditions of male bonding developed in the armed forces. Organizations such as the Boys' Brigade and the Boy Scouts provide a clearer illustration of the close relationship between the male body being moulded for romance and the male body being prepared for war. As we shall see in the next few pages, scouting is particularly interesting because of the way it linked military values and male comradeship.

Historians disagree about the militarist nature of boys' movements from the end of the century.[82] Certainly, it is easy to exaggerate the extent to which outdoor movements promoted values most commonly associated with warfare and it is clear that whatever degree of militarism may be discerned within British organizations, it was of a lower order than that emerging within other European countries.[83] However, most of the popular British movements adopted military-style organizational structures, promoted military skills and values (such as shooting and patriotism) and used military terminology.[84] For instance, in the Boys' Brigade (established in 1883) a distinction was made between the form of militarism that was 'the vile product of Prussianism' and 'the inculcation of the military spirit which stood for manliness, discipline, obedience, and the readiness to die for their country'.[85] The famous comment by the founder of the Boys' Brigade stands out: 'Call these boys, BOYS, which they are, and ask them to sit up in a Sunday School class, and no power on earth will make them do it; but put a fivepenny cap on them and call them soldiers, which they are not, and you can order them about till midnight.'[86] The Lads' Drill Association (1899) also aimed to provide 'systematic physical and military training to all British lads' and, in 1906, merged with the National Service League. The Church Lads' Brigade (1891) was linked with the Territorials.

A similar situation may be seen when we turn to the Boy Scouts. This was a very popular movement. In 1910, the Boy Scouts could claim a membership of 100,000 boys. By the end of the war, this number had more than doubled and by 1930 had reached 420,000. Many leading scouts saw themselves as assembling a 'National Army of the future'.[87] In *Scouting for Boys*, Robert Baden-Powell (founder of the Scouts) even provided his boys with instructions in how to kill a man: 'Aim first at the man, then, moving the muzzle a little faster than he is moving, and fire while moving it when it is pointing where he will be a second or two later, and the bullet will just get there at the same time as he does and will hit him.'[88] According to one pre-war member, the camps consisted of 'playing at soldiers . . . It was run on army lines and the people who controlled it were army officers.'[89] Troops were organized with 'military precision' and key words were 'turn-out', 'discipline' and 'morale'.[90] The training was acknowledged to be invaluable in wartime.[91] By exposing boys to military-type training, scouting could lead boys directly into the armed forces.[92] It is not surprising to discover that Lord Kitchener's message to the troops – a copy of which was given to each soldier early in the war – could have come straight out of a tract written by Baden-Powell. After a brief patriotic message, it concluded,

Be invariably courteous, considerate and kind. Never do anything likely to injure or destroy property, and always look upon looting as a disgraceful act. You are sure to meet with a welcome and to be trusted; your conduct must justify that welcome and trust. Your duty cannot be done unless your health is sound. So keep constantly on your guard against any excesses. In this new experience you may find temptations both in wine and women. You must resist both temptations, and, while treating women with perfect courtesy, you should avoid any intimacy. Do your duty bravely. Fear God. Honour the King.[93]

With the declaration of war in 1914, the militarist side of the scouting movement expanded, as it did in society in general. The day before being killed in the Battle of the Somme in July 1916, a scoutmaster wrote to a young boy who had belonged to his scouting troop, advising,

Out here tomorrow thousands & thousands of Englishmen will go to suffer & die in the fight for England & her allies. You would love to be here to see how gaily & gladly they go – doing their bit to smash the tyrant Joe. You Scouts cannot help out here. But you can help at home. And I hope that you and the other Wellingtons will always buck up & do your best to become brave Englishmen in the days ahead, fit & ready to take the place of those who fall today.[94]

Many boys took such advice seriously. To prepare for the ultimate sacrifice, 25,000 scouts worked as coast guards and patrolled telephone lines (thus freeing older men for the front lines).[95] A special war service badge was created for the 80,000 scouts who performed eighty-four hours' community service (for instance, collecting money for gifts to be sent to soldiers).[96] Many other scouts, however, were old enough to fight themselves. Of the 100,000 Boy Scouts who signed up, 10,000 were killed.[97]

Scouts believed that their training was of use in the war.[98] Baden-Powell liked to boast that 70 per cent of Boy Scouts went on to join the army compared with only 10 per cent of members of the Cadet Corps. In a drawing from *At Suvla Bay*, written by the scout John Hargrave, and published in 1916, the chief difference between the boy scout and the soldier is evident in the swaggering walk of the latter (illus. 35.) Leonard Humphries mused that it was 'most opportune that B.P. formed the Scouts when he did in view of the outbreak of the European War . . . in my own case the courses for the bandages that I had taken proved the greatest value that [*sic*] of First Aid helped me to save lives.'[99] For servicemen far from the front lines or in quiet sections, military life had much in common with pre-war experiences in outdoor movements. In a letter written from the trenches of France, Liddell Hart consoled his parents with the words that 'though one has to rough it far more than in England', the war reminded him of 'a great

I. Before going out. In Boy Scout uniform.

II. At Suvla Bay. We dressed as much like Boy Scouts as possible.

35 John Hargrave, 'Before going out . . . At Suvla Bay', monogrammed drawing from his *At Suvla Bay*, London, 1916.

picnic'.[100] Raymond Lodge and John Hare believed that the war made them and their friends look and feel like Robinson Crusoe.[101] Charles C. Ammons confessed that he enlisted because he yearned again for the 'open air life'.[102] It was commonly asserted that the value of outdoor training was never proved so clearly as at Suvla Bay (Gallipoli) where skills of stalking, map reading, understanding the stars and silence were paramount.[103] As an article in *The Times* in 1915 pointed out, boys who had been members of the Boys' Brigade and the Boy Scouts could be 'picked out for their soldierly qualities. They [had] been taught discipline, comradeship, obligation to others, trust, worthiness in carrying out orders, handiness and resource, and there could be no better equipment for the military life.'[104] Even after the war, when excessive emphasis on military training in outdoor movements was being questioned,[105] scout leaders might deny that scouting was 'of a military nature', but they still insisted that it was of 'undeniably great value to those ex-scouts who became soldiers'.[106]

It was within this tradition that the scouting movement (like the army, navy and air force) provided scope for male bonding. Scouting was all about 'Brotherliness'.[107] The camp provided a space for men outside the purview and rules of women. Boys were taught to live without feminine help. Their domestic skills (especially those of cooking) were prized.[108] In the all-male environment of camp, boys posed as protectors – not of women and children, but of fellow boys. Thus, Stanley Butler described his camping experiences in the quiet English countryside prior to the war: 'It was like an army camp – you wouldn't have an army camp anywhere without securing your boundary. You wouldn't just get into your tent and go to sleep and leave nobody outside to raise the alarm if anything happened. We had guard duty two hours on and four hours off during the night.'[109] The protection offered by one's mates at night, the shared tents, cups, food and the flickering campfires inspired physical intimacy. Like the armed forces, uniforms were an important part of this bonding process, as were states of undress. In this way, without self-consciousness, *Bristol Scouting* could describe the washing of a new (and dirty) recruit in the following words: 'the prisoner was apparently enjoying it, for he was grinning, and submitting tamely, standing on the grass stark naked while two Scouts thoroughly lathered him, paying particular attention to his ears and hair and neck'.[110] In the search for 'human beauty – the Good Animal – the Splendid Body', scouts eyed up each other's physique and distributed Beauty Prizes.[111] Scout leaders – like their military counterparts – relied on the efficacy of positive inducements to male bonding.

The End of Mateship

So far in this chapter we have looked at the way male bonding was stimulated within the armed forces through drawing attention to the aesthetic beauty of the group. This was not an exclusively military tradition, but one, as we have seen, that was adopted by a wide range of boys' clubs and organizations. There was a major difference, however, between male comradeship in peacetime and mateship in war. Although there was a certain amount of male bonding in wartime, such bonding was, however, contigent upon a wide range of conditions such as class and political identity; Irish servicemen were hence more likely to seek martial comradeship once they had been rejected by their nationalist contemporaries.[112] In this next section, the extent of comradeship will be questioned. To answer the question of how much bonding took, or did not take, place it is necessary to examine the broad institutional level as well as individual interactions between men sharing life in the armed forces. It will be argued that young men *expected* the war to heighten male bonding, but that wartime experiences placed too great a strain on this expectation. In other words, although it is possible to identify strands of male bonding in the writing of servicemen, for many men the crises of war proved too traumatic for its maintenance. While the war provided an intimate environment for love between men, it at same time exposed the fragility of brotherhood.

As we saw earlier in this chapter, it is easy to find retrospective assertions of mateship in the armed forces. To take one further example, from a source frequently used by historians: Sidney Rogerson believed that, despite

all differences in rank, we were comrades, brothers dwelling together in unity. We were privileged to see in each other that inner, ennobled self which in the grim, commercial struggle of peace-time is too frequently atrophied for lack of opportunity of expression. We could note the intense affection of soldier for certain officers, their absolute trust in them. We saw the love passing the love of women.[113]

Rogerson's comments seem to summarize the mateship argument. We should, however, view his assertions critically: he had been commissioned from Cambridge University in 1914; within three years he had been promoted to captain, and he was reminiscing from the standpoint of 1930. Much of the evidence written at the time, or by men who were less privileged than Rogerson, tells another story.

Of course, the ideology of male comradeship in war was never intended to subvert military rank and its associations with socio-economic class.[114] A few pages after the last quotation, Rogerson appears to change his tune slightly. Declaring himself to be 'liberal', he argues that when dealing with a largely conscripted army, it is absurd to adhere rigidly to the conventional forms of military discipline. However, he continues, the relaxation of pre-war military codes of behaviour

did not mean that an officer should rub shoulders with his men at every opportunity, or allow them to become familiar with him. It meant rather that he should step down from the pedestal on which his rank put him, and walk easily among his men, relying on his personality and the respect he had earned from

36 'T is the Trench . . .', cartoon from 'Captain Wideawake', *Jovial Jottings*, London, 1915.

them to give him the superior position he must occupy if he wished to lead. He had consequently to steer a delicate course between treating those under him as equals in humanity if inferiors in status, and losing their respect by becoming too much one of them.[115]

Men of lower military rank had harsher things to say. Divisional staff were regarded as 'a lot of girls tied onto bathing machines' and staff officers were described as 'fatheaded . . . white-faced . . . corpulent . . . facetious . . . boot-licking' men in contrast to 'real soldiers'.[116] The high officials behind the lines were 'stupid idiots'.[117] The 'well fed, fit and hearty . . . base wallahs' were certainly not comrades.[118] As a cartoon from *Jovial Jottings* saw it, the Other Ranks stood knee-deep in mud, firing at Germans a few feet away while 'the Staff' sat in safety writing memos (illus. 36). Russell L. Venables thought it 'strange' how 'the officers subverted the *esprit de corps* of the army by often promoting profane people to high rank'.[119] The sergeant mounted on a horse could call his marching men 'lazy swine', but what his men called him in reply can only be surmised.[120] The gulf between servicemen imposed by rank was unbridgeable. For instance, one night, John William Rowarth was detailed to go into no-man's-land to cut some German wire by his company commander, who was going on leave, as a souvenir. A frightened Rowarth bitterly mused, 'I had . . . to go into no mans [*sic*] land and cut a bit of wire, so that our Major could show it to his old woman, and she would be so proud of his bravery, she would let him have a bit of grummet, thats what some Irishmen called the blow-through [sex]. I hoped he would be like me, and when she was on her back waiting for him to up her, he could not get a hard on.'[121] With cynical humour, the trench paper, *The New Church Times*, informed subalterns that it was within their rights to kill adjutants since it was always possible to prove extenuating circumstances.[122] The corporal or sergeant aged twenty-three years could humiliate the conscript in his forties.[123] Officers censoring letters would jeer at the 'more sentimental patches' and they expressed contempt for 'the clumsy expression of a lot of heartsick youngsters fresh from home'.[124] Subservient servants crawled into dug-outs early in the morning and asked, 'What will you have, sir?' with as much sense of social prerogative as they would have had in a country house.[125] Class distinctions (as much as rank) were imported from the peacetime world directly into the trenches, cutting through vacuous notions of brotherhood.

It is not surprising that abandonment of military rank was not part of the mateship tradition. However, comradeship was also subverted by a host of other characteristics such as regiment, marital status, religion and ethnicity. Divisions between military units were strictly maintained – often on the grounds of physical differences. John Francis Jones described the feud between his own and a Scottish regiment as being based largely on the issue of cleanliness: 'They despised us for looking so clean, we despised them for looking so dirty.'[126] It was taking *esprit de corps* too far to interrupt another regiment at dinner.[127] Royal Army Medical Corps doctors treated with disdain civilian doctors in their hospitals and nurses in the Volunteer Aid Detachment.[128] When conscription was applied to married men in 1916, there was considerable bitterness amongst unmarried men when their married comrades complained. Single men were anxious to point out that they too had families to whom they were attached: parents, siblings, uncles, aunts. Furthermore, they hoped to start families of their own. Thus, although the unmarried Canon T. Guy Rogers sympathized with his married brethren, he confessed to his aunt in March 1916 that even he was 'getting a little tired of the distinction between married and single. Many here [were] a bit "fed up" with the grousing of the married. After all it [was] a question whether all these hosts of young men who might be prospective fathers, [were] not even a more valuable asset to the nation than the married men who ha[d] already gotten themselves families.'[129]

Not all unmarried servicemen lacked families: they were also not all white. Fighting men were also divided by race. The South African Native Labour Corps had nothing in common with most of the men in

37 Zulu war dance, at the South African Native Labour Corps war dance and sports, Dannes, France, 24 June 1917. [IWM Q2388]

the British Royal Army Corps (see illus. 37): the colour of their skins, their language, their customs and their clothes made identification of 'them' versus 'us' greater than a division between the Allies and Axis. During the war, there were over 98,000 Chinese, 82,000 Egyptians, 20,000 Indians, 9,000 British West Indians and 2,000 Mauritians, Maltese and Fijians, in the forces, in addition to nearly 122,000 other locally raised 'natives' and 35,000 'natives employed in substitution for British personnel' working for the British army in Labour corps.[130] White privates, however, resented taking orders from black officers. Batu Kindai Amgoza Ibn LoBagola's problems were even worse. He was not only a black African, he was also Jewish. When placed in charge of assigning Jewish troops at Kantara in Egypt, he faced great hostility: 'I was the only black amongst them. They were not willing to accept me as a Jew, because of their prejudice against my colour. All that made me feel wretched.'[131] Samuel Weingott's diary also testified to persecution for being Jewish.[132] F. M. Peckham described the fights that broke out between West Indians, South Africans, American Jews and Australians. He noted that there were also tensions between West Indian and African soldiers, the latter considering the West Indians to be 'black Scum'.[133] It did not matter how much troops from India were admired physically and for their martial prowess, they would always be regarded as savage: as in the instance related in the Revd Andrew Clark's diary in 1915 when he compared the souvenirs collected by a soldier in a Territorial unit (a bullet and a spike and badge from a German helmet) with those collected by an Indian soldier (German ears).[134] Similarly, in 1914, T. Corder Catchpool could describe the 'nigger' soldiers as

'hopeless. . .Their slow movements − such as in lighting a pipe, for example − often suggest a monkey to me almost as much as a man. And yet I am curiously fond of them. Wag your head at them as you go by, and you win the richest smile in the world, white teeth, thick lips, black eyes, all combine in the most bewitching production. They do not bear pain like the brave French boys.[135]

Chinese soldiers were teased, insulted and abused.[136] Soldiers born of German parents but who were naturalized citizens of Britain were removed from their comrades in the front line and placed in the 33rd Battalion Midshire Regiment ('Kaiser's Own') − much to their humiliation.[137] Place of birth divided men irreconcilably.

There was little fraternizing between Regular servicemen, Territorials and conscripted men. Again, the body was a major site of division. Physically (it was believed) these three groups could be easily distinguished. For instance, the Revd Montague A. Bere noted that it was possible to recognize Regular soldiers instantly by the fact that they were 'beautifully made . . . impressive'.[138] The clergyman was complimentary. More usually, the differences − physical, military and social − were grounds for snide comment.[139] Thus, Russell L. Venables could not understand how conscripted soldiers could ever be of any use.[140] Raymond Lodge wrote to his parents about the way Regular soldiers dreaded being mistaken for Kitcheners.[141] The Regular soldier Tommy W. Bacon had harsh comments about the Territorials, claiming that they were too highly educated and too imaginative to be effective warriors.[142] Ralph Creyke was also a member of the Regular army who was critical of the Territorials. He praised Kitchener for bypassing the Territorial Army and creating a separate military force since he regarded the Territorials as ill-disciplined: 'they [were] always going home for a bit & turning up again. I heard the other day of a Bn [sic] where 79 disappeared one night without leave − They turned up again in 3 days to a fortnight, quite calmly saying that they had been home to do a bit of work on the farm etc & seemed to think it quite natural.'[143] Territorial soldiers felt that they were being discriminated against in terms of promotion.[144] Equally pertinent was the distinction between the ex-Regular and the ex-hostilities soldier.[145] The separation between the volunteer and the conscripted soldier was maintained on demobilization with the issuing of the 1914–1915 Star for men who had been on active service prior to the introduction of conscription.[146]

If the male bonding thesis in wartime is to have any power, it is at the level of individual interactions at the Front. However, even here bonding was contingent. The administration of the war undermined any personal dream of comradeship since men could not be certain of remaining in close proximity to their pals. If the bureaucracy of war did not part men, death did.[147] Some military officers insisted that it was better if the men were not intimate. Brigadier Richard C. Foot commanded a battery that was made up of men from fourteen different Territorial Reserve forces. He approved of this diversity, claiming that it

proved a healthy origin for the Battery. There were few men whose families at home knew each other, and even few who could say that they came from the same village or town. Consequently, when a casualty occurred, while many servicemen's immediate friends might be depressed for a few days by his absence, it did not cause any general sentiment of loss or sorrow in the Battery. It was noticeable in units that were recruited from the same town that the death of a single individual could cause a wave of misery thoughout a whole Battalion; but this group of men, swept together into D/310 from all over the country had no such tie, and settled well together.[148]

Although handy for commanders, it embittered the soldiers. Despite the slogan 'Join the T.A. so that you can fight with your friends', Jack Houghton-Brown angrily found himself separated from his companions and 'weaned' from his battalion. He complained of the War Office that it

took no account of county morale . . . in the first week of my arrival, the original militia recruited from the county [Wiltshire] and trained at the Depot were all marched off 'en bloc' to the Worcester Regiment. These 150 men were the pride of the county. The Regiment had detached her best Officers and N.C.O.s to train them. Hours had been spent in teaching them the Wiltshire Regiment history. They were all made proud of their county Regiment and almost mutinied when told they had to go to another Unit.

Most exasperatingly, it was discovered that 200 Welshmen were sent to the Wiltshire Depot a fortnight later.[149] Similarly, James B. Lorimer indignantly informed his mother that his battalion was going to be divided to provide reinforcements to other battalions at the Front: 'It's pretty sickening in some ways and can't but take a certain amount of interest out of working up the efficiency of your men.'[150] In such a situation, the efficiency of communal pressures weakened. The RAMC were known as the 'Rob all My Comrades' men.[151] Rations were taken from hungry soldiers and sold.[152] Field glasses, pistols, kits, rum and other saleable valuables were pilfered.[153]

Earlier in this chapter, it was conceded that men in active service were rendered dependent upon each other for emotional as well as physical sustenance. However, the same wholesale physical turmoil that yearned to be soothed also necessitated emotional hardening. Men could not get too close – and if they did, they learnt to withdraw their affections just as wholeheartedly. As Walter Cobb put it,

My only particular chum was a Sorter from London who if anything hated the life more than I did . . . I had no other real chums – fellow soldiers – yes but companionship under conditions like ours was not really possible . . . we realised the hell overseas and could not hope to be one of the tiny minority to survive the repeated attacks of the line troops. Everything seemed on a day to day basis.[154]

Men learnt not to stop to help wounded men.[155] The pity a serviceman might feel for a man dying next to him could not be sustained if he too was wounded.[156] For many men, the words of W. Stephen King-Hall of HMS *Southampton* in a letter to the sister of a recently drowned sailor were appropriate: 'in these tremendous 22 hours, I can assure you that Death seemed a very small thing. Why in the first 30 minutes I saw two thousand gallant men lay down their lives.'[157] The stretcher-bearer Frank Dunham agreed, divulging in his diary on 26 May 1918 that 'one by one, our pals came and went; we were for ever making new friends, only to see the comradeship suddenly end'.[158] Stubborn love of one's male friends could be emotionally ruinous.

It is also easy to exaggerate the pleasures of what male comradeship did exist. Earlier, it was argued that wartime experiences demanded greater emotiveness between men, but the assumption that this strengthened bonds between them can be questioned. There was often a price to pay for any form of closeness. It could easily, for example, become irritating,[159] as in the case of Albert Andrews whose only comrades were drinkers. After one of their sprees, Andrews' feeling of illness made him consider teetotalism but, he noted, 'it was useless to say I would not drink or I would have no pals and nowhere to go'.[160] Other men found to their disgust that the 'drunkenness & language & gambling' were having an effect on them, and they eschewed all friendships as a consequence.[161] Many men did not 'fit in', and were lonely.[162] More frighteningly, masculine comradeship placed an immense burden on men to express martial values. Men might cry and hug each other with relief after a battle – but such displays were frowned on once a man was physically in pain: wounded men were expected to display stoicism.[163] Even complaining against mistreatment in military hospitals was avoided on the grounds that it exposed patients to accusations that they lacked 'pluck and self-sacrifice'.[164] The fear of being thought to be a coward was intense.[165] Emotional bonding could also be an impediment to openness. The rifleman Walter Shewry, who had been through the fighting at Loos and Hulloch, longed to unburden himself to his brother, a signaller, but was unable to: 'we just could not communicate – I just could not bring myself to tell him of my great misery and suffering nor of my fear and horror.'[166] Worse, comradeship could mean that you too died.[167] And if you did not, you could live with that guilt for years.[168]

There was another reason why male bonding failed: during the Great War, the armed forces were composed of civilians for whom the real world remained situated at home and for whom the post-war economic crisis created stresses for which mateship provided no answer. This can be seen most clearly in the memoirs of George Horton who had spent his entire life in the army. After the Boer War, he was discharged and returned to civilian life. He wrote,

> I wonder if you can imagine what it means to a man, after being nearly twenty years in one Regiment, knowing all its ways of working and nearly everyone in it, having travelled over nearly half of the world with it and taken part in all its ups and downs, seen men come and go, suddenly to sever his connections with it? It meant leaving all my old companions and comrades, some of whom I had known the whole of the time, and my thoughts were taken back to the days with them in India, Egypt and South Africa.

On leaving the army he felt 'very down on [his] luck . . . after travelling the world with one body of men, many of whom [he had] regarded as brothers'. In the period to the First World War, therefore, Horton attempted to retain his military friends and he frequently indulged his nostalgic memories. With the declaration of the 1914–18 war, Horton again served in the army. This turned out to be a very different experience, however. In his words: 'leaving the army, this time was very different . . . This time [he] was glad to get away in a sense, and get home again.'[169] In part, this change was due to his being older than other servicemen, but it also reflected the difficulties of stimulating male bonding in an army composed of civilian men for whom the male world of 'warriors' was ranked a long way behind the world of everyday domestic life.

So far in this chapter, we have considered the way in which male bonding was undermined in the relationships between men in the armed forces. This was not the only manner in which wartime experiences undermined male comradeship. The identity 'gender:

male' was badly shaken in situations where men killed men. No amount of training (and, as the war progressed, servicemen received less and less) could compensate for the shock of identifying their antagonists as men like themselves: 'big, handsome, fresh young men'.[170] It was disconcerting to discover that some of the men they were trying to maim or kill had lived in England – had even played in the same county cricket match.[171] Although many servicemen never saw a live German, the viewing of dead male Germans also discouraged devoting too much thought to the 'community of men'. Charlie C. May, whose letters testify to his intense love for his baby daughter, was devastated when he found (tucked into the pocket of a dead German) a child's Bible inscribed with the word 'Dada'. He laid bare his feelings in his diary:

It makes one feel that it would be well if kaisers and ambitious, place-seeking politicians and other such who make wars could be stricken down and peaceful, home-loving, ordinary men be left to live their lives in peace and in the sunshine of the love of wife and children. Perhaps that man may have been quite a blackguard or just a hateful, bullying, swaggering Prussian and, as such, something to loathe and detest. I do not know. All I am conscious of is that somewhere in his Fatherland there is a little child who called him 'Dada'. I have a little baby too.[172]

Respect for fathers was also shattered as soldiers agonized over having to kill 'old men with grey beards . . . [who were] not fit to have to fight'.[173] All the toughness-training in the world could not turn some men into killers.[174] War generated a callousness towards the bodies of other men that could not be lightly forgotten.[175] Propaganda photographs were unconvincing: one such photograph claims to show a British soldier giving a cigarette to a badly wounded German after the battle of Pilckem Ridge on 31 July 1917 (illus. 38). The famous example of fraternizing with the enemy on some parts of the Western Front at Christmas 1914 could not be repeated: at least not if the war was to be won.[176]

Returning to the Fold

Given the ultimate failure of wartime bonding, men after the war were faced with two choices: they could attempt to restructure pre-war male bonding using the spurious rhetoric of wartime comradeship or they could repudiate the rhetoric even further. The first response – that is, using the wartime rhetoric of male bonding in a new way within civilian groups – was attempted by ex-servicemen's associations such as the National Federation of Discharged and Demobilized Sailors and Soldiers, the National Association of Discharged Sailors and Soldiers,

38 The Battle of Pilckem Ridge, 31 July–2 August 1917. [IWM Q2629]

the Comrades of the Great War, the Officers' Association and the British Legion.[177] These groups are generally cited as examples of the strength of wartime bonding. Their own rhetoric supports this view. They claimed to be preserving the comradeship that had existed 'Over There': they wanted their wartime 'chums' back.[178] For instance, the Ex-Service Man's National Movement (1923) called for a return to the mutual dependence of wartime.[179] The Military Medalist Association pledged itself to be non-political and non-sectarian ('We shall possess one common bond, our Military Honours, and in that we are equally all comrades and pledged to foster and maintain that spirit of comradeship that existed "Over There"') and it exhorted its members to 'try to imagine that [they were] all in one Division or Corps and "zero" [was] fixed a few hours hence'. They had all been 'interdependent one upon the other *then*', and when they 'had gone over', they would not 'leave a wonderful Pal neglected. *Now* [their] comrades who ha[d] fallen upon evil times [were] like to the comrades [they had] not desert[ed] "over there".'[180] Similarly, in 1926, Kriegsgefangener, or the Association of

Ex-Prisoners of War, was established 'to keep alive that spirit of comradeship which alone made captivity endurable. Life in any camp would have been hard without the help of comrades.'[181] This rhetoric attracted some men. In particular, it appealed to men like General P.H. Henderson, an active member of the 84th Field Ambulance Old Comrades' Association who in 1965 still managed to exasperate his wife by declaring that the most enjoyable years of his life were during the Great War because it was there that he had 'made many friends who in [his] opinion were the very finest of the British Race'.[182]

However, this was a minority response. From the start, ex-servicemen's organizations had trouble recruiting members.[183] Their idea of comradeship followed wartime patterns and could not be called non-sectarian, non-political, and all-embracing. The mateship of comrades' societies was limited. Ex-servicemen suspected of cowardice, for instance, were excluded.[184] Men considering joining a comrades' organization had to choose from a large array of groups, all competing vigorously (and sometimes viciously) for limited resources. As shown in Chapter One, limbless ex-servicemen fought for preferential treatment against associations dominated by the able-bodied. In the *Northern Echo* (1936), 'Equality' agreed with the claim of the British Limbless Ex-Servicemen's Association that its members' pensions were too low, but he pointed out that this was the case also with the pensions of *all* ex-servicemen. 'Equality' pleaded that a 'wider claim of an all-round fifty per cent rise in pensions would breathe more of the true war spirit of comradeship'.[185] Class conflict was a further barrier to the development of these networks. Thus, the Ex-Services Welfare Society was concerned with ex-servicemen of a high social class, and demanded that class take precedence over military rank.[186] All these associations failed to elicit widespread support in part because their *raison d'être* was modelled too closely on a militaristic rhetoric of mateship. Outside the veteran organizations, some men attempted to maintain the idea of male bonding in the context of the war generation, but this flourished in private, nostalgic remembrances stripped of all the trappings of that community, rather than in groups. The once-a-year march to the Cenotaph was preceded and followed by isolation from the comrades.

The most common response to the failure of wartime experiences to heighten male bonding was the repudiation of wartime comradeship and a reiteration of the primacy of male-female relationships. This reaction was encouraged by the popularization of new psychological theories that placed a high premium on male-female relationships and stigmatized male-male relationships. Reunion with women – representing a return to older forms of intimacy – was the dominant ambition. As we shall see, however, the war changed the nature of this return. In particular, the sexual exchange between men and women had been questioned during war, and this questioning rendered the return to civilian domesticity after the war more difficult.

Although it is easy to exaggerate the extent to which women were sexually attracted to servicemen,[187] it is still true that, by putting on a military uniform, men obtained greater possibilities of sexual experimentation. Thus, from France, a man simply signing himself 'Jim' could ask Mrs Ethel Cox to 'Tell Fred's wife I will come and sleep with the two of you to keep you company I don't think I shall be shy four I have seen a lot of things over here.'[188] R. Graham Dixon had no trouble rationalizing it to himself. Although he described his attitudes to sex in the army as ambivalent, he noted,

We were not monks, but fighting soldiers and extraordinarily fit – fitter than we had been in our young lives, and fairly tough – certainly with an abundance of physical energy or . . . full of beans and bull-juice. Moreover we were constantly in the presence of death, and no man knew when his turn might come. I suppose that subconsciously we wanted as much of life as we could get while we still had life, and if bought love is no substitute for the real thing; it at any rate seemed better than nothing. And in any case it worked off steam! But the whole thing was compartmentalised – it was there, as it were, shut off from normal human relationships, and belonged to this lunatic world of war and to nowhere else. It had nothing to do with the world of home at all.[189]

Such a rationale worked in the armed forces in peacetime as well as during the war. If rates of venereal infection can be thought to provide any indication of the levels of sexual activity (and if we accept the War Office's view that their prophylactic campaign had failed), then the conscript armies were less prone to sensualism. Thus, in 1911 the annual rate of admission to military venereal hospitals were 61 to every 1,000 soldiers, while in 1916 it was under 37.[190] Despite venereal scares during the war (which were predominantly scares generated by Australian, Canadian and New Zealand military commands conscious of the fact that their servicemen were younger, less liable to be married and unable to return home while on leave), it is probably correct to argue that a majority of British servicemen never had casual sex with any woman during their active military service.[191] For the first time, women having sexual relationships with servicemen were more liable to be amateurs than professional prostitutes.[192] Although (behind the lines) the availability of sexually active women was greatly enhanced in wartime, access to them remained limited to periods of training and the occasional leave.[193] Even in training, access could be minimal: as 'Jim'

39 Men of the 5th Dragoon Guards at Rollencourt, 5 May 1917. [IWM Q5297]

reassured the 'girls of B-ham' in the following words, 'the boys are not flirting because, there's no girls I've [*sic*] only been out of camp twice since I've been here so you can tell what the surroundings are'.[194] Will H. Bowyer could conclude that the war had actually delayed the sexual maturity of himself and his friends, prolonging their period as 'innocent young men'.[195]

However, whether or not a particular serviceman actually took up any of the opportunities for casual sex during war, all were affected by it. The coy Frenchwoman, flirting with the expectant young lad and his embarrassed companion was a delightful fantasy for soldiers (see illus. 39). All servicemen were exposed to a sexual ethos far removed from that in the civilian world – and they responded in a variety of ways. James Murray loved and desired a woman called Agnes but the war kept him from actually making love to her. As he put it, 'I knew I would have been able to "make" her if I had wanted to at any time, but, as I knew also I might be killed on my next trip out to France, I decided she must stay virgin.'[196] War also preoccupied Sid T. Kemp: sex and marriage to his beloved Ethel were nothing in comparison with the questions of life and death. He recalled going home on leave before his first trip to France: 'I went home, Ethel had a few days off from work. That is when we should have married, but I didn't just think about it, and Ethel, like she always was, wouldn't ask for favours, so I had six days away from the army, but in all our minds was the one question: when would we be going to France?'[197] Another soldier disagreed: his impending military service in India just prior to the war made him desperate to marry. He wrote to his brother in 1914, 'I did intend having one [visit home] for the special purpose of picking up a decent woman for a wife as we go abroad the latter end of this year or the begining of the next so you see I have not much time to waste and I should like to be married before going if I don't it means being a bachelor for the remainder of my time which is not pleasant.'[198] More dramatically, E. Davidson wounded himself (his crime remained undetected) in order to be sent on leave so that he could get married. Although he confessed that he did not love his wife, he defended his marriage on two grounds: firstly, he wanted to 'know a woman in the biblical sense' before being killed and, secondly, if he survived he did not want to be 'without a wife'.[199] Other men also embraced the possibilities of sexual experimentation during war. According to James Williamson, when describing his period of training near Burly, 'there were plenty of girls in fact hundreds of them it [*sic*] was no use making appointments with a girl as some other girl generally grabbed you before you got to the appointed place'.[200]

With conscription, civilian men were removed from the secure, known environment of home and assigned to an institution where male sexuality attracted the attention of everyone from the commander-in-chief down. This was also an institution created to accommodate the needs of professional servicemen, not conscripts, and accustomed to enforcing rules regarding sexual access. Thus, only a certain proportion of Regular servicemen was allowed to marry, and marrying 'off the strength' was the subject of much discussion.[201] There were other, equally petty, rules such as the military order that army schoolmistresses could only marry servicemen above the rank of sergeant (the 'private may wink and ogle as he likes, the young guardsman in his brilliant walking-out dress may swagger himself to a standstill, the corporal and the lance-corporal and the cook and the drummer and the pay-clerk may employ a hundred blandishments to win the hand of the schoolmistress – all, all in vain', lamented the *Evening Express*).[202] Non-marital sexual intercourse was more acceptable to the Regular army: for the troops, the only considerations were its implications in terms of discipline and disease. Thus, General Frank Percy Crozier could assert that 'a man – or a boy . . . could not fight well unless he could love well'.[203] It was this attitude that confused and dismayed many new army men.[204] Harold Mellersh was an example of a man who resisted temptation. During his early days in the army, he struggled against his priggish upbringing after being forced to acknowledge that his fellow soldiers did all those things his mother had warned him against, yet were still 'good'.[205] Although accustomed to the fact that military service represented the first time away from home for many men, the authorities were less confident about handling the sexual lives of young men – many mere boys – who were civilians first and soldiers only temporarily. It was recognized that many of these young civilians would have their first sexual experiences during the war and the army, navy and air force were to provide them with their first lessons in sex.[206] Colin C. Stanley wrote to his wife about a lecture given while he was being trained at Aldershot, exclaiming, 'it was *hot*'.[207] It was an education that even married men could find enlightening.

A detailed example of the broader sexual education provided by wartime conditions can be found in the memoirs of the Cockney boy John William Rowarth. Here, he referred to himself in both the first and second person – sometimes even in the same sentence. Initially, Rowarth was shocked at the sexual talk of his fellow soldiers. He wrote,

the platoon started to talk of their love conquests, and one of my mates Said to me. Casey have you ever dipped your wick, what do you mean, I aint got no wick to dip, when the laughter had subsided, they put it more blunty had I ever made love to a girl, when I said no, oh you must be a bloody virgin, and when we get to France we will soon remedy that, and one of the blokes said if the French tarts are as tall as our Irish girls, Casey will have to lug a brick to stand on . . . This made me very angry, and I shouted, I aint going to have no truck with no French tarts. The Priest for the Battalion when I went to confession told me these Girls were very dirty, and they would give the pox, if I went with them. it is a mortal sin to do bad things to Girls.

However, even before going abroad, his ideas had relaxed somewhat. His first sexual encounter with a woman occurred on a hill overlooking Holyhead:

she was a bold Girl, who made all the advances, it was my very first sexual experience, and altho it was getting it seemed to take a hell of a time, The twighlight in North Wales is very lovely, and lying on the grass, with suuch a lovely Girl, who by the way she was acting was feeling very clucky, She was a lovely kisser, and thats all she wanted to do, and when my hand started to roam she stiffened up and murmured No, I just enjoy lying with you, it makes me feel very nice, but anything else, I must wait till I find mr Right.

This was not the end of his induction. Later, when he confessed to her that he was a virgin, she was aghast: 'Oh my Dear Have I rarlly found a virgin.' His humiliation was complete when he asked, 'a Virgin, wats a virgin, the only Virgin I know of is the Blessed Virgin Mary. since I have been in the Army, I have heard so many new words which frankly I dont understand. the Girl then said, lets change the subject.' Penetration did not occur until after he arrived in France – and, even then, his way was difficult. For one thing, he could not afford the prices charged in the first brothel he found and was ingloriously thrown out more than once. When Rowarth finally collected enough money to go to a whorehouse, he discovered that his problems had only just started:

I went limp. and even though this French hussy. tried everything she knew, even putting my thing in her mouth. I could not get hard, then she got very angry, am I not very beautiful to you, that you do not want to love me, you English are very cold, and do not know how to make love, I leave you now, get dressed, I have work to do. When I asked her for my five franks, I payed her, because I had not had any pleasure, well the way she acted, and screaming French abuse.

He was thrown out again. The next time he visited a brothel he managed to maintain his erection:

My whore was in a hurry, taking off a kind of slip, and like the other one lay without any clothes on, said hurry others are waiting. all this in very broken english, it took me a while to unbutton my tunic, undo my braces, take off my pants, and long underpants, I felt a little proud of my self because my member was standing out as stif as a ramrod, putting me on top of her, and guiding my stif un into her, she began to move her body, in a circular motion, and with making a move I ejaculated, I got the shock of my life, I was finished before I had started finished, the girl washed my business, said you were very quick and very good. I was hustled out the door and on the street, the queue was I thought longer than when I went.

When he told his mates that he had lost his virginity, he admitted that it was 'not as good as I thought, Its a bit like pulling your thing, but you have someone to talk to'. After such limited and unsatisfactory experiences, Rowarth became frightened when he was told that some '[women] urges you on, and when you try to force them, they cry rape, then its the case for the coppers'. He wrote, 'That made me think, I could be one of the unlucky ones, from then on no more Girls, no matter how much he was pempted [sic].'[208]

Rowarth's ambivalence was shared by others. Lieutenant Gareth Smithies Taylor picked up some French girls only because it was expected of him, but he deserted them at dinner because he found them 'hysterical and beastly'. 'I can't enjoy it,' he confessed.[209] Harold

Mellersh went to two brothels in St Omer. In the first, he was repelled by the moustached owner and her garish employees. In the second, when one pretty woman sat on his knee he was so embarrassed that all he could mutter was that she was wearing too much lipstick. The woman was offended and, again, it was expedient to leave.[210] Those more courageous than Mellersh were often disappointed with the speed with which they were expected to ejaculate and bid adieu.[211] Karl Engler was taken to a Maltese brothel but, despite the fact that he found the women attractive, he could not rouse any enthusiasm and ended up drinking too much instead.[212] G. A. Cook was not fooled by a French woman's 'face like an angel' and found the experience 'unpleasant & not even very interesting'. He wished that it was possible to remove the 'sordid element from vice', and returned to the trenches feeling that 'the front [had] its compensations'.[213] Rowland Luther laughed at the idea that the trenches could be 'safer than being with these creatures [prostitutes]', but fretted that it might be true.[214] John Cordy refused to have sex with a prostitute who had just pleasured two of his comrades.[215] While on leave in Amiens, Ernest Sheard and his friends repeatedly turned away women on the grounds that 'what [they] required were eggs and chips, not women'.[216] Another man, just out of the trenches, preferred a good night's sleep in a hotel to sex.[217] Many men were too tired even to masturbate.[218] Others felt that it was simply their duty to indulge in sexual intercourse while on leave – irrespective of desire.[219] Some rather pompous reasons were given for abstaining, such as Lawrence Gameson's explanation to himself in his diary as to why he did not bed a prostitute: 'the practice cuts dead against some cherished family traditions with which I yet see no reason to break'.[220] Some married men abstained from sex because of their desire to be faithful to their wives. Thus, four days before he went missing, Jack W. Mudd wrote to his wife, 'I hope, dear, you will always trust in me for I am always faithful – your face is always before me and I couldn't deny you.'[221] Many more men were genuinely frightened of contracting venereal disease.[222] Between 4 August 1914 and 11 November 1918, there were approximately 400,000 cases of VD in the British forces, and commanding officers threatened to inform the parents or wives of any man who contracted such a disease.[223] Less sensibly, some servicemen stayed clear of women because they believed that they were all spies.[224] Others were frightened of what *Pearson's Weekly* described as 'the woman tout' who 'like Bret Harte's heathen Chinee . . . ha[d]s many ways that [were] dark and tricks that [were] not nice' to trap unwary soldiers on leave.[225] Away from home, sexual intercourse could be a particularly frightening business.

The transition from this bewildering and threatening sexual environment to a post-war world peopled with familiar women was difficult – especially since many men and women harboured quite different visions of the opposite sex.[226] One wonders how the soldier who described to his loved ones in gory detail how the blood and hair of an unspecified number of Germans stuck to his bayonet (he had never been a within a mile of a German at the time of writing) could have lived up to his image when (and if) he returned home.[227] Long-distance love was also problematical. Wives suspected that their husbands had been unfaithful while in France and were fully prepared to 'have it out' as soon as they returned. Thus, one wife threatened to 'skin' her husband alive because she suspected that he had visited the type of 'French hussy' who seemed to think that her body 'looked best as born'.[228] Even the fidelity of women at home could bother some men. Reg Bailey wrote to his father from Salonica in July 1916. His letter is worth quoting at length for an insight into his predicament:

So, Nurse has written to you regarding my long silence. Well, I'm afraid I've got about a dozen unanswered letters of hers to hand, but although it is nearly 3 years since I have seen her, she seems to have woven quite a nice little war Romance to be enacted when I returned to Blightie, covered in glory and battle-scars and staggering under the weight of my hardly-won medals. But, I'm afraid Nurse's memory is a deal keener than mine. I only remember her as a bright cheery sort of person, who was always singing about Dawson's house. But, after an interval of a year or more, she rooted me out in the Army and we have corresponded and swapped yarns. But lately she has abandoned the impersonal strain and enthuses vastly over the Dear Old Country with the Dirty weather, and writes pages of gush which is all very tiresome and embarrasing [sic] to shy and retiring dispositions like my own.[229]

Other men – while equally nervous – were more keen to return to those who loved them and they anxiously reassured their loved ones (and themselves) about their ability to cope with the reunion. As 'Jack' mused in a letter to Miss D. Williams in November 1917, 'I have been abroad now over 2 yrs 4 months & not had the leisure of speaking to or taking a girl for a walk don't you think I have got out of practice but I think I shall be able to make up for lost time when I do return.'[230]

After the war, the generation of men who had fought were *more* liable to repudiate emotional expression outside the marital bond. For men, marriage had never been so popular. The war accentuated the female-male population imbalance so that the marriage rates of men exceeded those of women by around twenty per cent between 1916 and 1930.[231] There was increased emphasis on the importance of sex within marriage between the wars. Divorce rates rose dramatically after the

40 'Wilt thou have this woman for three years or for the duration of the war', drawing by M. F. Powis of the 3rd Echelon HQ, dated 21 August 1916, in the autograph album of a nurse, E. Campbell, in the 15th General Hospital, Egypt, 1916–17. [IWM Misc. 93 Item 1386]

'Wilt Thou have this woman for three years or for the duration of the war.'

M. F. Powis
3rd Echelon.
HQ.

21 Aug 1916.

war (there were three times as many divorces in 1919 as in 1913 and, as was joked in a contemporary drawing (illus. 40), wartime marriages were often 'for the duration of the war'), but this was not due to the repudiation of the marital tie, but an attempt to retreat from the rushed marriages of wartime and find a truly domestic space. There was a greater stress on domestic emotional ties as being necessary to the stability of the masculine personality – and male-to-male friendships were increasingly seen as undermining (rather than complementing) adult masculinity.

The male body was nourished within the domestic sphere. As I have shown elsewhere, domesticity was as much about men as women, especially when reduced hours of employment and improvements in wages and living standards made possible an adoption of the male domestic ideal for growing numbers of men.[232] The declaration of war provided many men with an opportunity to probe the depth of their commitment to domesticity: quite literally, it was an ideal for which they might risk their lives. Married and unmarried men alike declared that they were fighting for their families. Laurie Rowlands expressed the feelings of many men in a letter to 'Sweetheart Mine' on 5 February 1918 when he confessed that there was no thought of patriotism at the Front: 'I too have lost pretty nearly all the patriotism that I had left, it's just the thought of you all over there, you who love me and trust me to do *my* share in the job that is necessary for your safety and freedom. It's just *that* that keeps me going and enabled me to "stick it".'[233] This was more than merely public propaganda.

Ironically, defending this male domestic ideal meant being exiled from it, and returning home was not easy. For a sizeable minority of men the reconstruction of their civilian lives could only proceed slowly.[234] For them, the alienations of wartime were transferred to the peacetime economy. Three groups of ex-servicemen were particularly prone to flounder after the war. As was shown in Chapter One, the first group consisted of those who had been disabled or otherwise damaged by wartime experiences. W. G. Shipway had suffered illness and deprivation in a prisoner-of-war camp. His return to civilian society was exceptionally difficult: 'I was very depressed. I had lost touch with most of my friends who had survived and the others were working during the day. I spent hours practising on our three-quarter sized billiard table. This was no fun with no one to play with. I was suffering from recurrent jaundice and depression, with obsessions such as that my father was going to throw me out.'[235] The second group was of men who had enlisted immediately after leaving school and had no experience of adult civilian life to draw upon.[236] The third group was of men who had not maintained regular contact with people back in Britain. A photograph (illus. 41) shows the difficult conditions under which men frequently struggled to write back to their loved ones in Britain and elsewhere. Many servicemen such as Edward King found the task too difficult. In one of the few letters that King did write, he warns 'Libbie' not to expect letters from him: 'as for writing you dont get much heart to write things are always basy day and night . . . i wish you would not trubble about letters i should fell much better as i find got enough to look after myself fare some mounth to come.'[237] If King had survived the war, he would have found himself much less in touch with civilian life than servicemen who had maintained a regular correspondence.

Even servicemen who sustained frequent contact with family and friends back home might be temporarily bewildered or embittered by the chasm of difference between themselves and civilians.[238] The soldier in his hospital bed looks at his mother reading to him (illus. 42). She seems oblivious to his bewilderment and alienation. This was

41 Writing home, Oosttaverne Wood, battle of Messines Ridge, 11 June 1917.
[IWM Q2308]

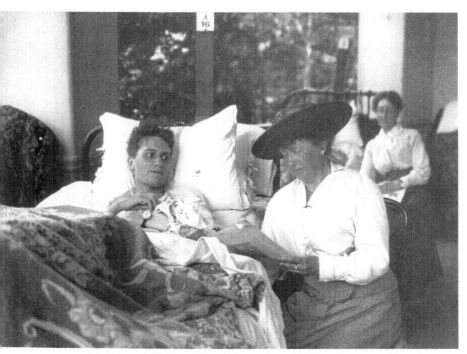

42 Mothers with their convalescent wounded sons in the Duchess of Westminster's
(No. 1 Red Cross) Hospital at Le Touquet, 18 June 1917. [IWM Q2409]

43 'C is the "Civvy" . . .', cartoon from 'Captain Wideawake', *Jovial Jottings*, London, 1915.

particularly the case while the war was still being fought. Thus, early in the morning of 20 May 1916, Lawrence Gameson scrawled these words in his diary, 'In the last lot [of wounded soldiers] is a surprisingly beautiful youth . . . long lashes, straight nose, finely finished limbs and so on. He was oozing frothy filth. It was all I could do to prevent him from drowning himself in his own juices.' Gameson then called on the 'woman who [had] wished [the youth] good-bye' to 'press now her lips to the clotted slime about his mouth'.[239] Less wrathfully, Harry Siepmann preferred spending his leave in French brothels to going back to England because the 'out-of-touch atmosphere of "patriotism" jarred so badly'.[240] The over-weight civilian who affirmed his dedication to the military cause in France while dressed in a fur coat, smoking a cigar and drinking a beer was one of the most painful characters for returned servicemen to meet (see the satirical view of this in illus. 43). Too often, those at home had accepted the 'fake photographs' of the 'laughing Tommy, doing his duty, always smiling'.[241] To be in the company of women was 'strange'.[242] In some cases, there was nothing to say.[243] The strain of war had 'desexed' men, rendering them impotent.[244] Pity in the eyes of women was resented.[245] So was women's power. Russell L. Venables returned to a London that seemed to be 'completely run' by women.[246] Arthur H. Hubbard was also aggrieved that 'the ladies were earning all the cash while we are away', and he reminded these ladies how much they owed to men.[247] It was widely felt that servicemen had paid too high a price in defence of their womenfolk. Ralph Scott expressed this sentiment in his diary for 18 August 1918 where he predicted that after the war people would forget men's sacrifices or simply 'make allowances'. He continued,

And the ladies for whom I gave my strength and more will leave me for the healthy, bouncing beggars who stayed at home . . . And, then, on howling winter evenings, our spirits might ride the cloud-wrack over these blood-soaked hills, shrieking and moaning with the wind, to drown the music of their dancing, so that they huddle together in terror, the empty-headed women and the weakneed [sic], worn-out men as we laugh at their petty, soulless lives.[248]

The rhetoric of the apocalypse expressed the desire for justice, for judgement.[249]

This, however, was a minority response. Most men returned gratefully, and happily, to the domestic fold. A sketch taken from a nurse's autograph book, although a crude copy of a popular postcard, is in its very primitiveness a more powerful symbol of man's desire (illus. 44). The removal of the intimate aspects of masculinity had encouraged further nostalgia for the domestic. Canon Ernest Courtenay Crosse recalled the 'shout of welcome' that went up from the ranks when 'the first grannie was sighted on our return to civilization'.[250] The lonely soldier correspondence scheme was enthusiastically adopted by

44 'It's a long, long way to Tipperary', drawing by Sgt T. W. Spratley, dated 26 October 1915, from the autograph book of a Canadian nurse, Miss M. Walker, 1915–17. [IWM Misc. 108 Item 1707]

some men.[251] Nursing sisters in military hospitals, as is well known, were adored.[252] In all-male environments, men reflected in their diaries that their girlfriends were their 'only pleasure[s] in life now', their 'mainstays'.[253] They gazed with longing at photographs of their wives.[254] They confessed that in the midst of battle, they could think of naught but their beloveds.[255] They luxuriated in that 'good married feeling'.[256]

After the war, their domestic sphere was reinstated. Married men returned to familiar beds; unmarried men sought companions. For these men, home was the ultimate retreat from the disciplines of military society. Whether healthy or disabled, men back from the war breathed more freely once they returned home. This relief was regarded as a major explanation for the reluctance of ex-servicemen to take advantage of offers to retrain for employment. In the words of the director of training for the Ministry of Pensions, 'They want[ed] to be back at their old homes, near their relatives and their wives' relatives.'[257] Similarly, a letter to the editor of *The Times* reminded people that the 'broken hero' desired only to 'go home to wife and children' or, if unmarried, to the 'old mother'.[258] As one serviceman declared, home represented 'Leisure, quiet, privacy, courtesy, relative luxury and comfort, forgetful of the army and all idiocy and petty oppression, muddle hurry [sic] and noise and squalor and discomfort, anxiety and worry . . . I never appreciated home before the war so much as I do now.'[259] It was the place a man could go to 'lick [his] wounds and recover [his] self-respect'.[260] It was 'order and cleanliness, most comforting to experience'.[261] Indeed, former comrades might be relegated to a shadowy part of a man's life. A year after the Armistice, a letter addressed to 'Dear Old Pal' and signed 'your old pal' began, 'I hope you will not think I have forgotten you as you have not heard from me since this time last year. Well . . . I have been married twelve months for Janry. 28, so – am becoming – quite a responsible married man. No doubt you will be surprised to hear that J. A. Johnson beat me by about a fortnight . . . Do you ever hear from any of the old boys? he is the only one I hear from . . .'[262] Women were replacing male comrades.

There was potentially another side to men's domesticity after the war. The experience of military life, during which men performed a wider range of domestic tasks than had been expected from them in civilian society, led to speculation about the impact of war on their attitude towards marriage and its associated chores. In 1917, for example, Ray Christopher wrote to his mother of a family friend who had been beating his wife, suggesting that the young man was sent to the Front to 'try knocking the Huns about instead of knocking his poor wife about'. To Christopher, it was 'pretty evident he [was] no man, first of all not having pluck enough to come out here and secondly hitting a woman'. Had the young man been at the Front 'for a short while, he would soon [have] learn[t] to appreciate the womenfolk of England'.[263] Writing in *Health and Efficiency* in 1919, Guy Thorne agreed that a change had taken place, but he identified a different cause. He wrote,

Before the war innumerable men wooed their brides with ardour and won them with strength of purpose. Their marriage was a stage in their career, something settled and achieved. They passed on to other ambitions . . . Now, a man who has spent the last year or two at the front will use married life very differently. After months of blood and mud, hunger and cold, noise which thrust itself between the skull and brain and beat out thought, lean death in all that tumult, he will escape to wife and love as the soul of a tortured martyr to heaven.

Thorne further believed that the war had taught men self-control: 'Is Mr Bull of the trenches going to loose his temper and raise Cain at home because his dinner is two minutes late? Is Private Greatheart, R.F.A., who has carried shells under fire for more days than he can count, going to let a tired wife carry coals while he reads the evening paper, as he did before the war?' The answer, according to Guy Thorne, was a resounding 'no'. Finally, he asserted that the war had done away with the helpless man about the house. Wartime experience in domestic chores had rendered him a perfect helpmate.[264]

Were these predictions realized? Many soldiers did admit that they had not appreciated the pleasures of their own domesticity until it had been taken from them. As Charlie May exclaimed in a diary addressed to his wife, 'Ah, Maudie, how little I realised where happiness lay till this old war came along and it was denied me. How limited is a man's mind. It does not allow him to enjoy life in the present but only to realise what moments have meant to him by looking back on them when they have passed.'[265] Similarly, Harry Thwaites professed to his wife that he was resigned to doing the housework when he returned: 'What i ear in the papers that all the women is doing mens work so when i come home i will have to stop at home and mind the babys and do the washing while you go to work that will be all right wont it.'[265] Some ex-servicemen increased their domestic labour after the war, as in the case, particularly, of those who had been disabled: their assumption of housework tasks enabled them to make a valuable contribution to their own domestic economy. Thus, the disabled pensioner James H. Kaye ended his letter to the Ministry of Pensions with the assurance that he was not simply sitting in a park but had just completed 'a good mornings housework'.[267] More common, however, was the retreat of men from the broad range of domestic jobs that they had performed during the war. This was not only true for those who had seen active service. During the war, J. McCarthy had been imprisoned for his conscientious objections. As the war came to an end, he fretted about one thing, the fact that his wife now knew that he could sew.[268] Mending one's trousers in a prison camp or outside a tent was fundamentally different from sewing on buttons in an armchair. Although the post-war world saw an increase in the amount of domestic labour carried out by men, it also saw greater resistance to their performing feminine types of housework. As I have shown elsewhere, men's housework became more 'manly' – concerned with gardening, household repairs and tasks considered particularly dirty or heavy – and the wartime extension of their domestic tasks had no lasting impact.[269]

As has been shown, earlier forms of male bonding were transferred into the war zones. The absence of women and the heightened dependence of men upon each other provided an environment and ethos where these bonds could be strengthened to their full potential. The social and geographical cohesion of the Pals' Battalion temporarily enabled the growth of male bonding, but these were decimated in the slaughter of the first day of the Battle of the Somme.[270] More typically, instead of being strengthened, the bonds snapped during the war. Wartime experiences proved too stressful to result in an expansion of masculine love. Not even the least important strand of male bonding – namely, the patriotic identification of man as fighter – could be sustained: the ex-servicemen's societies fractured into many parts. After the war, there was a return to earlier forms of intimacy. The greater value placed on male domesticity was as much the result of alterations in wages and the economy of employment as it was a rejection of the wartime experiences. It was impossible to apply military *esprit de corps* to men whose sense of identity remained lodged within their civilian domestic environment.

Four Inspecting

The demand for manpower and the economic constraints of wartime aroused public interest in the composition of the male body. We have already examined ways in which men responded to their urge to be regarded as beautiful rather than as simply functional. In the last chapter, the aesthetic responses of servicemen towards each other was a major theme. Employers and the state, however, were primarily concerned with the usefulness of the male body and both attempted to discipline men who failed to perform their assigned duties, recognizing, at the same time, that it was important to regulate behaviour in order to discourage shirking and malingering. This chapter considers the attempt to control men through manipulating their physical shape and fitness. Although the First World War did not create the impetus for state surveillance and discipline of the body, it intensified that surveillance, encouraged proliferation of regulatory institutions, and left a legacy that persisted throughout the inter-war years. After the war, although several organizations were dedicated to resisting militaristic ideals for the male physique, this involved no more than an attempt to exchange official forms of surveillance for equally restrictive, pseudo-scientific disciplines.

Surveillance

It was widely acknowledged that the state and employers had to accept some responsibility for the male physique. The military requirements of modern warfare provided governments with a powerful incentive to intervene in new areas of the economy – including the construction of men's bodies. Alan Peacock and Jack Wiseman have described this as the 'inspection effect' of wartime economies.[1] In Britain, alarm was greatly heightened by the Boer War in which the inspection of soldiers revealed that only 14,000 of the 20,000 volunteers were sufficiently fit to join the army.[2] The conviction that the British race was degenerating physically became increasingly prevalent.[3] Despondency was all the greater as it was recognized that the debilitated physique of working-class men was shared by their wealthier brothers.[4]

Although most historians have concentrated on the debates concerning physical degeneration around the time of the Boer War, the Great War heightened such anxieties.[5] This widespread disquiet was expressed in the Ministry of National Service's report of 1919. Here, it was noted, 'War is a stern taskmaster with whom no compromise is possible . . . convention, prejudice, self-satisfaction, apathy – all alike have to give way before the icy blast of war, which sweeps before it everything except hard facts . . . It has compelled us to take stock of the health and physique of our manhood; this stock-taking has brought us face to face with ugly facts.'[6] These 'ugly facts' were established through a complex series of physical examinations that classified men within the armed forces. Initially, the War Office imposed three categories: 'A' recruits were deemed fit for general service; 'B' recruits were fit for service abroad in a support capacity; and 'C' recruits were regarded as fit for service at home only. In 1917, this system was altered and four grades were adopted. Grade One contained the former category 'A' (or 'fit') recruits. Grade Two included men in categories 'B1' and 'C1'. These were men judged to be able to walk six miles 'with ease'. Grade Three men were unsuitable for combat. Men in the former categories 'B' and 'C' were placed in this grade. Finally, men in Grade Four were considered to be utterly unfit. The photographs (illus. 45) were published in the *British Parliamentary Papers* to show politicians the dramatic differences between men in the various 'grades'. The photographs themselves led to a resurgence of anxiety amongst a huge range of politicians, popularists and informed opinion. It is important to note that these grades were not solely intended to identify obviously diseased or disabled men. Within each of the categories, the shape of the body was crucial, as height, chest width and weight formed the basis for the decision.[7] Thus, in London during the first five months of war, over one-third of those rejected for military service were turned away because of defective chest measurements.[8] Of course, these statistics must be not read too literally. As the war progressed and manpower demands became desperate, standards were lowered. Hence, Edgar Hayland could complain to a friend that 'by one of the ways known only to the Army [his] category ha[d] been raised from C to A without any medical inspection'.[9] Despite such instances, nearly all young adult and middle-aged men in Britain had their bodies surveyed and categorized by medical officers at least once between 1914 and 1918 (see illus. 46). The results were devastating to both

SPECIMENS OF MEN IN EACH OF THE FOUR GRADES.

GRADE I.   GRADE II.   GRADE III.   GRADE IV.

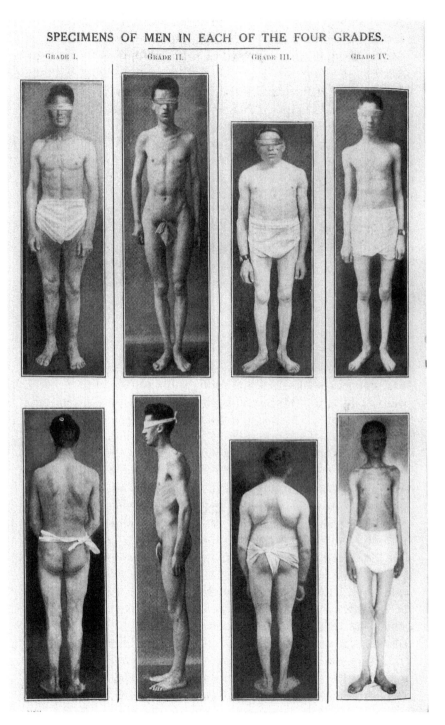

45 'Specimens of Men in each of the Four Grades'. [Par. Papers 1919 xxvi, 308]

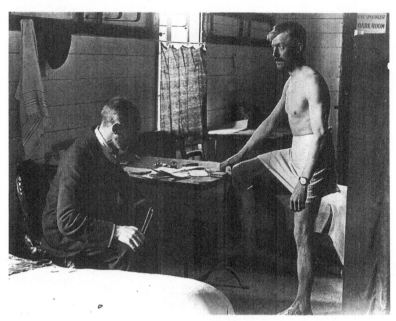

46 A medical officer examining a recruit. [IWM Q30062]

military and civilian commentators. In the final analysis, forty-two per cent of recruits were revealed to be in the last two grades.[10]

Despite the obviously mutilating impact of war on the bodies of so many young men, the armed forces maintained their reputation for improving men's physiques. Throughout the period, it was widely agreed that the physical training given to servicemen was efficacious in moulding the male body in the appropriate fashion. For instance, in 1899, E. Nobel Smith (the senior surgeon at the City Orthopaedic Hospital in London) catalogued the appalling condition of some men's bodies, before insisting that those drilled in the army were exceptions because their bodies had been 're-formed into more manly shapes'.[11] Empirical verification was provided in 1907 when army authorities re-measured over 15,000 infantrymen six months after they had enlisted and found that (on average) soldiers had grown by three-quarters of an inch, their chests had broadened by one inch and they had gained ten pounds in weight during their training.[12]

Similar observations were made during the First World War. National Service Medical Boards frequently passed unfit men into the armed forces in the belief that military drill and discipline would prove physically invigorating.[13] Charles E. Carrington noted that young men joining the Royal Warwicks in 1918 added, on average, an inch to their height and weighed an additional stone during their training.[14]

Servicemen in training commented on the changes in their own bodies: they were getting 'fitter and fitter' and military life was 'doing wonders' for them.[15] Middle-class men were particularly likely to experience dramatic changes in their physique once in the armed forces. Thus, Cecil Christopher wrote to his sister about a fellow employee who had just been involved in some heavy fighting:

In civilian life he was a most fastidious merchant in his likes and dislikes and always imagined he was ill, in fact getting a peppery little bachelor before his time. See him now, he eats anything that comes along, never reports sick and can do his 25 to 30 miles in full kit with the next man and up to now has never had to fall out on a long march. He is one fellow to whom the army has done a bit of good.[16]

Startling changes were also witnessed in working-class Salford where servicemen on leave astonished local residents: men were 'pounds – sometimes stones – heavier, taller, confident, clean and straight, they were hardly recognizable as the men who went away'.[17] Whatever its compensations in the markets of love and work, these benefits of war led some servicemen to complain that it encouraged civilians to doubt their 'stories of the Horrors of the Trenches'.[18] Of course, the proposal that military service improved the shape of men's bodies obscured an important issue: the war improved only those bodies that were not completely or partially decimated. In terms of public rhetoric, however, the physically scarred were set aside and the survivors used to bolster arguments that men's bodies had been 'made masculine' through military drill. It was the bodies of those who remained at home that symbolized all that was degenerate in the male physique.

It was only a small step from the belief that the armed forces improved men's physique to the proposal that military drill should be applied to the civilian population. From the turn of the century, but particularly from the First World War, the military body was acclaimed within civilian contexts. Military definitions of fitness were widely adopted. Civilians from all walks of life compared the 'A1' body with the 'C3' body. These comparisons took many forms. Military terminology provided rhyming syllables in popular songs.[19] It embellished political speeches – most famously in the case of the laments by the prime minister, Stanley Baldwin, in 1919 that 'we have discovered that there are too many C3 men', and his promise to make 'an increase in the numbers of A1 men part of the programme of Reconstruction'.[20] It was used to explain the failure of women to marry: thus, 'Jim' from Glasgow informed Marie Stopes that modern women did not marry 'for the simple reason that the biggest percentage of men [were] not in a fit or proper state to marry any girl, a fact proved by various Drs at the Military Tribunals . . .' Furthermore, 'we cant [sic] have a A.1 race, out of C.4 conditions. impossible'.[21] The language of the War Office prevailed.[22]

In addition, concern over the male physique was stimulated by three needs, all of which were central to the disciplines of warfare: military prowess, economic expansion and social stability. These rationales overlapped. Never far from the minds of promoters of physical training was the relationship between the masculine and the military body.[23] Thus, in 1914, the chief medical officer for the Board of Education could commend the 2,000 adult evening classes in physical training on the grounds that a 'recruit who ha[d] been accustomed to practise Swedish exercises [would] not only find that part of his training lightened', but that the physical development which resulted from the practice 'would be likelier to make him more suitable for military training as a whole'.[24] Obligatory physical jerks were said to be the solution to the question of military responsibilities.[25] National pride was at the centre of such debates. In 1922, Major Frederick William Stevens, a member of the executive committee of the Amateur Gymnastic Association, argued that only compulsory military drill could create a 'perfect human form in health and strength', a 'perfect race of men'. He continued, 'Our Empire should produce not merely a few players of a limited number of games, more or less athletic, but real athletes to take their place in the great game of life of the calibre for which our British temperament and natural disposition and mental and physical qualities fit us.'[26] Stevens was a typical physical training expert, entrepreneurial (his books were published by the Stevens' Exercise Equipment Service) and patriotic. W. Bruce Sutherland's photograph of his class in physical culture was entitled 'Training the New Army'. This indoor class was typical of those established around the time of the war (see illus. 47). Physical training was patriotic and chauvinistic: it prepared men's bodies for war.[27]

Linked to the military objective of physical training was the need for improved economic performance. The butchery witnessed on the battlefields made it even more crucial that those who survived should be fit to work for the nation.[28] The dysgenic effects of war were brought to the attention of the public, heightening fears that civilization was about to be plunged back into a period dominated by more brutal types of men.[29] Thus, the eugenist and dress reformer Caleb Williams Saleeby described walking through Hyde Park, gazing with 'homage and admiration and sorrow' at the 'splendid' physiques of servicemen in training. He reserved quite a different gaze for the

47 'Training the New Army – An Indoor Class', from W. Bruce Sutherland, *Physical Culture. The Bruce Sutherland System*, London, 1917.

'tramps and ne'er-do-wells, the broken-down tuberculous, rickety, alcoholic, and syphilitics who breathe[d] the same air, and loaf', and he sadly brooded over the fact that the 'brave, the vigorous, the healthy, the patriotic [were] taken and the others left'.[30] Truly, all hopes of an eugenic paradise would evaporate if the 'cream of the race' were taken and the 'skimming milk' left.[31]

Although wartime rhetoric was particularly prone to adopt the language of crisis, even in times of peace the British body was presented as competing with other – foreign – bodies. Two contrasting photographs show this fear most clearly (illus. 48). In the caption to the first, F. A. Hornibrook points to the 'military position of attention', asking readers to 'Note the pouter pigeon chest and hollow back.' In contrast, under the second photograph, he writes, 'Note the ease of attitude of the Polynesian native warrior.' The message was clear: in Britain, the military man was slightly ridiculous in comparison to the 'warrior' from the South Seas. In 1919, the sports coach Eustace Miles was especially eloquent on this point, insisting that physical fitness was important in the struggle against the 'yellow peril'. He further warned, 'we may soon have to compete against the millions of economically industrious, and skillful Orientals, disciplined, ready to obey orders faithfully, almost untiring . . . quickness we must have if we are to survive as a great nation'.[32] Only regular exercises could make men economically efficient.[33] This rationale worked at the individual as much as at the national level. The League of Health and Strength lamented that German, French, Russian, Italian and Turkish athletes had demonstrated their superiority over their British counterparts.[34] Physical training was required to strengthen the body in its fight against physical ailments.[35] It was the solution to the endemic ills of the British bowel.[36] The bodies of particular groups within society required coaching most urgently. Most obviously, blind and handicapped children were considered potential beneficiaries of a developing scientific discipline of physical training.[37] So were the unemployed.[38] And the middle-class businessman was not forgotten. Physical training was intended to give men a competitive edge in the world of employment. In a book entitled *Keeping Fit*, Colonel H. G. Mayes promised businessmen who were 'slightly the mental inferior' of their competitors a way to triumph through 'the sheer power of . . . virility'. As Mayes illustrated, 'A Man walks into a gathering of other men. Before his arrival there has been an air of lassitude about the meeting. This man, however, is fit, and the influence of his physical personality acts like a tonic upon his jaded fellows. I do not exaggerate. The man

Hana   *Underwood*

FIG. 4. The military position at attention. Note   FIG. 5. Note the ease of attitude of the Polynesian
   the pouter pigeon chest and hollow back.   native warrior shown here.

48 'The military position at attention' and 'The ease of attitude of the Polynesian warrior', from F. A. Hornibrook, *The Cultures of the Abdomen*, London, 1927.

who is well is the man who is noticed, the man who compels.'[39] The tutored male physique conquered all.

The male body required physical discipline not solely for the sake of a state threatened with military and economic collapse: it also required discipline in the pursuit of social harmony. The need for a morally cohesive citizenry demanded flinging aside the 'medieval dualistic conception' of body and mind.[40] In the words of the medical officer Edward Leech, physical training instructors had to be philosophers as much as athletes because caring for the body 'embrace[d] the care of the soul and mind of man . . . EXERCISE as understood at the King's Lancashire Military Convalescent Hospital [was] more *of a religion than a routine*.'[41] Again, this was not unique to the period after 1914. In discussions about physical deterioration at the turn of the century, it was also acknowledged that exercises provided 'mental and moral training'.[42] The Metropolitan Police had long regarded physical drill as crucial in the reform of juveniles convicted of various forms of disorderly conduct in the street.[43] During and after the war, the provision of playing fields was similarly thought to reduce juvenile crime.[44] It was believed that young boys taught to exercise their muscles correctly and regularly would be able to transfer this ability into control of their emotions.[45] Developing the 'gripping powers of the hand' would strengthen character and determination.[46] Physical training would teach boys to think in terms of group rather than personal interests and would help them to acquire 'habits of discipline, obedience, ready response and self-control'.[47] Furthermore, the actual development of the brain was promoted by motor activities.[48] This explained why physically disabled children were regarded as 'mentally retarded'.[49] Wilfrid Northfield (who had suffered a nervous breakdown while in France during the war) spoke for many when he declared, 'Whilst I admit the supremacy of mind in man, I am inclined from my observations to favour the opposite teachings of the Physical Culturalists – "Take care of the body and the mind will take care of itself".'[50] As Eustace Miles reminded his readers, 'the body [might] be a great deal more than "religious" people suppose[d]'.[51]

These different rationales for physical training were regarded as complementary rather than as competing. The concerns arising out of the war enhanced disquiet and provided pseudo-scientific data to bolster official anxieties. However, as we shall be examining in the next section, a shift occurred in what was considered the *type* of training most liable to result in the fulfilment of as many of these aims as possible. Competing systems of physical training included 'German' and 'Swedish' drill, in addition to what came to be called 'British' drill and

49 'Use Prof. Inch's Perfect System', from Albert Attila, *The Art of Weight-Lifting and Muscular Development*, London, 1903.

games.[52] The broad chronology may be sketched as follows: from the late nineteenth century to the First World War there was a movement away from German drill (comprising a variety of different exercises and sports but, most importantly, making use of apparatus such as Indian clubs, dumb-bells, horizontal and parallel bars, rings and the vaulting horse) towards Swedish drill (that is, free-standing exercises performed upon hearing words of command according to a definite 'table', or order).[53] In this shift, the focus of interest moved from the biceps and shoulders to the stomach, or from muscle-building to toning. The popularity of 'Prof. Inch' and his muscular development (as shown in the 1903 cartoon in illus. 49) was definitely out of fashion. The shift was followed by a process of modifying Swedish drill by introducing more flexibility and variety to the exercise tables. In other words, although Swedish drill remained a much more communal exercise than its German counterpart,[54] teachers were increasingly permitted to indulge their individual idiosyncrasies. Although generally accurate, this chronology can be misleading because it does not account for the different rates of change between grant-aided elementary schools, public schools and the armed forces. It also omits the main area of disputation, namely, the militaristic connotations of instruction.

Drilled Men

Britain was 'a land of sportsmen' – so read the legend. In practice, it was increasingly admitted that men 'talked sport, read sport, looked on life through sport spectacles . . . but – practised no form of sport themselves'.[55] In the 1930s, the Physical Education Committee estimated that nearly 91 per cent of boys aged between 14 and 18 years never engaged in any form of physical activity. Despite regional differences (for instance, 21 per cent of boys in Manchester participated in physical training compared with only 9 per cent of boys in Newcastle), the problems of physique was a national one and it was believed that the obvious place to remedy it was in the schools.[56]

The debate about the type of physical training that should be given to schoolboys was overlaid by a dispute concerning the militaristic nature of the exercises. In this chapter, the word 'militaristic' is to be interpreted narrowly as the involvement of military institutions (the army, navy, air force and War Office) in programmes of physical training, rather than the broader definition of militarist as referring to the inculcation of values such as discipline, obedience and patriotism.[57] Defined narrowly, physical training in schools frequently (although not inevitably) contained a significant militaristic component. The first mention of physical training in the code of regulations for elementary schools occurred in 1871 when it was agreed that students could perform 'military drill' for up to two hours a week. In 1883, the medical branch of the Board of Education recommended that schools adopt a form of German drill.[58] Although provision was made for instruction in physical training in all schools two years later, since it was left to the ordinary teaching staff to administer, training floundered.[59] Meanwhile, the London School Board had introduced Swedish drill (in 1881) for use by girls and four years later the first Swedish college in Britain was established.

Although, in 1890, the Board of Education had substituted the words 'suitable physical exercises' for 'military drill', and there was a shift in rationale from explicitly martial aims towards therapeutic medical ones (from 1907, administered by the School Medical Service), the involvement of military institutions in physical education was to increase after the turn of the century.[60] Revelations about the enfeebled state of the military body during the Boer War had shocked the War Office and Board of Education into concerted action. In 1901, the Physical Training Committee made provision for regular inspection of physical classes in schools. 'For the sake of economy', it had been agreed that nominations to the newly created posts of director of physical training and his divisional assistant should be restricted to employees of the War Office.[61] In 1902, after consultation with the War Office, the Board of Education issued a Model Course of Physical Training based on the Army Red Book. The crucial commands were military ones.[62]

Schools were clearly encouraged to employ instructors who had been trained in the Army Gymnastics Course.[63] As Captain J. C. Robertson reiterated in the monthly leaflet of the leading association dedicated to promoting Swedish drill, it was impossible to separate physical training from military needs.[64] In 1904, the Board of Education added certain elements of Swedish drill to its old army syllabus. Within two years, the Swedish system had been wholeheartedly adopted by the army and the Board of Education quickly followed suit.[65] In this way, between the Boer War and the First World War, the type of physical training in grant-aided elementary schools closely mirrored what was happening in military training camps.

This did not go unnoticed. The close relationship between the Board of Education and the War Office was regarded by many educationalists and parents as inappropriate.[66] Despite the high level of involvement in military organizations in British society prior to 1914 (for instance, in 1911, one in every 11 males aged between 17 and 25 years in Birmingham was a member of the Territorials and a further 1 in 25 was a member of the Army Special Reserve),[67] it was widely felt that drill sergeants were too ill-educated to teach children.[68] This was in fact forcibly argued by the person in charge of physical training in schools, the chief medical officer, George Newman. He was not against military drill *per se* – indeed, prior to the war he had stressed the need for non-militaristic physical training precisely on the grounds that it would render compulsory military service unnecessary – merely against it being used to mould the bodies of young boys.[69] As we shall see, he changed his mind during the war.

With the declaration of war, physical training became increasingly infused with the military ethos and the War Office's hold over schools tightened.[70] The prestige of the armed forces grew immeasurably.[71] The labour requirements of war were regarded as providing physical trainers and their pupils with an ideal opportunity for displaying their prowess. In the words of Harry Chapman in *Health and Vim* (1915), 'His whole life has been in training for such a moment as this. What matter if he cannot shoot straight? – he can learn that quickly. The main point is that his constitution is perfect, and he will be able to endure many of the hardships under which a weaker brother would give way . . . when it comes to a bayonet charge he is ever conspicuous.'[72] School instructors were already trained in the type of drill used in the army.[73] Physical instructors enlisted and were immediately given the rank of non-commissioned officers as army Swedish drill instructors.[74] Furthermore, as these men left to do their duty in the trenches, they were replaced by cadet NCOs, trained in gymnasia under the various army commands or by army instructors lent to schools for that purpose.[75] This policy was encouraged by the War Office 'in the hope of raising the physical standard of boys about to become officers in the army' and was continued after the war.[76] By 1918, George Newman had reversed his earlier hostility to instructors from the army physical training staff, since he saw them becoming more appropriate 'as military methods [had] been subject to considerable modification during the war and [had] become more recreative and informal'.[77] In addition, it became patriotic to employ ex-servicemen over civilian instructors. By 1923 more than one-third of physical training instructors in schools were ex-army or ex-navy instructors.[78] Even as late as 1935, one-third of physical instructors in preparatory schools were ex-army instructors.[79] The inspectorate was even more dominated by military men. On the eve of the Second World War, half of the male inspectors of physical training were either ex-military inspectors or had received their training in military schools.[80]

The declaration of war in 1914 had two other impacts on physical training for boys. Firstly, it led to increased concern within the Board of Education about the state of physical education in schools. As the person responsible for physical training in grant-aided elementary schools, Newman was particularly anxious that the wartime experiences were not lost. He regarded the war as creating the ideal moment for reform, warning that if the whole question were to be shelved until after the war there would be a tendency to return to the old routine: 'The opportunity [would] have vanished and reform when it [did] come [would] be more difficult to introduce.'[81] In his view, one of the great revelations of the war lay in the way it promoted games for *all* boys, regardless of class. Unlike in public schools, games had generally been frowned upon by the Board prior to the war. Although organized games such as cricket, football and hockey had been an accepted part of the school curricula since 1906, they were considered to be supplementary to drill.[82] Even in Newman's report for 1914, games were judged to be an inadequate way to mould boys' bodies because they did not provide 'systematic and duly proportioned exercise to each part of the body in turn'.[83] After observing the work of the Army Gymnastic Staff in France during the war, Newman changed his mind.[84] Not only were these games extremely popular amongst the servicemen (see illus. 50), but by 1917, he believed that the experience of games behind the front lines had also changed the attitudes of soldiers to physical activities. These men had previously been spectators, rather than players of games, but (according to Newman) the enthusiasm of the Army Gymnastic Staff led soldiers to resent the professionalism of games

50 Officers and men of the 26th Divisional Train playing football, Christmas Day, 1915. [IWM Q31575]

back in England, to wish to continue playing games when the war was over, and to express a desire to inculcate a love of games in their children as well.[85]

Newman failed, however, to get his dream of a 'nation of players' accepted more widely in the post-war world. Games were not universally adopted within grant-aided elementary schools for three reasons. Firstly, despite Newman's eagerness, many men in the Board of Education and local school authorities remained hostile to excessive attention being paid to games, claiming that they neglected the bodies of weaker boys, did not produce a balanced development since they were spasmodic rather than progressive, and were not suitable for boys of all ages and physical conditions.[86] Secondly, local authorities proved reluctant to employ Organizers of Physical Training. In 1923, only eighty-three authorities had made appointments.[87] This made it almost impossible to convince instructors who had been training in the armed forces to change their exercise tables and methods of teaching. Finally, there were practical considerations. Many schools lacked the facilities for games. In a survey of 135 grant-aided schools in 1923, sixty-three per cent of playing fields were either too small or too far away to be used by most of the boys. Only a quarter of schools possessed satisfactory accommodation for both games and Swedish drill.[88] Although the enterprising National Playing Fields' Association was founded in 1925, the provision of fields remained inadequate.[89]

The experience of the war had a second impact: it changed the rhetoric of dissenting groups within the community of physical instructors. So far, the story told in this chapter is a relatively simple one of the fluctuating involvement of military institutions in physical training classes as Swedish drill was progressively substituted for German drill. But it was a shift that did not occur without protest. Disaffected physical trainers contended that a modified form of German drill was more in keeping with British traditions of physical development. From the 1890s, the British College of Physical Education, the Gymnastic Teachers' Institute and the National Society of Physical Education had been promoting what they called British exercises.[90] These exercises were really a medley of German gymnastics (that is, the use of dumb-bells and horizontal bars) and callisthenics (movements to develop physical strength and grace). With the declaration of war, the Britishness of physical training for boys became a major issue. The supporters of British drill were forced to deal directly with the accusation that they were really promoting German drill under a different name.[91] Unity became important so that in the middle of the war the three colleges mentioned above combined to form the National Physical Training Association, the examining body of skilled gymnastic teachers, organized 'with the direct hope of being of service to the [Education] Authorities in connection with any national system of physical training which might be decided upon'.[92] Despite this avowal of service, it was strongly dedicated to opposing the Board of Education's emphasis on Swedish drill, as it considered that German drill was much superior. It deflected the accusation of promoting unpatriotic exercises from itself towards supporters of Swedish drill.[93] Boys' dislike of Swedish drill was said to be 'ingrained in [the] national temperament and . . . physical tastes'. In addition, 'Courage and daring and leadership, initiative, resourcefulness, self reliance and responsibility', were seen as 'the key note of all physical exercises of [the] Nation, on which account it [was] that they [were] valued here much more highly than throughout the world.'[94] In 1916, the association urged the Board of Education not to be prejudiced against British drill merely because it borrowed heavily from German systems of physical education, arguing that the 'one outstanding feature of the present European War as indeed of all previous Wars in which Germany [had] been engaged [had] been the German Gymnastic System without the effects of which the Germans [could] not have so prolonged their resistance'; the Germans in fact attributed their successes in previous wars to the effects of such a system.[95] The British were encouraged to beat the Germans at their own game, that is, by using similar techniques for developing the male physique.

These conflicts between the various schools of physical training are interesting for a number of reasons. At one level, the disagreement was about which élite was to dictate the ideal male body shape: here, governmental officials vied with athletes and popular sportsmen. In the words of Captain Francis Henry Grenfell, inspector of physical training for the Board of Education, the establishment of the 'so-called British system' side by side with the 'national system' would lead to chaos. 'Let individual British athletes adopt any system they like, but the schools should not be touched,' he pronounced.[96] The Board was sceptical about the motives of the promoters of British drill: as was explained to the president of the Board of Education, the National Physical Training Association had complained about the ascendancy of Swedish drill only because 'the common or garden gymnast or acrobat, whose ambition [was] to secure cups and silver medals at local shows, [found] his business losing favour'.[97]

At another level, the philosophy of physical education was at the centre of the conflict. Both governmental officials and professional gymnasts accused the other of emphasizing disconnected bodily parts as opposed to adopting a more holistic view of the body. According to Sir James Crichton-Browne (vice-president of the British College of Physical Education) in 1917, Swedish drill was unhealthily fixated on anatomy: it was, he said, 'too much of an anatomical system, having too exclusive regard to the actions of individual muscles, too little of a physiological system, having regard to their associated functional movements. Now anatomy as a basis is all very well, but in all vital questions it is physiology that really matters.'[98] Yet, in 1919, the supporters of Swedish drill criticized the German-British contingent equally harshly for insensitivity to the

physiological effect on the body of the student such as strengthening the vital organs, or increasing the venous or lymphatic circulation. Apparently all this system of gymnastic training aimed at was producing tricky, showy movements, in some cases developing immense strength in certain parts of the body, particularly in the arms and shoulder girdle but entirely ignoring any special hygienic considerations.[99]

The use of apparatus such as horizontal and parallel bars and rings were said to make for the uneven development of the body ('an unnatural hypertrophy of the muscles of the arms and shoulders and a great expansion in the girth of the chest . . . in short, the typical figure of the old-fashioned Drill Sergeant'). In contrast, Swedish drill made for a 'more pleasing physical appearance'.[100] In effect, however, there was one main difference between the two groups: the Board of Education's stress on reformed Swedish drill was more of a collectivist approach in contrast to the individualist emphasis of the supporters of British drill. While the opponents of the latter argued that the exercises developed the individual at the expense of the group, those in favour of it declared that they preferred individual initiative to the mechanical movements promoted in boys doing Swedish drill.[101]

Immediately after the war, a reaction to the involvement of military institutions in schools developed – affecting British, German and Swedish instructors alike. There were many reasons for this. The most common objection to drill was simply that it was boring, too formalist and placed excessive strain on young bodies.[102] It was considered particularly inappropriate for the two groups within society who were regarded as requiring special attention, namely, middle-aged men and children. The exercises were believed to be too difficult for middle-aged or elderly men who were becoming the targets of many books of physical training.[103] Children's bodies required an even kinder and more graduated system than those of older men.[104] By encouraging an exaggerated thrusting forward of the chest and curving the spine, drill (as conducted by army sergeants) was said to be contributing to children's poor posture.[105] In addition, in its moral mission, drill was said to be unsuitable for children because it imposed a discipline of 'mechanical obedience' rather than a discipline of self-control.[106] As one textbook declared, automatic movements were not educational.[107] In contrast to scouting, which offered the 'spirit of freedom, of active exercise in the open air, of initiative, of healthy emulation, of comradeship, of obedience without subservience', all forms of drill destroyed a boy's individuality.[108]

The unpopularity of drill was due more directly to wartime experiences. Men who had become accustomed to military drill between 1914 and 1919 quickly repudiated it. Demobilized soldiers consigned drill 'to a warm region', on the grounds not that it was ineffective, but that it was a relic from their military days which might have improved their bodies but at too great a cost.[109] When it was hinted that the Education Act of 1918 might include a clause imposing compulsory military drill in schools, thousands of individuals and organizations registered their protests.[110] It had become discreditable to be enthusiastic about soldiering.[111] The Board of Education had to allay suspicions that its attempts to expand physical training within grant-earning schools hid some 'militarist object', and accordingly it pleaded with instructors to give commands in a conversational tone, more like a superviser of games than an army sergeant.[112] It introduced more flexibility into the exercise tables and teachers were encouraged to supplement drill with games and other recreative exercises. They renamed the training 'reformed Swedish drill'.

Despite the hostility, military drill could not be cut entirely from the school curriculum. The shortage of physical instructors trained outside the armed forces compelled many schools to rely on men trained by the military. Other schools continued to use military exercise tables because they were the only ones familiar to the ex-service instructors or cadet NCOs taking the classes. As mentioned above, the main alternative to drill was games – and grant-aided schools lacked suitable recreational land.

The situation regarding physical training was very different in public schools. While grant-aided schools were attempting to move away from formal military drill by the 1920s, public schools retained their stress on games, supplemented by military drill, well into the century.[113] Indeed, physical training of the sort given in grant-aided elementary schools was regarded as 'the province of the sergeant or janitor' and was therefore accorded a much lower status than were games.[114] The slowness with which public schools adopted reformed Swedish drill was largely due to their failure to see any advantages in making the change. During the war, the War Office had promoted the use of boy instructors (trained under the various army commands or by army instructors) in public schools as well as in other schools. After the war, most headmasters were content to let this system continue. Military drill given by boy instructors was favoured on the grounds that it stimulated leadership skills and fostered a sense of responsibility amongst the boys. Moreover, it economized on instructors' wages.[115] Independent of any compulsory system of inspection, public schools retained military-style drill much longer than did grant-aided schools.

As we have already seen, in grant-aided schools, the attempts to separate physical training from military training was a feature of the years between 1919 and the early 1930s. From the 1930s, however, the physical training syllabus of the Board of Education and the War Office began moving closer together again.[116] The initiative came from the War Office which was anxious that 'pseudo-pacifism' had gone too far.[117] Its response to the de-militarization of physical training can be seen by looking at the Cadet Corps, whose fluctuating popularity (see below) illustrates the wider argument of this chapter concerning the vacillating fortunes of the male physique as moulded by military institutions.

The Cadet Corps had first received official recognition and financial support in 1908. During the war, this support was extended and the Corps was regarded as a valuable addition to military education. Between 1915 and 1919, the number of corps grew from 58 to 106.[118] The war was not only said to have increased their popularity, but also to be of invaluable use to aspiring officers.[119] After hostilities ended, however, the Corps came under increasing threat.[120] Teachers declared that they would rather see boys wearing cricket shirts and shorts than 'hideous khaki with its tragic associations'.[121] A typical incident occurred at a South Shields Education Committee meeting in May 1919 when a proposal to supply uniforms to the Cadet Corps was mooted. The meeting broke into disorder when Councillor Lawson pointed out that the British had 'been at war five years trying to destroy the same kind of training in Germany'. Alderman Dunlop agreed, declaring that although Prussian militarism had been destroyed, the military character of physical exercises in schools meant that they were 'simply making soldiers of the boys, and teaching them to kill'. Although two other members of the committee accused Lawson and Dunlop of exaggerating the seriousness of the militarist threat, the uniforms were never approved.[122] Corps were discontinued in many other schools all over England. At a conference attended by the old boys and staff of Wycliffe College in 1921, the college's Cadet Corps was dissolved on the grounds that the 'needs of education' were best served by scouting. Rather piously, W. A. Sibley summarized the consensus of the conference in the following words: 'we thought that the rigidity connected with the War Office control was not altogether in accord with our ideal of education, and not, perhaps, in accord with the League of Nations'.[123] A similar debate occurred at a meeting of the Litherland, Crosby, Formby and District Teachers' Association in 1926 when the King's Liverpool Regiment proposed establishing a cadet movement for boys aged between twelve and fourteen years. Despite a plea by one Mrs Lambert that military training should not be confused with militarism, and that cadet training provided valuable physical exercise and 'inculcated habits of obedience', the decision was swung by the ex-servicemen members of the association who reminded the other teachers that it was 'impossible to separate the ideas of military training and "militarism": the first naturally fused into the second'.[124] The vast majority of teachers voted against the proposal on the grounds that their duty was to teach boys to appreciate beauty, not to inculcate a 'warlike influence'.

Even more serious for the Corps, the War Office itself withdrew financial support in 1923.[125] This did not come as a complete shock as total army expenditure was being dramatically cut. In response, the cadets set out to convince the wider public that their camps were 'less military' than parents and teachers feared.[126] Rather, they argued, the real object of cadet work was training in citizenship: 'In a word, Cadet work brings about a greater sense of reality in School work, an increased measure of self-respect as the result of more effective discipline, and an increase in *esprit de corps* and sense of duty . . . Discipline, personal efficiency and a proper sense of patriotic feeling are not militarism.'[127] When the War Office threatened to withdraw *all* recognition from the Corps (which they did in October 1930), the cadets fought back more vigorously, led by the newly established British National Cadet Association which was presided over by the formidable Field-Marshal Lord Allenby. Once again, they attempted to distance their movement from any taint of war fever. At a meeting between the secretary of state for war and a deputation from the Corps in May 1930, Lieutenant-Colonel R. B. Wight (chairman of the Public Secondary Schools' Cadet Association) reiterated the claim that their movement was not militaristic: 'Discipline, the beauty of synchronized rhythmic movement, the appreciation of standing shouldertoshoulder [*sic*] with another fellow, pride in personal appearance, the duty owed to the group to which one belonged, the power of self-control and later the power of control of others and of leadership – these qualities . . . were well worth development.' Lieutenant-General Sir Hugh Jeud-wine (director general of the Territorial Army) supported him. He told the secretary of state for war that the training 'had not the slightest savour of militarism in it. What they taught was the value of unselfishness, endurance, sobriety, punctuality, obedience to auth-ority, cheerfulness under discomforts and reverses and the duty of keeping fit in body and mind.' Although he admitted that such training was valuable for an army, as it was certainly valuable for social reasons, he saw 'no militarism in that'. The force of his argument was weakened when he immediately added that boys who 'had a spice of the devil in them' needed 'something in the nature of a military savour'.[128] The rhetoric was less than convincing.

Gradually, however, the tide was turning. In 1931, a change of government meant that the Cadet Corps were once again given War Office approval and the military establishment again attempted to increase its influence within schools. At a meeting between Field-

Marshal Sir George H. Milne and the president of the Board of Education on 18 March 1932, concern was expressed about the condition of the national physique. Their fears had been heightened by the discovery that the physique of recruits from the élite establishments of Woolwich and Sandhurst was almost as poor as that of the recruits from the ranks. Milne claimed that rejection rates were so high that the War Office was being forced to review the maximum weight of baggage a soldier could be expected to carry. Although equally apprehensive about boys' physiques, the president of the Board of Education pointed out that the physical deterioration Milne had identified might not have been the fault of physical training in schools. Rather, deterioration could have taken place between leaving school at fourteen years of age and attempting to join the armed forces. Furthermore, the Board had no control over physical training in the public schools which supplied many of the officers for Woolwich and Sandhurst (and many of these public schools had spurned its recommendations).[129] The negotiations failed, so the War Office attempted to make its instructors of physical training more acceptable to schools by adopting, in 1935, the drill terminology of the Board of Education – not, as General P.H. Henderson indignantly reiterated, because they considered the board's system to be superior, but because they wanted to expand opportunities for ex-army instructors to enter the teaching profession.[130]

The real crisis rose to the surface from the mid-1930s with the prospect of another war looming up. Rearmament coincided with a debate over legislation to institute a more comprehensive system of physical training, which led to renewed accusations of militarism.[131] In May 1936, the War Office had sent the president of the Board of Education a proposal written by a retired lieutenant-colonel, R. J. Colson, in which he recommended establishing a Ministry for National Physical Training. Colson pointed out that although rearmament was taking place, the government had neglected to make adequate provision for preparing the male body for war. In his view, the majority of young men was feeble. Only one-quarter of men aged between fourteen and twenty-five years belonged to any of the existing voluntary movements in physical training and, of these, less than three per cent were 'really efficient' members. His proposed Ministry for National Physical Training was to be organized along military lines, with a central headquarters lording over county commanders, district commanders, officers and instructors. Not surprisingly, the proposal caused a flurry of anxiety within the Board of Education. Although not wholly unsympathetic, the Board could not endorse the establishment of a flagrantly militaristic new ministry. It shrank from the imagined response of the public to unadulterated military training being organized by a government department and declared that 'it ha[d] yet to be announced in this country that the object of physical fitness [was] to be a fit soldier'. The War Office was asked – politely – to stifle Colson since if his proposal were leaked to the press, it threatened to damn the Board of Education's entire physical training movement as militaristic.[132]

A compromise position was, however, reached. In January 1937, the government issued a white paper that proposed developing and extending facilities for physical activities. In June, the Physical Training and Recreation Act was passed, providing grants to local authorities.[133] While firmly disavowing any militarist aims, in 1938, the Board of Education launched the National Fitness Council. Within a year, it had provided grants worth nearly £1.5 million for swimming baths, clubs, recreation centres, youth hostels, playing fields and a host of other facilities for leisure.[134] Unfortunately, not everyone was persuaded by its denial of militarist motives. Were the council's activities the 'thin edge of the wedge of compulsion'? So high did public feeling run that when Sir Edward Grigg, chairman of the Somerset and Gloucester area committee, publicly declared himself in favour of the compulsory training of all young men, Lord Aberdare (chairman of the council) was forced to sack him on the grounds that he had pledged to keep militarism out of the fitness movement. Members of the General Council of the Trades Union Congress demanded reassurances from the National Fitness Council that they were not in any way linked to any military organization. The Trades Union Congress also wanted to ensure that the movement was not going to encourage 'mass habits and mass minds' at the expense of 'individual initiative and responsibility'. Sir Walter Citrine (general secretary of the Trades Union Congress) summarized the common feeling thus: 'anything approaching the militaristic bias of German physical training activities must be strongly resisted'.[135] The male body was to be prepared for war according to British traditions.

The Men's Movement

So far in this chapter we have reviewed shifts in the involvement of military institutions in systems of moulding the young male body, and in the rhetoric of patriotism surrounding these debates. Much of the conflict between German, Swedish and British exercises focused on the tension between collectivist as against individualist (or competitive) approaches to discipline the male body. The more communal approach of officials in the Board of Education earned them the most intense condemnation from a group of male teachers who contrasted what they regarded as feminine collectivism with masculine individualism. In this next section, these debates will be looked at more closely, especially in the light of what they reveal about the way the war was regarded as threatening rigid distinctions between masculine and feminine physiques.

As shown in the introduction, while there has been very little analysis of the impact of war on the construction of masculinity, its impact on women has been well researched. Although historians are divided about the extent to which the war led to any change in the status of women, it is clear that most people in the 1920s *believed* that the war had dramatically altered the relationship between the sexes. In the context of the male body, certain groups of men declared that the wartime economy had resulted in the supremacy of women over men. This belief was expressed particularly pugnaciously when physical training classes in schools were mentioned. Thus, it was asserted, the war had increased the power of female teachers in schools and within the Board of Education, consequently undermining manliness and, in particular, those aspects that were expressed through the male physique. The demilitarization of physical education and the substitution of gentler revised-Swedish exercises for the harsher German or British drill made certain groups of men fear that the male body was becoming feminized.[136] It was this threat that enabled Walter M. Gallichan to protest – in the middle of the war – that men were 'approaching a new type in which some of the feminine qualities are conspicuous'.[137] The effete boy portrayed in the *London Schoolmaster* in 1935 (illus. 51) was the product of a predominantly female teaching profession.

The male teachers referred to above decided to wage war on those factors they believed were feminizing the male body. The battle was directed by the National Association of Schoolmasters (NAS) or, as it styled itself, the 'men's movement', and was guided by ex-servicemen and instructors of physical training.[138] Its journal was to brag,

When men wavered, the sports-master came to the fore, the real men, those who had done big things in the war . . . Where sports-masters led, the victory is assured. Sport-masters are the real live men, men who know boy-nature, men who mix with men of other walks of life. They are the men who count. They are the greatest recruiters . . . Man-consciousness is essentially masculine: it touches the man: it is a reflex of manliness: it draws men to men: it means that *a man needs a man's union.*[139]

One sports-master put the case more racily: 'Sugar and birdseed is all

51 'Do you learn football?' 'No', cartoon from *London Schoolmaster*, vol. 13 no. 114, March 1935. ('Do you learn Football: No/Do you learn Boxing: No/Do you learn Cricket: No/Who's your Teacher: Miss Fanny Adams').

very well in a bird cage, but since injustice has opened the door of liberty, I prefer being an eagle to being a coddled canary.'[140] Another sports-master wrote, 'as in the old Army days, men like joining up with men, A Man's Union is a popular idea'.[141]

Although wartime experiences were regarded by the NAS as directly responsible for the need for a men's movement,[142] rumbles of this campaign could be heard before the war when a group of self-styled 'wild men' in Wales pitted themselves against the 'wild women' of the National Union of Teachers (NUT). In December 1913, these men organized themselves into the Cardiff Schoolmasters' Association. At this stage, however, the main issue was equal pay. The war heightened tensions (particularly when female teachers in the NUT began demanding to be given an equal share in the wartime additions to salaries granted by the London Education Authority), and added another item to their agenda, safeguarding the male physique.[143] Schoolmasters finally exploded at the annual conference of the NUT at Cheltenham in Easter 1919 when the plebiscite on equal pay revealed that 35,000 teachers had voted for equal pay, compared with 15,000 against. At a mass meeting on 31 May 1919, W. H. Thodag reminded his listeners that if women were given equal pay, they would 'become men's social superior: they would become goddesses and sit on Olympus'. If this happened, he 'did not know where the men would be'.[144] Alarm spread amongst male teachers and within a year the Cardiff group had merged with the Ex-Service Men's Teachers' Association and other disgruntled teachers to establish the NAS. Since their initial attempts to act as a pressure group within the NUT failed, by 1922 they had seceded from the union.[145] Although this action resulted in a drop in their membership from 72 per cent of all male teachers employed by the Local Education Committee to 51 per cent, by the end of the 1920s, the proportion had risen to 65 per cent.[146] In some areas – most notably in Liverpool – up to 95 per cent of male teachers were members.[147] According to these teachers, they were fighting the most menacing challenge to the virility of the nation.

It was no coincidence that their protest was provoked by what they considered to be a major threat to the male body. The scandal they identified was typical of the employment economy in war: in their view, women were sauntering into schools and taking control of the physical training of boys. Worse, female inspectors began scrutinizing the competence of ex-army drill instructors. How had women managed to insinuate themselves into positions of influence within boys' schools? For many men, the answer was obvious: women had abused the crisis of war. The schoolmaster had, in effect, been replaced by the schoolmistress. The schoolmasters' own evidence does not confirm this view. According to NAS statistics, the major shift had occurred before the turn of the century, not during the war. Prior to the 1870s, less than half of all teachers were women while, by the turn of the century, the proportion had risen to 70 per cent. However, the war had seen further increases in the proportion of female teachers. Immediately after it, the proportion of female teachers rose to 78 per cent and did not subsequently drop below 72 per cent.[148] Thus, in primary schools in the 1920s, only half of boys' classes were taught by men, and only one-twelfth of mixed classes.[149]

The Board of Education advised the women organizers of physical training to be tactful and begged the male instructors to acknowledge that there had been a 'great advance in scientific methods of physical training for children in recent years, and that they [could] learn a good deal about the new technique from a person specially qualified in the subject, even though that person [was] a woman'.[150] However, male indignation was shrill. Was this how their sacrifices in war were going to be repaid? As they described it, 'The REWARD OF PATRIOTISM. 20,000 Schoolmasters went to war. 1,800 Schoolmasters perished for England.'[151] They demanded the substitution of male instructors, claiming that the idea of female inspectors of physical training was 'repugnant', 'undignified', and an 'insult to common sense', especially since most male instructors hailed from the army.[152] Male teachers began refusing to allow female organizers to inspect their classes in physical education.[153] There was an outcry when Harold A. Lomas of Fareham Senior Boys' School in Hampshire was dismissed for refusing to parade his class before a female inspector. As a former member of the Royal Navy and a boxing champion, he argued that the proposed inspection went well beyond the realms of propriety.[154] Physical training involving discussing 'intimate matters' with boys – an inappropriate task for a woman.[155] It was quipped that a woman who could 'manage boys as well as any man' might be an 'admirable proprietress of a Wild West Saloon' but she should be kept out of British schools.[156] Physical training courses for schoolmistresses were not merely 'an antidote to the team spirit': they were the regimen to 'the tame spirit'.[157] Physical fitness was the 'foundation of character', but the predominance of female physical instructors robbed male teachers of their duty to develop 'qualities of manliness and sturdiness' in their young charges.[158] Truly, these schoolmasters asserted, it was an 'insult' for boys over the age of seven years to be taught by women.[159]

This was a war in which male teachers could not gain immediate victory. There were simply too few male inspectors of physical training. The central training institution for Swedish drill was the Ling Association which for a long time contained not one male member, not because men had been excluded but because, as the secretary of the association explained, 'they had had no applications from men teachers who were eligible'.[160] In 1916, of the 650 teachers of physical training, only 200 were men.[161] The Board of Education found it very difficult to entice men to their training camps and schools.[162] It was not until the mid-1930s that the imbalance of the sexes in physical training had been lessened, enabling the Physical Education Committee of the Board of Education to decree (partly in order to maintain 'good relations amongst teachers') that boys should be drilled only by male teachers, whenever possible.[163]

The NAS belonged to those minority movements examined in the last chapter that were attempting to induce comradeship between men in the post-war period. They could win widespread support only because the threat to their masculinity (in their view, a direct result of the war) was easy to identify. These men belonged to what they considered to be the 'war generation' and they regarded themselves physically and psychologically superior to the younger cohort of boys who had come under the 'dominant feminine influence'.[164] By the 1930s, the increase in crime among men aged between twenty and thirty years had come to be seen by these men as proof of the lamentable effect of boys being taught by women. According to Vernon Blunt in 1933, 'It [was] easier to smash a window, steal valuables, and drive off in a borrowed car, than to discipline oneself to work even though the wages be low.' Furthermore, because men in their forties and fifties had been educated by other men (and had been in the armed forces), they did not 'succumb to the temptation'.[165] Miss Cowdray, headmistress of the girls' school at Crouch End in north London, and an active supporter of the aims of the NAS, agreed. She argued that by 'barging' into boys' schools women teachers had 'helped to fill our prisons and keep our police busy'.[166] America was frequently cited as evidence of the dangers of this alleged matriarchal supremacy. By allowing women to teach boys, Britain was laying itself open to the 'gangsterdam' that had emerged out of America's 'gynaecocracy'.[167]

The schoolmasters did acknowledge, however, that not all men responded to their alleged emasculation with undisciplined behaviour. Indeed, quite the opposite: the greatest threat posed by the feminization of boys' physical training was that the male body would become domesticated.[168] In a pamphlet published by the NAS in 1927, Miss Marjorie Bowen argued that the average boy began,

with his first realization of his personality, to resent the feminine domination of nurse or mother; his greatest passion is to assert himself and escape the woman, whom he instinctively despises for lack of what he most admires – physical strength, an adventurous spirit, fearlessness, technical skill in machinery etc. – and for qualities which he detests – fussiness, gossiping, emotionalism, exaggeration, vanity and general pettiness, and frequently in the case of inferior and incompetent servants or nurses, deceit and injustice.[169]

This instinctive rejection of the feminine had, such people maintained, a physiological basis. The biologist and anti-feminist publicist Walter Heape in *Preparation for Marriage* (1914) provided pseudo-scientific confirmation. In Heape's view, all living beings survived 'by virtue of their ability to function' and the world consisted of two sexes with very distinctive roles. Crucially, men were expenders of energy: women conservers.[170] This functionalism was embraced by the schoolmasters. According to the London Schoolmasters' Association, debates about the relative strength of 'brain power' between men and women were unimportant. What mattered was that the minds of the two sexes were *different in kind* because they were governed by 'entirely different impulses inherent to sex'. The brain and nervous system were intimately associated with every other system of organs and, as the structure and function of these organs differed in men and women, so the nervous system and brain differed. One part of this argument has been referred to above: namely that since physical needs had an immediate and direct impact on the brain, the distinctive physical needs of women and men moulded their brains in different ways. In other words, since men expanded energy and women conserved it, there was a corresponding differentiation in the brain and in the whole nervous organization.

The other part of the biological theory of the London Schoolmasters' Association drew from the New Psychology of such sexologists as Havelock Ellis. According to the association, despite significant differentiation by function, both sexes shared some characteristics of the opposite sex. For instance, men contained predominantly male qualities with subordinate female qualities. If men were to function 'as they [were] intended', the masculine qualities needed to be nurtured. If they were exposed to an 'excessive' amount of feminine influence, they ran the risk of developing their subordinate qualities, resulting in the much feared figure of 'the effeminate man'.[171] In 1932, Meyrick Booth linked this idea explicitly with the New Psychology. In his view, it was irrefutable that 'the evolution of a stable [male] personality' involved 'freedom from undue maternal fixations'. If a boy's teacher were female, he ran the risk of being 'unconsciously led to react to her on an infantile emotional plane'.[172] Booth was anxious to stress to his readers that these ideas were not unique to the New Psychology. He reminded them of the anti-Freudian Dr Friedrich Wilhelm Foerster who had argued that 'nothing but the prevalence of a mechanical and unpsychological life-outlook' could possibly have accounted for the idea that women could, or should, be placed in authority over boys. He further stressed, 'Discipline, mental and moral, and indeed the whole course of character-building, is bound up with specifically masculine psychic forces.' Thus, in his view, it was a 'pure absurdity' to entertain the idea of interchangeability between the sexes in the teaching profession.[173] As one member of the NAS simplified the debate, 'an individual man might be less clever, less able to pass examinations, [might] even have less capacity for teaching than an individual woman, but nature ha[d] made him a man and a boy [was] a man in the making'.[174] Allowing boys to be taught by women condemned them to a life of 'maladjustment'.[175] It was by such arguments that male teachers justified excluding women from influence over the construction of boys' bodies.

Great Masculine Renunciation

This chapter has been concerned with examining attempts by the state, armed forces and the teaching profession to mould the male body through physical exercises. Wartime experiences have been portrayed as an important factor in the debates, particularly due to the way they increased the state's imperative to control and discipline the male body, and in the way the wartime employment market was believed to have feminized the young male body by empowering female teachers. The misogynist rhetoric of wartime masculinity (as expressed by the schoolmasters) was, however, only one response to the changing disciplines of masculinity. There was an alternative reaction, one that stressed the need of men to *embrace* certain aspects of war-induced feminism and thus free the male body from oppressive military and cultural regimes. For these commentators, men were not merely physical bodies performing their allotted civic and military functions efficiently. They were also men possessing aesthetic qualities and derisive of that 'remarkable repression of Narcissism' that had resulted in surrendering to women the sole claim to 'beauty and magnificence'.[176] In the last chapter, we looked at a number of fraternities dedicated to inspiring in young boys a consciousness of the unique and marvellous beauty of the male body.[177] Adult men had been exposed to similar sorts of disciplines during the war. These official attempts to improve the male physique encouraged men to rely on the conclusions of external examiners (such as medical orderlies and professional physical trainers). After the war, a number of groups was established for adult men that stressed the need for men to trust their own judgements, rejecting state and military disciplines.

In the context of this chapter, the most interesting of these groups was the Men's Dress Reform Party (MDRP),[178] which had grown out of a clothing sub-committee of the New Health Society, a creation of Sir Arbuthnot Lane. In 1929, this sub-committee consisted of William Ralph Inge, Alfred C. Jordan, Guy Kendall, Caleb Williams Saleeby, Richard Sickert, Ernest Thesiger and Leonard Williams. It was Lane's pupils (Jordan and Saleeby) who wrote the report that eventually led to the establishment of the MDRP. In their report, sartorial alternatives were set out. Instead of the starched collar, they promoted the Byron collar worn with a tie loosely knotted. Blouses were preferable to shirts and coats were only to be worn in the cold. Conventional trousers were condemned outright. Although they approved of the kilt, they decreed that modern industrial conditions made shorts the most practical type of clothing. Underclothing was to be loose. Hats should only be worn as protection against the rain or sun and sandals should replace shoes.[179] Most importantly, they called for the exercise of greater individuality in men's clothing.[180]

The war cannot be said to have directly led to the establishment of this organization. For one thing, it was founded ten years after the end of the hostilities. Furthermore, its members argued that it had not been the war that had heralded in a heinous modern age: this had happened more than a century earlier. Thus, John Carl Flugel, a psychologist from University College, London, contended that it was at the end of the eighteenth century that men had given up 'their right to all the brighter, gayer, more elaborate, and more varied forms of ornamentation, leaving these entirely to the use of women, and thereby making their own tailoring the more austere and ascetic of the arts'. He described this event as 'The Great Masculine Renunciation', or the occasion when men 'abandoned their claim to be considered beautiful. [They] henceforth aimed at being only useful.'[181]

However, the popularity of dress reform for men was an outcome of tensions harboured between 1914 and 1918. The MDRP was responding to four things, three of which it linked to men's experiences of warfare. Firstly, middle-class men were oppressed by the disciplines imposed by capitalist labour. Every night, they returned from work feeling 'hot, uncomfortable, tired and bad-tempered': the 'rather sad colours' they were forced to wear had a depressing effect.[182] Secondly, they were fettered by military-style uniformity in dress. Military uniforms were everywhere: in the street, tramcar, theatre, church, railway station.[183] Men had to be taught to be mortified rather than proud to find other men wearing identical clothes.[184] Furthermore, uniforms obliterated differences in class between the majority of men who remained in the lower ranks of the armed forces: as Michael MacDonagh recorded in his diary for 31 December 1914, when soldiers were seen in the streets it was impossible to tell from their appearances 'whether they [had] come from country houses and parsonages, or from labourers' cottages and artisan dwellings'.[185] This wartime equality needed to be eradicated. Thirdly, war-induced labour shortages and the need for the state to consult with working-class men during the crisis were regarded as having resulted in the rise of the working-classes: and this was oppressive to professional men. When Dean Inge sourly observed that it was the democratic forces of the French Revolution that had brought to an end the picturesqueness of men's attire – because gentlemen 'hoped to escape the guillotine by looking as bourgeois as possible' – he was really alluding to his fear that the time was coming when 'the unfortunate capitalist, reduced to burying his bond notes instead of investing, [might] find it expedient to try to pass for a trade unionist'.[186]

Finally, the female sex had risen supreme during the war. Just as men had become 'mere accessories' to women, so too men's clothing had become simply a foil to women's clothing.[187] Men needed to

52 James Thurber, 'I am
swift, I am beautiful, I am
naked', cartoon, from
Elizabeth Hawes, *Men Can
Take It*, New York, 1939.

"I am swift, I am beautiful, I am naked."

become 'as beautiful as women'.[188] Like the schoolmasters' associations, male liberation was their catch-cry: it was time to do away with
all symbols of masculine frustration.[189] To do this, they agreed on the
need to take inspiration from feminism. As the 'Lad o' London' noted
in 1928, 'Dress reform for men is long overdue and the chances are
small, unless we start with the boys and inspire them, as the girls have
been inspired in the past few years, with a fondness for light, loose
clothing which gives access to the air and freedom to the limbs.'[190]
Men's dress expressed imprisonment: women's expressed emanci-
pation.[191] Elizabeth Hawes commented on it in her book entitled *Men
Can Take It* (see illus. 52): men were oppressed by their clothing while
women had freedom of movement. Only by recovering male artistry
could men regain power and find happiness. It required men to actively
protest against their clothing (as in illus. 53, taken from *Punch* in 1924),
and stand defiantly against the horror and anger of women and dogs.
All symbols of men's inferiority to women were to be tackled. Hats, for
example, needed to be thrown away (or remodelled) so as not to cause
baldness.[192] The physical deformity caused by over-tight clothing had
to be eradicated.[193] Middle-aged men should never again faint because
of over-tight belts, stays and laces.[194] The practice of strangling young
boys with collars – causing them to talk 'like [. . .] adenoid[s]' and
appear 'like [. . .] tabloids' – had to be done away with.[195] In this way, a
new generation of men would rise from the ashes of war: élitist rather

MANNERS AND MODES.
A MASCULINE PROTEST.

53 'Manners and Modes: a masculine protest', cartoon from *Punch*, 8 October 1924.

than democratic; masculine, without any taint of femininity; beautiful, not deformed; regenerative, not destructive.

Although their primary purpose was the aesthetics of middle-age, there was an additional reason men needed to reform their dress: men's clothing was causing their health to degenerate. In this, the post-war dress reformers agreed with their predecessors, but they were divided over what promoted physical well-being. Sartorially, pre-war commentators had stressed the relationship between warmth and health.[196] Like animals, men had to be completely covered. Wool was favoured because it was the slowest conductor of heat and therefore was best at keeping the temperature of the body constant.[197] A well-dressed man should wear a flannel vest and drawers next to his skin, an upper shirt, as well as a complete suit of clothes. Thus, for male dress reformers in the 1890s, the chief flaws in men's dress included the fact that the waistcoat opened to show the shirt ('exposes the chest and throat unduly') and the way the coat opened behind ('permits the loin, when we sit, to be entirely without protection from the coat, which may explain the frequent occurrence of lumbago amongst men').[198] After the war, the emphasis changed. Post-war reformers complained that men were literally smothered in clothes: 'we swathe our bodies in unhygienic woollens so that the pores of the skin shall be clogged with minute fibres and thus rendered incapable of performing their proper duties as vomitories of impurities'.[199] The curative function of air and sunlight was considered axiomatic. The impetus for this ideology had been developing from the end of the nineteenth century. Smoke abatement committees had been established from the early 1880s, but achieved their greatest success in 1926 with the passing of the Public Health (Smoke Abatement) Act. Two years previously, the Sunlight League had been founded with the famous eugenist and leading male dress reformer Caleb Williams Saleeby as chairman. The invisible was important: it stained 'the surfaces and the depths' of men.[200] Public health authorities were exhorted to provide clinics for artificial sunlight treatment and local authorities were urged to build schools and houses that faced the sun.[201] Open-air swimming pools and sunbathing centres were established. It was the role of reformers to 'restore the sun's rays to town populations' by removing smoke, fumes and grit which emanated from house, mill and factory chimneys, as well as from trains.[202] The alderman David Adams wrote in 1932, 'To-day . . . we are returning to that most ancient of faiths, the worship of the Sun, in the ceremonial interblending his vital rays with our repetitive bodily framework.'[203] Or, as the nudist Harold Vincent blasphemed, 'God and the sun are identical.'[204]

Men's dress reform was regarded as crucial for physical well-being. Although, as we shall see, these arguments focused largely on the health and efficiency of middle-aged, middle-class men, the dress reformers bolstered their arguments with a rhetoric drawn from the well-established child welfare movement. Lack of sunlight and fresh air were held to be responsible for high levels of infant mortality.[205] They went further, arguing that exposure to sunlight would cure a wide range of illnesses, particularly rickets and tuberculosis.[206] If Britain was to compete with other nations, the problem of 'sun-starved' children needed to be overcome.[207] Sunlight treatment would prevent slum children from 'filling our hospitals and institutions', enabling them to 'play their part in the battle of life'.[208] The importance of fresh air for children was unquestioned.[209]

However, the chief concern of the dress reformers was with middle-aged men. The lack of sunshine was seen as being responsible for the sluggishness of sedentary workers. Men travelling in the London Underground were liable to suffer from 'tube-airculosis'.[210] Heavy winter clothing caused ill-health.[211] Men's bodies were tormented with rheumatism due to inefficient skin respiration through tight clothing.[212] Collars restricted circulation of blood to the brain and stunted its development.[213] Sunlight prevented disease by building up the body's resistance and restoring the health of the weak.[214] According to Saleeby, dress reform would offer 'a larger surface of skin for the life-giving action of the ultra-violet rays of sunlight, the most precious medicinal and hygienic agents in the world'.[215] Since darkness reduced work efficiency and increased the incidence of drunkenness, greater industrial efficiency clearly lay in exposing the body to the healthful rays of the sun.[216] Similarly, in 1928, Herbert N. Casson declared that men's clothing was partially responsible for the high rates of illness amongst working men. He reminded readers that in 1927 Great Britain lost 90 million working days through illness – that is, twelve times more working days were lost through illness than were lost through strikes.[217] This inefficiency of Britain's workers needed to be tackled if Britain were to compete with other nations. Casson further noted,

semi-naked races have no knowledge of science nor hygiene. They live in the midst of smells. They drink foul water. They know nothing of germs. But they live fairly long and are amazingly strong and healthy. Why? Because they have a *plus* which we lack. They have the Ultra-Violet rays on the skin of the whole body . . . The fact is that the bleached clothes-wrapped races are physically weaker than the natural-colour races. The dockers of London cannot compare, for strength and endurance, with the coolies of China and the natives of Africa. The law of compensation has made us pay dearly for our comfort and inventions.[218]

Sunbathing would regenerate the 'white' race.[219]

Leisured Bodies

These radical attempts to reform male states of dress and undress failed to win widespread support. By 1937, the New Health Society (which had provided accommodation, secretarial support and encouragement for the dress reformers) had been declared bankrupt, and nothing more was heard of them. The reasons for their failure to gain mass support are not difficult to understand. Members were often regarded as part of the looney fringe: photographs such as that published in the *Tailor and Cutter* (illus. 54) could only bring the movement into disrepute. Few men would be persuaded by 'H.S.L.' in *New Health* (1927) when he advocated that all English boys should wear the kilt, with the Highland bonnet, dirk, sporran and bright hose, on the grounds that it was the most hygienic and healthiest garment, in addition to being 'easily the most becoming of all boys' wear'.[220] For many, the clothes worn by the dress reformers themselves displayed extraordinarily bad taste: costumes resembling those worn by Lord Fauntleroy or monks could not command wide appeal. In the words of

54 The Men's Dress Reformers, photograph from *Tailor and Cutter*, 10 July 1931.

a former president of the Association of London Master Tailors, the clothes worn by male dress reformers were 'more suitable for Lotus-land than England'.[221] Even the editor of *New Health* – a journal that supported male dress reform – warned that the proposed designs showed a 'certain Puritanical austerity' and suggested that dress reformers try to 'coax rather than attempt to stampede' men into better ways.[222]

These aesthetic considerations seriously hampered the dress reformers. Even their advocacy of shorts met with ambivalence, if not outright hostility. Exposing the masculine leg was a source of anxiety for many men.[223] Thomas Macmillan 'hankered' after joining a Highland regiment with his friends, but could not do so because of the kilt: 'I had always enjoyed the manly game of football; but while it kept me fit, too large doses had left me with a pair of legs which, when honestly surveyed, limited my choice of regiment to one which did not wear the kilt. Being a true Highlander I resolved that since I could not grace the kilt I would not bring any disgrace upon it.'[224] Very few men could be said to 'have a leg'. The average man – with his 'bulbous, spindly, disproportionate, abnormal imperfect leg' – preferred conventionally styled trousers.[225] Equally, men's chests and bellies often did not merit display: they were 'discoloured and definitely ugly'.[226] For men without specially fashioned pectorals, partial nudity was to be avoided: even imagining men without collars and trousers was said to be 'horrible'.[227] Fleshly exposure was a breach of 'good taste': the sight of men sunbathing in Stratford-on-Avon was described as 'a horrid thing, and offend[ed] the aesthetic instincts . . . The human forms thus partially clothed were red, puce-purple, hairy, perspiring; they bulged in the wrong places, they were knock-kneed. They weren't indecent at all – just ugly.'[228] Only one man in ten was said to have a 'really pleasing figure'.[229] If the middle-aged man came into criticism, elderly men did so even more.[230] Clothes were necessary to hide 'defects', reducing everyone 'to a decent insignificance of physique'.[231] It was bad enough seeing men walking down Regent Street in the wrong clothes, without stripping them of clothes altogether.[232] Clothes were required to improve imaginings of the male body.[233]

Aesthetics were not the only considerations. Opponents of dress reform drew a connection between conventional male clothing and morality. For instance, in 1929, when dress reformers began attacking the uniforms of public schools (particularly of Eton), they were reminded of the 'natural conclusion' of their tinkering with tradition: 'The iconoclast who shatters the laws and customs of a Public School will make it easier for those who aim at national disruption and the destruction of the constitution.'[234] Dress reform in the army threatened the maintenance of discipline.[235] An extended discussion of this subject its to be found in an article published in the *Tailor and Cutter* on Christmas Day 1931, where the anonymous author contends that modern dress depended on 'restraint, on such articles of discipline and control as buttons, studs, and braces'. Such restraints were not noxious: they were the foundation upon which civilization rested and they protected men from savagery and decadence. The writer continued, 'A loosening of the bonds will gradually impel mankind to sag and droop bodily and spiritually. If laces are unfastened, ties loosened, and buttons banished, the whole structure of modern dress will come undone; it is not so wild as it sounds to say that society will also fall to pieces.' Efficiency in business depended on the civilizing effect of repressive clothing.[236] Or, as another writer put it, traditional men's clothing was important in 'keeping the social fabric together'.[237] The slow evolution of changes in men's dress ensured 'safety': sartorial conservatism checked social anarchy.[238]

It was recognized that male dignity rested on the clothes covering his body. Proposals to adopt the open-neck collar for the service dress in the army were rejected as unsoldierly, potentially making British officers the 'laughing stock of the French'.[239] The editor of the *Tailor and Cutter* reminded the dress reformers that 'the majesty of office [was] upheld by suitable attire . . . Take away or cut down trousers and some of the sobriety and importance of business men vanishe[d].' Truly, clothes were more than coverings or decorations: they were symbols. British men were to be manly and not turned into boy scouts or schoolboys.[240] Another accusation thrown at the male dress reformers was that they were 'effeminate' or 'perverted youths' who were avoiding their masculinity.[241] Thus, on Midsummer Night in 1932, D. Anthony Bradley spoke at a debate entitled 'Shall Man be Redressed?' His statement was unequivocal: 'The man who, alone in the jungle, changes into his dinner jacket does so to convince himself that he is not a savage – soft sloppy clothes are symbolic of a soft and sloppy race.' In his view, it did not matter what 'health cranks, exhibitionists or men of misplaced sex wore' but, '*man* – sturdy and virile man, capable of withstanding the rigours of a stiff shirt', had to maintain conservative standards of dress.[242]

As these comments would suggest, the dress reformers were competing with strong vested interests in the community, particularly the retail trade. Reformers attempted to allay the trade's suspicions by suggesting that the lighter materials and brighter colours of the proposed new men's clothing would necessitate more frequent changes of clothes. After all, they reasoned, a woman's dress bill far exceeded a man's.[243] Despite these reassurances, opposition was fierce. For one thing, it was pointed out that by reducing the amount of clothes worn thousands of people would be thrown out of employment.[244] In 1929, the National Federation of Merchant Tailors at their annual conference deplored the way dress reformers touted outside tailors' shops and demanded that the police and local authorities prohibited the practice. They also urged young ambitious men 'to be particular and precise in the matter of suitable dress on all occasions' and to take the advice of their tailors.[245]

The general failure of the movement to reform and loosen the rules applying to men's clothing should not be exaggerated. In one area it was successful: rules concerning the clothing of the leisured man were relaxed. This had started well before the war. By the late 1890s, lounge suits and even sports jackets could be seen in the dress circle at the theatre. In 1900 for the first time men arrived at the Goodwood Races dressed in flannel suits, navy blue blazers and white duck trousers with straw boaters.[246] The wearing of stays to improve the male figure had ceased in the first decade of the twentieth century.[247] Male dress etiquette was further relaxed by the scouting organizations' legitimation of shorts, at least for boys aged up to twelve.

The wartime economy speeded up this process. The difficulty of obtaining starch during the war encouraged the move to soft-collared shirts for both boys and men. For professional and white-collar workers, donning the khaki or blue uniform meant doing away with the collar and tie.[248] In some regions of the war, particularly Mesopotamia, adult men discovered the benefits of cutting down their trousers into shorts.[249] Even in France, at least one division actually wore shorts, which of course were advantageous in summer because they reduced louse-breeding areas, despite being unpleasant during mustard gas attacks (as A. Jack Abraham complained, 'scorched private parts can be very uncomfortable').[250] Many men took their wartime sartorial experiences back home with them.

With increased family-orientated leisure, especially at the beach and other resorts, a greater differentiation was made between men's casual and formal clothing. The popularization of beach resorts, coupled with the widening access to the seaside, increasingly legitimated semi-clothed sunbathing. The 'frowsy drabness and nit-wit regulations of the English holiday resort' were slowly being eradicated.[251] A case was easily made for men's dress reform in sport.[252] After the war, men's bathing costumes became shorter – stopping at the top of the thigh – and sleeveless with a round neck.[253] By the 1930s, the MDRP had convinced thirty-eight seaside resorts to allow men to wear only a bathing slip for mixed bathing.[254] The popularity of swimming increased as the provision of swimming pools was actively promoted by the Board of Education, Ministry of Health and local authorities.[255]

Men's clothes were increasingly made of lighter materials,[256] and the tanned body came into its own. In 1916, the senior medical officer for the Education Committee in the city of Nottingham marvelled at the appearance of soldiers on leave from 'Lord Kitchener's Open-Air School': he could 'hardly recognize [the] bronzed stalwart young fellow[s]'.[257] Men came back from the war proud of their bodies, tanned 'as . . . musty pea[s]'.[258] Indeed, the untanned body came to be regarded as unnatural.[259] Sunbathing centres for children were opened on the grounds that the brown baby was the healthy baby.[260] Areas of parks were allotted to sunbathing.[261] No longer did the white body indicate leisurely status: instead, the tanned body did so. Holiday-makers anxiously attempted to obtain this 'desirable insignia'.[262] To help, the vice-president of the Sunlight League, Sir

Leonard Hill, invented an apparatus to measure sunlight, and *The Times* published the results daily.[263] The tanned man was scarcely 'nude'.

The debates concerning functions and aesthetics of the male body in its various stages of dress and undress were not, as this chapter has attempted to show, restricted to the area of the military requirements. Although the immense manpower exigencies of the war led to a hitherto unsurpassed level of inspection, aesthetic pride had become an additional incentive for improving the male physique. It was therefore widely maintained that without physical training, 'the naked body of a modern grown man [was] not beautiful'.[264] The body was raw material that required sculpting. The ideal of the handsome male body expressed a reconstruction of manliness and a reassertion of masculinity over femininity. Before the war, the assertion tended to take the form of competition over the *healthy* body; after the war, competition became increasingly concerned with aesthetics and included a repudiation of the mutilations of wartime. Thus, the shape and texture of the male body was not simply emblematic of functional considerations: it could be suggestive of both power and attraction. Debates over the military purpose of the body focused more on whether masculine power should be explicit or latent. Militarist physical instructors and their pupils stressed the explicit superiority of muscular development: men more wary of accusations of bellicosity opted for the latent control of toning. But what was common to both groups was a view of the male body as an instrument of authority and status. They both strove to discipline the body in preparation for death.

Five Re-Membering

The most terrible words in all writing used to be 'There they crucified Him', but there is a sadder sentence now – 'I know not where they have laid Him' . . . Surely 'missing' is the cruelest word in the language. (Anonymous, *To My Unknown Warrior*, 1920.)[1]

The male body: dismembered on the battlefields, re-membered in peacetime. This chapter examines the corpse and the evocation of dead men in civic and religious rites. Death was not entirely in the hands of the Creator: it had many stage-managers. The aesthetics of the dead male body concerned people as much as the aesthetics of the living body. Acceptable levels of death and appropriate responses were negotiated between the state, various interest groups (such as the medical profession and funeral directors) and the bereaved. The First World War was to dramatically rearrange the theatre of death. Although there was nothing new in anonymous and unseemly endings, such degradation became ubiquitous in the carnage of this war. The war stimulated concern with the sanitizing of death, encouraging the spread of new hygienic procedures and popularizing the metaphor of purification, and so avoiding the fact of putrefaction. As before, the dead were not left to 'rest in peace'.

The urge to sanitize death extended to the male body when absent. This process will be illustrated by examining two of the most revered bodies in Britain: they were both male, both heroic and both lost. The first absent corpse belonged to the Unknown Warrior. Mourned by hundreds of thousands of bereaved parents, siblings, friends and lovers, the body of an unidentified serviceman was buried amidst ceremony at Westminster Abbey on 11 November 1920. For the mourners, this body evoked the unique features of those they had lost. The second absent corpse belonged to Horatio Herbert Kitchener who was drowned off the Orkney coast on 5 June 1916. His body was reconstructed in myth and in spirit, but never in the flesh. Then, in 1926, Kitchener's body was said to have been retrieved and to be awaiting the final sacrament in Westminster Abbey. These claims were later exposed to be part of an elaborate hoax. The debates in 1920 and 1926 surrounding the retrieval and 'laying to rest' of these two heroic corpses displayed a functional similarity: in both cases, men and women yearned to revitalize a decomposed male hero who was thought capable of soothing personal pain and stilling civic strife. A major shift had occurred between 1920 and 1926, however. In 1920, the search had been for a hero without worldly distinction; in 1926, it was for a figure of authority.

Withered Laurels

To whom did a body belong? Contending claims of ownership extended past death. As shall be seen in this section, there were a number of competitors for possession. Conventionally, family members claimed priority: burial insurance was intended to safeguard their interests; the correct appearance of the deceased reflected on their respectability; and they were the people who mediated between the dead body, the community and civic and religious officials.[2] For those deemed to be without family, the state had a particular interest. Under the Anatomy Act of 1832, the state legislated in the interests of anatomists to enable them to claim the bodies of homeless paupers for dissection. The war shifted the debates about access to the dead body – this time, however, predominantly *male* dead bodies. At a time when ownership of the body was related to access to a private domestic space within which to die, the removal of vast numbers of men away from the hearth was ominous. Family and friends struggled with the War Office for the bones of their loved ones. If we are to believe the pronouncements of spiritualist mediums, even dead servicemen returned to the physical world to insist on their continuing rights over their discarded flesh. However, during the war, the claims of military authorities over the bodies of men prevailed. Even after the cessation of hostilities, the War Office retained significant powers over the corpses of dead ex-servicemen and bereaved civilians were forced to seek new ways to lay their dead to rest.

During the war desperate manpower shortages meant that men's bodies became more unequivocally the property of the state. Conscription took away men's right to refuse to transfer ownership of their bodies to an institution in which the risk of being slaughtered was immeasurably increased. Furthermore, it promised them the ugliest death possible, and an equally unseemly burial. Despite censorship regulations, photographs of dead soldiers were widely circulated (see illus. 55). Of course, military rank (and its associations with social class)

55 Dead men on the battlefield at Guillemont Farm, September 1916. [IWM E (AUS) 4944)

mattered. Thus, Colonel James Lochhead Jack would have his boots and buttons polished before battle, explaining that a man should 'always die like a gentleman – clean and properly dressed'.[3] Rank and file servicemen had no such option. The bloodless deaths of young heroes in popular art (see illus. 56) mocked them. In 1917, the chaplain Geoffrey Gordon bitterly wrote,

You remember the picture of the Great Sacrifice, which at one time was to be seen in every shop window. A Young lad lies on the ground. A tiny bullet hole shows in his temple, and from it flows the faintest streak of blood. Over him hangs the shadowy figure of the Crucified . . . Like the young lad in the picture, the man whom I saw die had a bullet wound in the temple, but there the likeness ceased. Here was no calm death, but a ghastly mess of blood and brains and mud, on his face and in the surrounding trench; and in the stark horror of the moment I could not see the Crucified at all.[4]

Oscar P. Eckhard reflected how he had 'thought the majority of wounds were the neat little bullet hole which you could scarcely see, and that very few places were vital', but was appalled to discover that

'German bullets often [made] the most hideous wounds . . . they [might] leave a hole' that 'several fingers' could be put into.[5] Similarly, 'Ex-Private X' compared his experiences of civilian death with war death. His first sight of a wartime corpse was of one that had been 'dead just long enough to be offensive'. He continued, 'In my unadventurous life this was the first dead man I had ever seen, save for my father, who had laid smiling in his last sleep after months of weariness and pain. But this man was not smiling.'[6] What was wretched about death in war was not (according to Arthur West) the fact that men had been killed, but that wartime corpses were so 'limp and mean-looking: this [was] the devil of it, that a man [was] not only killed, but made to look so vile and filthy in death, so futile and meaningless' that the 'sight of him' was hated.[7]

War promised men the kind of death that 'removed [their] stomach[s], and left [them] a mangled heap of human flesh'.[8] Death was obscene: Scottish Highland kilts were blown up and putrefying

56 *The Great Sacrifice*, from *The Graphic*, 25 December 1914.

57 'Scottish Highlanders', from Ernest Friedrich, *War Against War!*, Seattle, 1987.

buttocks exposed (illus. 57). Men were roasted alive.[9] Death descended from the skies and disappeared without being sighted by those who survived.[10] It was like black magic: bodies continued walking after decapitation; shells burst and bodies simply vanished.[11] Men's bodies 'shattered': their jaws dropped and out poured 'so much blood'.[12] Aeroplane propellers sliced men into pieces.[13] In death, white soldiers turned blackish and black Senegalese soldiers turned whitish.[14] Bodies lay forever unburied, eaten by the dogs, birds and rats.[15] These ugly deaths were reserved for men in active service, and the experience of death dramatically widened between men and women.

Separated from family and friends, the 'laying to rest' of the serviceman's body became the duty of the state. As the war progressed, not only were a man's family, childhood friends and lovers absent, but it became less likely that military comrades would be present at the burial.[16] From 1915, attempts were made to bury the dead in military cemeteries. Graves were dug in advance.[17] Wartime burial became a matter of sanitation, morale and military exigency. Although not always possible, speed of burial was recognized as desirable, if only because the sight and stench of death upset those servicemen who remained alive.[18] Since the burying of their own dead took trained servicemen away from the fighting and engendered morbid thoughts, companies of Pioneer troops were organized to 'follow in the wake of the advancing infantry', burying the dead.[19]

These attempts to shield servicemen from visions of the ugly military death could clearly not succeed. At least 722,000 men in the British services were killed during the war: the unsightliness of their deaths was matched by the indignities of their burial. Occasionally, a decent funeral could be given. In 1915, the chaplain Owen Watkins described the rites over a motorcyclist scout who had been shot through the heart when he unintentionally rode through a German-occupied village in France: 'As soon as the Germans retired the villagers had lifted him tenderly into the cottage, straightened the fine young limbs into decent restfulness, and covered him with a clean white sheet. I found him, a bunch of newly gathered flowers on his breast, his face calm and determined, but looking strangely young.'[20] Similarly, the Anglican padre David Railton managed to collect blue flowers to drop on the grave of the first man he buried on the Western Front.[21]

Romantic gestures such as these were rare. Early in the war – and during major battles – soldiers were buried where they fell. William Clarke described the aftermath of the battle at Loos:

it had proved impossible to bury them all. They lay in the trenches where they'd fallen or had been slung and earth had just been put on top of them. When the rains came, it washed most of the earth away, you'd go along the trenches and you'd see a boot and puttee sticking out, or an arm or hand, sometimes faces. Not only would you see them, but you'd be walking on them, slipping and sliding.[22]

When hundreds of men were killed, mass graves had to be dug.[23] In his diary for 3 July 1916, Albert Andrews recorded his day's chore burying the dead after the Battle of the Somme: 'you put them in a hole ready dug with boots and everything on. You put in about 10 or 15, whatever the grave will hold, throw about 2 feet of earth on them and stick a wooden cross on the top.'[24] Worse, the dangers of battlefields meant that many men could not be buried – or only after a long wait.[25] According to some, the spirits of ex-servicemen were so disgusted by this tardiness that they returned to the earth in order to remind people that evil astral beings hovered over the battlefields 'gorging themselves on the blood' of these unburied men.[26] After heavy rain, corpses floated down the trenches,[27] and were also sometimes used to patch up the sides of trenches.[28] Graves were robbed and games played with skulls and bones.[29]

Under such circumstances, notions of decency had to be altered. Burial parties attempted to give 'those poor bleeding pieces of earth' a Christian burial by reading sections from the Book of Common Prayer over mass graves.[30] Even if the words could not be heard over the roar of shells, the burial service was recited.[31] Despite rules forbidding ministers, chaplains and priests from burying men of different denominations, confusion over the religious beliefs of the deceased (and the shortage of religious ministers of any denomination) did not prevent some kind of religious service being performed over the dead.[32] In Mesopotamia, a decent grave meant one that was not only unnamed, but unmarked as well, in order to reduce the risk of bodies being unearthed in a search for clothes and blankets.[33] In military hospitals, the shortage of coffins rendered canvas sheets 'decent' burial cloth-ing.[34] Indeed, to be buried in 'some old sacking' was described in one war diary as 'fairly decent'.[35] Conventional rites of civilian burial could not be maintained in wartime: but, whenever possible, some form of ritual was enacted.

The contrast between the anonymous, mutilated corpse on the battlefield and the personalized, integrated corpse at home should not be exaggerated. In civilian life, the ideal death occurred between clean sheets, in a familiar bedroom, surrounded by family and friends. The bereaved strove to lay out a 'handsome corpse' that could be photo-graphed and whose likeness could be kept on the mantelpiece.[36] This was not always possible, however, since the beautiful death required a network of family and friends, a fellowship to which not all men could claim membership. Sixteen thousand people died in workhouses each year.[37] Each year, nearly 100 people were known to have been murdered, and suffered the indignities of having their bodies photo-graphed from every angle, dusted for fingerprints, dissected and disembowelled on coroner's benches.[38] An unknown number of men met their end in public streets where pedestrians, rescuers and medical staff rifled their pockets for each last penny.[39] The neglected dead had their bodies tipped from their 'final resting places' to make room for storage sheds. Their bones were tossed about and referred to as 'ham-shank[s]', or ended up being sold at auctions or exhibited in public houses.[40] Even more bizarre fates might be in store – such as the set of newly born, newly dead quadruplets (said to be 'disgusting objects') displayed in an undertaker's window in Hoxton, in London, in 1920 for the entertainment of 300 curious bystanders, and as an advertise-ment.[41] These were the tarnished bodies: ugly and untidy cadavers.

The bodies most at risk belonged to paupers. For them, questions about ownership were particularly pertinent. In 1832, the Anatomy Act had been passed: henceforth, the disposal of dead bodies lay in the hands of the executor or 'other Party . . . having lawful possession of the body of any deceased person'. One group that had lawful possession over the bodies of a large number of people was that of the Poor Law Guardians.[42] Around the time of the war, approximately sixteen per cent of people dying in Poor Law institutions in Britain were unclaimed by relatives or friends: their bodies came to be at the disposal of the elected representatives on the Board of Guardians.[43] From 1832, therefore, the state possessed a mechanism by which it hoped to entice Guardians to hand over the bodies of paupers to the medical profession who wished to use them in the training of medical students and in conducting research. The demand for bodies was high during the nineteenth century, but (as shown in Chapter One) the surgical requirements of the Great War vastly increased the need for men with a good grasp of anatomy. After the war, greater surgical intervention into the lives of the physically disabled maintained this need.[44] Between 1892 and 1897, 1907 and 1912, 1917 and 1926 and 1932 and 1938, the supply of bodies was deemed to be seriously inadequate and attempts to persuade people to donate their bodies prior to death – either on the grounds that this would obviate the danger of being buried alive or for more noble motives – had obviously failed.[45] Less than four per cent of corpses dissected in anatomy schools had been bequeathed. Clearly, pauper bodies under the control of Poor Law Guardians were a potentially rich source of supply and the Inspectors of Anatomy (William H. Bennett from 1892 and Alexander Macphail from 1921) set out to reap the harvest. The anonymous, mutilated bodies laid out on dissecting tables in the Department of Anatomy at the University of Cambridge (illus. 58) were the bodies of the un-loved poor.

Thus, the state, in alliance with the medical profession, claimed to have rights over the bodies of certain paupers and, as in the case of servicemen (another group conventionally regarded as of low status within society), used this claim to justify procedures that were considered unacceptable for other civilians. The state still had to work through the elected representatives on the Boards of Guardians for whom the exposure of paupers to anonymous mutilation on dissecting benches in anatomy schools was a delicate political issue.[46] In 1919, men responsible for the gathering of corpses were told to adhere to three rules: these were to avoid admitting on paper to supporting dissection, to ensure that third parties initiated all public discussions and, thirdly, never to explicitly call for corpses in the hearing of anyone 'of whose discretion [they were] not certain'.[47] Yet, many Guardians would only declare a body to be unclaimed if no relation or friends had visited within the previous twelve months – and increasingly few paupers fitted this criterion. From 1908, old age pensions had made elderly people more valuable to their families. A declining death rate and the growing popularity of insurance and funeral societies contributed to a reduction in the supply of bodies. Foreign pastors began claiming the bodies of the 'alien' dead. By reducing the practice of

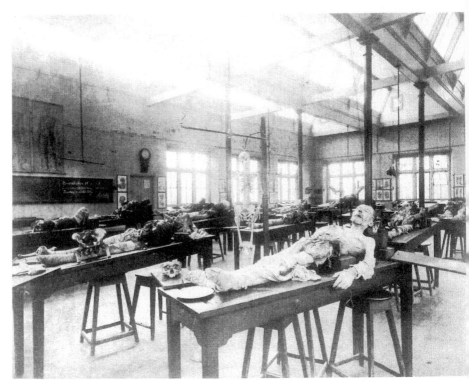

58 The Dissecting Room in the Department of Anatomy at Cambridge University, *c.* 1888–93. [CMAC L2687]

tramping in search of employment, the dole created a more geographically stable population of paupers who were therefore more likely to be surrounded by family and friends as they neared the end of their earthly lives.[48] An even greater number of bodies was rendered unsuitable for anatomical teaching by the zeal of medical officers for post-mortems, especially during the influenza epidemic of 1919.[49]

Socialist and labour spokesmen, as well as many religious groups (particularly the Christian Scientists) were intensely opposed to the appropriation of paupers' bodies by anatomists.[50] More significantly, Boards of Guardians, masters of workhouses and inspectors of the poor resisted donating the bodies of their paupers to anatomy schools. Poor Law institutions such as those in London might send less than half of all unclaimed bodies to medical schools and, in the provinces, less than one-quarter was sent.[51] From a cynical point of view, the reluctance of Poor Law officials to donate bodies might have been due to their resentment towards the medical profession over the Insurance Acts, the fact that it had been made illegal to pay them for their pains in donating bodies and a desire not to alienate voters. On the other hand, the Guardians may have been genuinely reluctant to subject the poor dead to this final indignity. Their meetings were often split over the issue, particularly between those who argued that it was better to 'dissect a dead body than a live dog', against those who insisted that it was 'bad enough to conscript live bodies without taking the dead ones'.[52]

In reply to arguments about desecration, those responsible for dissection laid increasing emphasis on the reverential treatment given to cadavers. Boards of Guardians were assured that 'the most offensive bodies' were made 'fairly sweet' by being embalmed.[53] People were informed that, after examination, body parts were returned to the 'shell' and given an 'ordinary burial service' according to the religious persuasion of the deceased.[54] Few were convinced. Scandals continually rocked public confidence in the Inspectorate of Anatomy. There was an outcry when it was discovered that in some schools (such as the London Hospital Medical School) insufficient care was taken to ensure that the separated parts of an individual's body were returned to the correct 'shell'.[55] Guardians often took it upon themselves to verify the claims made by the inspectorate. In July 1923, the Hammersmith Guardians monitored one such burial and discovered that no service was held in the chapel at the cemetery and only a few words said at the graveside. Furthermore, the body had been enclosed not in a proper coffin but in a cheap deal box, the handles of which fell off when it was moved; and the coffin had been brought to the cemetery in a 'one ton Ford van painted black' rather than in a funeral hearse.[56] Such investigations served to convince many Guardians that the Inspectorate of Anatomy and the medical profession did not warrant their claim over the bodies of paupers.

For the poor, however, the fear was not merely of being dissected. Even if spared that indignity, pauper burials were fates to be avoided if at all possible. Indeed, they closely resembled those of the war. In 1932, for instance, the secretary of the British Undertakers' Association described one such occasion: 'A common interment is a grave dug ten, fifteen or twenty feet deep and the bodies are put in one after another. There will be about eight adult persons in that grave, and they will finish off the top with a layer of four children so that there may be twelve to sixteen people in one grave . . . People talk about pit burials, that is what are called common interments.'[57] Thus, the mass-burials on the battlefields were 'common interments'.

Furthermore, the wartime economy led to a deterioration in the treatment of the civilian dead body, particularly if it was poor. Civilian undertakers found it difficult to maintain pre-war standards of decency in their burial customs. This was exemplified by the claim of the Mersey District Funeral Directors' Association that, as a result of the manpower demands of war, the number of men in the funeral business had been reduced by half. Coffin-makers accustomed to working fifty hours a week found themselves working seventy-three hours and the shortage of gravediggers forced cemetery authorities to extend the notice required for the opening of a grave from twenty-four hours to thirty-six.[58] In an attempt to draw the government's attention to the problem, a deputation from the British Undertakers' Association informed officials at the War Office on 15 January 1917 that in the previous week there had been 2,000 deaths in London and that wholesale coffin traders had been forced to refuse help to the British military authorities in France in order to meet the demand. Despite these precautions, many bodies remained without coffins for five to six days, and the deputation recalled a case in which a body remained coffin-less for twelve days in a crowded tenement house.[59] Many funeral businesses came to depend on the labour of women and black people – a state of affairs that was considered far from satisfactory, if not downright indecent.[60] The War Office and other ministers of state were unsympathetic. Thus, when the British Undertakers' Association lobbied against more undertakers being called into the armed forces, their fierce critic Sir John Paget retorted that they ought to cut down all 'unnecessary extravagancies'. As far as he was concerned, 'All those fellows in top-hats and black ties walking along by the hearse might be working at the benches in the shops.' They could be seen 'going along the streets with a lot of swagger'. The sight disgusted him.[61] Given the scale of death in the war zones, it is perhaps not surprising that the government was unable to summon much sympathy for the domestic dead and their professional representatives.

Fairly similar conflicts over the appropriate treatment of dead bodies continued after the war. The chief difference was that the war itself had temporarily altered the population at risk of an ugly death. No longer was it restricted to paupers. Men of course predominated more than ever. The anonymous, mutilated death came to be the fate of the young (76 per cent of the men who died on active military service were under the age of 30 years) and the middle classes (in the first year of war, 14 per cent of officers were killed compared with 6 per cent of servicemen in the other ranks). For paupers, the indignities of death were scarcely changed by the disciplines of war. After 1919, a new enthusiasm on the part of medical officers and the Inspectorate of Anatomy, coupled with the burgeoning prestige of surgery, increased intervention into their dead bodies. The need to safeguard the bodies of the wealthy continued to put the bodies of the poor at risk.

Purely Dead

The allure of a clean death was pervasive. The vision of death during war – painful, humiliating, ugly – intensified the urge for its immaculate counterpart. Although the war stimulated debate over the purification of corpses, burial reform did not start with the war.[62] Long before 1914, organizations such as the Church Burial, Funeral and Mourning Reform Association and the Church of England Funeral Reform Association had attempted to coax the bereaved into adopting simple and cheap funeral practices. In particular, they had targeted crépe clothing, the 'great solidity of coffins', and the 'excessive burden of floral tributes'.[63] The dramatic crisis of death and burial resulting from this war spread the appeal of their entreaties so that, to take a bizarre example, by the mid-1930s, the Ministry of Health was forced to accede to the request of the 'large number of people' who objected to seeing their friends and relations 'screwed down in wooden boxes', by agreeing to permit burials in wicker coffins 'picked with new mown hay'.[64] This, however, was a short-lived fad. The most significant changes occurred not in coffin design, but in funeral custom. Although the traditions of a boisterous wake survived in some areas, the dead body was increasingly liable to be accorded a respectful silence – even awe – rather than a heartbreaking keening. As the war progressed and black clothes began casting a shadow over public places, the bereaved were implored to adopt cheaper and more varied mourning apparel.[65] Thus, Mrs Edward Lyttelton proposed that crépe be exchanged for a purple armlet while Arthur Balfour, the Duchess of Devonshire, and the Marchioness of Lansdowne suggested that a white armlet should be worn instead (according to them, the colour white best expressed 'the pride we feel in knowing that those who are nearest and dearest have given their lives in their country's cause').[66] At St Paul's, at Easter 1918, Dean Inge pleaded with his listeners to stop 'parading' bereavement.[67] It was claimed that some dead servicemen felt so strongly about burial reform that they asked their spiritualist mediums to convey to their loved ones their agony when attending their own funerals. One spirit was said to be grieving over his earthly home because it was 'reeking with flowers, nasty old flowers too, with funeral bows on them', added to which, 'his mother and even that dear little sister . . . [were] draped in black'.[68] Another spirit (called Bob) allegedly begged the bereaved not to mourn, on the grounds that every tear was like 'torture' for dead men. He elaborated: 'tell the mothers and fathers and sisters and wives to stop crying. No man can stand the sight of tears, the sound of sobs. They feel it much worse here . . . for heaven's sake (this is literally for heaven's sake) beg the mourners to stop crying and to cease wearing black clothes.'[69] Some parents achieved the correct balance and (if one believes the spiritualists) their sons returned to thank them. Thus, it was reported that Rex Ward's spirit rejoiced in the unornate, simple ceremony in which he was honoured: 'The service seemed to soothe me. I felt as though I were hopelessly distraught, and it acted like soothing music might on a person suffering from mental worry on earth.'[70] The War Office may have been able to dictate the manner of many men's deaths and burials, but on the home front bereaved family and friends, spiritualist representatives of dead servicemen and various social institutions negotiated the appropriate expressions of mourning.

Although the ubiquitousness of death and mourning during the war led to a simplifying of funeral practices in Britain (they were never again so elaborate), the war had another impact. Perhaps it is not surprising that the generation that witnessed such a public exhibition of mouldering bodies on the battlefields should shrink away from the language of putrefaction. This recoil is most evident in the rhetoric used by people promoting a new hygienic discipline over the body: namely, cremation. In Britain, the movement for cremation had begun in the nineteenth century, but it was only in the inter-war years that it became an important part of British funeral practices. Founded in 1874 by Sir Henry Thompson, the Cremation Society was initially concerned with issues of contagion and epidemics. By 1910, its president was the dominant champion of public health, Sir Charles Cameron. Due to the society's efforts, the first crematorium in Britain was built in Woking in 1879, although it was not permitted to operate until 1885. It was followed by crematoria in Manchester, Glasgow, Liverpool, Hull, Darlington and Leicester in the decade after 1892. Cremation remained, however, a minority movement. In the 1890s, there were between 100 and 240 cremations annually.[71] Between 1917 and the mid-1920s, the number of cremations still remained fewer than 3,000.[72] However, by the mid-1930s, this figure had risen to over 11,000 and by the beginning of the Second World War, the number of cremations had reached nearly 20,000 annually.[73]

In terms of discussion of the male body and war, it is important to notice the change of rhetoric concerning cremation between the 1890s and the 1930s. Before the war, those in favour of cremation stressed the nastiness of burial. It was 'defilement' and 'degradation of the body'.[74] The 'horror of decomposition' was reiterated.[75] Those who allowed the 'human frame' to undergo a 'slow and disgusting decay', which gave off an 'offensive odour to distress [the bereaved] with the thoughts of corruption', were accused of scarcely meriting to be called Christians.[76] The body was said to be too sacred to become the 'food of worms'.[77] Most importantly, burial was dangerous: it exuded unhealthy gases and promoted epidemics.[78] Equally frightening, burial could come precipitately to the unlucky majority who were not members of the Association for the Prevention of Premature Burial.[79]

Men's experiences during the war shifted the emphasis of this rhetoric, the three strands of which appear in the posters issued by the Cremation Society (illus. 59, 60, 61). These posters represent the three arguments in favour of cremation: pragmatic economics ('the provision of large and costly cemeteries will be unnecessary'), public health ('Dispose of the dead without danger to the living'), and personal purification ('Purification by fire'). By the end of the Great War, it was no longer seemly to remind men of bodies lying on the battlefields turning yellow, grey or blue as they underwent 'the indignity of slow decomposition'.[80] Instead of physical decay, cremationists increasingly adopted a rhetoric concerned with the flames of purification.[81] Quite literally, the human body was 'purified by fire'.[82] Man's ashes were rendered 'pearly white . . . intact and pure' and 'delicate, white ash'.[83] The body was 'never handled' but underwent purification alone: 'as the heat [was] generated in a separate furnace, there [was] no contact with the actual fuel, and consequently no possibility of any foreign matter becoming mixed with the human ashes. Everything that [went] into the heated chamber [came] out of it, the flesh as gas drawn upwards into the air, and the bones as dust and ashes cleansed of all pollution.'[84] Cremation perpetrated no assault on the body. As one pre-war promoter of cremation explained, the 'bath of heat is as painless as a bath of the fragrance of summer roses would be'.[85] The relationship between Englishness and rural England which was strengthened as the result of wartime experiences had an impact on the practices accompanying this rhetoric.[86] The argument that the individual's remains should 'rest peacefully in the sunlight among the birds, the flowers, and the trees; Nature's monument', gained in appeal, so ashes came increasingly (from the 1920s) to be scattered in gardens of rest.[87] This practice was said to represent a return to 'the beautiful old custom of having the Dead in the place where he [had] worship [ped]'.[88] Emphasis was placed no longer on the misery and the mouldering, but on the departure of a purified body to a higher world. A writer in the *Brighton and Hove Herald* in 1934 used old words to

59, 60, 61 Three posters issued by the Cremation Society, from P. Herbert Jones and George A. Noble's *Cremation in Great Britain*, London, 1931.

convey a new route to death: 'Death is robbed of its sting, and it is not the grave that has the victory.'[89]

Cremation, therefore, entailed a different view of death. This may be further examined by briefly mentioning the design of crematoria. In 1931, the designer Albert Freeman spoke of his ambition to develop an architecture of death that was 'not repulsive' but was 'imposing, suggestive of its meaning, and fitting to mark the transition from the earlier to the later – and modern – custom of disposal of the dead'.[90] In the same year, another designer, H. T. Herring, urged people to reject 'the old conception that the great passing over [should] be surrounded by signs of decay'. He railed against the

bare, cold, comfortless buildings; the grounds strewn with an endless sea of derelict graves; the withering flowers, speaking emblems of those now forgotten; the depressing feelings of decay and dreariness. All this must be omitted from this new conception. A fresh start must be made on entirely different lines, rather implying from the life around that those near and dear are not dead but have only passed on.[91]

Spacious grounds, gardens of rest, large car parks, the new Romanesque architecture, dignified chapels decorated in subdued colours, comfortable seating: these were at the opposite pole to wartime burial.

It was precisely this simplicity that was eventually achieved in the war cemeteries. The problem of burial has already been discussed. The bereaved did not give up their rights over the burial of their loved ones. Early in 1915, the exhumation of bodies was banned for the duration of the war. Instead, the dead were to be buried in centralized war cemeteries close to where they had died. The bones of German servicemen (which had often laid alongside those of their British counterparts) were removed.[92] Henry Williamson wrote, 'The bones of the slain may lie side by side at peace in wartime, but in peacetime they are religiously separated into nations again, each to its place: the British to the white gardens "that are forever England", and the others to – the Labyrinthe.'[93] Furthermore, in 1918 the Imperial War Graves Commission decided to substitute uniform headstones for the simple wooden crosses in military cemeteries. Although there were clearly financial reasons for this decision, such uniformity also aimed to cater to the variety of religious beliefs amongst the servicemen as well as impose an aesthetic discipline.

The decision was not greeted with universal approval. There were two issues at stake: to whom did the rights over the 'laying to rest' of servicemen belong and, if this right were claimed by the state, would the dead be dishonoured? In a war fought to a large degree by civilians rather than professional soldiers, civilian treatment of the dead was imperative. Despite much anguish (especially when American bodies began to be repatriated), it was generally agreed that the demands of equity and economy made repatriation of the dead back to Britain inappropriate. Protest was registered strongly, however, when it was revealed that the Imperial War Graves Commission intended to adhere rigorously to its uniform pattern of gravestones. No variation was to be allowed whether in size, design, expense or material. Bereaved families all over the country began to claim that they had prior rights over their dead loved ones. These views were expressed strongly in a debate in the House of Commons in 1920. The parliamentarian Sir James Remnant stated,

I am anxious that there should be equality for all, and that the right which is inalienable to every man, the right to do as he likes with his own dead, should not be taken away. Relatives should long treat their own loved ones in their own distinctive way, and I hope the House of Commons will hesitate long before it allows the right to be taken away or any interference with it. The dead are certainly not the property of the State or of any particular regiment; the dead belong to their own relatives.[94]

A report in *The Times* made a similar point: 'It is equally repugnant to British feeling that even in death the family should surrender all rights over the individual to the state, and that private memorials should therefore be prohibited.'[95] This was 'bureaucratic tyranny and nothing else'.[96] As shown earlier, the state did possess certain rights over the dead, and the commissioners' opponents pleaded with them to 'confine their attention to those graves where there [were] no relations to see to the last sad rites'.[97]

The second issue was over honouring the dead. The neglect of war graves after the Boer War led many to question whether the centralized graves scattered around the war zones were to be cared for.[98] Another question concerned the function of war cemeteries and whether they had been constructed for the sake of 'idle tourists' or 'bereaved relatives'.[99] Most important, however, was the question of whether they were to be centres of familial mourning or memorials to the war.[100] The Imperial War Graves Commission struggled to combine both. In part, the tension was the funereal equivalent to the modernist versus anti-modernist tension within the language of mourning. The commission was opting for the stark realities of modernity while many of the bereaved sought the romantic myths of traditional British funeral practices. This is illustrated in Sir James Remnant's speech in the House of Commons:

The War Graves Commission say that you must have uniformity in order to produce a sufficiently artistic effect. I doubt if that really be a serious contention. We know that in our village churchyards there is a great want of uniformity, all members of society, whether fortunate or unfortunate, being able to put up what headstone they like, and there in God's Acre beauty still remains and is a joy for ever to those who look upon it.[101]

The hierarchical myth of Merrie England did not represent the experience of death and mourning amongst poor, urban dwellers.

Despite the criticisms against the plans of the Imperial War Graves Commission, the House of Commons eventually supported the commission's proposals. In addition, many of the bereaved in fact approved of its modernist designs. By emphasizing the contrast between the worlds of war and peace, the uniformly constructed war cemeteries were an attempt to console the bereaved, and for many people they were successful. Thus, in 1931 the loyal batman to Captain Burnaby visited his master's war grave in France. He wrote to Burnaby's widow, 'I am sorry to say I broke down . . . I must say every thing looks very peaceful where he is resting and the birds are singing and peaceful. the Evening when he was being Buried there was A great Bombartment and we could hardly hear the Service So every thing is completely change [sic].'[102] Lady Burnaby also received a letter from the secretary to the Queen's Royal Regiment concerning the site of her husband's grave:

It is a beautiful spot & such a haven of peace & rest. Situated by the side of a country lane & surrounded by cornfields, no better spot could have been selected . . . as I understand you have never visited the cemetery, I can only appeal to you to do so some day. It would I feel sure give you some consolation & perhaps a little happiness to see this peaceful little cemetery. To rest awhile with him who was so Dear to you. To listen to the songs of the birds above & to come away knowing that he rests in peace.[103]

Consolation required the invention of a language and aesthetics of death that denied the realities of war.

Whether or not the starkness of the war cemeteries was appreciated by the bereaved, another response was required. Families and local communities reacted to mass bereavement by constructing war memorials, which took many forms, the most popular being the Christian cross, obelisk and lifelike statues of servicemen.[104] Although financial considerations constantly imposed restraints, and religious and political rhetoric overlaid all decisions, each community framed its decision on the form of memorial in broader moral terms.[105] Thus, in Llandudno it was felt that 'any memorial of a pronounced warlike or realistic character should be avoided', and an obelisk was chosen because it was the type which had 'been used as a commemorative monument by successive civilisations for nearly 4,000 years'.[106] The war memorial committee of Colwyn Bay disagreed: it decisively opted for a bronze figure of a soldier, stressing that the figure was to contain 'no suggestion of callousness or brutality associated with war' but was to be 'typical . . . Called from his uneventful civil pursuits by the stern voice of duty, he [was to carry] with him the refinement of his ordinary life, whilst the knowledge of the horrors and possibilities of War enhance[d] his valour'.[107] Many more communities chose a simple cross.[108] Paramount in these rites was the repudiation of the military death and its link with pauperism: the war dead were sanitized, their civilian status emphasized and the pre-war celebratory aspects of death repudiated.

Missing Men

So far in this chapter we have looked at how the military exigencies of war altered the way men experienced death and what happened to their bodies after that death. The ugly death was not solely a product of the war but was part of the common lot for paupers in times of peace. The Great War prompted a revulsion from the celebratory nature of burial, encouraged greater simplicity in mourning customs and stimulated a move towards *personal* hygienic practices (as opposed to the *public* health-hygiene arguments earlier in the century). We turn now to a special group of men for whom the conventional rites of burial were delayed. In battle, male bodies were often dismembered to such a degree that identification was rendered impossible: the force of an explosion might blow them to small pieces, or bury them under a ton of soil. The sea swallowed its sailors. Continuous fighting made burial squads too fearful to rescue men's 'shells'. Sometimes a disappearance was merely administrative as, for instance, in the clerical oversight that meant that Edgar Oswald Gale vanished from all records – even from the lists of those who fought in the war – for well over half a century.[109] The War Graves Commission was unable to keep the registers up to date, and mistakes were made.[110] Uncertainty was endemic. Thus, Edward Ridley confessed to his mother, 'I told you in my last letter that Goschen was killed on Christmas Eve. I am now told that it is not certain he is dead. He was badly wounded in the legs and head by a shell and had to be left in a trench when we were evacuating. It is just possible that he is a wounded prisoner, he is reported "missing". The odds are[, however,] he is dead.'[111] The contingency of death was particularly frustrating for civilians. Molly C. Thompson could obtain no accurate information about the fate of her fiancé: 'I have now 6 dates that he was killed on & not anything personal belonging to him nor has

62 Grave of an unknown British soldier, Thiepval, September 1916. [IWM Q1540]

he ever been buried. It is all so very trying but I have not given him up. I feel quite sure that he will return to me.'[112] Similarly, another woman's husband was reported missing. The War Office officially pronounced him dead, the Red Cross announced that he had been picked up alive, and a member of her husband's regiment visited her with what he claimed were her husband's dying words. Rather than trust these reports, the woman visited a clairvoyant who informed her that her husband was badly wounded in a hospital in Münster. The clairvoyant's vision was vindicated, and eventually she received a letter from her husband.[113] Of those men reported missing after major battles, however, less than one-quarter was later identified.[114] Menin Gate at Ypres lists over 50,000 names of the missing dead; at Thiepval, there are 73,000; at Tyne Cot, 35,000; and so on. On the battlefields and in the seas of this war, the bodies of over 200,000 men were never recovered. Men buried in graves probably never attained the status of being buried in one of the cemeteries to the 'missing' (see illus. 62). Although care was clearly taken to erect a crude cross, the mud probably buried all public memory of their sacrifice.

Few of these men lacked family or friends to mourn. While recovering in hospital, Arthur Schuman recalled being visited by the distressed parents of a soldier who had been reported missing. He informed them of their son's death and noted that they were 'very glad' that he 'had seen him killed instantly'.[115] The *Daily Express* was not incorrect when it stated that greater distress was caused over the missing than over the dead.[116] As Mary MacLeod Moore wrote in July 1917, ' "Killed" is final; "Wounded" means hope and possibilities; "Prisoner of war" implies a reunion in the glad time when peace comes again to a stricken world; but "Missing" is terrible. In that one word the soldier's friends see him swallowed up behind a cloud through which pierces no ray of light.'[117] Four years after the war ended, the popular sentimental poet John Cotton concluded a poem entitled 'Among the Missing' with the following lines:

> After a battle – when the roll was read –
> And no sure word to my sad question came;
> If taken prisoner, or if life was fled
> None knew . . .
> Drear months have passed; I wear now on my head
> The widow's crape, though some there are who blame;
> Distress and doubt oft set my mind aflame;
> But loyal love pleads – 'do not deem him dead;
> He may return; by Hope be comforted,
> Tho "Missing" marks as yet your dear one's name'.[118]

Hundreds of thousands of households received telegrams or letters stating, 'Regret – No Trace'. A year later, they would receive a letter from the Red Cross deeming their loved one 'presumed dead'.[119] Parents and friends responded to the verdict 'missing' in many ways. Occasionally, a bereaved parent would threaten chaplains with legal action for not finding their son and giving him a Christian burial.[120] More commonly, people grieved in silence, while others lived in hope that their young men might turn up injured in a hospital or in a prisoner-of-war camp.[121] Few did.[122]

As has already been suggested, there was another response to the verdict of missing: searching the spiritual world for signs of their continued existence. In this context, conventional Christianity had little to offer. Margaret Jarvis's pain was manifest in a letter she penned to a female friend in 1918 after hearing of her son's death: 'I am just all to pieces at present. My boy was all I had in the world, & I honestly did trust that God would keep him safe, & he believed it too, all through these horrible six months, I trusted . . . my poor boy, he was so good, why did God make him suffer so.'[123] Small numbers of men took the

63 A New Zealand chaplain celebrating Holy Communion in the field near the firing line. [IWM Q79042]

sacraments (see illus. 63). Despite valiant attempts by religious hierarchies to fulfil their spiritual duties, there were simply too few of them (there was one chaplain to over 1,000 servicemen), chaplains wore officers' uniforms (which alienated them from the rank and file), and distinctions of class, education and military prowess led many servicemen to regard these 'men of God' as obsequious and immature. Religious doubt even seemed to be exacerbated within the armed forces. As John William Rowarth exclaimed in his usual vivid fashion, 'you know, nobody loves me no even jesus, this Flipping Bloody, bleeding Army has almost made me lose my Faith in God, and Mary, and Joseph. and now by my blaspheme, I have committed another Mortal sin'.[124] Even the kindly Revd Charles Ivor Sinclair Hood could think of no words of comfort in the midst of the carnage except that 'Paradise must be a wonderful place with so many friends there.'[125] Hiram Sturdy's cry after the Battle of the Somme was echoed by many other men: 'Jesus Christ do you see all this and let it go on.'[126]

For some, it was fortunate that conventional Christianity did not hold a monopoly on spirituality. Wartime traumas opened the door to spiritual experimentation. Life in the armed forces led many men to place their trust in amulets, charms and protective tunics.[127] One soldier who remembered nothing except 'running like hell for 2 days'

64 Print of *The White Comrade*, reproduced from a painting by G. Hillyard Swinstead, RI, with a verse by 'V.H.S.', London, 1915.

during the retreat from Mons, also swore to having seen the Angel of Mons.[128] Visions of the Virgin Mary, God, Jesus and angels were not uncommon. A print from 1915 (illus. 64) shows one popular representation of the meeting of servicemen and supernatural: Jesus looks down encouragingly at the soldier helping a wounded man to safety. 'The White Comrade' represents brotherhood in times of need. There are two comrades in the picture: Jesus and the Red Cross worker. In addition to living substitutes for Jesus, there were the spirits of dead servicemen who claimed (through their mediums) that they remained on the battlefield, 'doing a man's part still . . . bring[ing] comfort and aid to the wounded'.[129] 'Friends in White' lay next to men in shell-holes during battle.[130] A similar process occurred on the home front. A. Wyatt Tilby described the change when, in 1918, he contended that the war had been preceded by an age of prosperity and security: 'We still confessed ourselves miserable sinners in church, but we laid less emphasis on the misery than our ancestors, and for the most excellent reason. We had conquered this world, and we desired no other.' The war changed everything. Bewildered people once again sought out spiritual consolation: 'The churches filled again, but they had no new message, and they are often accused of failing in the presentment of the old. Men and women, and more particularly those women who had lost their men, looked elsewhere for sympathy.'[131]

For many bereaved men and women, disparate religious beliefs could be assembled together by spiritualism. This was not merely a phenomenon of the war, but the experience of war heightened the appeal of spiritual practices.[132] Although its popularity was in decline by the 1930s, by that time it had been so successful in filling the gap left by the absent menfolk that the Church of England found it necessary to establish a special committee to investigate.[133] For many people affected by the war, spiritualism offered the bereaved a way to accept the death of their loved ones while simultaneously asserting their continued 'existence' in another sphere. It made plausible the Christian belief in 'life after death'. Thus, mothers had visions of their sons, and their descriptions of these visions were poignantly maternal (for instance, one mother was particularly comforted when the spirit of her missing son appeared with 'his hair . . . beautifully brushed').[134] As this vision suggests, spiritualism was concerned with both the spiritual and the physical worlds. On the spiritual plane, it asserted that 'the Spiritual alone is Real'.[135] By stressing that inordinate grief was detrimental to the spirit of the departed, it provided a way for the living to start again.[136] Indeed, it was imperative for the living to overcome their grief since the sorrow of family and friends was said to hinder the progress of the spirit, 'casting a shadow over the brilliant outlook of eternity'.[137] Perhaps more importantly, it blocked communication between loved ones in 'This' and 'The Other' worlds. As the scientist and leading spiritualist Sir Oliver Lodge insisted, 'LOVE BRIDGES THE CHASM', and love was made manifest by spiritualist communication, not bereavement.[138]

On the physical plane, spirits – allegedly communicating through their mediums – constantly reassured their listeners of the ease of death. The body was a 'shell' that was easily discarded.[139] Many spirits claimed that they only became aware that they had died because of the joy of being reunited with departed friends and by the sudden absence of pain (according to 'Bob', 'Mother, the soul leaves the body as a boy jumps out of a school door'), or, as another spirit heartened his audience during a session of automatic writing, if the bereaved could 'realise the immediate *relief* – though the passing may be sharp, of the spirit released from the body – they could not wish their loved ones back again. In the awful holocaust, the carnage and the slaughter which the Hun has brought into Europe, and elsewhere – this is the saving thought, – Release!!'[140] The dead soldier, a Private Dowding, agreed. He divulged to his medium that physical death was

nothing. There is really no cause to fear . . . Something struck hard, hard, hard, against my neck. Shall I ever lose the memory of that hardness? It is the only unpleasant incident that I can remember. I fell, and as I did so, without passing through any apparent interval of unconsciousness, I found myself outside myself! . . . You see what a small thing is death, even the violent death of war! . . . no horror, no long-drawn suffering, no conflicts.[141]

Such interpretations, of course, prompted questions regarding the enemy, whether the Germans would also not suffer in death, and whether they too would attain peace, even pleasure, in the afterlife. Another dead soldier provided the answer to these questions in a session of automatic writing on 4 June 1916. He declared that dead Germans were

too weary of life on earth to be able to grasp the beauty that awaits them and some are very fine souls who have been compelled against their better judgement to fight the whole of Europe. Others are too brutal for our gospel, they go to their own place – attracted thither by a wonderful law of attraction, which is to be the extension and fulfilment of the same law of like, or repulsion, which we went through on earth.[142]

Death separated men from their enemies, not their friends.

Crucially, spiritualism was the transcendental equivalent to cremation. In both, the body of the beloved was purified in death. There was no mortification, no putrefaction. And these immaculate bodies were not eradicated: indeed, for the bereaved who recognized the extent to which so many men's bodies had been mutilated in war, it was a comfort to know that all the 'pieces' had been 'put back together'. The best description of this process was provided by the spirit of the dead Raymond Lodge. He communicated to his family that his body was 'very similar' to the one he had possessed when alive. Like a comforting midwife, he informed them that he had eyelashes, eyebrows and a tongue. There were two things absent, however: in contrast to the bloodiness of war, those in the 'Other World' did not bleed. Nor did they possess anuses.[143] According to Lodge, if a limb were lost in battle just prior to death, that limb was immediately restored on entering the 'Other World'. In the after-life, those people disabled from birth had to wait much longer as their limbs had to *grow* back in perfect form.[144] This was religious belief at its most pragmatic.

Two Unknowable Bodies

The distress of the family and friends of missing soldiers, sailors and airmen demanded a civic as well as a spiritual response. In reply to the great hunger for information expressed by thousands of sorrowing parents, siblings and friends, the Red Cross and Order of St John established the Wounded and Missing Enquiry Department to which the War Office would send lists of missing soldiers. During the war, staff at searching stations at Boulogne, Calais, Rouen, Havre, Le Treport and Etaples answered over 342,000 enquiries, wrote nearly 385,000 reports and interviewed between four and five million servicemen at the battlefront, in hospitals and on trains about the whereabouts of missing soldiers.[145] A similar function was performed by the War Registration Commission which was founded by the Red Cross worker Fabian Ware a few months after war was declared. In March 1915, the commission was officially recognized by the War Office and it became the Imperial War Graves Commission.[146]

The problems faced by the searchers of the Wounded and Missing Enquiry Department and members of the War Graves Commission were formidable. In 1918, there were still half a million unmarked British graves in the war zones. A photograph shows two members of the 400-strong Graves Registration Unit searching for missing bodies at Anzac (illus. 65). They found headstones in places where there were no bodies: they found a number of bodies buried under only one headstone.[147] Graves were numbered, but there was no list matching numbers with names.[148] They had to be detectives as much as searchers. Relationships with the families of the deceased were often fraught. While travelling with the War Graves Commission in 1919, Major Arthur Lees complained that the bereaved were 'a little inconsiderate about enquiries'. He received 'dozens each day' and the day before had 'heard a very Welsh voice down the phone asking [him] to take him, to see the grave of Pte Davis', who had 'seemed quite hurt when [he had] told him that there were a mere 3,5000 [*sic*] corpses

65 The Revd. Charles Pierrepont, MC, working with the Graves Registration Unit at Gallipoli. [IWM Q14444]

[t]here including many Davises & [that he] wanted something more definite as all the information he had was that he was killed on Gallipoli'.[149] Private Davis would have had a better chance of being found had he been promoted prior to death. As before the war, not all corpses were allocated the same status.[150] Thus, in the Wounded and Missing Enquiry Department, the families of officers were indulged. A secretary for the Red Cross Department boasted about their famous Watching List which consisted of cards listing every officer at the Front. Every day, these cards were checked with admission lists to hospitals. As soon as an officer entered any military hospital, they would send a reassuring message to the family.[151] Missing officers could be found more rapidly.

At the end of the hostilities, the hopes of the families of missing men were shattered. The war padre David Railton recognized that some kind of public funeral was needed to facilitate mourning, so in October 1920 he persuaded the Dean of Westminster Abbey to speak to King George v about interring in the abbey an unidentified body from the battlefields of France. Although the king did not initially approve of the scheme, the persuasive voice of Lloyd George changed his mind and Lord Curzon was placed in charge of proceedings. Arrangements were highly ritualized, even masonic. Six bodies were exhumed from Ypres,

Cambrai, Arras, the Somme, the Aisne and the Marne and taken to Ypres where a blindfolded officer selected one of the coffins. This unidentified body was then transported to Britain in a coffin made of oak from a tree at Hampton Court Palace. The coffin is shown in Illustration 66. After resting in a temporary chapel in Victoria Station overnight, on the morning of 11 November the body was carried with much ceremony to Westminster Abbey where it was interred in French soil under the statue of Lord Chatham. The inscription simply read: 'An Unknown Warrior'. The war padre had accurately understood bereavement. In the week after Armistice Day in 1920, between half a million and one million people visited this tomb.[152] The Unknown Warrior stood in for all the missing dead.

If the heroic warrior in 1920 was lowly, meek and innocent, by 1926 the celebrated dead meant something very different. In what came to be known as the 'Kitchener Hoax', the Unknown 'Lost' Warrior was exchanged for the most Well-Known 'Lost' Warrior: Kitchener of Khartoum. As we shall see in the following pages, similar motifs emerged, but the heroic body was no longer the anonymous, muddied one returned from the battlefield but became the water-cleansed body of a statesman. The renowned military leader was substituted for the working man.

Disliked by the War Office and the political administration, Kitchener was revered by the masses. His reputation was enhanced by the manner of his death: he was drowned on 5 June 1916 when HMS *Hampshire* struck a mine off Orkney on its way to Russia. One and a half million people bought copies of the *Daily Mirror* to read of the announcement of his death.[153] Despite the abundance of reverential elegies, many people were concerned that this great man had not been sufficiently honoured.[154] The demand for information may be judged by the fact that within a year, five biographies had been published along with collections of his writings.[155] When the war was over, this interest revived. Statues were unveiled to commemorate his life and death.[156] In the 1920s, S. Stuart Starritt, Victor Wallace Germains and Reginald, Viscount Esher, each published their own defences of Kitchener's life.[157] Even poets devoted stanzas to Kitchener.[158] Alongside these valedictory works, there developed a vast literature of conspiracy.[159] The coyness of the Admiralty led to questions in Parliament demanding an official enquiry.[160] Many refused to believe that Kitchener could actually die (although such scepticism was also expressed about the deaths of Emperor Nero, Charles I, Marie-Antoinette and Oscar Wilde).[161] A journalist named Frank Power reported that some of his acquaintances believed that Kitchener had

66 Coffin of the Unknown Warrior, Westminster Abbey. [IWM Q31492]

not sailed on the *Hampshire* but had been impersonated on the ship by a look-alike substitute. He claimed to know people who had recently seen Kitchener striding down Whitehall or around the War Office. More incredibly, Kitchener was believed to have been recognized in disguise as 'the Chinese general who has ridden, almost roughshod, over his enemies'.[162] Equally fanciful was the idea that Kitchener had been spirited away to a cave on some remote island of the Hebrides where he lay 'plunged, like King Arthur or Barbarossa into an enchanted sleep from which he would presently awake'.[163] Despite the fact that one of Kitchener's sisters failed to get in touch with him during seances (which convinced her that he was alive), at least three spiritualists reported speaking to Kitchener's spirit – two wrote books relating their discussions, and one offered to prove to the Metropolitan Police that the 'old soldier' was indeed dead by bringing forward witnesses who had seen his 'materialized spirit torn through [her] while under a trance'.[164]

These sightings climaxed in 1926, thanks to the efforts of the journalist Frank Power, who had discarded the name Arthur Vectis Freeman for his blunter pseudonym. Aged forty-four in 1926, he believed he had a vocation in law, earned his living as a typist and shorthand writer, and ended his career as an undischarged bankrupt. He was not the originator of the hoax. The plan to reverently 'lay to rest' the missing Kitchener had been conceived in 1921 when the publicity agent Singleton Gates had been approached by Norman Ramsey of the film corporation Screen Plays and asked whether he would promote an unreleased film entitled *How Kitchener was Betrayed*. The film dealt with the betrayal of Kitchener by an unnamed woman and it insinuated that the Germans were aware through the influence of Rasputin of Kitchener's presence on the *Hampshire*. Gates arranged a private viewing, to which he invited members of both Houses of Parliament, representatives from the War Office and the Admiralty and Kitchener's sisters. The audience was unfortunately angered by the portrayal of Kitchener and advised Ramsey to scrap the film and produce a completely different one – with a 'patriotic' message. Since Frank Power (or Arthur Freeman as he was still called) had attended the screening, he was invited by Gates and Ramsey to discuss the way in which they could deal with the hostility generated by it. Gates suggested that the film could be rehabilitated if they found Kitchener's body. Speculating on the possibility that it had been washed ashore in Norway, the three men concocted a story about discovering the 'sea-soaked epaulette of an officer of the British Army upon which were the insignia of the rank of Field Marshal' in a

Norwegian fisherman's hut. The fisherman – whose name they had invented by combining the Christian name of a Norwegian hotel proprietor with the surname of another – had then apparently shown them the burial mound of the man from whose body he had cut the epaulette. Although the story was published in a 'morning paper', it did nothing to revive the fortunes of the film. A ban by the London County Council rendered it practically worthless, and it was eventually sold to Frank Power.

With the exception of one unsuccessful attempt to show the film in 1922, nothing more was heard of it or Kitchener's body until 1926 when Frank Power launched a defamatory attack on the Admiralty, claiming that it had brazenly thrown away the great soldier's life through a series of blunders. In public speeches, newspaper articles and two books, Power claimed that Kitchener had been betrayed and that, contrary to Admiralty assertions, Kitchener's presence on the *Hampshire* had been widely known: it had been discussed in Russia a month before his departure. Going even further, Power hinted at a direct conspiracy to kill Kitchener. Although he conceded that the *Hampshire* had fouled a German mine, he argued that there had been two additional explosions – from *inside* the ship. With dramatic rhetoric, he provided graphic descriptions of Kitchener's final fight for life, clinging to a rock on Orkney, before being slain by a spy.[165] Power was to conclude a number of his speeches and writings in the following vein:

I am going to Norway to prove in the most conclusive possible way that Lord Kitchener is dead, but I shall still hope for the final vindication of the great soldier, to which his sacrificial passing alone entitles him, a last resting place in Westminster Abbey; and, without rancour and without hate but simply as an act of British justice, I shall hope for the final confusion of those whose hands have struck in the dark.[166]

Before fulfilling his sacred mission, the right atmosphere had to be created. Power enlisted the support of eighty-nine branches of the British Legion.[167] In 1926, he exhibited another film, this time entitled *The Tragedy of the 'Hampshire'*, at the London Opera House. The occasion was declared to be a mass-meeting to press for the establishment of a court of enquiry to look into the tragedy. At the meeting, some of the survivors from the *Hampshire* appeared on the stage to hysterical cheering. Power then asked the audience to vote on a resolution demanding an official enquiry into Kitchener's death. There was only one hiccup in the proceedings. On his declaration that the resolution had been passed unanimously, one brave man stood up to register his objection and was booed down with cries of 'Traitor!'

and 'Throw him out!' In the end, 2,000 people signed a petition for the publication of the full report on the disaster.

After this meeting, Power left the country and, within a few days, claimed to have chanced upon Kitchener's burial site. He wrote, 'With care and reverence, and after reading some passages from a beautiful illuminated prayer book specially arranged for my pilgrimage by a lady who was an intimate friend of the late Earl, I removed the pieces of wood which covered all that remains of Lord Kitchener.'[168] Torn by conflicting desires to look as though he was able to ensure a safe return of the body, and to publicize what he claimed was an event of national importance, Power approached a Mr Foster of Crystal Productions who employed a cinematographic operator to accompany him back to Norway to film scenic shots of the area. In the name of secrecy, the operator was not told of the purpose of the mission, but proved willing to film Power in a graveyard containing British dead. Power directed his attention to a gravestone inscribed with the words 'Known Only Unto God', which was duly filmed. The cinematographic operator also participated in the filming of a mock funeral procession at Stavanger when the coffin containing what were said to be the remains of Lord Kitchener was allegedly taken on board a ship bound for England.

Power arrived back in London by train, accompanied by a long packing case that he had brought back with him as excess baggage. Once at Waterloo Station, the packing case – identified as a coffin by a porter who consequently demanded a higher tip – was transported in the most modern manner (by motor-hearse) to a nearby chapel where it remained all night, draped in a Union Jack with lighted candles burning at its head and flanked by a simple wooden cross. Power then informed the prime minister, Stanley Baldwin, of his intention to lay Kitchener to rest in Westminster Abbey. What he forgot was the need for a burial certificate, which meant that a coroner had to examine the remains. Early the following morning, the police swooped: as a crowd gathered, they removed the coffin to Lambeth mortuary and with a great show of publicity – this time not generated by Power – they opened the coffin, exposing an empty box unevenly spread with fresh tar. Power was brazenly unrepentant: he declared that at some stage between leaving the chapel and arriving at the coroner's court, Lord Kitchener's remains had been surreptitiously removed.

He was not believed. The press expressed the widespread fury. The hoax was said to have poured scorn not only on the sentiments of Kitchener's family, but on thousands of men and women who cherished a 'deep veneration of the memory of the great soldier who [had] sacrificed his life to the country's need during the war'.[169] The reaction of a man signing himself 'One who was Gulled' when writing to the Metropolitan Police was unexceptional: he demanded that Power be shot.[170] The hoax offended the myth of Kitchener's true grave: it denied the 'majestic tragedy of Kitchener's death, the solitary grandeur of his green grave, the lonely splendour of his tremendous vanishing in the storm'.[171] The journalist James Douglas denounced Power and his accomplices for possessing 'the corrupted minds of scoundrels and the depraved cunning of cads'. They were men who had 'stooped to the lowest depths of cupidity and callous heartlessness in their exploitation of national reverence and national gratitude for the hero of its direst and dark sacrifice'. Douglas lamented the impotence of the law to punish Power, and called on the 'insulted race' to brand everyone associated with the hoax as 'outcasts from our blood and our breed'.[172] Furthermore, it was sacrilege. Only eight years since 'the last British soldier or sailor or airman [had] laid down his life for us', Douglas rallied his readers to 'live again through the agony of 1914' and to recollect how Kitchener had been 'the heart of us, the soul of us, the faith of us, the endurance of us, the stark, strong strength of us, our tower of power, our flash of foresight, our visionary with the long view, our organizer of willing service, our maker of patience, and our architect of perseverance'.[173] A nation that could nourish a man capable of such a hoax against the nation's 'holiest shrines' was certainly degenerate.[174] Edmund Burke's words were recalled: 'It is gone, that sensibility of principle, that chastity of honour.'[175] Technically, however, Power had not been guilty of any offence, and he simply disappeared from the public eye, disgraced.

Renown and Unknown Warriors

Despite being in the middle of a test-match, the return of Kitchener's remains and the ensuing exposure of the hoax hit the news. It came near the end of a bad year. In May there had been the General Strike and the miners were still 'out'; one and a half million people were unemployed; another war was predicted. It was a time when a comrade of Kitchener – a survivor of the *Hampshire* disaster – could be forced onto the dole.[176] Furthermore, since the war, discontent about the funerals of ex-servicemen was growing as military authorities began demanding changes in the regulations that granted a military funeral party to ex-servicemen who died of wounds or diseases attributable to military service.[177] On the grounds that applications for military funerals were numerous and increasing, that many had to be refused because of the shortage of troops, that training and military duties generally were being interfered with by the need to organize funeral parties, and that constant funeral duties were 'morbid in effect on the soldier', the War Office decided not to provide troops at the funerals of ex-servicemen who had died of their wounds.[178]

It was within this context that Power's hoax proved irresistible. The idea that Britain's last national hero – the defender of the empire, the 'Lion of the Seas', the man who was trusted when he cried, 'Your Country Needs YOU' – was going to rise again, if not in living flesh then symbolically through his ashes, was enticing. The thought that he was going to be accorded a grand funeral was even better. In this time of crisis, many people recalled that of 5 June ten years earlier when the nation had been in the midst of a nightmarish war that did not seem to be coming to an end. In 1916, Kitchener represented all that Britain was proud of; in 1926, he represented all that had been lost. His name was synonymous with devotion to king and country; he personified British military prowess; he was 'the greatest Liberal statesman'; 'a giant among men'.[179] By 'smashing the Mahdi', he had paid the debt owed to Charles Gordon in the Indian campaign; with Earl Roberts he had redeemed the situation in South Africa; in 1914 he had created 'one of the iron armies of the world' – a 'deathless army, fortified and made perfect by his genius, which [had beaten] down the doors of death'.[180] Writing about Kitchener in 1926, W. E. Hayter Preston recalled those days immediately after news came of Kitchener's drowning a decade earlier: 'nobody could realize that Kitchener was dead. In those dark days the most tragic, because the most human, voice I heard was that of a private soldier in France. He said to me: "It's only a blind and Kitchener's all right. He's putting the Russians in order; and the Jerry'll know it soon." '[181] When the General Strike was announced on the radio and the prime minister pleaded for calm, the feelings of a small group of military and professional men were echoed throughout the country: '[Baldwin's] message sounded woefully inadequate. Babel broke loose. An elderly dame gave us our cue by saying that she wished Kitchener were alive. We were lost sheep bleating for a shepherd.'[182] In those dark, divisive days in 1926, only a hero such as Kitchener could put everything in order again.

Frank Power emphasized Kitchener's symbolic importance. For him, the discovery of Kitchener's remains would have been a reminder of the important ideals of life, of 'loyal and ungrudging service, of the consideration of supreme gifts to God and to the King' in 'a time of unrest and disillusionment'.[183] Kitchener fulfilled the desire for a leader who was 'above poverty-strife' and 'all petty controversies'.[184]

The bringing back of his remains was the 'homecoming of a noble Englishman' to the 'final resting place that he himself would have wished, in the England that he loved and served, and in the heart of the great city': that is, near to the Unknown Warrior in Westminster Abbey.[185]

Kitchener was the right kind of hero for the mid-1920s. Like the sons and lovers of men and women throughout Britain, he was a hero whose sacrifice in dying in the performance of duty had not been sufficiently recognized.[186] Like the death of every other mother's son during war, his own was democratic: nobody was indispensable.[187] Yet the tragedy of Kitchener's death was publicly potent: only he could 'pull us through'.[188] He was 'cool', 'intolerant of the trivial and petty', possessing a 'hard will' and a 'hard constitution, combined with untiring energy'.[189] This was the man who could reduce his critics to 'a little group of submissively inquiring Greeks' with his authoritative pronouncements.[190] He was 'the complete soldier': assuredly not one of the insipid malingerers – this warrior was truly masculine, even in death.[191] Thus, when Power had first looked upon what he was to claim were Kitchener's remains, he noted that it was 'apparent . . . at once' that he was looking at a 'well-made, tall man'. And one of the Norwegians who helped him uncover the grave was said to have exclaimed in his limited English, 'Ah, this was a fine man!'[192]

The press were quick to make use of the comparisons between the bodies of Kitchener and the Unknown Warrior. The *Star* entitled its article on the hoax 'John Brown's Body', proclaiming, 'We do not know whether Lord Kitchener's body "lies moldering in the grave" of an "unknown warrior", or under the restless waves of the North Atlantic.'[193] On the street, the British were portrayed as responding to the (claimed) return of Kitchener's remains in a manner reminiscent of their response to the Unknown Warrior. For instance, when the unheralded and unidentified coffin said to be containing Kitchener's corpse was taken from Waterloo Station to the chapel, onlookers responded to the 'modest little procession' with a respect that 'could not have been greater had it been known that this was the funeral cortège of Lord Kitchener himself'. Men doffed their hats; scores of servicemen stood and saluted; women 'stopped with a glance of tender pride'. Truly, 'K of K [*sic*] would have wished in his heart no higher tribute than that instinctively paid to a soldier passing to his rest.'[194] This description echoed that of six years earlier when the *Manchester Guardian* had described the silence that descended on 11 November 1920 as the Unknown Warrior was taken to Westminster Abbey: 'Someone took off his hat, and with a nervous hesitancy the rest of the men bared their heads also. Here and there an old soldier could be detected slipping unconsciously into the posture of "attention". An elderly woman not far away, wiped her eyes and the man beside her looked white and stern.'[195] In 1920, and then again in 1926, English men and women stood reverently to lay to rest their sons whose graves were unknown.

The need to 'lay to rest', to take the 'sting out of death', to honour, glorify and hush memories scarred by international or civil war was as alive in 1926 as it had been in 1920.[196] Of course, Kitchener had already been honoured – with titles and medals – so a burial in Westminster Abbey was to be anticipated. The Unknown Warrior was much more in need of the honour of burial in the famed abbey. In a prayer to her lost husband during the ceremony on 11 November, an unnamed widow expressed this need for a civic adulation of dead loved ones when she told of the pride felt by her husband's father:

He had been so ambitious for you. He had sacrificed so much for you. You realized for him to-day the best of all his dreams – and so much more. For even he had never pictured you lying amongst the greatest of his people's heroes, beside Royal bones, taking your own proud place in his country's history, yourself history too. Buried in Westminster Abbey – my son John . . . I knew he would make his mark but – Westminster Abbey, beside Pitt and Gladstone, David Livingstone and Cromwell, in sight of Poet's Corner – my son John.[197]

England publicly embraced her missing sons.

This widow's prayer to her lost husband suggests other similarities between the events in 1920 and 1926. In both cases, the bereaved accused an all-powerful officialdom of responsibility for the death of their loved ones, and of indifference to finding their remains. Power accused officialdom of 'evasion, quibblings and procrastination'.[198] He claimed that there was 'no need for [him] to explain how it came about that it should have been left to [him], a private citizen, to engage in a mission which [had] resulted in the finding of Lord Kitchener's grave'.[199] Power's indictment of officialdom was echoed by the widow: 'I am sure the authorities did all they could, but oh, I am so thankful that the long and bitter disappointment of opening official envelopes is ended. I am so thankful that I shall never again have to read those cruel words, "Regret – No Trace"; that I can now forget those awful reference numbers running into hundreds of thousands.'[200] The widow's rebuke was echoed by another person – adopting the name 'Disappointed' – who wrote to *The Times* to ask if it might be possible for the War Office to 'show some little interest' in the missing men – if only to 'relieve [the] anxiety' of the bereaved.[201] The relentlessly humble demeanour of the bereaved in communication with state officials only served to draw attention to their moral superiority.

There was another reason for the potency of both of these accounts which relates to discussions earlier in this chapter concerning the filthiness of death in wartime. The modesty of death during battle made the need to honour the dead serviceman after war by a majestic display more urgent. Kitchener's grave was described as a 'cairn of stones', a 'little mound beside some others with headstones . . . and an inscription on one was "Known only to God" '.[202] Although it failed, Power's mission was to honour Kitchener in an ostentatious ceremony worthy of the warrior's status. Similarly, the Unknown Warrior was described thus:

> They little dreamt, who threw
> The hasty earth upon him, whom none knew –
> A broken glume, a flotsam cast aside –
> He should be type and pick of all who died.
> Or was he dragged from Ypres' muddied sea?
> Whichever be,
> A Prince of men, through crowds that massed the street,
> He rode triumphant; charioted to meet
> New obsequies in other soil than France
> With king, lords, people; all that can romance
> With death and trick her. Hither was he brought
> That matched, unnamed, our mightiest dead, who wrought
> Not more, nay less. This stately pile is his,
> His mausoleum, for a myriad eyes
> To wonder on.[203]

The body of the loved one had to be found, carried over the waves, and brought back home to the final resting place in the heart of London. Power claimed to be returning Kitchener's body 'to the resting place that he himself would have wished, in the England that he loved and served, and in the heart of the great city'.[204] In the same year as the Kitchener scandal, but concerned with the Unknown Warrior, E. H. Carrier put it more poetically,

> But when at last the War has passed
> They found him in his lowly grave;
> Round his chill form the Flag they cast
> And bore him home across the wave!
> A shrine they made and homage paid:
> The laurel wreath, the sacred gloom!
> And while an Empire watch, they laid
> The Unknown Warrior in his tomb.[205]

What was being represented was not an unknown warrior – for every mother, father, sister, brother and friend recalled the face belonging to the body buried on 11 November – but the unknown grave. Memorials to Kitchener echoed the words of the bereaved:

> Mother, where sleeps this Kitchener of ours?
> Vainly escutcheon sought for many hours
> In House of England's mighty dead – no tomb
> Marks spot of His – whom England mourned in gloom . . .
> O Mother mine, where sleeps our Kitchener?[206]

Another poem repeated this sentiment, and took it one step further. Instead of the anonymous dead, in this poem, we are given the heroic man, laid to rest in the entire sea:

> Well nigh two years have passed since beat of drum
> Unleashed the dogs of War, when Europe woke
> To scenes of blood and fire, and Mars' fell stroke
> Lay low young lives, whose no name can sum,
> But ah! did ever shock so sudden come
> To dwellers in these isles, as when there broke
> The news – 'The Pillar of our Armies' hope
> Is drown'd in waters which no line can plumb.'
>
> Will no one tell me whether reef or mine,
> Or merely mighty winds, with crested seas,
> Shipwrecked the *Hampshire* in that surging brine
> Which ebbs and flows around the Orcades?
> As not the cause – What boots it to repine –
> Our flag still braves the battle and the breeze.[207]

Finally, both the Unknown Warrior and Kitchener epitomized manly valour in a world seen to be desperately in need of heroism. As shown in Chapter Two, the rhetoric of courage and strength flourished more on the home front than on the battlefield. Fighting men repeated endlessly the refrain: where was heroism in the suicidal missions of misguided young men? Where was heroism in the pitiful deaths of soldiers mistakenly shot by their own side?[208] However, on the home front, the sacrifice of the heroic male body had two aspects. There was a special group of sacrificing warriors. These were men offering their bodies to save particular friends. In a poem called 'Jim (Royal Flying Corps) 1917', Georgette Agnew eulogized one such hero:

> Dauntless of death, above the pale clouds' net
> You led your bold patrol, and died
> Saving a comrade, enemy-beset –
> Ah! England such a gallant act will not forget;
> Your name stands glorified.[209]

The *Manchester Guardian* reported a similar instance in 1914 where after a charge of the Irish and Coldstream Guards, a soldier discovered that his 'chum' had been wounded and would not be rescued until morning: 'I'll go and keep him company, for he'll be terribly lonely out there by himself,' he said. By morning, both were dead.[210] These were the soldiers of whom it could be said, 'He saved others, himself he could not save.'[211] Similar stories abound.

Not everyone could attain such a distinctive death, even if they felt the urge to do so. The contradictions between sacrifice and duty were expressed by the war correspondent Dixon Scott, in May 1915, after he had been offered a job as a staff captain in England:

Tempting? Not a bit. It's the other that's tempting – the bloodshed and beastliness and the chittering nerves and even the sickness and death. Can't explain it entirely. But there it is. It's partly due to one's new realization of the *littleness* of individual death. With all these disappearances, one can't keep feeling awfully afraid of it . . . Or am I a sentimental fool? Perhaps – but I begin to believe so in heroism, in the truth of the most romantic, melodramatic, sort [sic] of it. I've met so many instances. These beggars do die spectacularly: Even the wounded do it as though to slow music; nurses and doctors have told me the queerest tales. They may, of course, be victims of their own ideas of what is romantically acceptable – Another reason for getting out oneself.[212]

The heroes Scott was writing about were men who, faced with the inevitable, chose to submit to their concept of the noble death, and gave their bodies to their country.

Heroic sacrifice was commonplace in war: indeed, when the chaplain T. W. Pym condemned the extent of petty theft in the trenches, he brooded over the fact that soldiers seemed more willing to sacrifice their bodies than small luxuries like a razor or blanket.[213] Sacrifice of the body was expected. Albert Andrews noted in his diary for 24 June 1916 that on leaving the front line trenches, soldiers were subjected to a fifteen-minute sermon on how Christ had given his life for others and how they were required to do the same.[214] All soldiers, sailors and airmen who died (except those who were executed after courts-martial) were placed into this heroic tradition because it required no special action of valour.[215] In war, the mere fact of dying was ennobling. There was, however, a hierarchy, part of which can be seen in Oscar P. Eckhard's musings over the death of his friend Eric Simon. In his diary, Eckhard wrote, 'If he had been killed in an attack it would not seem quite so awful; but to be killed while just walking along a trench or supervising a working party, perhaps by a stray bullet a mile behind the firing line – that is horrible.' Despite not being killed in an attack, a lower status of nobility could be conferred on the dead: 'Yet it somehow invests him with a nobility which he might not have achieved in half a century of humdrum life in times of peace. In fact it ennobles the whole Simon family,' he continued.[216] As was suggested in Chapter One, an even lower rank of heroic death belonged to the servicemen dying of disease. The heroic death in war was important to those who lived. Henry Buckmaster informed his mother of the death of his brother, her other son, and exhorted her to be brave: 'You must also remember that Nevill's sacrifice is a greater deed that winning any medal.'[217] In another letter, the mother of a dead soldier enjoined her sister not to grieve: 'Dear Gareth chose to put himself in the foremost place of danger, and has given his life willingly, so it is not for me to feel any regrets. I often thought how honoured a woman must feel like the mother of a great man – and now I know that this veil has fallen on me.'[218] Other men reminded themselves to cast aside their bitterness at the slaughter and remember that 'it [was] [their] country's freedom which [was their] goal'.[219]

The Unknown Warrior and Kitchener were both part of this tradition. The *Manchester Guardian* described the ceremonies on 11 November in the following words:

Primarily the supreme ceremony of yesterday was a tribute to the common man, to that same, sound, good-hearted, enduring humanity which we like to think is the stuff that goes to make an Englishman . . . This man was not a hero, except as all who died for their country and the world's good in that great time were heroes. He was just one of the multitude who did heroic things and died heroically.[220]

Kitchener's death was similarly heroic – its minor variations made it more, not less, appealing to people. His death was only exceptional because his life was sanctified: he gave his sublime life for those merely human. He was 'superhuman . . . a giant among men'.[221] Kitchener, the Unknown Warrior and all the heroic dead resembled Jesus. On the bodies of the killed were the 'marks of Jesus'.[222] When the Kitchener hoax was exposed, James Douglas wrote, 'They gambled on the great soldier's coffin and diced upon his shroud.'[223] Again, while preparing to attend the ceremonies on 11 November, the grieving mother of a lost soldier recalled how she was 'unmoved' by the Good Friday lesson earlier in the year: 'My body used to shrink and tremble at the words and I think I realized physically a little of what "crucified with Christ" meant, but to-day for the first time, my thoughts wandered and a soldier battered, broken on the wire took the place of Christ on the Cross.'[224]

Both the Unknown Warrior and the Kitchener hoax had been planned for the comfort of the bereaved rather than to give solace to those who had risked their bodies. In the case of the Unknown Warrior, living servicemen were incapable of persuading themselves that the anonymous body could statistically ever 'actually be' the body of the beloved. In the case of the Kitchener hoax, no ex-servicemen were mentioned. In the juggle between competing sacrifices – that of the bereaved as opposed to that of those men who fought – the bereaved triumphed.

However, there was one major difference between these two accounts concerning missing men. Both events were planned for the benefit of the bereaved but only in the first case was honour given to the mass of the bereaved. Although the committee that planned the ceremonies had privately intended to exhume a 1914 corpse belonging to a member of the Regular army, the body honoured in the ceremonies on 11 November was repeatedly said to belong as much to the dead son of a greengrocer as to the dead son of an aristocrat.[225] Contemporary reports consistently pointed out that the Unknown Warrior could have been anyone's loved one: he could have been one who had died somewhere on the Yser or in Ypres, Londrecies, Le Cateau, Loos, Neuve Chapelle or the Somme. He could have been an Ulsterman, a New Zealander, a Scotsman, an Irishman, a Welshman, a South African, a Newfoundlander or a man from Middlesex. He could have been a Christian or a Sikh.[226] As *The Times* editorial proclaimed on 11 November 1920, the ceremonies were 'impersonal, or, more truly, they are personal to us all . . . They are a tribute to no single name; to no General whose genius inspired our Armies; to no warrior whose prowess won renown among his fellows. They are a tribute to "the glorious dead", equal in their glory as in death . . . The Unknown Warrior is in a special sense an emblem of "the plain man", of the masses of the people.'[227] In 1926, however, the dead man was conspicuously heroic and illustrious. At a time when the validity of sacrifice itself was being questioned, the stress that Power's hoax placed on one of the warmongers helped to legitimate the fact that this was also the Kitchener who had sacrificed their own sons. Between the war and 1926, a shift had occurred in the construction of masculinity: the image of manliness stimulated by the Kitchener affair was more rather than less heroic.

The male body was subjected to callous treatment during war and then to the renewed sanitizing disciplines of peace. At the same time, the ceremonies honouring male bodies remained inadequate. The spiritualists as well as the hoaxer were all too willing to exploit sorrow as a commodity. The services at Westminster Abbey enabled the bereaved to visualize those they had lost not in the muddied fields of Flanders but in the purifying atmosphere of a place of worship. The consciences of the bereaved were put at rest without their needing to ask whether the sacrifice had been necessary. The Kitchener hoax infuriated commentators because Frank Power had defiled Kitchener's body by attempting to remove it from the embrace of the cold clean waves to some sordid little room of an undertaker. None of these commentators, however, was disputing the need for an authoritative hero to inspire patriotism and embody discipline. The radical potentiality of the desire for mutual support that surfaced briefly, and for only a minority of men, under the stressful conditions of modern warfare quickly disappeared in peacetime. In fact, when in 1920 Padre David Railton attempted to have the Unknown Warrior named the 'Unknown Comrade', his proposal was rejected out of hand.[228]

Wartime experiences and imaginings were utterly new for two groups of men. The dead experienced the war absolutely, and hundreds of thousands of men's bodies were literally dismembered. In the flesh, this was irrevocable. Mutilated men returned to a country which rapidly forgot this corporeal crisis. Although the war dramatically changed the technologies and techniques applied to the maimed, men responded to their physical handicaps in conventional ways. Within a few years, their status as warriors had been forgotten and society had relegated them to the lowly position of disabled children and injured workmen. While the signs by which the older generation of men attempted (and failed) to demonstrate its masculinity could be worn on its sleeves in the form of shiny medals, or were evident in the stumbling gait of the wounded, the younger generation flaunted its muscles and asserted its strength in a symbolic display of bellicosity. Although fathers could not compete with their sons' swollen biceps and thighs, both generations shared a concern with individual, fragmented bodily parts. It was by this process of fragmentation and fetishization that the male body regained respect.

For those servicemen who returned 'whole', their military experiences had exposed them to disciplines that were 'new' only in the sense that they were now being applied to a much broader section of the population. This can be seen in class as much as sectoral terms. Firstly, despite fundamental differences between the experiences of officers compared with men in the other ranks, the war saw a narrowing in the way men of all classes experienced their own corporeality. The way in which a respectable clerk and a miner at the turn of the century lived through their bodies became less differentiated during the war. Although the range of 'masculinities' remained extremely wide, military experiences led to a greater sharing of gender identities between men of different classes, ages and localities. Secondly, while

Victorian Britain was becoming increasingly militarist, the war dramatically enhanced this trend as the techniques used to discipline men within military contexts were applied to civilian workers between the wars. Debates about the relationship between the 'body' and the 'mind' enabled employers and managers to label shirking workers as neurasthenic, and industrial psychology taught them how to control their workers more effectively. The body came to be inspected by a huge army of self-designated experts. Military and civilian disciplines, which had been moving closer together since fears of degeneration at the time of the South African War, were firmly fused.

The individual man retreated to familiar spaces of desire and empowerment. Wartime experiences led to an increased yearning amongst the male sex for a domesticity that was far from oppressive statist and military interventions, but that very domesticity failed to substitute a more effective conjugal bonding. The ability of lovers to communicate kindly to each other was as limited as male bonding in the trenches. Those fortunate enough to attain domestic contentment regarded their happiness with astonishment. Organizations devoted to forging 'modern' masculinities inspired only a handful of men: more typically, they were to enthusiastically embrace familiar roles and desires. In the inter-war years, attempts to remember the wartime body and to reconstruct a new type of masculinity failed to provide an alternative to either Kitchener or the Unknown Warrior. Instead, as the threat of another war intensified, the sacrifice of a new generation of men, their bodies trained to a still higher standard of discipline, was offered up once again. The dismembered man was Everyman.

References

Introduction: Embodiment

1 Gayle Rubin, 'The Traffic in Women: Notes on the "Political Economy" of Sex', in Rayna Reiter, ed., *Towards an Anthropology of Women* (New York, 1975), 80.

2 For a sensitive discussion of the 'constructionist' position, see David M. Halperin, 'Is there a History of Sexuality?' *History and Theory. Studies in the Philosophy of History*, XXVIII (1989), 257–74. For influential applications of constructionist models, see Michel Foucault, *Discipline and Punish* (London, 1977), and *The History of Sexuality. Vol. 1: An Introduction*, translated by Robert Hurley (New York, 1978).

3 Robert H. MacDonald, *Sons of the Empire. The Frontier and the Boy Scout Movement, 1890–1918* (Toronto, 1993); J. A. Mangan, *Athleticism in the Victorian and Edwardian Public Schools* (Cambridge, 1981); Peter Parker, *The Old Lie: the Great War and the Public School Ethos* (London, 1987); Michael Rosenthal, *The Character Factory: Baden-Powell and the Origins of the Boy Scouts Movement* (London, 1986); John Springhall, *Youth, Empire and Society: British Youth Movements 1883 to 1940* (London, 1977); John Springhall, 'Building Character in the British Boy: The Attempt to Extend Christian Manliness to Working-Class Adolescents, 1880–1914', in J. A. Mangan and James Walvin, eds, *Manliness and Morality* (Manchester, 1987), 52–74; Norman Vance, *The Sinews of the Spirit: The Ideal of Christian Manliness in Victorian Literature and Religious Thought* (Cambridge, 1985); Allen Warren, 'Popular Manliness: Baden-Powell, Scouting and the Development of Manly Character', in Mangan and Walvin, eds, *Manliness and Morality*, 199–219.

4 Kelly Boyd, 'Knowing Your Place. The Tensions of Manliness in Boys' Stories Papers, 1918–39', in John Tosh and Michael Roper, *Manful Assertions* (London, 1991), 145–67; John R. Gillis, *Youth and History. Tradition and Change in European Age Relations 1770 – Present* (New York, 1981); Stephen Humphries, *Hooligans and Rebels. An Oral History of Working-Class Childhood and Youth 1889–1939* (Oxford, 1981); John O. Springhall, *Coming of Age. Adolescence in Britain 1860–1960* (Dublin, 1986).

5 Ronald Hyam, *Empire and Sexuality. The British Experience* (Manchester, 1992); John MacKenzie, 'The Imperial Pioneer and Hunter and the British Masculine Stereotype in Late Victorian and Edwardian Times', in Mangan and Walvin, eds, *Manliness and Morality*, 176–98; John MacKenzie, *Imperialism and Popular Culture* (Manchester, 1986); J. A. Mangan, *The Games Ethic and Imperialism* (Harmondsworth, 1985); George L. Mosse, *Nationalism and Sexuality: Respectability and Abnormal Sexuality in Modern Europe*, (New York, 1985); idem, *Fallen Soldiers. Reshaping the Memory of the World Wars* (New York, 1990).

6 Stefan Collini, '"Manly Fellows": Fawcett, Stephen, and the Liberal Temper',

and Boyd Hilton, 'Manliness, Masculinity and the Mid-Victorian Temperament', both in Lawrence Goldman, ed., *The Blind Victorian: Henry Fawcett and British Liberalism* (Cambridge, 1989), 41–59 and 60–70.

7 David Newsome, *Godliness and Good Learning: Four Studies of a Victorian Ideal* (London, 1961), and Vance, *Sinews of the Spirit*.

8 Frank Mort, *Dangerous Sexualities: Medico-Moral Politics in England since 1830* (London, 1987); Mosse, *Nationalism and Sexuality*; Jeffrey Weeks, *Coming Out: Homosexual Politics in Britain from the Nineteenth Century to the Present* (London, 1977); Jeffrey Weeks, *Sex, Politics and Society. The Regulation of Sexuality since 1800* (London, 1981).

9 Joanna Bourke, *Working-Class Cultures in Britain 1890–1960: Gender, Class and Ethnicity* (London, 1994); Elizabeth Roberts, *A Woman's Place. An Oral History of Working-Class Women 1840–1940* (Oxford, 1984); John Tosh, 'Domesticity and Manliness in the Victorian Middle Class. The Family of Edward White Benson', in Tosh and Roper, eds, *Manful Assertions*, 44–73; David Vincent, 'Love and Death and the Nineteenth-Century Working Class', *Social History*, 5.2 (May 1980), 223–47.

10 Roy Porter, 'History of the Body', in Peter Burke, ed., *New Perspectives on Historical Writing* (Pennsylvania, 1991), 225.

11 Very little has been written on masculinity and the First World War. The exception are Mosse's books, *Nationalism and Sexuality* and *Fallen Soldiers*, which focus on Germany and France but make perceptive comparisons with Britain. Some work has been done on masculinity in the literature of the war. For instance, Alfredo Bonadeo, *Mark of the Beast. Death and Degradation in the Literature of the Great War* (Lexington, 1989) links masculinity in wartime with manly degradation. Adrian Caesar's *Taking It Like a Man. Suffering, Sexuality, and the War Poets* (Manchester, 1993) looks at the life and writings of Rupert Brooke, Siegfried Sassoon, Wilfred Owen and Robert Graves and draws a relationship between masculinity in wartime and sado-masochism.

12 The best are in John Tosh, 'Domesticity and Manliness in the Victorian Middle Class. The Family of Edward White Benson', in Tosh and Roper, eds, *Manful Assertions*, 44–73; John Tosh and Michael Roper, 'Introduction: Historians and the Politics of Masculinity', in Tosh and Roper, eds, *Manful Assertions*, 1–24; and Mangan and Walvin, eds, *Manliness and Morality*.

13 Lynne Segal, *Slow Motion: Changing Masculinities, Changing Men* (London, 1990), and Victor J. Seidler, *Rediscovering Masculinity: Reason, Language and Sexuality* (London, 1989), 21.

14 Tosh and Roper, 'Introduction: Historians and the Politics of Masculinity', in Tosh and Roper, eds, *Manful Assertions*, 9.

15 Graham Dawson, *Soldier Heroes. British Adventure, Empire and the Imagining of Masculinity* (London, 1994).

16 Ian Beckett, 'Frocks and Brasshats', in Brian Bond, ed., *The First World War and British Military History* (Oxford, 1991), 89–112. See the defence of the use of oral history by Peter Simkins, 'Everymen at War: Recent Interpretations of the Front Line Experiences', in Bond, ed., *The First World War and British Military History*, 288–313.

17 Jack Christie, 'Undiminished Memories', in Michael Hall, *Sacrifice on the Somme* (Newtownabbey, 1993), 22.

18 J. M. Bourne, *Britain and the Great War 1914–1918* (London, 1989), 244.

19 Ralph Scott, *A Soldier's Diary* (London, 1923), 174.

20 Revd John M. Connor, 'Diary', 21 November 1914, IWM 87/10/1.

21 J. L. Hammond, 'The War and the Mind of Great Britain', *Atlantic Monthly*, CXXIII (March 1919), 356.

22 J. F. Rutherford, *Talking with the Dead?* (London, 1920), 47.

23 Arthur Marwick, *War and Social Change in the Twentieth Century* (London, 1974).

24 Jay Winter, *The Great War and the British People* (London, 1986). See also Deborah Dwork, *War is Good For Babies and Other Young Children. A History of the Infant and Child Welfare Movement in England 1898–1918* (London, 1987); Ruth Barrington, *Health, Medicine and Politics in Ireland 1900–1970* (Dublin, 1987); Jay Winter, 'Some Paradoxes of the Great War', in Richard Wall and Jay Winter, eds, *The Upheaval of War: Family, Work and Welfare in Europe 1914–1918* (Cambridge, 1988), 9–42.

25 Deborah Thom, 'Wishes, Anxieties, Play, and Gestures: Child Guidance in Inter-War Britain', in Roger Cooter, ed., *In the Name of the Child. Health and Welfare 1880–1940* (London, 1992), 200–19, and Cathy Unwin and Elaine Sharland, 'From Bodies to Minds in Childcare Literature. Advice to Parents in Inter-War Britain', in Cooter, ed., *In the Name of the Child*, 174–99.

26 Sara Josephine Baker, *Fighting for Life* (Huntingdon, 1980), first published 1939, 165.

27 For the argument that the war dramatically and permanently expanded provision for scientific and technological research, see Guy Hartcup, *The War of Invention. Scientific Developments 1914–1918* (London, 1988); Roy Macleod and Kay Macleod, 'War and Economic Development: Government and the Optical Industry in Britain, 1914–18', in Jay M. Winter, ed., *War and Economic Development* (Cambridge, 1975), 165–203; Michael Pattison, 'Scientists, Government and Invention: The Experience of the Inventions Board 1915–1918', in Peter H. Liddle, ed., *Home Fires and Foreign Fields. British Social and Military Experience in the First World War* (London, 1985), 83–100. The impact of war has been questioned by Roger Cooter, 'War and Modern Medicine', in W. F. Bynum and Roy Porter, eds, *Companion Encyclopedia of the History of Medicine* (London, 1993), 1536–73, and D. E. M. Edgerton, 'Science and War', in R. C. Olby, G. N. Cantor, J. R. R. Christie and M. J. S. Hodge, eds, *Companion to the History of Modern Science* (London, 1990), 934–45.

28 Alisdair Reid, 'Dilution, Trade Unionism and the State in Britain During the First World War', in S. Tolliday and J. Zeitlin, eds, *Shop Floor Bargaining and the State: Historical and Comparative Perspectives* (Cambridge, 1985), 46–74, and Alisdair Reid, 'World War One and the Working Class in Britain', in Arthur Marwick, ed., *Total War and Social Change* (London, 1988), 16–24.

29 W. H. Greenleaf, *The British Political Tradition. Vol. 1. The Rise of Collectivism* (London, 1983), 47–77; Alan T. Peacock and Jack Wiseman, *The Growth of Public Expenditure in the United Kingdom* (London, 1961), xxi–xxv; Jay Winter, 'Some Paradoxes of the Great War', in Wall and Winter, eds, *The Upheaval of War*, 453. For other changes in institutions, see Gaynor Kavanagh, 'The First World War and Its Implications for Education in British Museums', *History of Education*, XVII.2 (1988), 163–76. For a cautious statement about the failure of the state to change dramatically as a consequence of the war, see J. M. Bourne, *Britain and the Great War 1914–1918* (London, 1989), 236–40.

30 Marc Ferro, *The Great War* (London, 1973); Gerd Hardach, *The First World War* (London, 1977); David Sweet, 'The Domestic Scene: Parliament and People', in Liddle, ed., *Home Fires and Foreign Fields*, 9–19. A fascinating comparative dimension may be found in Russell Lawrence Barsh, 'American Indians in the Great War', *Ethnohistory*, XXXVIII.3 (Summer 1991), 276–303.

31 Gary S. Messenger, 'An Inheritance Worth Remembering: The British Approach to Official Propaganda during the First World War', *Historical Journal of Film, Radio and Television*, XIII.2 (1993), 117–27; Philip M. Taylor, 'Introduction: Britain and the Cinema in the First World War', *Historical Journal of Film, Radio and Television*, XIII.2 (1993), 115–16; Bernard Waites,

'The Government of the Home Front and the "Moral Economy" of the Working Class', in Liddle, ed., *Home Fires and Foreign Fields*, 175–93.

32 James F. McMillan, 'World War One and Women in France', in Marwick, ed., *Total War and Social Change*, 1–15, and Sarah M. Gilbert and Susan Gubar, *No Man's Land. The Place of the Woman Writer in the Twentieth Century. Vol. 2. Sexchanges* (New Haven, 1989), 318. Also see R. J. Adams, *Arms and the Wizard: Lloyd George and the Ministry of Munitions, 1915–16* (London, 1978); Carl Chinn, *They Worked All Their Lives: Women of the Urban Poor in England 1880–1939* (Manchester, 1988), 165; Sandra Stanley Holton, *Feminism and Democracy: Women's Suffrage and Reform Politics in Britain 1900–1918* (Cambridge, 1986); David Mitchell, *Women on the Warpath: The Story of the Women of the First World War* (London, 1966); Robert Roberts, *The Classic Slum: Salford Life in the First Quarter of the Century* (Manchester, 1971), 162; Penny Summerfield and Gail Braybon, *Out of the Cage: Women's Experience in Two World Wars* (London, 1987); Angela Woollacott, *On Her Their Lives Depend. Munition Worker in the Great War* (Berkeley, 1994).

33 Arthur Marwick, *The Deluge: British Society and the First World War*, 2nd edn, (London, 1991), 147.

34 Deirdre Beddoe, *Back to Home and Duty* (London, 1989), chapter 3; Gail Braybon, *Women Workers in the First World War: The British Experience* (London, 1981); Miriam Glucksmann, *Women Assemble: Women Workers and the New Industries in Inter-war Britain* (London, 1990); Jenny Gould, 'Women's Military Services in First World War Britain', in Margaret R. Higonnet et al., eds, *Behind the Lines* (New Haven, 1987), 114–25; Arthur Marwick, *Women at War 1914–1918* (London, 1977); Susan Pedersen, 'Gender, Welfare and Citizenship in Britain during the Great War', *American Historical Review*, XCV.4 (October 1990), 983–1006; Denise Riley, 'Some Peculiarities of Social Policy Concerning Women in Wartime and Post-war Britain', in Higonnet et al., eds, *Behind the Lines*, 260–71; Denise Riley, 'War in the Nursery', *Feminist Review*, II, 1979; Sylvia Walby, *Patriarchy at Work: Patriarchal and Capitalist Relations in Employment* (Cambridge, 1986); Deborah Thom, 'Women and Work in Wartime Britain', in Wall and Winter, ed., *The Upheaval of War*, 297–326.

35 The phrase is from Angela Woollacott, *On Her Their Lives Depend. Munition Workers in the Great War* (Berkeley, 1994). There is a great deal about the gendering of war and women: for instance, see Miriam Cooke and Angela Woollacott, eds, *Gendering War Talk* (Princeton, 1993); Higonnet et al., eds, *Behind the Lines*; Helen Cooper et al. (eds), *Arms and the Women: War, Gender and Literary Representation* (Chapel Hill, 1989).

36 Paul Fussell, *The Great War and Modern Memory* (London, 1975).

37 Eric J. Leed, *No Man's Land. Combat and Identity in World War One* (Cambridge, 1979), 193.

38 Ibid., 193.

39 Samuel Hynes, 'The Irony and the Pity', *Times Literary Supplement*, 18 December 1981, 1469.

40 Idem, *A War Imagined. The First World War and English Culture* (London, 1992), x.

41 John Cruikshank, *Variations on Catastrophe. Some French Responses to the Great War* (Oxford, 1982). See also Malcolm Bradbury, 'The Denuded Place: War and Form in *Parade's End* and *U.S.A.*', in Holger Klein, ed., *The First World War in Fiction* (London, 1976), 193–209, and David Harvey, *The Condition of Postmodernity: An Enquiry into the Origins of Cultural Change* (Oxford, 1989).

42 Modris Eksteins, *Rites of Spring. The Great War and the Birth of the Modern Age* (London, 1989).

43 Peter Buitenhuis, *The Great War of Words. Literature as Propaganda 1914–18 and After* (London, 1989), 179–80.

44 Ian Beckett, 'The British Army, 1914–1918: The Illusion of Change', in John Turner, ed., *Britain and the First World War* (London, 1988), 99–116.

45 For analyses on the importance of the war in Irish political history, see D. G. Boyce, 'British Opinion, Ireland, and the War, 1916–1918', *Historical Journal*, XVII (1974), 575–93; David Fitzpatrick, ed., *Ireland and the First World War* (Dublin, 1986); idem, ed., *Revolution? Ireland 1917–1923* (Dublin, 1990). For a discussion on the impact of the war on Irish arts and literature, see Keith Jeffery, 'The Great War in Modern Irish Memory', in T. G. Fraser and Keith Jeffery, eds, *Men, Women and War* (Dublin, 1993), 136–57.

46 The best summary is in Jay M. Winter, *The Experience of World War I* (Oxford, 1988), 226–9. See also Ian Beckett, 'The British Army, 1914–1918: The Illusion of Change', in Turner, ed., *Britain and the First World War*, 116, and Keith Jeffery, 'The Post-War Army', in Ian Beckett and Keith Simpson, eds, *Nation in Arms* (Manchester, 1985), 211–34.

47 Letter from Paul Nash to his wife, 16 November 1917, quoted in Paul Edwards, *Wyndham Lewis: Art and War* (London, 1992), 36. Similar words were written by Wilfred Owen in a letter to his mother on 4 October 1918: Harold Owen and John Bell, eds, *Collected Letters* (London, 1967), 580.

48 Andrew Rutherford, *The Literature of War, Five Studies in Heroic Virtue* (London, 1978).

49 Ted Bogacz, '"A Tyranny of Words": Language, Poetry, and Antimodernism in England in the First World War', *Journal of Modern History*, LVIII (September 1986), 643–68.

50 Jay Winter, *Sites of Memory, Sites of Mourning. The Place of the Great War In European Cultural History* (Cambridge, 1995).

51 Leed, *No Man's Land*, xi.

52 Hynes, *A War Imagined*, x.

53 Harry Siepmann, 'Rising with the Guns. Reminisces [*sic*] of the First World War Compiled from the Letters and Diaries of Capt. Harry Siepmann, RFA', 301, IWM 85/43/1.

54 This is not to deny the dramatic impact of the war on the development of psychoanalytical theory: Freud was forced to reformulate his ideas regarding aggression and the death instinct as a result of the war: S. Freud, 'Beyond the Pleasure Principle', *Collected Papers* (London, 1920).

55 W. Graham Wallace, 'Copy of Typescript Memoir of his Service', 1935, 39, Liddell Hart Centre for Military Archives.

56 Stuart Sillars, *Art and Survival in the First World War* (Basingstoke, 1987), 154–5.

57 Douglas Haig was British commander-in-chief on the Western Front. Cited in J. M. Bourne, *Britain and the Great War 1914–1918* (London, 1989), 208.

58 *Post Office. Report of the Postmaster-General of the Post Office 1914–15* [Cd. 7955], H. C. 1914–16, XXXII, 5, and *Post Office. Report of the Postmaster-General on the Post Office 1915–16* [Cd. 8424], H. C. 1916, XIV, 2.

59 For a comment to this effect, see Henry Gother Courtney, 'Letters', letter to his sister Kathleen, 1 December 1916, Birmingham University Library no. 8/148.

60 For instance, Courtney told his sister that he kept a diary in addition to writing to his family most days. He wrote, 'I have tried to make the diary complementary to letters, putting in it what can't be said in letters at the time': Courtney, ibid., letter to his sister Kathleen, 21 December 1916, Birmingham University Library no. 8/153. It was often possible to avoid the censor by giving letters to servicemen on leave: see Courtney, letter of 25 November 1916,

Birmingham University Library no. 8/14, and J. Allson, 'Letter', undated, IWM 85/15/1.

61 Henry Gother Courtney, 'Letters', letter to his mother, 3 December 1914, Birmingham University Library no. 8/17.

62 Miss D. Williams, 'Letters', letter to her from 'Jack' who is in Palestine, 23 November 1917, IWM 85/4/1.

63 Throughout the present study, quotations from correspondence illustrate this point (especially in Chapters One and Five). For a particularly good example, see Henry Gother Courtney, 'Letters', Birmingham University Library.

64 Brian Finney, *The Inner I. British Literary Autobiography of the Twentieth Century* (London, 1985), 169.

65 For a detailed, theoretical analysis of the dual mentality of people writing 'home', see David Fitzpatrick, *Oceans of Consolation, Personal Accounts of Irish Migration to Australia* (Ithaca, 1994).

66 Leed, *No Man's Land*, 200.

67 Klaus Theweleit, *Male Fantasies*, 2 vols (Minneapolis, 1987).

68 Comment by 'Corporal Frederick W' in Clifford Nixon, 'A Touch of Memory. Transcription of an Autograph Book, 1914–1915', 13 July 1915, 23, IWM Misc 163 Item 2508.

69 Leed, *No Man's Land*, 194–5.

70 Mosse, *Nationalism and Sexuality*, 127–8.

71 Gilbert and Gubar, *No Man's Land, Vol. 2*, 262–3.

72 Survey of film-goers in the late 1930s: Jeffery Richards and Dorothy Sheridan, eds, *Mass-Observation at the Movies* (London, 1987), 45, 82, 100–2.

73 Fussell, *The Great War and Modern Memory*, 279–80.

74 Martin Taylor, *Lads. Love Poetry of the Trenches* (London, 1989), 34. Fussell, *The Great War and Modern Memory*, traces this homoerotic tradition from the aesthetic movement and the Uranian poets until the war.

75 Taylor, *Lads*, 26.

76 The most clear exposition of the thesis that male comradeship led to the downfall of heterosexual love can be found in Taylor, *Lads*, 53.

77 Caesar, *Taking It Like a Man*, 234. See also p. 225.

78 Winter, *Sites of Memory, Sites of Mourning*.

79 In the context of literary representations, Andrew Rutherford's *Literature of War, Studies in Heroic Virtue* (Basingstoke, 1989), has identified the variations in terms of a shift from the hero as subaltern (Kipling) to the hero as intellectual (T. E. Lawrence) to the hero as the common man (the Western Front). Although I accept his general schema, in my argument the order of the last two is reversed, for the hero as common man (in my version, the Unknown Warrior) precedes the hero as intellectual (or, in my version, the hero as leader: Lord Kitchener).

80 M. M. Postan, 'Some Social Consequences of the Hundred Years' War', *Economic History Review*, XII (1942), 4.

81 For further discussion, see Roger Cooter, 'War and Modern Medicine', in Bynum and Porter eds, *Companion Encylopedia of the History of Medicine*, 1536–73, and Roger Cooter and Steve Sturdy, 'Science, Scientific Management and the Medical Revolution in Britain *c.* 1870–1948', unpublished paper, 1994, 8.

82 Arthur Marwick, 'Introduction', in Marwick, ed., *Total War and Social Change*, xi.

83 Charles Edmunds Carrington [pseud. Charles Edmunds], *Soldiers from the Wars Returning* (London, 1965), 250.

84 Cited in Taylor, *Lads*, 55.

85 'F.A.V.', *Combed Out* (London, 1920), 132.

86 This stress on diversity is also made by Tony Ashworth, *Trench Warfare 1914–*

1918: The Live and Let Live System (London, 1980), 21–2; Ian Beckett, 'The
Territorial Force in the Great War', in Liddle, ed., *Home Fires and Foreign
Fields*, 21–37; Ian Beckett, 'The British Army, 1914–1918: The Illusion of
Change', in Turner, ed., *Britain and the First World War*, 106–7; Keith Robbins,
The First World War (Oxford, 1984), 150–1; Keith Simpson, 'The British
Soldier on the Western Front', in Liddle, *Home Fires and Foreign Fields*, 143–5.

87 Denis Winter, *Death's Men. Soldiers of the Great War* (London, 1978), 20.
88 Ibid., 20.
89 For instance, see Richard B. Speed, *Prisoners, Diplomats and the Great War. A
Study in the Diplomacy of Captivity* (New York, 1990).
90 Jay M. Winter, 'Britain's "Lost Generation" of the First World War', *Population
Studies*, XXXI.3 (1977), 450.
91 For instance, see the superb book by Robert Weldon Whalen, *Bitter Wounds.
German Victims of the Great War, 1914–1939* (Ithaca, 1984). His discussion of
the treatment of the German war-injured provides an interesting comparison
with my own.
92 Winter, *Sites of Memory, Sites of Mourning*.
93 *General Annual Reports on the British Army for the Period from 1 October 1913 to
30 September 1919* [Cmd. 1193], (London, 1921).
94 Henry Gother Courtney, 'Letters', letter to his sister Kathleen, 2 December
1916, Birmingham University Library no. 8/148.
95 For an excellent comparative analysis of soldiers and sailors, see David
Englander and James Osborne, 'Jack, Tommy, and Henry Dubb: The Armed
Forces and the Working Class', *Historical Journal*, XXI.3 (1978), 593–621.
96 Winter, 'Britain's "Lost Generation" of the First World War', 450.
97 Bryan Ranft, 'The Royal Navy and the War at Sea', in Turner, ed., *Britain and
the First World War*, 53–69, provides an interesting and only slightly less
pessimistic account of the navy's influence on the war. Also see A. Marder,
From Dreadnought to Scapa Flow, v (London, 1970), 192–4.
98 Michael Paris, 'The Rise of the Airmen: The Origins of Air Force Elitism,
*c.*1890–1918', *Journal of Contemporary History*, XXVIII (1993), 123–41.
99 Roger Cooter, 'War and Modern Medicine', in Bynum and Porter, eds,
Companion Encyclopedia of the History of Medicine, 1536–73.
100 The best discussion of both art and film is undoubtedly Winter, *Sites of Memory,
Sites of Mourning*. For art, see Paul Edwards, *Wyndham Lewis: Art and War*
(London, 1992); John Ferguson, *The Arts in Britain in World War One* (London,
1980); M. R. D. Foot, *Art and War. Twentieth-Century Warfare as Depicted by
War Artists* (London, 1990); Charles Harrison, *English Art and Modernism 1900–
1939* (Bloomington, Indiana, 1981); Imperial War Museum, *A Concise Catalogue
to Paintings, Drawings, and Sculpture of the First World War, 1914–1918* (London,
1924); Elizabeth Louise Kahn, 'Art From the Front, Death Imagined and the
Neglected Majority', *Art History*, VIII.2 (1985); Sue Malvern, '"War As It Is":
The Art of Muirhead Bone, C. R. W. Nevinson and Paul Nash, 1916–17', *Art
History*, IX.4 (1986), 487–515; Tom Normand, *Wyndham Lewis. The Artist
Holding the Mirror Up to Politics* (Cambridge, 1992); Stuart Sillars, *Art and
Survival in First World War Britain* (Basingstoke, 1987). For film, see the special
issue devoted to film and the First World War in *Historical Journal of Film,
Radio and Television*, XIII.3 (1993); Kevin Brownlow, *The History of the British
Film 1914–1918* (London, 1948); Cate Haste, *Keep the Home Fires Burning.
Propaganda in the First World War* (London, 1977); Nicholas P. Hitey, '"The
British Army Film", "You!" and "For the Empire": Reconstructed Propaganda
Films 1914–1916', *Historical Journal of Film, Radio and Television*, V.2 (1985);
Nicholas Reeves, *Official British Film Propaganda during the First World War*
(London, 1986); M. L. Sanders, 'British Film Propaganda in Russia, 1916–

1918', *Historical Journal of Film, Radio and Television*, III.2 (1983), 117–29; and, for a comparative example, see Eberhard Demm, 'Propaganda and Caricature in the First World War', *Journal of Contemporary History*, XXVIII (1993), 163–92.

101 Lowell Thomas, *With Lawrence in Arabia* (London, 1925), 17.

102 Graham Dawson, 'The Blond Bedouin, Lawrence of Arabia, Imperial Adventure and the Imagining of English-British Masculinity', in Roper and Tosh, eds, *Manful Assertions*, 114.

103 Ibid., 114; John M. MacKenzie, 'T. E. Lawrence: The Myth and the Message', in Robert Giddings, ed., *Literature and Imperialism* (Basingstoke, 1991), 150–81; Brian Holder Reid, 'T. E. Lawrence and his Biographers', in Brian Bond, ed., *The First World War and British Military History* (Oxford, 1991), 227–59. For a brief, but perceptive study, see Mosse, *Nationalism and Sexuality*, 120–5.

104 Fussell, *The Great War and Modern Memory* and Gilbert and Gubar, *No Man's Land*, vol. 2. Also see the historians cited in the footnotes concerned with literature and the war experience.

105 The most important work on metaphors of the body as machine is Anson Rabinbach, *The Human Motor: Energy, Fatigue, and the Origins of Modernity* (Berkeley, 1992). He argues that metaphors of the machine were applied to the body, heightened by concerns about the 'wastage' of labour. Also see Karen Lucic, *Charles Sheeler and the Cult of the Machine* (London, 1991) for a discussion of the importance of 'the machine' in American discourse between the wars.

106 For examples, see Frank Constantine and Peyton Skipwith (introducers), *C. R. W. Nevinson, War Paintings 1914–1918* (Sheffield, 1972), and Paul Edwards, *Wyndham Lewis: Art and War* (London, 1992).

Chapter One: Mutilating

1 Wilfred Willett, 'Memoirs', 81, IWM 82/1/1. This fear of mutilation was frequently expressed. For example, see Warwick Deeping, *No Hero – This* (London, 1936), 2.

2 Hazel Thompson Clements, 'Diaries', 22 May 1915, in IWM 86/76/1.

3 Calculated from the *General Annual Reports on the British Army (Including the Territorial Force from the Date of Embodiment) for the Period from 1st October, 1913, to 30th September, 1919. Prepared by Command of the Army Command* [Cmd. 1193], H. C. 1921, XX, 71.

4 Jay M. Winter, 'Britain's "Lost Generation" of the First World War', *Population Studies*, XXXI.3 (1977), 451.

5 G. Howson, *Handbook for the Limbless* (London, 1922), xii. For similar statistics, see H. H. C. Baird, *A Handbook for the Limbless. For the General Guidance of Ex-Service Men who have lost One or More Limbs* (London, 1921), 1, and Ernest Muirhead Little, *Artificial Limbs and Amputation Stumps. A Practical Handbook* (London, 1922), 23–4.

6 'Convalescent Centres. Memorandum by the Ministry of Pensions', 6 October 1920, PRO PIN15/35.

7 *Copies of Reports made to the Prime Minister by the British Legion regarding the Condition of Ex-Service Men and of his Reply* [Cmd. 5738], H. C. 1937–38, X, 30.

8 *British Limbless Ex-Service Men's Association. Annual Report and Accounts for the Year ended 31st December, 1977*, 1.

9 P. Duval, *War Wounds of the Lung: Notes on their Surgical Treatment at the Front* (Bristol, 1918), 3, and H. P. Pickerill, *Facial Surgery* (Edinburgh, 1924), 77.

10 Frederick Watson, *Civilization and the Cripple* (London, 1930), 19.

11 James Henry Dible, 'Diary', 9, IWM Con Shelf. He continued, 'On the contrary: I have played hockey at Etaples, golf at Etretat, cricket at St. Omer.'

12 Sir Charles Burtchaell, 'Translation of Criticism by Dr Doyan of the French Army Medical Service, July 1915: The Distribution of the Wounded', 1915, 2, CMAC RAMC 446/11.

13 'F.A.V.', *Combed Out* (London, 1920), 59.

14 Edward T. Devine, *Disabled Soldiers and Sailors. Pensions and Training* (New York, 1991), 9.

15 Ibid., 11. See also 'Copy of a Letter from Colonel Arthur Lee, M. P., to Lord Kitchener', 21 October 1914, 4, PRO WO159/16; letter from Lord Esher to Kitchener, 30 September 1914, 3–4, PRO 30/57/59; Sir W. Herringham, *A Physician in France* (London, 1919), 78–80; Redmond McLaughlin, *The Royal Army Medical Corps* (London, 1972), 35: Owen Richards, 'The Development of Casualty Clearing Stations', *Guys Hospital Reports*, LXX (1922), 116.

16 See Sir Anthony Bowlby, 'War Diary', throughout diary, CMAC RAMC/2008/7/2; H. M. W. Gray, *The Early Treatment of War Wounds* (London, 1919), 1; Ronald Raven, 'Gas Gangrene', in E. Fletcher and R. W. Raven, eds, *War Wounds and Injuries* (London, 1940), 20.

17 War Office, *General Principles guiding the Treatment of Wounds of War. Conclusions adopted by the Inter-Allied Surgical Conference held in Paris, March and May, 1917* (London, 1917), 14–15.

18 Harold Upcott, 'Diary', 16 November 1916 and 28 July 1916, in CMAC RAMC 1101 Box 224. For detailed descriptions of the difficulties faced by surgeons during the war, see 'Minutes of the Meeting of the Third Corps Medical Society [On the Western Front]', in CMAC RAMC 2053 Box 430.

19 T. J. Mitchell and G. M. Smith, *Medical Services, Casualties and Medical Statistics of the Great War* (London, 1931), 284, analysis of 1,043,653 casualties. Approximately 10 per cent of men who experienced amputations died, compared with only 3 per cent of men who suffered injuries to their arms or legs which did not require amputation. Note, however, that 16 per cent of men who suffered injuries to their chest died, and 43 per cent of those who suffered injuries to their abdomen died.

20 Caroline E. Playne, *Britain Holds On 1917, 1918* (London, 1933), 76–7.

21 Jim Wolveridge, *Ain't It Grand (Or This was Stepney)* (London, 1981), 19. Also see Revd Andrew Clark, *Echoes of the Great War. The Diary of the Reverend Andrew Clark 1914–1919*, ed. by James Munson (Oxford, 1985), 193, 21 May 1917, and Frederick Watson, *Civilization and the Cripple* (London, 1930), 21.

22 Researchers used a wide variety of definitions, often lumping together physically handicapped people with the 'mentally defective' and introducing criteria such as the ability to be self-supporting. The statistics should, therefore, be regarded as 'guesses' as much as 'accurate estimates'. For instance, while the Central Council for Crippled Children believed that there were 200,000 crippled children in Britain, the *Lancet* (14 June 1924, 122) gave a figure closer to 100,000. The *Board of Education. Annual Report of the Chief Medical Officer of the Board of Education, 1919* [Cmd. 995], H. C. 1920, XV, 102–3 concluded that there were (on average) 8.6 crippled children to every 1,000 children in Britain: in country areas this figure dropped to 3.5 per 1,000 but it reached 22.9 per 1,000 in Swinton and Pendlebury. See also *Ministry of National Service 1917–19. Report Vol. 1. Upon the Physical Examination of Men of Military Age by National Service Military Boards from November 1st, 1917-October 31st, 1918* [Cmd. 504], H. C. 1919, XXVI, 24–5. For detailed analysis, see Roger Cooter, *Surgery and Society in Peace and War* (Manchester, 1993).

23 Central Council for the Care of Cripples, *Handbook on the Welfare of Cripples, 1937* (London, 1937), 14–15.

24 G. R. Girdlestone, 'The Work of the Central Committee for the Care of Cripples', *Cripples' Journal*, III.9 (July 1926), 2.

25 Central Council for the Care of Cripples, *Handbook on the Welfare of Cripples*, 19. In the 1911 census of cripples in Birmingham, forty-two per cent were under the age of sixteen years: *City of Birmingham Education Committee. Report of a Special Sub-Committee of Enquiry concerning Physically-Defective Adults and Children presented to the Education Committee 27th October, 1911* (Birmingham, 1911), 12. It should be noted, however, that in Birmingham the proportion of 'cripples' over the age of sixty-five years was severely underestimated because such people were categorized as 'senile'. Three-quarters of elementary school children in 1932 had spine defects according to Dorothy Wood and M. C. Bywaters, 'An Enquiry into the Posture of Children attending Public Elementary Schools', 9 November 1932, 42, in PRO ED50/61.

26 For the estimate of rickets, see Alfred F. Hess, *Rickets including Osteomalacia and Tetany* (London, 1930), 46.

27 *Ministry of Transport. Road Accidents involving Personal Injury – Great Britain 1938*, [106], H. C. 1938–39, XXI, 9. 'Serious' injuries referred to fractures, concussion, internal injuries, crushing, severe cuts and laceration and severe general shock necessitating medical treatments.

28 R. H. Anglin Whitelock, *Football Injuries* (London, 1904), 3.

29 Noted in Peter Parker, *The Old Lie* (London, 1987), 212.

30 Bertie A. Pond, 'Old Soldiers Never Die', 34, IWM 78/27/1, and the unsorted papers of Donald Hunter, 'Papers', Box 45, file 'Occupational Stigmata', CAMC uncatalogued.

31 Edwin Brock, *Here. Now. Always* (London, 1977), 40 and 47; James Allen Bullock, *Bowers Row: Recollections of a Mining Village* (East Ardsley, 1976), 86; Max Bygraves, *I Wanna Tell You a Story* (London, 1976); Sam Clarke, *An East End Cabinet Maker* (London, 1983), 13; Walter H. Davies, *Ups and Downs* (Swansea, 1975), 50; Harry Gibbs, *'Box On'* (London, 1981), 10; Ronald Goldman, ed., *Breakthrough: Autobiographical Account of the Education of Some Socially Disadvantaged Children* (London, 1968), 19 and 75; Nigel Gray, *The Worst of Times: An Oral History of the Great Depression in Britain* (London, 1985), 89; Ken Howarth, ed., *Dark Days: Memories of the Lancashire and Cheshire Coalmining Industry* (Manchester, 1978), 50–1; Reginal Lee, *The Town That Died* (London, 1975), 33–4; Pat O'Mara, *The Autobiography of a Liverpool Irish Slummy* (London, 1972), first pub. 1934, 78; Arthur Sturgess, *A Northamptonshire Lad* (Northampton, 1982), 2. For more on the importance of boxing, see Stan Shipley, 'Tom Causer of Bermondsey: A Boxer Hero of the 1890s', *History Workshop*, XV, Spring 1983. For contemporary discussions, see John Edwin, *I'm Going – What Then?* (Bognor Regis, 1978), 6; Ralph L. Finn, *Spring in Aldgate* (London, 1968), 120–1; Maurice Levinson, *The Trouble with Yesterday* (London, 1946), 81–3; Spike Mays, *Reuben's Corner* (London, 1969), 45; Dorothy Scannell, *Mother Knows Best: An East End Childhood* (Bath, 1974), 151.

32 'Boxing at Wonderland', *The Sporting Life*, 23 July 1902, PRO MEPO2/555; Robert Fitzsimmons, *Physical Culture and Self Defence* (London, 1902), 64; Wilfred Northfield, *Conquest of Nerves. The Inspiring Record of a Personal Triumph over Neurasthenia* (London, 1933), 24–5; Boy Scouts, *Boy Scouts and What They Do. As Illustrated at the Imperial Scout Exhibition and Rally held in Birmingham, July, 1913* (London, 1913), 32.

33 For the relationship between sport and war, see Sir Walter Kirke, 'Papers', speech given to the London Division (Territorial Army) Boxing Tournament, undated, Liddell Hart Centre for Military Archives, Kirke 16/4. For the severity of the injuries see Levison, *The Trouble with Yesterday*, 81–3, whose bout in a boxing ring resulted in six weeks in hospital.

34 For detailed discussion, see the uncatalogued papers of Donald Hunter in the

CMAC. Very little was said about the risk of mutilation for women working in munitions factories: see Angela Woollacott, *On Her Their Lives Depend. Munition Workers in the Great War* (Berkeley, 1994), chapter three.

35 *Building Accidents Committee. Report of the Departmental Committee Appointed to Inquire into the Dangers Attendant on Building Operations. With Draft for Regulations, Minutes of Evidence, and Appendices* [Cd. 3848], H. C. 1908, XI, vii.

36 Ibid., 66, evidence by P. Flanagan, secretary of the Federated Builders' Labourers.

37 *Journal of Industrial Welfare*, September 1925, 331; 'The Work of the Manor House', n.d., MRC MSS 292/842.1/2; 'Wounded While Working', *A.U.C.E. Journal*, XII.6 (December 1919), 136, MRC MSS 292/143/6.

38 Mitchell and Smith, *Medical Services*, 277, 279 and 282, analysis of 1,043,653 casualties. In the case of the ages, I have excluded men whose ages were not known.

39 Artificial Limb Service, *Artificial Limbs and their Uses. Report of a Survey among Patients of the Artificial Limb Service* (London, 1984), 1.

40 Steve Humphries and Pamela Gordon, *Out of Sight. The Experience of Disability 1900–1950* (Plymouth, 1992).

41 Mitchell and Smith, *Medical Services*, 279, analysis of 1,043,653 casualties. As we will be seeing in Chapter Two, official statistics on self-inflicted wounds were underestimates: most went undetected.

42 *Great Advance. Tales from the Somme Battlefield told by Wounded Officers and Men on their Arrival at Southampton from the Front* (London, 1916), 12.

43 Ian Rashan, 'The Spirit of the Bayonet', *The Blimp. Being The Souvenir of 'F' Coy No. 2 O.C.B. Christ's College – Ridley Hall July – October 1917* (Cambridge, 1917), 42–3, Cambridge Central Library (Local Records Collection) C45.5, and Alfred Downes, 'Notes taken at Southern Army School of Instruction, Brentwood Course, Birmingham, Commencing Oct. 16. 1916', unpaginated, lecture entitled 'Bayonet Fighting', Birmingham City Archives MSS 547.

44 'Guild of the Brave Poor Things' (London, 1901), 7, Bristol Record Office 39842/PM/4.

45 Ada Vachell, 'City of Bristol Guild of the Brave Poor Things. A New Scheme', n.d., 1, Bristol Record Office 39842/PM/6. See also idem, 'Visiting' (London, 1905), Bristol Record Office 39842/A/3. Vachell was president of the City of Bristol Guild of the Brave Poor Things.

46 'Committee Book of the City of Bristol Guild of the Poor Things', minutes for 6 April and 22 September 1905, Bristol Record Office 39842/A/1A.

47 Ibid., executive meeting minutes for 3 February 1916, Bristol Record Office 39842/A/1B.

48 *City of Bristol Guild of the Handicapped (Guild of the Brave Poor Things). The Story of 1917* (Bristol, 1917), 3–4, Bristol Record Office 39842/A/2A.

49 For instance, in 1906 the medical officer under the Swansea Local Education Authority warned about the 'serious moral aspect' of all physical defects because physical disabilities weakening a person's self-respect decreased his self-reliance, and made him deceitful: *Inter-Departmental Committee on Medical Inspection and Feeding of Children attending Public Elementary Schools. Minutes of Evidence . . . Vol. II – List of Witnesses, Minutes of Evidence, Appendices, and Index* [Cd. 2784], H. C. 1906, XLVII, 159, evidence by Dr Rhys Davies.

50 *Building Accidents Committee. Report of the Departmental Committee appointed to inquire into the Dangers Attendant on Building Operations. With Draft for Regulations. Minutes of Evidence, and Appendices* [Cd. 3848], H. C. 1908, XI, 72, evidence by William Bullen, a building contractor in Liverpool. See the Trades Union Congress papers on the National Safety Week (19–24 May 1930) which

often suggested that disabilities were caused by workers' carelessness: MRC MSS 292/142/4.

51 Archibald McKendrick, *Malingering and its Detection under the Workmen's Compensation and Other Acts* (Edinburgh, 1912), 7.

52 'Sir Auckland Geddes' Speech at Meeting held in St George's Hall, Liverpool', 15 March 1918, 8–9, PRO NATS1/78; Central Council for the Care of Cripples, *Handbook on the Welfare of Cripples. 1937*, 6 and 18; J. Lawson Dick, *Defective Housing and the Growth of Children* (London, 1919), 23; idem, *Rickets. A Study of Economic Conditions and their Effects on the Health of the Nation* (London, 1922), 9; Agnes Hunt, 'A Plea for the Adult Cripple', *Cripples' Journal*, III.10 (October 1926), 92; T. P. O'Connor, 'Made, Not Born', *Cripples' Journal*, II.2 (October 1925), 94–7; Evelyn C. Pearce, *A Textbook of Orthopaedic Nursing* (London, 1927), xvi; Frederick Watson, 'The Cripple and Modern Conditions', *Cripples' Journal*, III.10 (October 1926), 127.

53 Report from J. J. Cox, commissioner of Medical Services, North West Region, to the chief commissioner of Medical Services in the Ministry of National Service, 27 September 1918, 3, PRO NATS1/764; Girdlestone, 'The Work of the Central Committee for the Care of Cripples', 2; Alfred Lodington Jackson, *A Short Paper on the Proper Safeguarding of Handicap in the Case of Persons who are afflicted from Birth* (Ramsgate, 1928), 1–2; Robert J. Parr, *Maimed or Whole? A Statement relating to the Operations on Children* (London, 1912); Evelyn C. Pearce, *A Textbook of Orthopaedic Nursing* (London, 1927), xvii–xviii.

54 A. G. Hunt, 'Baschurch and After. II. Fourteen Years On', *Cripples' Journal*, I.2 (October 1924), 86. Also see 'Record Book of the Handicapped', in 'Bristol Guild of the Handicapped Papers, *c.* 1900–1940', Bristol Record Office 39842/A/3 in which the respectability (or otherwise) of the family was noted before many of the children were admitted.

55 Howson, *Handbook of the Limbless*, 48.

56 Minute to Minister of Pensions from Matthew Nathan, 18 April 1917, PRO PIN15/1147.

57 John Francis Jones, 'N.C.O.', 1934, 81, Liddell Hart Centre for Military Archives; 'Mark VII', *A Subaltern on the Somme in 1916* (London, 1927), 51; W. A. Quinton, 'Memoirs', 1929, 53, IWM 79/35/1; Dorothy Scholes, 'Papers', unpaginated scrapbook, comment by Driver Heath, in the Edward Hall Collection, Wigan Archives Service D/DZ.EHC; Hiram Sturdy, 'Illustrated Account of his Service on the Western Front with the Royal Regiment of Artillery', 19–20, IWM Con Shelf; Daniel Sweeney, letter on 4 December 1917, in Michael Moynihan, ed., *Greater Love. Letters Home 1914–1918* (London, 1980), 72.

58 Revd Andrew Clark, *Echoes of the Great War. The Diary of the Reverend Andrew Clark 1914–1919*, ed. James Munson (Oxford, 1985), 20, 28 September 1914; Clements, 'Diaries', 12 April 1915, IWM 86/76/1; W. P. Nevill, 'Letters and Papers', vol. III, 727, undated newspaper cutting, 'Glorious East Surreys', IWM Con Shelf.

59 *Departmental Committee on Workmen's Compensation. Minutes of Evidence. Vol. I. 30th July to 9th December, 1919* [Cmd. 908], H. C. 1920, XXVI, 514, evidence by C. F. A. Hore, assistant secretary to the Ministry of Pensions.

60 Mrs C. W. [Grace] Kimmins, 'The Heritage Craft Schools, Chailey', *Cripples' Journal*, I.4 (April 1925), 269.

61 Little, *Artificial Limbs and Amputation Stumps*, vi. He was also the first president of the Royal Society of Medicine and the leading doctor in charge of the limbless of Queen Mary's Convalescent Auxiliary Hospital.

62 'Report as to the Practice of Medicine and Surgery by Unidentified Persons in the United Kingdom' (London, 1910), 86, CMAC SA/BMA/C405 Box 114.

Also see pp. 8 and 65–86. This evidence must be placed in perspective: it was part of a debate concerned with the professionalization of orthopaedics. It was important for these men to exaggerate the incompetence of traditional bone-setters.

63 See the speech by Sir Robert Jones in 'British Orthopaedic Association', *British Medical Journal*, 31 October 1925, 799–800, CMAC SA/BMA/C.193 Box 75; 'Scrutator', 'The Problem of the Adult Cripple', *Cripples' Journal*, II.6 (October 1925), 97; *Birmingham and District Cripples' Union* (November 1911), letter headed 'Dear Sir or Madam'; *Birmingham and District Cripples' Union. Fifteenth Annual Report 1913–14* (Birmingham, 1914), 11; *Birmingham Cripples' Union Seventeenth Annual Report from April 1st, 1915 to March 31st, 1916* (Birmingham, 1916), 9.

64 *Report of the Central Council for the Care of Cripples for 1931* (London, 1931), 9, and *Report of the Central Council for the Care of Cripples for 1935* (London, 1935), 11.

65 The total number of male cripples examined was 546. Of these, 39 per cent of those aged between 16 and 30 years were employed, compared with nearly 20 per cent of those aged between 30 and 45 years, less than 15 per cent for those aged between 45 and 60 years, and 5 per cent of those aged over 60 years: *City of Birmingham Education Committee*.

66 'Somerset Miners' Association Papers 1868–1964', 'Coal Mines (Minimum Wage) Act, 1912. Somerset Joint District Board', 17 May 1913, rule no. 2, University of Bristol Special Collections, uncatalogued.

67 *City of Birmingham Education Committee*, 20.

68 For further analysis, see Cooter, *Surgery and Society in Peace and War*. Also see the comments made in *Report of the Central Committee for the Care of Cripples for Years 1922 and 1923* (London, 1923), 32, and *Report of the Central Council for the Care of Cripples for 1930* (London, 1930), 8.

69 *Inter-Departmental Committee on Medical Inspection and Feeding of Children Attending Public Elementary Schools. Minutes of Evidence . . . Vol. II – List of Witnesses. Minutes of Evidence, Appendices, and Index* [Cd. 2784], H. C. 1906, XLVII, 128, evidence by Dr J. Kerr, medical officer, Education, under the London County Council. He was referring to 'mentally defective' children, many of whom were actually physically disabled.

70 There is further discussion of this in Seth Koven, 'Remembering and Dismemberment: Crippled Children, Wounded Soldiers, and the Great War in Great Britain', *American Historical Review*, XCIX.4 (October 1994), 1167–1202. For a contemporary reference, see *Birmingham and District Cripples' Union. Sixteenth Annual Report from April 1st, 1914 to March 31st, 1915* (Birmingham, 1915), 21 and 28.

71 See Cooter, *Surgery and Society in Peace and War*. For statistics on the decline of rickets as a cause of crippling, see *Board of Education. Annual Report for 1914 of the Chief Medical Officer of the Board of Education* [Cd. 8055], H. C. 1914–16, XVIII, 185.

72 Report from J. J. Cox, commissioner of Medical Services, North West Region, to the chief commissioner of Medical Services in the Ministry of National Service, 27 September 1918, 4, PRO NATS1/764.

73 Robert Mitchell, *What can be done to train Disabled Sailors and Soldiers in Technical Institutions* (London, 1916), 6.

74 For an example, see the report of the strike by disabled ex-servicemen at Lord Roberts' Workshop in 1917, in 'Disabled Soldiers' Strike. The Split of the Age', *Daily Post*, 1 October 1917.

75 The Disabled Society had been established in 1921 with the sole aim of improving the position of limbless ex-servicemen, not civilians.

76 Emanuel Miller, A. T. M. Wilson and Eric Wittleaver, 'Clinical Case Studies and their Relationships, including the Psychosomatic Disorders', in Emanuel Miller, ed., *The Neuroses in War* (London, 1940), 81.

77 John Calder, *The Vanishing Willows. The Story of Erskine Hospital* (Bishopton, Renfrewshire, 1982), 19.

78 Although this was generally the case, by 1927 there were a few cases where the wooden limb was lighter: *Lancet*, 2 April 1927, 630 and 735.

79 Howson, *Handbook for the Limbless*, 47–8.

80 Ibid., 19.

81 Ibid., 17.

82 'The Pensions Ministry and Artificial Limbs', *Lancet*, 22 December 1928, 1324. For a small percentage of limbless men, the wooden artificial limb remained the most suitable one.

83 Introduction by Edward Marshall, in H. H. Thomas, *Help for Wounded Heroes* (London, 1920), 1–2.

84 Daniel Robinson, 'Artificial Limbs and Some Difficulties', *Reveille*, II (November 1918), 273.

85 Ibid., 273.

86 Ministry of Pensions, *Artificial Limbs. Report of the Departmental Committee Appointed by the Ministry of Pensions* (London, 1944), 14.

87 Lieutenant-General Goodwin, 'What the War Office is Doing', *Reveille*, II (November 1918), 222. This is contradicted in Ministry of Pensions, *Artificial Limbs. Report of the Departmental Committee appointed by the Ministry of Pensions* (London, 1944), 13, where it was said that the average one-armed or armless man would prefer a hand – even though it was not as useful as an appliance and was much heavier and more uncomfortable.

88 George A. Ponsonby, 'The Full Use of Artificial Limbs', *Lancet*, 19 March 1921, and Howson, *Handbook for the Limbless*, 49. Ponsonby was a legless ex-serviceman.

89 H. H. C. Baird, *An Unexpected and Far-Reaching Development in regard to Light Metal Limbs for the Legless* (Bridge, Nr Canterbury, 1924), 25.

90 At the outbreak of the Second World War, the Ministry Limb Service was extended to include the Ministry of Labour casualties. In 1944, under the Education Act, this service was extended to children of school age. The Disabled Pensions (Employment) Act of 1944 placed upon the Ministry of Labour and National Service the responsibility for finding employment for disabled persons by establishing courses of industrial rehabilitation and vocational courses, establishing workshops for those persons so severely disabled to be incapable of entering competitive employment, and by requiring employers to engage a proportion of disabled workers. In July 1948 when the National Health Service came into operation, 30,000 civilian amputees came under the care of the Ministry of Pensions (R. Ham and L. Cotton, *Limb Amputation* (London, 1991), 159). During the first year of the National Health Service, 5,960 war pensioners and 8,106 civilian patients were fitted with artificial limbs and arms. With the deaths of Great War amputees in the following couple of years, the number of artificial limbs supplied to them declined to 3,771 while those suppled to civilian patients doubled to 16,142: Leon Gillis, *Artificial Limbs* (London, 1957), 83.

91 Little, *Artificial Limbs and Amputation Stumps*, 161.

92 *Bristol Crippled Children's Society. Second Annual Report* (Bristol, 1924), 7, Bristol Record Office 39428/1 and the letter from the general secretary of the Bristol Crippled Children's Society to 'Sir', 13 September 1929, Bristol Record Office 39428.

93 A. Gwynne James, 'Letter to the Editor: Orthopaedics in Industrial Life',

Recalled to Life, II (September 1917), 299. The writer hoped that this would change.

94 *Departmental Committee on Workmen's Compensation. Minutes of Evidence. Vol. I. 30th July to 9th December, 1919* [Cmd. 908], H. C. 1920, XXVI, 106, evidence by Frank Hall, representing the Miner's Federation of Great Britain.

95 The Committee recommended that employers should provide artificial limbs, but this was ignored: *Departmental Committee on Workmen's Compensation. Report to the Right Honourable The Secretary of State of the Home Department by the Departmental Committee appointed to inquire into the System of Compensation for Injuries to Workmen*, [Cmd. 816], H. C. 1920, XXVI.

96 *Departmental Committee on Workmen's Compensation. Minutes of Evidence. Vol. II. 10th December 1919, to 28th May, 1920* [Cmd. 909], H. C. 1920, XXVI, 55, evidence by Thomas May Smith, director of Messrs A. Boake, Roberts and Co., wholesale chemical manufacturers of Stratford. See also ibid., 423, evidence by Michael Brett, secretary of the Shipping Federation since 1901 and *Departmental Committee on Workmen's Compensation. Minutes of Evidence. Vol. I. 30th July to 9th December, 1919* [Cmd. 908], H. C. 1920, XXVI, 275, 314 and 327, evidence by His Honour Judge B. Fossett Lock, William Hall (representing Sir W. G. Armstrong, Whitworth and Co.), and Andrew Cairns Baird (solicitor in Glasgow and secretary for the Scottish Conference of Friendly and Approved Societies).

97 *Departmental Committee on Workmen's Compensation. Minutes of Evidence. Vol. II. 10th December 1919, to 28th May, 1920* [Cmd. 909], H. C. 1920, XXVI, 40, evidence by Charles Frederick Allsop, representing the shipowning firm of Furness, Withy and Co.

98 *Departmental Committee on Workmen's Compensation. Minutes of Evidence. Vol. I. 30th July to 9th December, 1919* [Cmd. 908], H. C. 1920, XXVI, 501, evidence by Edmund Hibbert, chief spokesman of the representatives of the ordinary members of the Board of Management of the Lancashire and Cheshire Miners' Permanent Relief Society. For more on the attitudes of trade unions, see *Departmental Committee on Workmen's Compensation. Minutes of Evidence. Vol. I. 30th July to 9th December, 1919* [Cmd. 908], H. C. 1920, XXVI, 109, evidence by James Henson, representing the National Sailors' and Firemens' Union; 'Trades Union Congress General Council. Minutes of the First Meeting (1924–1925) of the Joint Workmen's Compensation Committee Representing the Trades Union Congress, The Labour Party, and the Parliamentary Labour Party . . . 6th November, 1924', 2, MRC MSS 292/143.1/1; 'Compensation Act 1923. Proposed Alterations', MRC MSS 292/143/4.

99 *Departmental Committee on Workmen's Compensation. Minutes of Evidence. Vol. I. 30th July to 9th December, 1919* [Cmd. 908], H. C. 1920, XXVI, 106, evidence by Frank Hall, representing the Miner's Federation of Great Britain.

100 'Somerset Miners' Association Papers', 'Somerset Miners' Welfare Hospital and Convalescent Committee. Minutes of the Management Committee held May 3rd 1934 following a Meeting of District Welfare Committee', University of Bristol Special Collections, uncatalogued. They discussed their policy in the minutes for 5 May 1936 and in their annual meeting on 3 March 1939 agreed to provide the full cost for the *first* artificial limb.

101 *Departmental Committee on Workmen's Compensation. Minutes of Evidence. Vol. I. 30th July to 9th December, 1919* [Cmd. 908], H. C. 1920, XXVI, 283–4, evidence by Henry Eustace Mitton, on behalf of various colliery companies not belonging to Mutual Indemnity Associations.

102 Ibid., 125, evidence by Samuel Charlton, assistant general secretary of the National Union of Railwaymen.

103 J. L. Smyth (secretary of the Trades Union Congress Social Insurance

Department), 'Industrial Accidents and Rehabilitation', speech to the Cripples' Training College in 1935, 2, MRC MSS 292/146.9/1. For more on the treatment of disabled workmen as 'criminals in the dock', see the letter from George T. Barrow (former bus inspector of Castle Douglas), to J. L. Smythe, secretary of the Trades Union Congress Social Insurance Department, 11 November 1935, MRC MSS 292/143/1.

104 'Bishop Sutton Compensation Cases', letter from H. Harvey to Mr Swift, secretary of the Somerset Miners' Association, on 20 February 1923 and the letter from John Clarke to Mr Swift, undated but September 1927, 'Somerset Miners' Assocation Papers', University of Bristol Special Collections, uncatalogued.

105 'Memorandum of Interview. County Court Cases and Medical Referees', 21 April 1933, 1, and *John Smith Has an Accident* (London, 1933), both in MRC MSS 292/143/1.

106 Letters from Michael McAleer to Sir T. Legge of the Trades Union Congress, 24 February, 4 March and 18 December 1930, MRC MSS 292/841.6.

107 A. G. Hunt, 'Baschurch and After. III. During the War', *Cripples' Journal*, 1.3 (January 1924), 180.

108 *Report of the Central Committee for the Care of Cripples. From its Inception to December, 1921* (London, 1921), 18.

109 Ada Vachell, 'Story of the City of Bristol Guild of the Poor Things', 1897, 8–13, Bristol Record Office 39842/A/2(a). Also see *Guild of the Brave Poor Things* (London, 1901), 5–8, Bristol Record Office 39842/PM/4.

110 *Guild of the Brave Poor Things* (London, 1901), 10 and 27, Bristol Record Office 39842/PM/4.

111 Contrary to the meaning of the word 'surgery' today, in this period there were two types of 'surgical' intervention: operative and conservative. When the word 'surgical' is used in this chapter, the operative surgery is meant. For a discussion of the distinctions, see Cooter, *Surgery and Society in Peace and War*, 20–3. For increased surgical intervention into the lives of disabled civilians as a result of the war, see *Birmingham Cripples' Union. 23rd Annual Report from April 1st, 1921, to March 31st 1922* (Birmingham, 1922), 7; 'Birmingham (Selly Oak) Hospital Management Committee. The Royal Orthopaedic Hospital Birmingham. The Woodlands, Northfield 1909–1949' (Birmingham, 1949), 1; *Board of Education. Annual Report of the Chief Medical Officer of the Board of Education, 1919* [Cmd. 995], H. C. 1920, XV, 101; 'Memorandum Prepared for the Use of Ministry of Health', November 1925, 2, PRO ED50/59; Royal Cripples' Hospital, *You Can Help to Perform this Miracle* (Birmingham, 1939), 5; Frederick Watson, *The Cripple* (London, 1926), 10.

112 Frederick Watson, *Civilization and the Cripple* (London, 1930), 19–20.

113 Cooter, *Surgery and Society in Peace and War*, 108.

114 Watson, *The Cripple*, 10–1.

115 Watson, *Civilization and the Cripple*, 21.

116 *Departmental Committee on Workmen's Compensation. Minutes of Evidence. Vol. II. 10th December 1919, to 28th May, 1920* [Cmd. 909], H. C. 1920, XXVI, 424, evidence by J. Smith Whitaker, senior medical officer of the Ministry of Health, and medical adviser to the National Health Insurance Joint Committee.

117 *Departmental Committee on Workmen's Compensation. Minutes of Evidence. Vol. II. 10th December 1919, to 28th May, 1920* [Cmd. 909], H. C. 1920, XXVI, 381, evidence by Bernard Gilbert, secretary of the Industrial Orthopaedic Society. Also see the papers of the Manor House Hospital which documents its transfer to the Industrial Orthopaedic Society, MRC MSS 292/842.1/1–2.

118 'Memorandum Prepared for the Use of Ministry of Health', November 1925, 3, PRO ED50/9.

119 Ibid., 2–3.
120 Minute from A. H. Wood to L. G. Duke, 28 August 1923, PRO ED50/172, Part 5.
121 *First and Second Special Reports from the Select Committee on Pensions. Together with the Proceedings of the Committee and Minutes of Evidence and Appendices* [247], H. C. 1919, VI, 88, evidence by Sir L. Worthington-Evans, the minister of pensions.
122 'Cripples' Training', report of a meeting with a Miss Simpson and a Miss Turner of the Central Council for the Care of Cripples, 2 May 1938, PRO AST10/17. They were referring to those who were only slightly handicapped. Also see the reply of the Midland District of the National Union of General and Municipal Workers to a request by the Trades Union Congress to answer certain questions about disabled workmen in 1937: MRC MSS 292/146.9/1.
123 *City of Bristol Guild of the Handicapped. The Story of 1920* (Bristol, 1920), 9, Bristol Record Office 39842/A/2(b), and *City of Bristol Guild of the Handicapped. The Story of 1921* (Bristol, 1921), 4, Bristol Record Office 39842/A/2(b).
124 British Medical Association, 'Report of Committee on the Diagnosis and Certification of Miners' Nystagmus' (London, 1936), 5, CMAC SA/BMA/C.151 Box 67.
125 *Report of the Departmental Committee on Compensation for Disabled Sailors and Soldiers Under the Workmen's Compensation Act, 1906* [Cmd. 49], H. C. 1919, XXXI, 3–4.
126 Ibid., 3–4. It did not worry employers in the following industries: cotton spinning, calico printing, bleaching, dyeing and finishing trades and flint-glass makers.
127 For 'foreigners', see *First and Second Special Reports from the Select Committee on Pensions. Together with the Proceedings of the Committee and Minutes of Evidence and Appendices* [247], H. C. 1919, VI, 399, evidence by S. E. J. Brady of the Industry and Manufacturing Branch of the Board of Trade. For women, see same report, p. 206, evidence by H. M. Fraser.
128 'The Making of a Cripple', *Cripples' Journal*, II.8 (April 1926), 290.
129 'Scrutator', 'The Problem of the Adult Cripple', *Cripples' Journal*, II.6 (October 1925), 100.
130 John Galsworthy, 'So Comes the Sacred Work', *American Journal of Care for Cripples*, VII.2 (1918), 88.
131 Watson, *Civilization and the Cripple*, 20.
132 Ministry of Labour, Employment and Insurance Report, 'After-Care Association for Blind, Deaf, and Crippled Children', 1928, paragraph 33, PRO LAB2/178/ETJ503/1929.
133 'Sussex East. Chailey The Heritage Craft Schools Nos. 29132 and 1256', visit by Mr Lumsden, 19 November 1935, 7–8, PRO ED32/785.
134 Rowland Myrddyn Luther, 'The Poppies are Blood Red', 33, IWM 87/8/7.
135 Lawrence Gameson, 'Papers', 27, IWM Con Shelf.
136 This is in contrast to the much more optimistic account of the limbless after the American Civil War: Laurann Figg and Jane Farrell-Beck, 'Amputation in the Civil War: Physical and Social Dimensions', *Journal of the History of Medicine and Allied Sciences*, XLVIII.4 (October 1993), 454–75.
137 The best discussions can be found in Ted Bogacz, '"A Tyranny of Words": Language, Poetry, and Antimodernism in England in the First World War', *Journal of Modern History*, 58 (September 1986), 642–68, and Paul Fussell, *The Great War and Modern Memory* (London, 1975).
138 Minute of 3 March 1920, PRO LAB2/221/EDX209/5/1920.
139 Introduction by Edward Marshall, in Thomas, *Help for Wounded Heroes*, 1.

140 'The Volunteer', in Robert W. Service, *Rhymes of a Red-Cross Man* (London, 1916), 16.

141 'The Disabled Soldier', *Liverpool Chronicle*, 27 June 1917.

142 E. M. Corner, 'The Phantom Limbs of Amputees', *Practitioner*, CIV (February 1920), 81–4; R. D. Langdale-Kelham and George Perkins, *Amputations and Artificial Limbs* (London, 1942), 44; Louis Minski, 'Psychological Reactions to Injury', in William Brown Doherty and Dagobert D. Runes, eds, *Rehabilitation of the War Injured. A Symposium* (London, 1945), 117–18; W. R. D. Mitchell, 'The After-Care of Amputations', in Doherty and Runes, eds, *Rehabilitation of the War Injured*, 368.

143 Amy Baker of Burley, letter to the editor, *The Times*, 2 February 1917; M. Creach-Henry and D. Marten, *The Unknown Warrior* (London, 1923), 5; 'For Men Broken in Our Wars', *The Times*, 21 July 1915; 'No Charity, Please!', *Liverpool Chronicle*, 6 June 1917; PRO PIN15/15. There are many examples of the phrases 'broken heroes' or 'broken warriors' in Liverpool Council of Social Service, 'Cuttings from National Newspapers 1910–17', Liverpool Record Office 361 COU/1/16; 'Broken Soldiers. The Curative Workshop Scheme', *The Times*, 2 February 1917; *City of Bristol Guild of the Handicapped (Guild of the Poor Brave Things). The Story of 1917* (Bristol, 1917), 3–4, Bristol Record Office 39842/A/2A.

144 A. T. Wilkinson, 'Account of His Life in South London during the First World War', 1976, 1, IWM 78/51/1. Also see the comments on this song by Alistair L. Crerar, in a letter to his sister Dorothy, 27 October 1916, IWM Con Shelf; Lawrence Gameson, 'Papers', 30, diary for 9 July 1916, IWM Con Shelf; Arthur Schuman, 'Memories', 8, IWM 82/1/1; S. Wakefield in the autograph album from the Soldiers' Club, IWM Misc. 3 Item 20.

145 For instance, see Siegfried Sassoon's poem, 'Does it Matter?' which goes, 'Does it matter? losing your legs? / For people will always be kind, / And you need not show that you mind / When the others come in after hunting / To gobble their muffins and eggs.'

146 *First and Second Special Reports from the Select Committee on Pensions Together with the Proceedings of the Committee and Minutes of Evidence and Appendices* [247], H. C. 1919, VI. 38, evidence by Colonel Yates, MP and secretary of the Parliamentary Army Committee. According to Mitchell and Smith, *Medical Services*, 276, analysis of 1,043,653 casualties, 28 per cent of injured or ill men returning from France suffered from wounds compared with between 5 and 9 per cent of men returning from Mesopotamia, Macedonia, Palestine and Egypt.

147 This was not unique to the First World War, but occurred during the Crimean and Boer wars as well.

148 Sir Thomas Lewis, letter from Lewis to the secretary of the Disabilities Committee, 28 April 1920, CMAC PP/Lew/C1/8.

149 Lawrence Gameson, 'Papers', 82, IWM Con Shelf.

150 Ibid., 170.

151 'War Emergency Workers' National Committee', resolution from the Bradford and District Trades and Labour Council, 19 September 1916, Labour History Archive (Manchester) WNC 24/1/207.

152 Eugenics Education Society Council Minute Book 1914–1918, 16 May 1916, cited by Richard A. Soloway, *Demography and Degeneration. Eugenics and the Declining Birthrate in Twentieth-Century Britain* (Chapel Hill, 1990), 145.

153 'Disabled Soldiers' Pensions', *Daily Post*, 1 March 1916, and the letter from Sir A. G. Boscawen to the Ministry of Pensions, 29 September 1917, PRO PIN15/570.

154 *First and Second Special Reports from the Select Committee on Pensions. Together*

with the Proceedings of the Committee and Minutes of Evidence and Appendices [247], H. C. 1919, VI, 204, evidence by H. M. Fraser.

155 E. M. Spearing, *From Cambridge to Camiers under the Red Cross* (Cambridge, 1917), 34.

156 Revd Montague A. Bere, 'Papers', letter to his wife, 18 September 1917, IWM, 66/96/1. Dr Mark Harrison points out that the exception was servicemen with venereal disease.

157 *Departmental Committee on Workmen's Compensation. Minutes of Evidence. Vol. I. 30th July to 9th December, 1919* [Cmd. 908], H. C. 1920, XXVI, 506, evidence by C. F. A. Hore, assistant secretary to the Ministry of Pensions.

158 Report by C. F. A. Hore, to the Committee on the Employment of Severely Disabled Men, 16 December 1920, 2, PRO PIN15/33.

159 'The Debt of Honour', *The Times*, 12 December 1920, quoted by Baird, *An Unexpected and Far-Reaching Development*, 14–15. Also see Howson, *Handbook for the Limbless*, 48.

160 'Our Broken Soldiers. Why Mr Cain's Offer was Refused?', *Liverpool Chronicle*, 9 August 1916, Liverpool Council of Social Service, 'Cuttings from National Newspapers 1910–17', Liverpool Record Office 361 COU 1/6.

161 'Braces in the News', *Tailor and Cutter*, 26 August 1932, 883.

162 G. H. Slade, *Two Sticks* (London, 1923), 96.

163 Caroline E. Playne, *Britain Holds On 1917, 1918* (London, 1933), 76–7.

164 Gameson, 'Papers', 8–12, IWM Con Shelf.

165 Ibid., 81.

166 Letter from Hugh Wansey Bayly to *Morning Post*, 25 October 1926, cited in Bayly, *Triple Challenge or, War, Whirligigs and Windmills* (London, 1930), 278. He attended appeal tribunals to aid pensioners.

167 'Deputation of Members of Parliament, on War Pension. Wednesday, the 3rd February, 1937', PRO PIN15/1410.

168 'War Emergency Workers' National Committee', newspaper clipping by George N. Barnes (MP), 'Pensions and Allowances', *Daily News and Leader*, 28 March 1916, 4, Labour History Archive (Manchester) WNC 24/1/136.

169 'War Emergency Workers' National Committee', letter from the Llanelly and District Labour Association, 26 March 1916, Labour History Archive (Manchester) WNC 24/1/133.

170 Minute from the regional director, 29 May 1920, PRO PIN56/24.

171 'Representation from County Donegal Local Committee in Lifford', 31 March 1920, to H. G. Stevenson, Ministry of Pensions in Belfast, PRO PIN56/24.

172 Revd Montague A. Bere, 'Papers', letter of 31 July 1918, IWM 66/96/1.

173 'Notes', *American Journal of Care for Cripples*, VII.2 (1918), 174.

174 Letter from G. Chandley, honorary general secretary to the British Limbless Ex-Service Men's Association, to Prime Minister C. Neville Chamberlain, 12 September 1938, PRO PIN15/1416.

175 'War Emergency Workers' National Committee', letter from A. F. Berne of Southsea, formerly of the Inniskillen Fusiliers, to the Labour Party, 28 February 1918, Labour History Archive (Manchester) WNC 24/1/332. See also, 'No Charity, Please!', *Liverpool Chronicle*, 6 June 1917, and 'Durham', letter to the editor, *The Times*, 23 January 1917.

176 'Memorandum on Pensions for Invalided Soldiers', initialled 'H. W. F.', 1 March 1916, 1, PRO WO32/11209.

177 A. Jack Abraham, '1914–1918: Memoirs of a Non-Hero', *c.*1973, 85, IWM P191; Henry Buckmaster, 'Letters', to his mother, 10 December 1917, 35, Wigan Archives Service; Clements, 'Diaries', 22 May 1915, IWM 86/76/1; Albert V. Conn. 'Memories', 1974, 46, IWM 81/41/1; Mrs Ethel Cox, 'Letters and Other Papers', letter from 'Jim', 15 March 1916, Birmingham City Archive

MSS 1546/1/15; Millais Culpin, *Recent Advances in the Study of the Psychoneuroses* (London, 1931), 25; idem, *Psychoneurosis of War and Peace* (Cambridge, 1920), 32–3; *Happy Though Wounded! The Book of the Third London General Hospital* (London, 1917), IWM Misc. 85 Item 1275; Arthur E. Kaye, 'Papers and Letter', letter from J. W. Lowry to Kaye, 27 October 1917, IWM 82/11/1; Miller, Wilson and Wittleaver, 'Clinical Case Studies', 79; Mrs F. J. Prime, 'Letters to Mrs Prime from Servicemen', letter from 'Reg', 30 September 1917, Cambridge University Library ADD 7660; T. A. Ross, *Lectures on War Neuroses* (London, 1941), 64–5; T. Ray Sutherland, 'Miscellaneous Papers', letter to his mother, 11 April 1917, Birmingham City Archives MSS 771; Norman Austin Taylor, 'Letters', letter to his sister Joyce, August 1915 (no day given), IWM 90/28/1; E. Gardiner Williams, 'Supplement to Pic from France', 8–9, Liverpool Record Office Acc. 2175.

178 Conn, 'Memories', 52, IWM 81/41/1. On p. 74 he almost gives an arm for the war.

179 Clark, *Echoes of the Great War*, 76, 18 August 1915.

180 For the most thorough analysis of the variety of reasons for joining, see B. C. Croucher, 'British Working-Class Attitudes to War and National Defence, 1902–1914', 2 vols, Ph.D. thesis, University College, Swansea, 1992.

181 *Departmental Committee on Workmen's Compensation. Minutes of Evidence. Vol. I. 30th July to 9th December, 1919* [Cmd. 908], H. C. 1920, XXVI, 505, evidence by C. F. A. Hore, assistant secretary to the Ministry of Pensions.

182 'Home Office Workmen's Compensation Scheme 1935, Notes of a Meeting held on Thursday, 16th January 1936. Evidence by Mr. Glover and Dr. Stewart on Behalf of the Ministry of Pensions', 15, PRO PIN15/130.

183 Ibid., 9.

184 'Home Office Workmen's Compensation Scheme 1935, Notes of a Meeting held on Thursday, 16th January 1936. Evidence by Mr. Glover and Dr. Stewart on Behalf of the Ministry of Pensions', 7–8, PRO PIN15/130.

185 Devine, *Disabled Soldiers and Sailors*, 169–70.

186 Russell Jones, 'Workmen's Compensation. Report to Joint Committee', 1925, 4, MRC MSS 292/143/4; 'Our Industrial Correspondent', 'State Clinics for Injured Workmen', *Daily Herald*, 18 January 1936, CMAC SA/BMA/C150 Box 67; Alfred Riley, 'Paper Read to the Executive of the Painters' Amalgamation, in Answer to a Request by Them For Suggestions on the Amendment of the Workmen's Compensation Acts. On the 28th Day of January, 1928', 6–7, MRC MSS 292/143/4; 'Workmen's Compensation Act. Summary of Replies Received from Unions in Response to Circular Sent Out 16th June, 1934', MRC MSS 292/143/4.

187 Letter from G. Knight of Papworth to T. Knight who passed it on to J. L. Smythe, secretary of the Trades Union Congress Social Insurance Department, 19 December 1935, MRC MSS 292/143.

188 *Departmental Committee on Workmen's Compensation. Minutes of Evidence. Vol. I. 30th July to 9th December, 1919* [Cmd. 908], H. C. 1920, XXVI, 43, comment by A. C. Farquharson during the evidence of Miss Susan Lawrence of the National Federation of Women Workers.

189 *Departmental Committee on Workmen's Compensation. Minutes of Evidence. Vol. II. 10th December, 1919, to 28th May, 1920* [Cmd. 909], H. C. 1920, XXVI, evidence by Robert Barrie Walker, member of the Parliamentary Committee of the Trades Union Congress. Also see *Departmental Committee on Workmen's Compensation. Minutes of Evidence. Vol. I. 30th July to 9th December, 1919* [Cmd. 908], H. C. 1920, XXVI, 15, evidence by William Shaw, chairman of the Scottish Trades Union Congress.

190 *Departmental Committee on Workmen's Compensation. Minutes of Evidence. Vol. II.*

10th December, 1919, to 28th May, 1920 [Cmd. 909], H. C. 1920, XXVI, 103–4, evidence by George W. Booth, director and secretary of the insurance company, Messrs J. Lyons and Co.

191 *Departmental Committee on Workmen's Compensation. Minutes of Evidence. Vol. I. 30th July to 9th December, 1919* [Cmd. 908], H. C. 1920, XXVI, 506, evidence by C. R. A. Hore, assistant secretary to the Ministry of Pensions.

192 'Report of Sub-Committee on Wound Gratuities and Pensions for Officers', 20 February 1918, 1, PRO WO32/2791.

193 *First and Second Special Reports from the Select Committee on Pensions. Together with the Proceedings of the Committee and Minutes of Evidence and Appendices* [247], H. C. 1919, VI, 206, evidence by Mr Siddall.

194 *Ministry of Pensions. Second Annual Report of the Minister of Pensions. From 31st March, 1918, to 31st March 1918* [39], H. C. 1920, XXII, 86. This statistic includes both permanent and 'conditional' alternative pensions. Many of these 'conditional' pensions would have subsequently been invalidated.

195 *Departmental Committee on Workmen's Compensation. Minutes of Evidence. Vol. I. 30th July to 9th December, 1919* [Cmd. 908], H. C. 1920, XXVI, 511, evidence by C. F. A. Hore, assistant secretary to the Ministry of Pensions.

196 *Report from the Select Committee on Pensions Together with the Proceedings of the Committee, Minutes of Evidence and Appendices* [185], H. C. 1920, VII, 56, evidence by H. Wolfe, principal assistant secretary of the Ministry of Labour and responsible for the Civil Liabilities Department.

197 *First and Second Special Reports from the Select Committee on Pensions. Together with the Proceedings of the Committee and Minutes of Evidence and Appendices* [247], H. C. 1919, VI, 287, evidence by J. M. Hogge.

198 Petition to the Treasury from twenty-four widows in Malta, 30 April 1935, PRO PIN15/699.

199 See PRO PIN71/1027 for lengthy correspondence about the restriction.

200 For protests about this rule, see 'War Emergency Workers' National Committee', resolution from the Bradford and District Trades and Labour Council, 19 September 1916, Labour History Archive (Manchester) WNC 24/1/207. Also see WNC 24/1/281ia. For further discussions of entitlement, see PRO PIN15/1054; PIN15/2432; PIN15/2431; PIN15/2434. For front-line threats, see Ralph I. Smith, 'Enlistment', 5, IWM 86/36/1.

201 Letter from W. F. Menzies, the medical superintendent of the County Mental Hospital in Cheddleton, Leek (Staffordshire) to the Ministry of Pensions, 25 October 1917, PRO PIN15/870.

202 Letter from Gerald McDonnell to J. H. Thomas, 13 July 1935, PRO PIN15/663. Spelling and punctuation as in original.

203 'Treatment of British Ex-Service Men in the Irish Free State', 'Report from Dublin', 22 June 1936, 1, PRO15/758.

204 *First and Second Special Reports from the Select Committee on Pensions. Together with the Proceedings of the Committee and Minutes of Evidence and Appendices* [247], H. C. 1919, VI, 373–4, evidence by W. G. Fallon, secretary of the City of Dublin War Pension Committee. Also see *Report from the Select Committee on Pensions. Together with the Proceedings of the Committee. Minutes of Evidence and Appendices* [185], H. C. 1920, VIII, 93 and 98, evidence by Gordon Campbell, secretary of the Irish Department of the Ministry of Labour.

205 Niall MacFhionnghaile, *Donegal, Ireland and the First World War* (Leitrim, 1987), 136.

206 Harold E. Mellersh, 'Schoolboy into War', 118, IWM Con Shelf.

207 See the speech by Sir Robert Jones, 'British Orthopaedic Association', *British Medical Journal*, 31 October 1925, 799–800. CMAC SA/BMA/C.193 Box 75.

208 No author given, February 1917, 2, PRO NATS1/742.

209 Devine, *Disabled Soldiers and Sailors*, 185, and Mitchell, *What Can Be Done*, 56.

210 Devine, *Disabled Soldiers and Sailors*, 158; Douglas C. McMurtie, 'Experience in the Re-Education of Disabled Soldiers in Great Britain', *American Journal of Care for Cripples*, VIII.6 (1919), 427; Mitchell, *What Can Be Done*, 56; Donald C. Norris, 'The Care of the Injured Industrial Worker', *News Letter. Circulated by the Central Council for the Care of Cripples*, V (January 1941), 4.

211 L. V. Shairp, 'The Re-Education of Disabled Soldiers', *Edinburgh Review*, CCXXV.459 (January 1917), 129.

212 McMurtie, 'Experience in the Re-Education of Disabled Soldiers in Great Britain', 426. Also see Lord Charnwood, 'A General Survey', *Recalled to Life*, II (September 1917), 220; Devine, *Disabled Soldiers and Sailors*, 182; minute from Matthew Nathan, 18 April 1917, PRO PIN15/1147.

213 'Crippled Heroes', *Liverpool Chronicle*, 4 May 1917, Liverpool Council of Social Service, 'Cuttings from National Newspapers 1910–17', Liverpool Record Office 361 COU 2/2.

214 Letter to the editor, from Amy Baker of Burley, *The Times*, 2 February 1917.

215 Devine, *Disabled Soldiers and Sailors*, 187.

216 For instance, see Liverpool Council of Social Service, 'Cuttings from National Newspapers 1910–17', Liverpool Record Office 361 COU 2/2.

217 Hiram Sturdy, 'Illustrated Account of his Service on the Western Front with the Royal Regiment of Artillery', 30, IWM Con Shelf.

218 E. Longfield, honorary general secretary of the United Council of Disabled Ex-Servicemen's Associations, Manchester, *New Chronicle*, 21 April 1938, PRO PIN15/1417. For the financial implications of such debates (and a taste of the bitterness they engendered), see the letter from H. Parker of the Treasury, to A. E. Kingham, of the Ministry of Labour, 7 April 1939, in reference to a delegation from the British Legion, PRO LAB20/6; 'Report of the Ex-Regular Soldier Re-Settlement Committee', December 1931, 5, PRO WO32/4227; minutes of the Committee on Employment of Ex-Professional Sailors, Sailors and Airmen, 1921, PRO WO32/422.

219 Clark, *Echoes of the Great War*, 21 May 1917.

220 Letter from Colonel Townsend of the North Western Region Pension Board, to J. E. Bury, Ministry of Pensions, 3 June 1925, PRO PIN15/11.

221 L. V. Shairp, 'The Re-Education of Disabled Soldiers', *Edinburgh Review*, CCXXV.459 (January 1917), 124–5.

222 Letter from D. M. MacLean, *Edinburgh Evening Dispatch*, 9 March 1916, PRO PIN15/2142. Also see *Edinburgh Evening Dispatch*, 13 March 1916 and the minute from I. Fletcher Porter, 27 January 1919, PRO PIN15/1059.

223 'The Axe for Cripples', *Lancet*, 14 April 1923, 778, and *Birmingham Cripples' Union. Twenty-Second Annual Report for April 1st, 1920, to March 31st, 1921* (Birmingham, 1921), 10.

224 Central Council for the Disabled, *A Record of Fifty Years' Service to the Disabled From 1919 to 1969* (London, 1970), 19. Also see *Birmingham Cripples' Union. Twenty-First Annual Report from April 1st, 1919, to March 31st, 1920* (Birmingham, 1920), 18.

225 'Points in the Administration of the West Ham Union', 31 July 1929, 9, PRO MH79/264.

226 Letter from W. H. Baker of Tunbridge Wells, to the War Pensions Department, 1 June 1937, PRO PIN15/38.

227 'Ex-Servicemen's Claim for Adequate Pensions', *Wigan Observer*, 26 February 1938.

228 Quoting from a letter from Sir Frederick Milner, *The Times*, 25 April 1924, in Bayly, *Triple Challenge*, 276.

229 PRO LAB2/1524/ED1484/6/1920; LAB2/1199/2332/64/1920; letter from

Edgar J. Smith, a one-armed ex-soldier, to the Ministry of Pensions, 25 July 1918, PRO PIN15/3372; F. George, *The Position of Ex-Service Man. Past. Present. Future* (Aldershot, 1921), 5; *First and Second Special Reports from the Select Committee on Pensions. Together with the Proceedings of the Committee and Minutes of Evidence and Appendices* [247], H. C. 1919, VI, 312–23. An important source is the very large file containing completed surveys on disabled employees carried out by the Trades Union Congress in 1937; MRC MSS 292/146.9/1.

230 'Memorandum of Interview. Care of Cripples', 10 January 1934, MRC MSS 292/841.6.

231 Kaye, 'Papers and Letters', letter to Mrs Kaye from Nurse J. Badger, 29 January 1917, IWM 82/11/1.

232 *First and Second Special Reports from the Select Committee on Pensions. Together with the Proceedings of the Committee and Minutes of Evidence and Appendices* [247], H. C. 1919, VI, 476, evidence by Mrs E. M. R. Shakespear, honorary secretary of the Birmingham Local War Pensions Committee and honorary secretary of the General Association, representing all the Local War Pension Committees.

233 John Galsworthy, 'Letters Additional', letter to V. C. Buckley, 31 July 1918, University of Birmingham Library (Heslop Room) JGL Add.61.

234 Cecil Webb-Johnson, *The Care of the Child from Birth to Puberty* (London, 1930), 13, and 'The Making of a Cripple. An Authentic Document', *Cripples' Journal*, 2.8 (April 1926), 285–93.

235 Joanna Bourke, *Working-Class Cultures in Britain 1890–1960: Gender, Class and Ethnicity* (London, 1994).

236 'Converting the Public', *Cripples' Journal*, 1.3 (January 1925), 121.

237 The extent to which ex-servicemen were prematurely aged was extensively debated. For examples, see *Copies of Reports made to the Prime Minister by the British Legion regarding the Condition of Ex-Service Men and of his Reply* [Cmd. 5738], H. C. 1937–38, X, and Sir Thomas Lewis, 'Papers', CMAC PP/LEW/C1/9.

238 M. Creach-Henry and D. Marten, *The Unknown Warrior* (London, 1923), 5.

Chapter Two: Malingering

1 Miss Dorothy Scholes, 'Papers of Miss Dorothy Scoles', scrapbook belonging to Dorothy Scholes, nurse at a military hospital, Edward Hall Collection, Wigan Archives Service D/DZ.EHC. Wounded soldiers described how they were injured. Unnamed entry. Punctuation and spelling as in original.

2 For some techniques to get into the army when not entitled to, see A. Bassett Jones and Llewellyn J. Llewellyn, *Malingering or the Simulation of Disease* (London, 1917), 14. For accounts of how unfit men managed to get into the army, see Sir Edward Henry Lionel Beddington, 'My Life', 1960, 10, Liddell Hart Centre for Military Archives; Sid T. Kemp, 'Remembrance. The 6th Royal West Kent Regiment 1914–1916', 4, IWM 85/28/1; R. Loudon, 'My Life in the First World War', 4, IWM 87/17/1; James Murray, 'To Passchendaele and Back', 1976, 53, IWM P457; Stewart Richie, 'La Grande Guerre. Some Notes on the Life of a Stretcher Bearer', 1, CMAC RAMC 1740 Box 351; G. Skelton, 'Memories', 29, IWM 79/17/1; E. Gardiner Williams, 'Background to Requirement', 4, Liverpool Records Office Acc. 2175; James Williamson, 'Memoirs', c.1948, 1, IWM P443.

3 W. Clarke, 'Memoir', 6, IWM 87/18/1, and H. A. Munro, 'Diary', 20 May 1915, IWM P374.

4 Revd Ernest Courtenay Crosse, 'The History of the Chaplain's Department in the War 1914–1918. Section I. With an Infantry Battalion at the Front', 1919, 10, IWM 80/22/1. For other discussions of this, see James Bannerman

Lorimer, 'Letters in War-Time', letter to his mother, 6 September 1916, IWM
96/193/1; Ernest Lye, 'A Worm's Eye View of Suvla Bay', c.1920s, 22, IWM
81/9/1; Thomas Macmillan, 'The War to End War: 1914–1918', 1935, 44,
IWM Con Shelf; A. G. May, 'Personal Experiences of the War Years 1915–
1917', 22, IWM 88/46/1; Sir (Charles) Geoffrey Vickers, 'Diaries and
Correspondence 1915–40', diary for 15 January 1917, Liddell Hart Centre for
Military Archives.

5 For a file on men who carried out the threat, see PRO PIN15/807. For other
examples, see Hubert Costello-Bowen, 'Diary', 30 December 1914, IWM 86/
19/1; Macmillan, 'The War to End War', 68, IWM Con Shelf; R. L. MacKay,
'Diary', 2 January 1917, IWM P374; Canon T. Guy Rogers, 'Letters to his
Aunt', 12 January 1916, IWM Con Shelf. For official discussions, see Ministry
of Pensions, Minute Sheet, 1 January 1917, PRO PIN 15/807; letter from
George Chrystal to E. Phillips of the Treasury, PRO PIN15/810; 'Men's
Suicide Cases. Questions of Pensions and Allowances to Widows and
Dependants', 'Draft', c.1920, 2, PRO PIN15/810.

6 *War Emergency Workers' National Committee*, letter to WNC from Mr Egglishaw,
of the The Rectory Cottage, Houghton-le-Spring, 9 July 1915, pleading on
behalf of these young men, Labour History Archive, Manchester, WNC1/3/
12/8i. For a similar example, see *War Emergency Workers' National Committee*,
letter to T. J. Macnamara, MP, of the Admiralty, from the WNC, 15 December
1914, Labour History Archive, Manchester, WNC1/3/7/3.

7 Letter to the editor by Lieutenant-Colonel Frank Garrett (retired officer in the
Territorials), 'The Territorial Army', *The Times*, 4 September 1926.

8 Lancashire War Pensions Committee, Minute Book, 11 December 1914, 8–9,
meeting of the County Relief Committee, Lancashire Record Office, Preston,
CC/WPM/2.

9 Valentine Fleming, 'Letters', letter to 'Randolfo', 6 December 1914, IWM 90/
28.1.

10 J. H. Mitchell, 'The Worker's Point of View. x. Pit-Head Baths: Their Effect
on the Worker', *Human Factor, The Journal of the National Institute of Industrial
Psychology*, VI (1932), 457.

11 Jones and Llewellyn, *Malingering*, 12; Sir William Chance, *Industrial Unrest. The
Reports of the Commissioners (July 1917), Collected and Epitomised* (London, 1917),
9; Sir John Collie, 'The Effects of Recent Legislation upon Sickness and
Accident Claims', *Practitioner*, XCVII (July 1916), 301; Charles S. Myers, *Mind
and Work. The Psychological Factors in Industry and Commerce* (London, 1920),
111–18; idem., *A Psychologist's Point of View. Twelve Semi-Popular Addresses on
Various Subjects* (London, 1933), 148–50; T. H. Pear, *Fitness for Work* (London,
1928), 92–3; A. G. Woodward, *Personal Management* (London, 1938), 96 and
100–2.

12 See Joanna Bourke, *Working-Class Cultures in Britain 1890–1960; Gender, Class
and Ethnicity* (London, 1994). A particularly interesting example of the public
relationship between striking and malingering can be seen in the Metropolitan
Police Papers concerning the 1918 police strike: PRO MEPO3/2574A and
MEPO3/254.

13 Bert Rudge, 'Transcript of Interview', March 1980, 19–20, IWM 85/39/1.

14 Hiram Sturdy, 'Illustrated Account of his Service on the Western Front with
the Royal Regiment of Artillery', 14, IWM. Punctuation as in original.

15 War Office, *Statistics of the Military Effort of the British Empire during the Great
War* (London, 1922), 643.

16 Robert H. Ahrenfeldt, *Psychiatry in the British Army in the Second World War*
(London, 1958), 273.

17 S. Bradbury, 'War Diary', 1923, 2 and 11, IWM 81/35/1; John M. Cordy, 'My

Memories of the First World War', 5, IWM 86/30/1; E. A. McKechnie, 'Reminiscences of the Great War, 1914–18', 50–1, IWM 88/27/1; Samuel Weingott, 'Diary', 3 January 1915, IWM 91/3/1.

18 Robert W. F. Johnston, 'Some Experiences in the Great War of 1914–1918', 44, IWM 82/38/1.

19 For instance, see Charles Callender, 'Memoirs', 1972, 3–4, IWM 73/186/1, and Weingott, 'Diary', 7 April 1915, IWM 91/3/1. Since the 'group' aspects of shirking were identical to those in malingering, more examples will be given below.

20 For a comparison of war and civil malingering, see Henry Waite, 'Medically Unfit', *Practitioner*, XCI (January 1916), 123, and William Wallace, 'Methods of examining the Vision of Recruits and Soldiers, with special reference to Assumed and Real Defects', *Journal of the Royal Army Medical Corps*, XXVI.4 (April 1916), 477–8.

21 Sir John Collie, *Malingering and Feigned Sickness*, 2nd edn (London, 1917), 24 and 377.

22 Alan W. Sichel, 'A New Test Type for the Detection of Malingerers in the Army', *Journal of the Royal Army Medical Corps*, XXX.3 (March 1918), 326.

23 Collie, *Malingering*, 378.

24 Donald C. Norris, 'Malingering', in William Brown Doherty and Dagobert D. Runes, eds, *Rehabilitation of the War Injured. A Symposium* (London, 1945), 126. See the variations to this 'trick', in Collie, *Malingering*, 377.

25 T. A. Ross, *Lectures on War Neuroses* (London, 1941), 28.

26 Walter Emanuel and John Hassall, *Keep Smiling. More News by Liarless for German Homes* (London, c.1914–19), 10.

27 Hazel Thompson Clements, 'Diaries', 23 August 1916; 2 September 1916; 4 September 1916; 17 September 1916; 20 September 1916; 5 October 1916; 30 November 1916; 10 December 1916; 22 December 1916; 2 January 1917; 20 July 1918, punctuation, spelling, and capitalization as in original, IWM 86/76/1. His diaries from late 1916 to demobilization in 1919 contain several examples of malingering. For other examples of prolonging incapacity, see Les J. T. Matthews, 'A Sapper recalls 1914–1919. Egypt, Gallipoli, Palestine', 20, IWM 85/32/1, and T. A. Silver, 'Stapenhill Darby and Joan Club. Minute Book', unpaginated, IWM 74/108/1.

28 John William Rowarth, 'The Misfit Soldier', 32 and 41, IWM 80/40/1. Punctuation as in original.

29 David William Jabez Andrews, 'Diary', 13–23 September 1915, 11, CMAC RAMC 2021 Box 424.

30 Cited from F. P. Roe's manuscript memoirs by Peter H. Liddle, *The Soldiers' War 1914–1918* (London, 1988), 87. For other examples of self-inflicted wounds, see McKechnie, 'Reminiscences, 40, IWM 88/27/1, and Munro, 'Diary', 20 June 1915, IWM P374.

31 John Francis Jones, 'N.C.O.', 63, Liddell Hart Centre for Military Archives.

32 A. J. Jamieson, 'German Offensive on the Somme – 21–2 March 1918', 1977, 4, IWM 88/52/1.

33 C. E. Stuttard, 'Papers', letter from him to the editor of *Southport Visitor*, 8 October 1960, IWM 90/7/1. Also see Stokes, C.B., 'Papers', letter to wife on 2 May 1915, file CB54/5, IWM 93/23/6.

34 W. A. Quinton, 'Memoirs', 1929, 53, IWM 79/35/1.

35 David Starrett, 'Batman', 54, IWM 79/35/1.

36 Collie, *Malingering*, 368. Also see Guy Chapman, *A Passionate Prodigality. Fragments of an Autobiography* (London, 1933), 122; Sir Wyndham Childs, *Episodes and Reflections* (London, 1930), 166; Clark, *Echoes of the Great War*, 92–3; Arthur H. Hubbard, 'Letters Written May–November 1916', letter to Nellie

and Ivy, 29 June 1916, IWM Con Shelf; G. W. C. Hughes, 'Papers', 16, IWM P127; Walter Norris Nicholson, *Behind the Lines. An Account of Administrative Staffwork in the British Army 1914–18* (London, 1939), 289–90.

37 Ralph H. Covernton, 'Fifty Odd Years of Memoirs', 76, Liddell Hart Centre for Military Archives.

38 Maberley S. Esler, 'Memoirs', 49, IWM 74/102/1. Also see Jones, 'N.C.O.', 358, Liddell Hart Centre for Military Archives and Williamson, 'Memoirs', c.1948, 38–9, IWM P443.

39 Begg, *Surgery on Trestle*, 54–5.

40 Norris, 'Malingering', in Doherty and Runes, eds, *Rehabilitation*.

41 Begg, *Surgery*, 80.

42 Ernest Sheard, 'Manuscript Memoirs', vol. 7, 997, IWM P285.

43 Collie, *Malingering*, 368–9.

44 Ibid., 373.

45 Alec Bishop, 'Look Back With Pleasure', vol. 1, 13, Liddell Hart Centre for Military Archives.

46 Collie, *Malingering*, 373.

47 A. Jack Abraham, '1914–1918: Memories of a Non-Hero', c.1973, 112, IWM P191.

48 Begg, *Surgery*, 53.

49 Collie, *Malingering*, 378, and Millais Culpin, *Recent Advances in the Study of the Psychoneuroses* (London, 1931), 18.

50 Jim Goodies, 'Letter to His Wife', in the papers of the Goodies family, Manchester City Council Local Studies Unit Misc. 752/2, and Norris, 'Malingering', in Doherty and Runes, eds, *Rehabilitation*.

51 Sichel, 'A New Test', 326.

52 War Office, *Statistics*, 643.

53 Childs, *Episodes and Reflections*, 166. For a detailed examination, see David Englander and James Osborne, 'Jack, Tommy and Henry Dubb: The Armed Forces and the Working Class', *Historical Journal*, XXI.3 (1978), 598.

54 'Records of the 55th (West Lancashire) Division 1916–1919', Liverpool Record Office 356 FIFI–2–28.

55 This can be seen throughout the diaries of Clements, 'Diaries', IWM 86/76/1. See the entries for 25 August 1916, 19 November 1916 and 22 January 1917. The idea that malingering was ubiquitous was widespread; see Guy Buckeridge, 'Memoirs of my Army Service in the Great War', c.1920s, 13, IWM P273.

56 Rogers, 'Letters to his Aunt', in his brown notebook, IWM Con Shelf. Punctuation and spelling has been corrected.

57 Jim Wolveridge, *Ain't It Grand (Or Was This Stepney?)* (London, 1976), 19.

58 Jones and Llewellyn, *Malingering*, vii, 14 and 53–5; Collie, *Malingering*, 380; Sichel, 'A New Test', 326; Waite, 'Medically Unfit', 123; Wallace, 'Methods of Examining', 477–8; idem, 'The Vision of the Soldier, with special reference to Malingering', *Journal of the Royal Army Medical Corps*, XXXVII.1 (July 1921), 41.

59 The most famous being Collie, *Malingering*, and Archibald McKendrick, *Malingering and its Detection under the Workmen's Compensation and other Acts* (Edinburgh, 1912).

60 Charles S. Myers, *Mind and Work. The Psychological Factors in Industry and Commerce* (London, 1920), 118.

61 Jones and Llewellyn, *Malingering*, vii.

62 Ibid., 10–11, and McKendrick, *Malingering*, 7. The idea that malingering was a consequence of provision for compensation was common and was reiterated throughout the *Departmental Committee on Workmen's Compensation. Minutes of Evidence. Vol. 1. 30th July to 9th December, 1919* [Cmd. 908], H. C. 1920, XXVI,

and *Departmental Committee on Workmen's Compensation. Minutes of Evidence. Vol. II. 10th December 1919, to 28th May, 1920* [Cmd. 909], H. C. 1920, XXVI.

63 For histories of industrial compensation, see P. W. J. Bartrip, *Workmen's Compensation in Twentieth-Century Britain* (Aldershot, 1987), and Helen Bolderson, *Social Security, Disability and Rehabilitation. Conflicts in the Development of Social Policy, 1914–1946* (London, 1991).

64 Jones and Llewellyn, *Malingering*, 25–6.

65 Ibid., 26–7. For a similar argument regarding the way lump-sum payments encouraged malingering, see 'Minutes of Medico–Political Committee. 18th March, 1936', CMAC SA/BMA/C149 Box 66.

66 *Departmental Committee on Workmen's Compensation. Minutes of Evidence. Vol. I. 30th July to 9th December, 1919* [Cmd. 908], H. C. 1920, XXVI, 67, evidence by George Harold Stuart Bunning, chairman of the Parliamentary Committee of the Trades Union Congress.

67 Jones and Llewellyn, *Malingering*, v, and Sir John Collie, 'The Effects of Recent Legislation upon Sickness and Accident Claims', *Practitioner*, XCVII (July 1916), 15.

68 *Departmental Committee on Workmen's Compensation. Minutes of Evidence. Vol. I. 30th July to 9th December, 1919* [Cmd. 908], H. C. 1920, XXVI, 14, evidence by William Shaw, chairman of the Scottish Trades Union Congress, and Wilfred Willett, 'Memoirs', 26, IWM 82/1/1.

69 Ibid., 354–5, evidence by Hubert Kenrick Beale, a Birmingham solicitor in the firm of Beale and Co., solicitors to the Midland Railway Company. Beale did not consider that the decline in accidents might be due to changing working practices rather than to malingering, nor that patriotic fervour might lead 'genuinely' injured workers to remain at work. See also the evidence of Sydney Septimus Ayles of the finance department, Ministry of Munitions, on p. 30. The relationship between malingering and wages was also discussed in Edward Mansfield Brockbank, *Incapacity or Disablement in its Medical Aspects* (London, 1926), 94.

70 *Departmental Committee on Workmen's Compensation. Minutes of Evidence. Vol. I. 30th July to 9th December, 1919* [Cmd. 908], H. C. 1920, XXVI, 94, evidence by George Barker, member of the National Executive Committee of the Miners' Federation of Great Britain.

71 Cited in Sir John Collie, 'Neurasthenia: What it costs the State', *Journal of the Royal Army Medical Corps*, XXVI.4 (April 1916), 528.

72 Sir John Collie, 'The Effects of Recent Legislation upon Sickness and Accident Claims', *Practitioner*, XCVII (July 1916), 1–2. The number of accidents increased from 326,701 to 472,408 and the amount paid in compensation increased from less than £2.1 million to £3.4 million.

73 Brockbank, *Incapacity*, 14.

74 Collie, 'The Effects of Recent Legislation,' 15.

75 Collie, *Malingering*, 7.

76 For a cautious statement, see Jones and Llewellyn, *Malingering*, 18.

77 Wallace, 'The Vision of the Soldier', 43. For a more lengthy discussion of the role of military doctors, see Mark Harrison, *Medicine and British Warfare: The Royal Army Medical Corps, 1898–1918*, forthcoming, and his lecture delivered at the University of Nijmegen entitled 'Disease, Medicine and Dissent in the Indian Army during the First World War', unpublished.

78 Dr Henry Cohen, 'The Nature, Method and Purpose of Diagnosis', undated, 7, in the uncatalogued papers of Donald Hunter, CMAC Box 45.

79 *Report of the War Office Committee of Enquiry into 'Shell-Shock'* [Cmd 1734], H. C. 1922, XII, 132.

80 McKendrick, *Malingering*, 68.

81 Munro, 'Diary', 20 June 1915, IWM P374.

82 T. Lister Llewellyn, *Miners' Nystagmus. Its Causes and Prevention* (London, 1912), 122.

83 *Departmental Committee on Workmen's Compensation. Minutes of Evidence. Vol. I. 30th July to 9th December, 1919* [Cmd. 908], H. C. 1920, XXVI, 109, evidence by James Henson, representing the National Sailors' and Firemen's Union.

84 Jones and Llewellyn, *Malingering*, 51, and W. R. Inge, *Diary of a Dean. St. Paul's 1911–1934* (London, 1949), 8 January 1917, 35. This was also true for industrial malingering: Pear, *Fitness for Work*, 85–6. For racial characteristics, see Colin Robert Ballard, 'Letters', letter to his mother, 31 December 1914, Liddell Hart Centre for Military Archives iv/8; Bradbury, 'War Diary', 1923, 94, copy of a letter from F. W. Bewshew, IWM 81/35/1; Richard C. Foot, 'Once a Gunner', 8, IWM 86/57/1; Gameson, 'Papers', 23, diary for 16 July 1916, IWM Con Shelf; John Hare, 'War Diary, September to December 1914', 4 May 1914, 6, CMAC RAMC 1327 Box 288; Johnston, 'Some Experiences', section entitled 'The British Army Officer and the Great War', 11, IWM 82/38/1; Walter Norris Nicholson, *Behind the Lines. An Account of Administrative Staffwork in the British Army 1914–18* (London, 1939), 240; 'Orellius', 'Our London Lads', unlocated press cutting in the papers of Edwin Taylor, 'Papers', CMAC RAMC 1803 Box 361; Sturdy, 'Illustrated Account', 23–4, IWM Con Shelf.

85 Jones and Llewellyn, *Malingering*, 69–73; Frederick Walker Mott, *War Neuroses and Shell-Shock* (London, 1919), 218; William Wallace, 'Methods of Examining', 480.

86 McKendrick, *Malingering*, 68.

87 Norris, 'Malingering', in Doherty and Runes, eds, *Rehabilitation*.

88 Wallace, 'Methods of Examining', 481.

89 Sichel, 'A New Test'.

90 Arthur F. Hurst, *Medical Diseases of the War*, 2nd edn (London, 1918), 28; Jones and Llewellyn, *Malingering*, 82; Charles S. Myers, *Shell-Shock in France 1914–18. Based on a War Diary* (Cambridge, 1940), 51–3.

91 Jones and Llewellyn, *Malingering*, 83.

92 Ibid., 83–8.

93 McKendrick, *Malingering*, 15.

94 Collie, *Malingering*, 376.

95 Ibid., 4 and 30. For similar statements, see Jones and Llewellyn, *Malingering*, 40–1.

96 J. C. Dunn, *The War the Infantry Knew 1914–1919* (London, 1987), 410, diary of a medical officer, 15 October 1914.

97 Dunn, *The War*, 585.

98 Charles Cyril Ammons, 'Service in the First World War', 6, CMAC RAMC 1599 Box 337; Kemp, 'Remembrance', 9, IWM 85/28/1; 'Mark VII' [pseud. Mark Plowman], *A Subaltern on the Somme in 1916* (London, 1927), 55; William Charles Sims, 'Diary 1 August 1916–2 September 1918', 22, 19 and 22 November 1917, Bristol Record Office 40340; Arthur Graeme West, *The Diary of a Dead Officer* (London, 1918), 11 July 1916, 41.

99 Anonymous diary, 'Mesopotamian Diary. With the 5th Buffs along the Tigris 1915–1916', *The Great War. The Illustrated Journal of First World War History*, 3.1, part 6 (November 1990), 29.

100 James Henry Dible, 'First World War Account', 48, IWM Con Shelf. In his attitude to men suffering from neurasthenia, however, his sympathy reached its limit although he preferred to 'treat' these men himself than to see them punished. He wrote, 'I cannot abide these neurasthenic people. R.A.M.C officers call them "Scrimshankers": but that is the R.A.M.C.'s second most

frequent disease. No doubt they suffer and their woes are very real to themselves: all the same they exasperate me beyond endurance but I rather prefer to kick them out of my presence with a few well rubbed words of worldly wisdom than to hand them over to their N.C.O.s as scrimshankers' (p. 29).

101 'Shell-Shock. Proceedings of a Court of Enquiry dealing with the Failure of a Part of an Infantry Battalion to carry out a Raid', July 1915, in Sir Charles Burtchaell, 'Papers and Reports', CMAC RAMC/446/18.

102 Starrett, 'Batman', 34–5, IWM 79/35/1.

103 Stephen Graham, *A Private in the Guards* (London, 1919), 18, and R. L. Mackay, 'Diary', 1 August 1917 and 31 July 1917, IWM P374. No statistics exist for men who were 'unofficially' shot while running away. For the official statistics, see War Office, *Statistics*, 648. There were 266 cases of executions for desertion. For further discussion of the death penalty, see Anthony Babington, *For the Sake of Example: Capital Courts Martial 1914–1920* (London, 1983); William Moore, *The Thin Yellow Line* (London, 1974); Julian Putkowski and Julian Sykes, *Shot at Dawn* (Barnsley, 1989).

104 Childs, *Episodes*, 145.

105 James Lochhead Jack, *General Jack's Diary 1914–1918* (London, 1964), 56. See also *Report of the Committee constituted by the Army Council to enquire into the Law and Rules of Procedure regulating Military Courts-Martial* [Cmd 428], H. C. 1919, x.

106 Andrews, 'Diary', 30 September 1915, 8, CMAC RAMC 2021 Box 424.

107 Ahrenfeldt, *Psychiatry*, 271.

108 Jones, 'N.C.O.', 101, Liddell Hart Centre for Military Archives. Also see 'Mark VII', *A Subaltern*, 95–6.

109 Chapman, *A Passionate Prodigality*, 81.

110 Reginald S. Cockburn, 'Diary and Recollections', 114, IWM P258.

111 Ibid., diary for 6 May 1917, 64, IWM P258, and A. E. Perriman, 'Memoirs', 1976, 9–10, IWM 80/43/1.

112 Sturdy, 'Illustrated Account', 22, IWM Con Shelf. Also see Maurice Healey, 'Death Penalty in the Army', *The Times*, 1 April 1927.

113 'Ex-Private X', *War is War* (London, 1930), 74.

114 Thomas Macmillan, 'The War to End War: 1914–1918', 1935, 169, IWM Con Shelf.

115 'Diary of an Unidentified Soldier in the Border Regiment, 1914–15', 6 March 1915, IWM Misc. 550.

116 Quinton, 'Memoirs', 1929, 60–3, and continuing in the unnumbered, handwritten pages, IWM 79/35/1.

117 Nicholson, *Behind the Lines*, 289. For examples of the difficulties experienced by commanders, see C. L. Spencer, 'Some Private Recollections of a Base Wallah, 1914–1919', 1933, 146, Liddell Hart Centre for Military Archives.

118 Alex Knight, 'Letters', letter to his mother, 17 October 1916, IWM Con Shelf.

119 Jones, 'N. C. O.', 63, Liddell Hart Centre for Military Archives.

120 Graham, *A Private in the Guards*, 155. When this story was told, it was added that at the next battle, the sergeant-major who had sentenced the boy to death was severely wounded and while he 'lay on the battlefield in mortal agony', no one would give him a drink of water. Some even spat on him as they marched past.

121 Bayly, *Triple Challenge*, 155.

122 Frank Dunham, *The Long Carry. The Journal of Stretcher Bearer Frank Dunham 1916–18*, ed. R. H. Haigh and P. W. Turner (Oxford, 1970), 181.

123 Childs, *Episodes*, 166; letter from J. S. Middleton to the Llanelly and District Labour Association, 12 November 1916, in War Emergency Workers' National Committee Papers, Labour History Archive (Manchester) WNC24/1/225;

minutes on 8 October 1918, 6 August 1919 and 25 August 1919, PRO PIN15/
1381; 'Ministry of Pensions. Method of Dealing with Cases of Accidental
Injuries and also Certain Cases of Disease or Death', undated but 1919, PRO
PIN15/1381; letter from George Chrystal, 13 July 1921, PRO PIN15/1381;
minute from Matthew Nathan, 28 June, no year, PRO PIN15/1399; *First and
Second Special Reports from the Select Committee on Pensions. Together with the
Proceedings of the Committee and Minutes of Evidence and Appendices* [247.], H. C.
1919, VI, 193, evidence by Mrs Ethel M. Wood.

124 Ashley Gibson, *Postscript to Adventure* (London, 1930), 176.

125 Jack, *General Jack's Diary*, 111.

126 Letter from Sir Douglas Haig, general officer commanding-in-chief, British
Armies in France, to the secretary of the War Office, 4 December 1916, 1–2,
PRO WO32/5400.

127 PRO WO32/5460.

128 Childs, *Episodes*, 145.

129 Letter from Haig, to the secretary of the War Office, 4 December 1916, 3,
PRO WO32/5400.

130 Minute from 'A.G.', 11 December 1916, PRO WO32/5460 and letter from
Haig to the secretary of the War Office, 4 December 1916, 3, PRO WO32/
5400.

131 Rowarth, 'The Misfit Soldier', 31, IWM 80/40/1.

132 Rowland Myrddyn Luther, 'The Poppies are Blood Red', 11, IWM 87/8/1.

133 Letter to the secretary of the War Office, from G. F. Milne, general officer
commanding-in-chief of the British Force in Salonica, 2, PRO WO32/5400.

134 'Desirability or Otherwise of Retaining F.P. No. 1. Précis of Interviews with W.
O., N. C. O.s, and Men', 1919, 1, PRO WO32/5461.

135 Letter from G. F. Milne, general officer commanding-in-chief, British Salonika
Force, to the secretary of the War Office, 20 December 1916, 2, PRO WO32/
5400. For a similar argument, see letter from Haig to the secretary of the War
Office, 4 December 1916, 1–2, PRO WO32/5400.

136 For protesting letters in 1916 and 1917, see PRO WO32/5460 and WO32/
5400.

137 See Robert Blatchford, 'My Case against Crucifixions', no location given but
possibly *Evening Standard*, PRO WO32/5400. Also see his story in *Sunday
Chronicle*, 29 October 1916, and the defence of 5 November.

138 Letter from Miss Fanny C. Grieve to the Home Office (who passed it on to the
War Office), 8 January 1917, PRO WO32/5460.

139 PRO WO32/5460: 28 March 1917; PRO WO32/5460: 26 February 1917.

140 'Mark VII', *A Subaltern*, 30. Also see R. A. Ford, 'Dilly', 4, IWM.

141 Letter to Lloyd George from F. Hardy of Forest Hill, London, 19 November
1916, PRO WO32/5460. Also see newspaper clipping, Roy Horniman of
Kensington, London, 'Field Punishment', *Daily News*, undated, probably
November 1916, PRO WO32/5460.

142 Ernest Sheard, 'Manuscript Memoirs', vol. 1, 51, IWM P285, and Guy
Buckeridge, 'Memoirs of my Army Service in the Great War', *c.*1920s, 74,
IWM P273.

143 Horniman, 'Field Punishment'.

144 'Desirability or Otherwise of Retaining F.P. No. 1. Précis of Interviews with W.
O., N. C. O.s and Men', 1919, 1, PRO WO32/5461.

145 Roy Horniman of Kensington, London, 'Field Punishment', *Daily News*,
undated, probably November 1916, PRO WO32/5460. See also Lawrence
Gameson, 'Papers', 85, IWM Con Shelf.

146 'Desirability or Otherwise of Retaining F. P. No. 1. Précis of Interviews with
W. O., N. C. O.s and Men', 1919, 1, PRO WO32/5461.

147 Gameson, 'Papers', 11, diary for 20 May 1916, IWM Con Shelf.

148 Lye, 'A Worm's Eye View', 7 and 33. IWM 81/9/1.

149 W. R. Acklam, 'Diary September 1916 – December 1918', 3 May 1918, IWM LS Box No. 83/23/1.

150 A. R. Brennan, 'Diary', undated, November 1916, IWM P262, and Macmillan, 'The War to End War', 71, IWM Con Shelf.

151 John Theodore Foxell, 'Diaries', entries for April–May 1916, IWM 91/24/1.

152 Silver, 'Stapenhill Darby and Joan Club', unpaginated, IWM 74/108/1, entire manuscript written in capital letters with many spelling errors.

153 Ibid.

154 Clements, 'Diaries', 22 October 1915 and 26 January 1917, IWM 86/76/1.

155 A. Caseby, 'Jottings from the Spiritual Side of the Army', c. 1920, unpaginated, IWM 78/4/1. Callender, 'Memoirs', 14, IWM 73/186/1 records his shock at the harshness of the punishment (Field Punishment No. 1 for three months) meted out to a soldier for urinating in the snow.

156 Russell L. Venables, 'The Great War 1914–1918: Diary', undated entry for 1916, 16–17, IWM 76/225/1.

157 Abraham, '1914–1918', 55, IWM P191; Johnston, 'Some Experiences', 36, IWM 82/38/1; Quinton, 'Memoirs', 1929, 22, IWM 79/35/1; Wilfred Watkins, 'Reminiscences of Wilfred Watkins (1897–1979) of Treharris, South Wales', recorded in 1970, 7, IWM 91/3/1.

158 Cockburn, 'Diary', 48, diary for 31 March 1918, IWM P258; Jones, 'N.C.O.', 171, Liddell Hart Centre for Military Archives; Mackay, 'Diary', 3 August 1917, IWM P374.

159 Costello-Bowen, 'Diary', 27 December 1914, IWM 86/19/1.

160 Begg, Surgery, 80.

161 Clements, 'Diaries', 6 September and 17 December 1916, IWM 86/76/1, and Gameson, 'Papers', 23, diary for 10 June 1916, IWM Con Shelf.

162 Begg, Surgery, 56. Also see p. 53.

163 Clements, 'Diaries', 17 October 1915, IWM 86/76/1.

164 Macmillan, 'The War to End War', 19, IWM Con Shelf.

165 Wolveridge, Ain't It Grand, 19. For further discussion of the rules which legitimated (or otherwise) malingering within the Other Ranks, see my 'Swinging the Lead: Malingering, Australian Soldiers and the Great War', Journal of The Australian War Memorial, 26 (April 1995), 10–18.

166 Collie, Malingering, 36–7.

167 In 1908, 18 per cent of the claims for compensation which reached court were decided in favour of the employer. By 1913, this had increased to nearly one quarter: Collie, Malingering, 36–7.

168 Somerset Miners' Association, 'Papers 1868–1964', newspaper cutting entitled 'A Miner's Injury', Bath and Wilts Chronicle and Herald, 16 May 1927, and an unidentified newspaper cutting entitled 'A Poisoned Thumb', 19 May 1927, University of Bristol Library Special Collections, uncatalogued.

169 McKendrick, Malingering, 14.

170 Ahrenfeldt, Psychiatry, 27; W. D. Chambers, 'Mental Wards with the British Expeditionary Force: A Review of Ten Months' Experience', Journal of Mental Science, lxv (July 1919), 161; Waite, 'Medically Unfit', 120–21.

171 Lord Moran, The Anatomy of Courage (London, 1945), 166.

172 F. M. Earle and A. Macrae, Tests of Mechanical Ability (London, 1929); F. M. Earle and F. Gow, The Measurement of Manual Dexterities (London, 1930); F. M. Earle and J. Kilgour, A Vocational Guidance Research in Fife (London, 1935); F. M. Earle, Methods of Choosing A Career (London, 1931); Bernard Musico, Lectures on Industrial Psychology, 2nd edn revised (London, 1920), 104–52; and

Charles S. Myers, *Present-Day Applications of Psychology with special reference to Industry, Education and Nervous Breakdown* (London, 1918), 10–16.

173 Woodward, *Personnel Management*, 15.

174 Henry J. Welch and Charles S. Myers, *Ten Years of Industrial Psychology. An Account of the First Decade of the National Institute of Industrial Psychology* (London, 1932), 207, and Woodward, *Personnel Management*, 148–59.

175 Winifred Spielman, 'Square Pegs and Square Holes', in Charles S. Myers, ed., *Industrial Psychology* (London, 1929), 194. See also Charles S. Myers, *Industrial Psychology in Great Britain* (London, 1926); W. Spielman Raphael, C. B. Frisby and L. I. Hunt, *Industrial Psychology Applied to the Office* (London, 1934), 3–30; Welch and Myers, *Ten Years*, 207–37.

176 H. G. Maule and May Smith, *Industrial Psychology and the Laundry Trade* (London, 1947), v.

177 Leonard P. Lockhart, 'Industrial Problems from the Standpoint of General Practice', August 1931, 3, in National Institute of Industrial Psychology Papers, LSE NIIP 16/5.

178 Charles S. Myers, 'Introduction', in Myers, ed., *Industrial Psychology* (London, 1929), 9.

179 Ibid., 11.

180 See Welch and Myers, *Ten Years*, 2, and every issue of *Journal of the National Institute of Industrial Psychology*.

181 Herbert N. Casson, *Handbook for Foremen* (London, 1928), 96; F. W. Lawe, 'The Economic Aspects of Industrial Psychology', in Myers, ed., *Industrial Psychology*, 227; idem, *A Psychologist's Point of View*, 152–3.

182 Casson, *Handbook for Foremen*, 95.

183 For a discussion of why Taylorism was not significant in Britain, see Robert Fitzgerald, *British Labour Management and Industrial Welfare 1846–1939* (London, 1988), 7–8, and Craig R. Littler, *The Development of the Labour Process in Capitalist Societies* (London, 1982).

184 Myers, *Mind and Work*, 116, and idem, *A Psychologist's Point of View*, 152–3.

185 Jones and Llewellyn, *Malingering*, vii; Elizabeth Livingstone and John D. Handyside, *Two Studies in Supervision* (London, 1953); J. H. Mitchell, 'The Worker's Point of View. x. Pit-Heads Baths: Their Effect on the Worker', *Human Factor. The Journal of the National Institute of Industrial Psychology*, VI (1932), 457; Woodward, *Personnel Management*, 70–87.

186 Ibid., 158.

187 'Proposed National Institute of Industrial Psychology and Physiology Applied to Commerce and Industry. Statements illustrating some of the work to be undertaken by the Institute' (London: NIIP, n.d.), 3, in National Institute of Industrial Psychology Papers, LSE NIIP 16/3; Myers, *Present-Day Applications*, 10–16; Pear, *Fitness for Work*, 138–43; J. Ramsay and R. E. Rawson, *Rest-Pauses and Refreshments in Industry* (London, 1939).

188 W. R. Dunlop, *An Investigation of Certain Processes and Conditions on Farms* (London, 1927), 70, and Spielman Raphael, Frisby and Hunt, *Industrial Psychology applied to the Office*, 67.

189 Myers, 'Introduction', in Myers, ed., *Industrial Psychology*, 14.

190 John Baynes, *Morale. A Study of Men and Courage. The Second Scottish Rifles at the Battle of Neuve Chapelle 1915* (London, 1987), 253–4.

191 Digby Bell, 'Sport. Its Function in Industry', *Journal of Industrial Welfare*, II.4 (April 1920), 108–11.

192 T. B. Miles, *Industrial Unrest. Its Cause and Suggested Cure* (London, 1923). Also see *Departmental Committee on Workmen's Compensation. Minutes of Evidence. Vol. I. 30th July to 9th December, 1919* [Cmd. 908], H. C. 1920, XXVI, 265, evidence by B. Fossett Lock, county court judge for the Hull Circuit.

193 Collie, 'The Effects of Recent Legislation,' 20, and Jones and Llewellyn, *Malingering*, 31–2.

194 Harold Clegg, 'Memoirs', 76, IWM 88/18/1; Frank Gray, *The Confessions of a Private* (Oxford, 1920), 35–6; Sir Basil Liddell Hart, letter to his parents, 17 October 1915, Liddell Hart Centre for Military Archives 7/1915/17, and letter to his parents, 18 October 1915, Liddell Hart Centre for Military Archives 7/1915/8; Hubbard, letter to Nellie and Ivy, 29 June 1916, IWM Con Shelf, Rogers, 'Letters to his Aunt', 23 October 1915, IWM Con Shelf.

195 Clegg, 'Memoirs', 76, IWM 88/18/1. Also see Buckeridge, 'Memoirs', 93, IWM P273; 'Ex-Private X', *War is War*, 117–18; Christopher Hughes, 'The Forgotten Army', 1925, 27, IWM 82/25/1.

196 For instance, see Clements, 'Diaries', 18 June 1915, IWM 86/76/1.

197 'A Lover of Decency', 'Correspondence', *New Church Times* (a trench paper), I.1, 17 April 1916, CMAC RAMC 479 Box 97.

198 'F. A. V.', *Combed Out* (London, 1920), 77. Also see 'Nurses' Autograph Album, Highbury Hospital, First World War', poem by J. H. Jones, 'The War and Slackers', IWM Misc 124 Item 1938.

199 Henry Gother Courtney, 'Letters', letter no. 8/81 to his sister on 17 July 1915, University Library Archive, no. 8/142; Walter Tom King, 'Letters', to his brother, 22 May 1917, IWM 89/7/1; Johnston, 'Some Experiences', section entitled 'The British Army Officer and the Great War', 9, IWM 82/38/1; Arthur C. L. D. Lees, 'Diary and Letters', letter to his wife, 17 October 1919, IWM 91/22/1; Luther, 'The Poppies', 11, IWM 87/8/1.

200 F. A. MacKenzie, *Canada's Day of Glory* (Toronto, 1918), 331. Also see J. L. Jack, *General Jack's Diary 1914–1918* (London, 1964), entry for 18 March 1915.

201 Jones, 'N. C. O.', 356, Liddell Hart Centre for Military Archives.

202 R. G. Macdonald Ladell, 'Medical Psychology: Pre-War-Time and Post-War', in Sir Walter Langdon-Brown, R. G. Macdonald Ladell, Frank Gray and F. G. Crookshank, eds, *The Place of Psychology in the Medical Curriculum and Other Papers* (London, 1936), 21.

203 Sir W. P. MacPherson, Sir W. P. Herringham, T. R. Elliott and A. Balfour, *Medical Services. Diseases of the War, Volume II* (London, 1923), 2.

204 Elaine Showalter, *The Female Malady: Women, Madness and English Culture 1830–1980* (London, 1987), 63.

205 Thomas W. Salmon, 'The Care and Treatment of Mental Diseases and War Neuroses ("Shell Shock") in the British Army', *Mental Hygiene*, I.4 (October 1917).

206 Ibid., 518.

207 Showalter, *The Female Malady*, 63.

208 The best discussion of this committee is given in Ted Bogacz, 'War Neurosis and Cultural Change in England, 1914–22: The Work of the War Office Committee of Enquiry into "Shell-Shock"', *Journal of Contemporary History*, XXIV (1989), 227–56.

209 McPherson, Herringham, Elliott, and Balfour, *Medical Services*, 8.

210 Showalter, *The Female Malady*, 63.

211 Mott, *War Neuroses*, 162.

212 'Ex-Private X', *War is War*, 97–8.

213 Rowarth, 'The Misfit Soldier', 33, IWM, 80/40/1.

214 Salmon, 'The Care and Treatment', 516.

215 Moran, *The Anatomy of Courage*, 186.

216 Abrahams, '1914–1918, 84, IWM P191. Also see Luther, 'The Poppies', 27b, IWM 87/8/1.

217 McKendrick, *Malingering*, 25–6.

218 Salmon, 'The Care and Treatment', 527–8.
219 Ibid., 527–8. Also see Maurice Nicoll and J. A. M. Alcock, 'Neurosis of War', *Medical Annual. A Yearbook of Treatment and Practitioner's Index 1920, 38th Year.* (Bristol, 1920), 253.
220 Mott, *War Neuroses*, 179. Also see Salmon, 'The Care and Treatment', 528.
221 Hurst, *Medical Diseases*, 28–9. Also see Collie, 'Neurasthenia': 530.
222 James J. Healy, 'The Diagnosis and Estimation of the Degree of Neurasthenia by means of Perimetric Examination of the Eyes', *Journal of the Royal Army Medical Corps*, XXXIV.2 (February 1920), 143.
223 Charles S. Myers, *Shell Shock in France 1914–18. Based on a War Diary* (Cambridge, 1940), 40–1.
224 Salmon, 'The Care and Treatment', War, 528.
225 Jones and Llewellyn, *Malingering*, 12–13. See also H. Norman Barnett, *Accidental Injuries to Workmen with reference to Workmen's Compensation Act, 1906* (London, 1909), 114–15, and Collie, 'Neurasthenia', 526.
226 Salmon, 'The Care and Treatment of Mental Diseases', 527. For another discussion of 'shell-shocked' men being shot for desertion, see Conn, 'Memories', 41, IWM 81/41/1.
227 George Rutherford Jeffrey, 'Some Points of Interest in connection with the Psychoneuroses of War', *Journal of Mental Science*, LXVI.273 (April 1920), 133. According to one study in 1917, one-fifth of 731 men suffering from neurasthenia returned to the Front after leaving hospital: Salmon, 'The Care and Treatment', 525.
228 Shulamit Ramon, *Psychiatry in Britain. Meaning and Policy* (London, 1985), 62.
229 O. P. Napier Pearn, 'Psychoses in the Expeditionary Forces', *Journal of Mental Science*, LXV (April 1919), 103 and 105.
230 W. D. Chambers, 'Mental Wards with the British Expeditionary Force: A Review of Ten Months' Experience', *Journal of Mental Science*, LXV (July 1919), 158.
231 Jeffrey, 'Some Points of Interest', 133, and Pearn, 'Psychoses', 103 and 105.
232 Esler, 'Memoirs', 74–5, IWM 74/102/1; Rogers, 'Letters to his Aunt', 31 May 1916, IWM Con Shelf; Starrett, 'Batman', 57, IWM 79/35/1.
233 Salmon, 'The Care and Treatment', 514–15. The higher ratio of officers to other ranks was confirmed by MacPherson, Herringham, Elliott and Balfour, *Medical Services. Diseases of the War. Volume II*, 17. The discrepancy may partially reflect the greater likelihood that officers would receive lengthier treatment.
234 MacPherson, Herringham, Elliott, and Balfour, *Medical Services. Diseases of the War, Volume II*, 17–18. See also Sir Robert Armstrong-Jones, 'The Psychology of Fear and the Effects of Panic Fear in War Time', *Journal of Mental Science*, LXIII.262 (July 1917), 369; Collie, *Malingering*, 186; Sir Frederick Walker Mott, 'Body and Mind: The Origin of Dualism', *Mental Hygiene*, VI. 4 (October 1922), 684; Myers, *Shell Shock*, 40; W. H. R. Rivers, 'War Neurosis and Military Training', *Mental Hygiene*, II.4 (October 1918), 514–17; William Aldren Turner, 'Neuroses and Psychoses of War', *Journal of the Royal Army Medical Corps*, XXXI.5 (November 1918), 400–1 and 410.
235 Millais Culpin, *Recent Advances in the Study of the Psychoneuroses* (London, 1931), 25.
236 Healy, 'The Diagnosis and Estimation of the Degree of Neurasthenia', 143.
237 *Report of the War Office Committee of Enquiry into 'Shell-Shock'* [Cmd 1734], H. C. 1922, XII, 43, evidence by Dr William Brown, neurologist for the 4th and 5th Armies, France.
238 *Departmental Committee on Workmen's Compensation. Minutes of Evidence. Vol. I. 30th July to 9th December, 1919* [Cmd. 908], H. C. 1920, XXVI, 238, evidence by

Arthur Henry Leech. general manager of the Northern Employers' Mutual Indemnity Co. in Wigan.

239 *Departmental Committee on Workmen's Compensation. Minutes of Evidence. Vol. II. 10th December 1919, to 28th May, 1920* [Cmd. 909], H. C. 1920, XXVI, 431, evidence by Michael Brett, secretary of the Shipping Mining Federation since 1901. Also see *Departmental Committee on Workmen's Compensation. Minutes of Evidence. Vol. I. 30th July to 9th December, 1919* [Cmd. 908], H. C. 1920, XXVI, 67, evidence by George Harold Stuart Bunning, chairman of the Parliamentary Committee of the Trades Union Congress.

240 *Departmental Committee on Workmen's Compensation. Minutes of Evidence. Vol. I. 30th July to 9th December, 1919* [Cmd. 908], H. C. 1920, XXVI, 98, evidence by George Baker, member of the National Executive Committee of the Miners' Federation of Great Britain.

241 Brockbank, *Incapacity*, 93.

242 Lockhart, 'Industrial Problems', August 1931, 6, in National Institute of Industrial Psychology Papers, LSE NIIP 16/5.

243 Brockbank, *Incapacity*, 86.

244 Revd Victor Tanner's diary for 26 September 1916, in Michael Moynihan, ed., *God is on our Side* (London, 1983), 161.

245 In Michael Moynihan, ed., *Greater Love. Letters Home 1914–1818* (London, 1980), 83.

246 For discussions of the organic and the psychological explanations, see H. Campbell, 'War Neurosis', *Practitioner*, XCVI (1916), 501–9; Culpin, *Recent Advances*, 15; Wilfred Garton, 'Shell-Shock and its Treatment by Cerebrospinal Galvanism', *Journal of the Royal Army Corps Medical Corps*, XXVIII.5 (May 1917), 600–1; W. Harris, *Nerve Injuries and Shock* (London, 1915); R. G. Macdonald Ladell, 'Medical Psychology: Pre-War, War-Time and Post-War', in Sir Walter Langdon-Brown, R. G. Macdonald Ladell, Frank Gray and F. G. Crookshank, eds, *The Place of Psychology in the Medical Curriculum and Other Papers* (London, 1936), 21; W. Milligan and F. H. Westmacott, 'Warfare Injuries and Neuroses', *Journal of Laryngology, Rhineology, and Otology*, XXX (1915), 297–303; Frederick Walker Mott, 'The Effects of High Explosives upon the Central Nervous System', *Lancet*, I (1916), 331–8, 441–9, 545–3; Maurice Nicoll and J. A. M. Alcock, 'Neurosis of War', *Medical Annual. A Yearbook of Treatment and Practitioner's Index 1920, 38th Year* (Bristol, 1920), 255; J. H. Parsons, 'The Psychology of Traumatic Amblyopia following the Explosion of Shells', *Lancet* (1915), 697–701; W. A. Turner, 'Remarks on Cases of Nervous and Mental Shock', *Lancet*, I (1915), 833–5.

247 Sir Wilmot Herringham, *A Physician in France* (London, 1919), 140, and Mott, *War Neuroses*, 2–3.

248 J. Mitchell Clarke, 'Some Neuroses of the War', *Bristol Medico-Chirurgical Journal*, XXXIV, July 1916, 49–72.

249 Myers, *Shell Shock*. Also see D. Forsyth, 'Functional Nerve Disease and the Shock of Battle', *Lancet*, II (1915), 1399–1403.

250 Pearn, 'Psychoses', 101.

251 Sir Frederick Walker Mott, 'Body and Mind: The Origin of Dualism', *Mental Hygiene*, VI.4 (October 1922), 684. See also Ladell, 'Medical Psychology' in Langdon-Brown, Ladell, Gray and Crookshank, eds, *The Place of Psychology*, 24.

252 Nicoll, 'Neurosis of War', 302–3. Also Rivers, 'War Neurosis and Military Training', 515–16, and Turner, 'Neuroses and Psychoses of War', 405.

253 E. Fryer Ballard, 'Some Notes on Battle Psycho-Neuroses', *Journal of Mental Science*, LXII.262 (July 1917), 402–3.

254 Dr Ernest Jones, 'War Shock and Freud's Theory of the Neuroses', in S.

Ferenczi, Karl Abraham, Ernest Simmel and Ernest Jones, eds, *Psycho-Analysis and the War Neuroses* (London, 1921), 47–8.

255 James B. Mennell, 'Massage as a Therapeutic Agent in the Treatment of Neurasthenia', *Practitioner*, XCII.547 (January 1914), 101.

256 Wilfred Garton, 'Shell-Shock and Its Treatment by Cerebrospinal Galvanism', *Journal of the Royal Army Medical Corps*, XXVIII.5 (May 1917), 601.

257 Collie, *Malingering*, 374. Also see R. H. Norgate, 'The Effects of War on the Mental Condition of Citizens of Bristol', *Bristol Medico-Chirurgical Journal*, XXXVII, March 1920, 106.

258 Quoted in Eric J. Leed, *No Man's Land: Combat and Identity in World War One* (New York, 1979), 174. See L. R. Yealland, *Hysterical Disorders of Warfare* (London, 1918).

259 Collie, *Malingering*, 9, and Norris, 'Malingering', in Doherty and Runes, eds, *Rehabilitation*.

260 For a discussion, see *Report of the War Office Committee of Enquiry into 'Shell-Shock'* [Cmd. 1734], H. C. 1922, XII, 125–36.

261 Charles S. Myers, 'Contributions to the Study of Shell Shock: (II) Being an Account of Certain Cases Treated by Hypnosis', *Journal of the Royal Army Medical Corps*, XXVI.5 (May 1916), 652, and J. B. Tombleson, 'An Account of Twenty Cases Treated by Hypnotic Suggestion', *Journal of the Royal Medical Corps*, XXIX.3 (September 1917), 340–6.

262 Nicoll and Alcock, 'Neurosis of War', 254–5. Even organicists might use 'suggestion'. Garton – a strong believer in the organic explanation – wrote, 'The cure of neurasthenia by suggestion in some cases is not an inexplicable contradiction, for it is conceivable that the paralysis of the nervi nervorum may be of just that extent that recovery is only prevented by the mental depression consequent on the condition maintaining a state of lowered vitality': Garton, 'Shell-Shock' 601. See also Jeffrey, 'Some Points of Interest', 140.

263 For a discussion of the effect of such treatment, see Collie, *Malingering*, 193, and C. Stanford Read, 'A Survey of War Neuro-Psychiatry', *Mental Hygiene*, II (1918), 360.

264 Jeffrey, 'Some Points of Interest', 140.

265 Cited approvingly in Salmon, 'The Care and Treatment', 525. Similar arguments were used by Canadian doctors according to D. Marton and G. Wright, *Winning the Second Battle: Canadian Veterans and the Return to Civilian Life* (Toronto, 1987), 75.

266 Norgate, 'The Effects of War" 106–7.

267 Rose I. Patry, *Daily Drill for the Voice. A Book of Exercises composed to help Men whose Speech has been affected by Shell-Shock or other Causes* (London, 1917), preface.

268 Brockbank, *Incapacity*, 94. According to spiritualist mediums, in the 'astral plane', dead servicemen suffering from shell-shock were also treated by being taken to cheerful surroundings where their attention could be distracted from their own condition and the happenings on the earth: J. S. M. Ward, *A Subaltern in Spirit Land* (London, 1920), 239.

269 Albert William Andrews' diary for 8 July 1916, in Richardson, *Orders are Orders*, 53–4.

270 Herringham, *A Physician in France*, 135–6.

271 The term 'wound' came to be used to describe these men. For instance, see *The Times* for 24 April 1915 and 25 May 1915: examples given in Bogacz, 'War Neurosis and Cultural Change', 234.

272 Herringham, *A Physician in France*, 140.

273 G. S. Patton, *War as I knew It* (Boston, 1947), 340. Also see pp. 381–2.

274 Moran, *The Anatomy of Courage*, 186–7.

275 T. W. Standwell, 'Are You a Potential Post-War Criminal?', *Health and Strength*, 24 January 1920, 62. See also J. Mitchell Clarke, 'Some Neuroses of the War', *Bristol Medico-Chirurgical Journal*, XXXIV, July 1916, 42–72.

276 Mott, *War Neuroses*, 110.

277 Ibid., 107 and 111.

278 Pearn, 'Psychoses in the Expeditionary Forces', 101.

279 William Robinson, 'The Future of Service Patients in Mental Hospitals', *Journal of Mental Science*, LXVII.276 (January 1921), 40. Also see Turner, 'Neuroses and Psychoses of War', 399–400.

280 Robinson, 'The Future of Service Patients', 41.

281 Sir George H. Savage, 'Mental Disabilities for War Service', *Journal of Mental Science*, LXII.259 (October 1916), 654.

282 D. K. Henderson, 'War Psychoses: An Analysis of 202 Cases of Mental Disorder occurring in Home Troops', *Journal of Mental Science*, LXIV (April 1918), 186.

283 This is contrary to Martin Stone's argument that the 'monolithic theory of hereditary degeneration upon which Victorian psychiatry had based its social and scientific vision was significantly dented as young men of respectable and proven character were reduced to mental wrecks after a few months to the trenches': Stone, 'Shellshock and the Psychologists', in W. F. Bynum, Roy Porter and Michael Shepherd, eds, *The Anatomy of Madness. Essays in the History of Psychiatry. Vol. II. Institutions and Society* (London, 1985), 245. I would argue that this was only 'for the duration of the war'.

284 T. Brown, 'Shell Shock in the Canadian Expeditionary Force, 1914–1918: Canadian Psychiatry in the Great War', in C. G. Roland, ed., *Health, Disease and Medicine, Essays in Canadian History* (Toronto, 1984), 308–32; R. D. Hinshelwood, 'Psychodynamic Psychiatry Before World War I', in German E. Berrios and Hugh Freeman, eds, *150 Years of British Psychiatry, 1841–1991* (London, 1991), 197–205; Harold Merskey, 'Shell-Shock', 245–67; Malcolm Pines, 'The Development of the Psychodynamic Movement', 206–31; Shulamit Ramon, *Psychiatry in Britain. Meaning and Policy* (London, 1985); Stone, 'Shellshock and the Psychologists', 242–71. For a history of the growth of psychiatry to the First World War, see A. Scull, *Museums of Madness* (London, 1979).

285 H. V. Dicks, *Fifty Years of the Tavistock Clinic* (London, 1970), 3. During the war, the founder of the Tavistock Clinic, Hugh Crichton-Miller, had been officer-in-charge of functional nervous patients at the 21st General Hospital, Alexandria and, in 1917, had been appointed consultant in 'shell-shock' at the 4th London General Hospital.

286 Janet Oppenheim, *'Shattered Nerves'. Doctors, Patients, and Depression in Victorian England* (Oxford, 1991); Pines, 'The Development of the Psychodynamic Movement'; Ramon, *Psychiatry in Britain*; Stone, 'Shellshock and the Psychologists', 244–5; Jeffery Weeks, *Sex, Politics and Society. The Regulation of Sexuality since 1800* (London, 1981), 155.

287 *Lancet*, September 1917.

288 Myers, *Present-Day Applications*, 44.

289 For three superbly argued and contrary views, see Bogacz, 'War Neurosis and Cultural Change', 227–56; Merskey, 'Shell-Shock', 245–67; Stone, 'Shellshock and the Psychologists', 242–71.

290 Montague David Eder, *War Shock* (London, 1917), i.

291 In 1915, forty-two per cent of asylum medical staff had been accepted into the military services: Kathleen Jones, *A History of the Mental Health Services* (London, 1972), 229–30. Also see Savage, 'Mental Disabilities for War Service', 654, and Robinson, 'The Future of Service Patients', 41.

292 R. Mayou, 'The History of General Hospital Psychiatry', *British Journal of Psychiatry*, CLV (1989), 746–76.
293 Dicks, *Fifty Years*, 1.
294 Ramon, *Psychiatry*, 87.
295 Sir Robert Armstrong Jones in *Lancet*, II (1920), 402–4.
296 Oppenheim, *'Shattered Nerves'*, 15.
297 The Maudsley Hospital was the exception to the rule requiring patients being admitted to mental institutions to be certified insane prior to 1930.
298 Ramon, *Psychiatry*, 80 and 87.
299 Ahrenfeldt, *Psychiatry*, 15–16. He was a major in the Royal Army Medical Corps and the deputy assistant director of Army Psychiatry.
300 William C. Menninger, 'Psychiatric Experience in the War, 1941–1946', *American Journal of Psychiatry*, CIII (1947), 577–86. He was the chief consultant in Neuropsychiatry to the surgeon general of the US army and was discussing the American experience.
301 Oppenheim, *'Shattered Nerves'*, 152.
302 Luther, 'The Poppies are Blood Red', 37, IWM 87/8/1.
303 Anonymous letter to Marie Stopes, 8 March 1923, from Brighton, in Marie C. Stopes, 'Papers', CMAC PP/MCS/A1.
304 Arthur Kenneth Chesterton, *Adventures in Dramatic Appreciation* (London, 1931), 19.
305 Scholes, 'Papers' Edward Hall Collection, Wigan Archives Service D/DZ.EHC, scrapbook belonging to Dorothy Scholes, nurse at a military hospital. In this scrapbook, wounded soldiers described how they were injured. Extract written by J. S. Barrett. Spelling as in original. See also 'Nurse's Autograph Album, Malta, 1915–1916', IWM Misc. 154 Item 2396. 'Sham pain' is also spelt and pronounced 'champagne'.
306 Fleming, 'Letters', letter to 'Randolfo', 6 December 1914, IWM 90/28/1.

Chapter Three: Bonding

1 Irene Barnes, *A Peace Scout* (London, 1911), 29–30.
2 See the Introduction for a discussion of this theme. For two poignant examples, see the handwritten poem on a scrap of paper, probably written by A. L. Grice about a pal who was killed at Mons, IWM Misc. 130 Item 2001, and Florence Cook, 'Memoirs and Souvenirs', autograph album from the First Birmingham War Hospital, entry by a serviceman from the First Battalion of Royal Dublin Fusiliers, Birmingham City Archives MSS 1473/1.
3 For a discussion of this process, see Guy Chapman, *A Passionate Prodigality. Fragments of an Autobiography* (London, 1933), 3. It took Chapman more than a decade after leaving the army to start thinking of himself separately from the battalion. For a fascinating example of this, see the certificate given by the brigadier-general commanding the 29th Division Artillery to all servicemen being demobilized, in W. M. Floyd, 'Papers', IWM 87/33/1.
4 See J. M. Bourne, *Britain and the Great War 1914–1918* (London, 1989), 217.
5 Alfred Downes, 'Notes taken at Southern Army School of Instruction, Brentwood. Course commencing Oct 16. 1916', first lecture, 17 October 1916, on 'Discipline', Birmingham City Archives MSS 547.
6 PRO HO45/14373/587272. For interesting examples of the failure to develop *esprit de corps* in the early months of the war because of the shortage of uniforms, see Peter Simpkins, *Kitchener's Army. The Raising of the New Armies, 1914–16* (Manchester, 1988), 263–4.
7 Reginald George Garrod, 'Experiences of a 1913 Soldier', 1, IWM 79/44/1. Also see H. J. Coombes, 'The Baton', 2, IWM PP/MCR/119.

8 George Henry Hewins, *The Dillen. Memories of a Man of Stratford-upon-Avon* (London, 1981), 57, from the Salford working class. T. A. Silver, 'Stapenhill Darby and Joan Club. Minute Book', unpaginated, IWM 74/108/1, wrote of his pride in wearing the scarlet uniform and his distress when war declared and this uniform was changed to what he describes as 'Karkee'. Also see Charles H. Mapp, 'Memoirs of Charles H. Mapp, MBE', September 1976, 8, Liddle Collection, Leeds, and Wilfred Willett, 'Memoirs', 3, IWM 82/1/1.

9 Pat O'Mara, *The Autobiography of a Liverpool Irish Slummy* (London, 1972), first published 1934, 193.

10 R. L. Venables, 'The Great War 1914–1918: Diary', undated entry for 1915, 2, IWM 76/225/1. Also see James Murray, 'To Passchendaele and Back', 1976, 53, IWM P457, and E. A. Godson, *The Great War 1914–18. Incidents, Experiences, Impressions and Comments of a Junior Officer* (Hertford, n.d.), 16.

11 John Hargrave, *At Suvla Bay. Being the Notes and Sketches of Scenes, Characters and Adventures of the Dardanelles Campaign* (London, 1916), 1.

12 For instance, see Guy Buckeridge, 'Memoirs of my Army Service in the Great War', *c.*1920s, 36, IWM P273; Hargrave, *At Suvla Bay*, 1; Thomas Macmillan, 'The War to End War: 1914–1918', 1935, IWM Con Shelf; F. M. Mitchell, 'First World War Account', 12, IWM 75/3/1; David Starrett, 'Batman', 43, 62, 121 and 136 IWM 79/35/1. For examples of the shame of male nakedness in peacetime, see Catherine Cookson, *Our Kate* (London, 1969), 52; Grace Foakes, *My Part of the River* (London, 1974), 62; Kilmacormick Workers' Educational Association History Group, *A Danger down the Streets. Memories of Life on the Old Backstreets Community of Enniskillen* (Belfast, 1988), 26–7; Spike Mays, *Reuben's Corner* (London, 1969), 177. It is interesting to note that this desire for privacy amongst men was most noticeable amongst miners and can be seen in their opposition to pit-head baths: for instance, see Ken Howarth, ed., *Dark Days: Memories of the Lancashire and Cheshire Coalmining Industry* (Manchester, 1978), 47; Bill Johnstone, *Coal Dust in my Blood. The Autobiography of a Coal Miner* (Victoria, 1980), 18; E. R. Manley, *Meet the Miner* (North Wakefield, 1947), 45–6. In the 'Memorandum by the Secretary for Mines', 8 July 1924, 1, PRO POWE20/15 we are told that the prejudice against exposing the naked body was pronounced, except among the younger miners 'and particularly those who have been in the army'.

13 A. Jack Abraham, '1914–1918: Memoirs of a Non-Hero', *c.* 1973, 40, IWM P191; Lawrence Gameson, 'Papers', 225, IWM Con Shelf; C. B. Stokes, 'Papers', letter to his wife, 6 May 1915, file CBS 4/5, IWM 93/23/6.

14 Charlie C. May, 'Diaries', 28 December 1916, IWM 91/23/1. Also see David Starrett, 'Batman', 43, IWM 79/35/1.

15 Maberley S. Esler, 'Memoirs', 47, IWM 74/102/1.

16 H. J. Palmer, letter from Blumistead (or Plumistead), 'To the Officer in Command', 26 June 1915, IWM 91/5/1.

17 For an account of the 'Grimsby Chums', or the 10th Battalion, the Lincolnshire Regiment, see C. H. Emerson, 'Papers', IWM P115.

18 Charles Cyril Ammons, 'Service in the First War', 2, CMAC RAMC 1599 Box 337; H. T. Bolton, 'Diaries', unpaginated and undated, his first diary, IWM P262; Walter Cobb, 'Memories of the Old 59 Squadron 1914–1918. Walter's Contribution. Part I', 1, IWM 73/188/1; A. J. Jamieson, 'Some Reminiscences', 1980, 1–2, IWM 88/52/1; Sid T. Kemp, 'Remembrance. The 6th Royal West Kent Regiment 1914–1916', 3–4, IWM 85/28/1; Vernon Rhodes, 'Reminiscences of World War One', 5, IWM 88/57/1; Arthur Schuman, 'Memoirs', 1, IWM 82/1/1; Ernest Sheard, 'Manuscript Memoirs', vol. 1, 1, and vol. 2, 313–15, IWM P285.

19 Simpkins, *Kitchener's Army*, 79 and 82–3.

20 Ralph Ernest Barnwell, 'Notes written during the World War 1914–1918', 1–2, IWM 85/7/1.

21 Jack Houghton-Brown, 'Farmer-Soldier', 1945, 110, Liddell Hart Centre for Military Archives.

22 Macmillan, 'The War to End War', 6, IWM Con Shelf. Also see W. A. Quinton, 'Memoirs', 1929, 11, IWM 79/35/1.

23 For one example, see Buckeridge, 'Memoirs', 9, IWM P273.

24 Ibid., 25–6.

25 Throughout William Walls, 'Diary', Book I, Wigan Archives Service D/DZ A 76/1. For instance, see 31 May 1916, 5 and 26 June 1916. When his closest friend Joe was hospitalized in October and November 1916, Walls spent the entire time with a high fever.

26 Letter from Basil Liddell Hart to his parents on 10 November 1915, Liddell Hart Centre for Military Archives 7/1915/27. Also see Reginald S. Cockburn, 'Diary and Memoirs', 81, diary for 12 July 1917, IWM P258.

27 Letter from Sir Basil Liddell Hart to his parents on 9 September 1915 and 27 May 1916, envelope labelled 'To be opened in the event of my death', Liddell Hart Centre for Miliary Archives 7/1915/9.

28 John Francis Jones, 'N. C. O.', 1934, 14, Liddell Hart Centre for Military Archives. Also see Quinton, 'Memoirs', 56, IWM 79/35/1.

29 Revd C. E. G. Parry Okeden, 'Letters', letter to his wife, 7 April 1918, IWM 90/7/1. Stewart's body was never found.

30 Gameson, 'Papers', 105–6, IWM Con Shelf. This idea can be seen in many of the quotations. To take another example, W. A. Quinton regarded intimate male friendship as something that flowered under the stress of wartime but which lay 'dormant in the monotonous round of everyday civilian-life': 'Memoirs', 56, IWM 79/35/1.

31 Revd Andrew Clark, *Echoes of the Great War. The Diary of the Reverend Andrew Clark 1914–1919*, ed. James Munson (Oxford, 1985), 252, 9 October 1918. Also see W. Cecil Christopher, 'Letters', letter from Christopher to his sister Val, 22 May 1916, IWM 88/11/1.

32 Walls, 'Diary', 11 March 1916, Book I, Wigan Archives Service D/DZ A 76/1; Sir W. G. MacPherson, Sir W. H. Horrocks and W. W. O. Beveridge, *Medical Services. Hygiene of the War. Vol. I* (London, 1923), 317–18.

33 Chapman, *A Passionate Prodigality*, 23.

34 George Bradshaw, 'Letters Home', letter from Clipstone Camp, Nottinghamshire, Manchester County Council Local Studies Unit M267/3/3/1.

35 R. Nevill Buckmaster, 'Letters', letter to his mother on 14 June 1917, Wigan Archives Service.

36 Henry Gother Courtney, 'Letters', letter to his sister Kathleen, 22 October 1915, Birmingham University Library no. 8/104.

37 Walls, 'Diary', 1 January 1916, Book I, Wigan Archives Service D/DZ A 76/1.

38 War diary of the Revd Maurice Murray, from Flanders, no date except 1917, in Michael Moynihan, ed., *God on Our Side* (London, 1983), 138. Also see Cyril Ammons, 'Service in the First War', 11, CMAC RAMC 1599 Box 337; Revd Montague A. Bere, 'Papers', letter of 16 November 1917, IWM 66/96/1; Cockburn, 'Diary and Memoirs', 116–17, IWM P258; John M. Cordy, 'My Memories of the First World War', 29, IWM 86/30/1; Gameson, 'Papers', 223, IWM Con Shelf; W. C. F. Harland, 'Reminiscences', 14, CMAC RAMC 1590 Box 336; A. J. Jamieson, 'Meteran May/August 1918', 6 IWM 88/52/1; John William Rowarth, 'The Misfit Soldier', 38, IWM 80/40/1; Starrett, 'Batman', 61, IWM 79/35/1; W. G. Shipway, 'My Memories of the First World War', 31, IWM 90/37/1. For an interesting set of papers re.

entertaining the troops, see Charles Hill, 'Papers', Birmingham City Archives MSS 1430/4 and 5.

39 J. C. Dunn, *The War the Infantry Knew* (London, 1987), 410, diary of a medical officer, 15 October 1914.

40 E. A. McKechnie, 'Reminiscences of the Great War, 1914–18', 3, IWM 88/27/1.

41 Chapman, *A Passionate Prodigality*, 131. Also see Basil Clarke, 'How the Wounded are brought Home', *The Great War*, viii.132, 24 February 1917, 312; Alfred M. Hale, *The Ordeal of Alfred M. Hale. The Memoirs of a Soldier Servant*, ed. Paul Fussell (London, 1975), written *c*.1922, 53; J. W. B. Merewether and Sir Frederick Smith, *The Indian Corps in France* (London, 1917), 471.

42 Quinton, 'Memoirs', 56, IWM 79/35/1.

43 Walls, 'Diary', 3 and 24 March 1916 and 19 August 1916, Book 1, Wigan Archives Service D/DZ A 76/1.

44 Miss D. Williams, 'Letters', letter from 'Jack' in Palestine, 23 November 1917, IWM 85/4/1. See also Abraham, '1914–1918' 15, IWM P191 and (in Boer War) George Horton, *A Brief Outline of My Travels and Doings whilst serving in the Army from 1884 to 1918* (Belfast, 1982), 45.

45 Henry Gervis, *Arms and the Doctors. Being the Military Experiences of a Middle-Aged Medical Man* (London, 1920), 45–6.

46 Lawrence Anthony Humphries, 'The War of 1914–1918. A Note on the Period of Fighting during the Great German Attack of 21st: March to 5th: April 1915', 1–8, Liddell Hart Centre for Military Archives. Punctuation and spelling as in original.

47 Walls, 'Diary', 8 July 1916, Book 1, Wigan Archives Service D/DZ A 76/1.

48 Sturdy, 'Illustrated Account', 72, IWM Con Shelf.

49 For instance, see Jones,'N. C. O.', 157, Liddell Hart Centre for Military Archives, where a corporal and a private lie on either side of an injured man in the snow in order to keep him warm and alive.

50 Quinton, 'Memoirs', 56, IWM 79/35/1. Also see A. R. Brennan, 'Diary', 1 July 1916, IWM P262, and Ralph I. Smith, 'Enlistment', unpaginated, IWM 86/36/1.

51 Jack W. Mudd, 'Letters', letter to his wife, 22 October 1917, IWM 82/3/1.

52 A. C. Warsop, 'One Man's War', 1965, 13, IWM 86/2/1.

53 Jones, 'N. C. O.', 15, Liddell Hart Centre for Military Archives.

54 Richard C. Foot, 'Once a Gunner', 125, IWM 86/57/1.

55 Mary Macleod Moore, 'Missing', *Sunday Times*, 8 July 1917.

56 Revd John M. Connor, 'Diary', 21 November 1914, IWM 87/10/1.

57 C. H. Cox, 'Account of his Experiences in the Honourable Artillery Company on the Western Front in 1917', *c*.1950s, 2, IWM 88/11/1.

58 John A. Boullier, *Jottings by a Gunner and Chaplain* (London, 1917), 29. For similar examples, see Henry Wynyard Kaye, 'A Young Officer's Account of Nervous Breakdown during the Second Battle of Ypres, 1915', 2, CMAC RAMC 739/20, and Ernest Sheard, 'Manuscript Memoirs', vol. 1, 58, IWM P285.

59 Connor, 'Diary', 22 November 1914, IWM 87/10/1. For a very similar example, see Okeden, 'Letters', letter to his wife, 7 April 1918, IWM 90/7/1.

60 Cox, 'Account of his Experiences', 3, IWM 88/11/1. Also see Niall MacFhionnghaile, *Donegal, Ireland and the First World War* (Leitrim, 1987), 78.

61 David Houston Fenton and William Charles Fenton, 'Letters and Documents', letter from David H. Fenton to the mother of a fellow soldier, IWM 87/13/1.

62 Macmillan, 'The War to End War', 61, IWM Con Shelf. In this account, the word 'companions' has been crossed out and the word 'inseparable' kept. Much to the disgust of the soldiers, the chaplains wished to separate the two friends.

63 For a discussion of the failure of 'muscular Christianity' amongst the working class, see Stuart Barlow. 'The Diffusion of "Rugby" Football in the Industrialized Context of Rochdale, 1868–90: A Conflict of Ethical Values', *International Journal of the History of Sport*, x.1 (April 1993), 49–67.

64 *Health and Strength: Leaguerers' Guide, c.* 1935, 7–10.

65 *Health and Strength Annual*, 1910, 5.

66 Ibid., 1928, 35–40.

67 Ibid., 1911, 6. League members were allowed 'moderate use of the weed if extreme youth is pass'.

68 Ibid., 1908, 4.

69 George Hackenschmidt, *The Way to Live. Health and Physical Fitness* (London, 1908), 9.

70 Health and Strength, *Correct Breathing for Health. Chest and Lung Development*, (London, 1908), 38; Albert Parker, 'What is it doing for me?', *Health and Vim* (February 1913), 76; C. H. Rolph [pseud. Cecil Rolph Hewitt], *London Particulars* (Oxford, 1980), 45; Peter C. Vigor, *Memories Are Made of This* (Luton, 1983), 76.

71 *Health and Strength Annual*, 1908, 4. See also *Health and Strength Annual*, 1908, 3, and A. Wallace-Jones, *50 Exercises for Health and Strength* (London, 1914), 15.

72 William R. Lucas, *Physical Culture Simplified* (London, 1931), 86.

73 Chas T. Trevor, *How to develop Powerful Arms* (London, 1944), 3–4.

74 Parker, 'What is it doing for me?', 76.

75 'Uncle Bob', *How to develop Arms* (London, 1910), 7.

76 Lionel Stebbing, 'Virility: The Master Power. How to develop and retain it', *Health and Strength Annual* (1932), 51.

77 Trevor, *How to develop Powerful Arms*, 3–4.

78 Edward Aston, *How to develop a Powerful Grip* (London, 1946), 4. He was designated 'Britain's Strongest Man' between 1911 and 1934.

79 'G.H.W.', 'What is Strength?', *Health and Vim*, February 1913, 60.

80 Pat O'Mara, *The Autobiography of a Liverpool Irish Slummy*, first pub. 1934 (London, 1972), 132–3.

81 Max Bygraves, *I Wanna Tell You a Story* (London, 1976), 39.

82 The following historians stress the militarist nature of boys' movements: Michael D. Blanch, 'Imperialism, Nationalism and Organised Youth', in John Clarke, Chas Critcher and Richard Johnson, eds, *Working-Class Culture – Studies in History and Theory* (London, 1979), 103–20; J. R. Gillis, 'Conformity and Rebellion: Contrasting Styles of English and German Youth, 1900–1933', *History of Education Quarterly*, XIII.2 (1973), 249–60; Samuel Hynes, *The Edwardian Turn of Mind*, (London, 1968), 27; Michael Rosenthal, 'Knights and Retainers: the Earliest Version of Baden-Powell's Boy Scout Scheme', *Journal of Contemporary History*, XV (1980); John O. Springhall, 'Baden-Powell and the Scout Movement before 1920: Citizen Training of Soldiers of the Future?', *English Historical Review*, CII (October 1987), 934–42; John O. Springhall, 'The Boy Scouts, Class and Militarism in Relation to British Young Movements 1908–1930', *International Review of Social History*, XVI (1971), 125–58; John O. Springhall, 'Lord Meath, Youth and Scouts', *Journal of Contemporary History*, V.4 (1970), 97–111. The following historians disagree: Martin Dedman, 'Baden-Powell, Militarism, and the "Invisible Contributors" to the Boy Scout Scheme, 1904–1920', *Twentieth-Century British History*, IV.3 (1993), 201–23; and Allen Warren, 'Sir Robert Baden-Powell, the Scout Movement, and Citizen Training in Great Britain, 1900–1920', *English Historical Review*, CI (1986), 376–98.

83 Within the United Kingdom, the exception, of course, was Ireland which had a

well-established militarist tradition: see the work of David Fitzpatrick, 'Militarism in Ireland, 1900–1921', in Thomas J. Bartlett and Keith Jefferys (eds), *A Military History of Ireland* (Cambridge, forthcoming 1996). In Britain, there were a few outdoor movements that were explicitly anti-militarist: for example, the Order of Woodcraft Chivalry and Kibbo Kift. They never became popular.

84 Michael Rosenthal's warning about the use of the word 'militarism' must be noted. He has pointed out recently (*The Character Factory: Baden-Powell and the Origins of the Boys Scouts Movement* (London, 1986), 192–3) that the word 'militarism' can be used to encompass a wide range of meanings, from the promotion of military values to the use of military-style drill.

85 'Prince Albert and the Boys' Brigade', *The Times*, 9 May 1919, 9.

86 Quoted in Victor Bailey, 'Bibles and Dummy Rifles: The Boys' Brigade', *History Today*, October 1983.

87 Robert Baden-Powell, letter to the editor, *The Times*, 8 May 1913, 6.

88 Idem, *Scouting for Boys* (London, 1967), 249.

89 Stanley Butler, 'Peppard, The Hindenburg Line, and Return', 1985, 15, IWM 86/2/1.

90 Houghton-Brown, 'Farmer-Soldier', 10, Liddell Hart Centre for Military Archives.

91 Christopher W. Hughes, 'The Forgotten Army', 1925, 25, IWM 82/25/1.

92 Sir Basil Liddell Hart admitted to a friend in 1957 that his interest in scouting had stimulated his military ideas: letter to D. Crinnell-Milne of 28 February 1957, unlisted in a section entitled 'Added' in 8/252–355, Liddell Hart Centre for Military Archives.

93 E. C. Mercer, 'Letters and Papers', a leaflet from Lord Kitchener, IWM 92/52/1.

94 A. W. Wyatt, 'Letters to a Lambeth Scout', letter to A. W. Wyatt from his scoutmaster, Captain M. Gammon, 20 June 1916, IWM 87/33/1.

95 For an example, see Abraham, '1914–1918' 1, IWM P191.

96 W. J. Batchelder and David Balfour, *'Be Prepared!' The Story of Baden-Powell* (London, 1938), 252–3, and the editorial, *The Times*, 11 February 1919, 11.

97 Boy Scouts' Association, *Boy Scouts and Citizenship. The Handbook of the Great International Jamboree. Olympia, July 30th to August 7th, 1920* (London, 1920), 45. This chapter concentrates on Robert Baden-Powell's Boy Scouts. This should not lead us to forget groups such as the Jewish Lads' Brigade. About one-third of British Jews who died during the First World War were members of the brigade: Richard A. Voeltz, 'A Good Jew and a Good Englishman: The Jewish Lads' Brigade, 1894–1922', *Journal of Contemporary History*, XXIII.1 (1988), 124.

98 For instance, see Revd Montague A. Bere, 'Papers', letter to his wife, 12 September 1917, IWM 66/96/1; Revd Andrew Clark, *Echoes of the Great War. The Diary of the Reverend Andrew Clark 1914–1919*, ed. James Munson (Oxford, 1985), 21 November 1914, 34; Frederick L. Newnham, 'Scouting during World War I', 1979, 5, IWM 91/11/1; Mary Pakington, *Boy Scout Pageant of all Nations Illustrating Scouting Past and Present* (unpaginated, 1923), 48; For an opposite view, see the cynical comment of 'Ex-Private X', *War is War* (London, 1930), 34–5, who jeered at two scouts whose attempts to transplant the scouting camp to the trenches failed to prevent them from being killed.

99 Leonard Humphreys, 'An Early Note on Sir Robert Baden-Powell and Scouting 1907–1911', 4, Liverpool Local History and Record Office H369.42/HUM.

100 Christopher, letter to his mother, 16 December 1915, IWM 88/11/1, and letter

from Sir Basil Liddell Hart in France to his parents on 29 September 1915, Liddell Hart Centre for Military Archives 7/15/3.

101 W. B. G. Angus, 'Papers', letter number 10, 28 July 1915, IWM 69/3/1; John Hare, 'War Diary, September to December 1914', 3, n.d., 1914, CMAC RAMC 1327 Box 288; letter from Raymond Lodge to his family, 3 April 1915, in Sir Oliver J. Lodge, *Raymond or Life After Death* (London, 1918), 18.

102 Ammons, 'Service in the First War', 2, CMAC RAMC 1599 Box 337.

103 Hargrave, *At Suvla Bay*, 157.

104 'Boys and the War. Patriotic Lessons', *The Times*, 24 March 1915. Rosenthal, *The Character Factory*, 202, quoting Robert Baden-Powell's comparison of the proportion of scouts and members of Cadet Corps who later joined the military services.

105 Speech by Mr Morton of Leeds Modern School, in Boy Scouts' Association, *Report of a Conference of Schoolmasters held at the Imperial Headquarters on Thursday, April 10th, 1924* (London, 1924), 24. Even prior to the war, parental suspicions about the military side of the scouts caused recruitment problems: see Robert Baden-Powell's letter to the editor, *The Times*, 8 May 1913, 6.

106 Batchelder and Balfour, *'Be Prepared!'*, 262.

107 This is repeated throughout Pakington, *Boy Scout Pageant*.

108 *Boy Scouts and What They Do. As Illustrated at the Imperial Scout Exhibition and Rally held at Birmingham, July 1913: – With an introduction by the Chief Scout* (London, 1913), 33–4. Also see Lincoln Green, *Camp Cookery. A Book for Boy Scouts* (London, 1914), 4, and 'Papers of the Grantchester Scouts', 'Extracts from the Parish Magazine', August 1917, Cambridgeshire Record Office P79/28/51.

109 Butler, 'Peppard', 15, IWM 86/2/1.

110 'Editorial Chat', *Bristol Scouting*, July 1924, 94. Also see Birmingham Boys' and Girl's Union, *Camp Camp* (Birmingham, *c.* 1925), 1.

111 Butler, 'Peppard', 16, IWM 86/2/1, and John Hargrave, *The Confession of the Kibbo Kift. A Declaration and General Exposition of the Work of the Kindred* (London, 1927), 87.

112 For instance, Jack Christie, 'Undiminished Memories', in Michael Hall, ed., *Sacrifice on the Somme* (Newtownabbey, 1993), 22. He joined the 36th [Ulster] Division in 1914. He rejoiced in the comradeship: 'the comradeship that came out of it, was something that had to grow . . . would you believe that after the first of July, after the battle, after all the horror, when I went home on leave I found that I was missing my comrades. The funny thing in a way, was that your old friends, your old pals that you knew before the war, who hadn't joined up, didn't want you. And I just wanted to be back with my boys again, with my comrades.'

113 Sidney Rogerson, *Twelve Days* (Norwich, 1930), 60.

114 Writing about Germany, George Mosse makes a similar point: 'Social distinctions were supposed to vanish as the German people stood united, but in reality in the best of cases they were merely transformed into a hierarchy of function – that is, of command and obedience – rather than of status' (*Fallen Soldiers. Reshaping the Memory of the World Wars* (New York, 1990), 65). See also the letter from E. Howard, general secretary of the Ex-Services' Welfare Society, to Dr Cunningham-Brown of the Medical Services Department of the Ministry of Pensions, 23 April 1923, PRO PIN15/2498, and Hiram Sturdy, 'Illustrated Account of his Service on the Western Front with the Royal Regiment of Artillery', 10–1, IWM Con Shelf. This was also true in the scouts where 'brotherhood' did not mean equality: see Hugh Goodacre, *The Boy Scout Movement* (Leicester, 1924), 19.

115 Rogerson, *Twelve Days*, 87–8.

116 T. H. Clayton-Nunn, 'Diary: 30-3-15 to 25-5-18', 8 August 1915 and 11 November 1917, Liddle Collection, Leeds. Also see Bere 'Papers', letter to his wife, 14 August 1917, IWM 66/96/1, and Hazel Thompson Clements, 'Diaries', 26 November 1915, IWM 86/76/1. For a defence of the commanders during the war, see John Terraine, 'British Military Leadership in the First World War', in Peter H. Liddle, ed., *Home Fires and Foreign Fields. British Social and Military Experience in the First World War* (London, 1985), 39–51.

117 William Clarke, 'Random Recollections of '14/'18', 13, Liddle Collection, Leeds.

118 Sheard, 'Manuscript Memoirs', vol. 5, 748–53, IWM P285. See also Jones, 'N.C.O.', 143, 101–4 and 294, Liddell Hart Centre for Military Archives; Robert W. F. Johnston, 'Some Experiences in the Great War of 1914–1918', section entitled 'The British Army Officer and the Great War', 6. IWM 82/38/1; May, 'Diaries', 21 April 1916, IWM 91/23/1; 'VADs Autograph Album, First World War', IWM Misc. 4 Item 48.

119 Venables, 'The Great War 1914–1918: Diary', undated entry for 1919, 95, IWM 76/225/1.

120 Buckeridge, 'Memoirs', 62, IWM P273.

121 Rowarth, 'The Misfit Soldier', 19, IWM 90/40/1.

122 'Answers to Correspondents', *New Church Times* (trench paper), 1.1, 17 April 1916, unpaginated, CMAC RAMC 479 Box 97.

123 'Memorandum from the General Head Quarters to all Commands and Inspectors', 3 July 1917, PRO NATS1/750, and Stephen Graham, *A Private in the Guards* (London, 1919), 28.

124 Kemp, 'Remembrance', 23, IWM 85/28/1, and Harry Siepmann, 'Rising with the Guns. Reminisces [*sic*] of the First World War Compiled from the Letters and Diaries of Capt. Harry Siepmann, RFA', 97, IWM 85/43/1.

125 Letter from Raymond Lodge to his family, 1 September 1915, in Lodge, *Raymond*, 67.

126 Jones, 'N.C.O.', 91, Liddell Hart Centre for Military Archives. For tension between England and Scottish sailors, see Macmillan, 'The War to End War', 22, IWM Con Shelf.

127 Letter to the editor from 'Major General', 'Regimental Dinners', *The Times*, 26 June 1926, and letter to the editor from 'Centurion', 'Regimental Dinners', *The Times*, 1 July 1926.

128 Sir Charles Burtchaell, 'Papers and Reports', letter of 27 July 1917, CMAC RAMC 446/13.

129 Canon T. Guy Rogers, letter to his aunt, 21 March 1916, IWM Con Shelf. For similar sentiments, see Hale, *The Ordeal*, 30.

130 War Office, *Statistics of the Military Effort of the British Empire during the Great War* (London, 1922), 160.

131 Bata Kindai Amgoza Ibn LoBagola, *Lobagola. An African Savage's Own Story* (New York, 1930).

132 Samuel Weingott, 'Dairy', 18 March 1915, IWM 91/3/1.

133 F. M. Peckham, 'Memoirs of an Old Contemptible 1912–1920', 29, IWM P316. Also see Tommy Jordan, 'Undiminished Memories', in Michael Hall, ed., *Sacrifice on the Somme* (Newtownabbey, 1993), 24.

134 Clark, *Echoes*, 44, 21 January 1915. Also see J. W. B. Merewether and Sir Frederick Smith, *The Indian Corps in France* (London, 1917), 110–11 and 471.

135 T. Corder Catchpool, *On Two Fronts* (London, 1918), 28, letter of 15 November 1914.

136 Frank Dunham, *The Long Carry. The Journal of Stretcher Bearer Frank Durnham 1916–18*, ed. R. H. Haigh and P. W. Turner (Oxford, 1970), 42; 'Ex-Private

X', *War is War* (London, 1930), 104; W. N. Nicholson, *Behind the Lines. An Account of Administrative Staffwork in the British Army 1914–18* (London, 1939), 240. For a passionate reply, see letter to the editor from twelve Chinese sailors, 'Chinese Sailors', *Daily Post*, 3 October 1916, in Liverpool Council of Social Service, 'Cuttings from National Newspapers 1910–17', Liverpool Record Office 361 COU 1/6.

137 Maximilian A. Mugge, *The War Diary of a Square Peg* (London, 1920), 74 and 85.
138 Bere, 'Papers', letter of 7 November 1917, IWM 66/96/1.
139 Johnston, 'Some Experiences', section entitled 'The British Army Officer and the Great War', 4, IWM 82/38/1.
140 Venables, 'The Great War', undated entry for 1916, 33, IWM 76/225/1.
141 Letter from Raymond Lodge to his family, 7 July 1915, in Lodge, *Raymond*, 54–5.
142 Tommy W. Bacon. 'Letters', letter to Bacon from his nephew, Ralph Creyke, 20 December 1914, IWM P391. Also see his letter 26 January 1915.
143 Ibid., 26 January 1915.
144 Ian Beckett, 'The Territorial Force in the Great War', in Liddle, ed., *Home Fires*, 29–32. However, Beckett also notes that the great need for servicemen during the war meant that men moved between different types of units and the distinctions were blurred.
145 For instance, see letter from H. Parker of the Treasury to A. E. Kingham, Ministry of Labour, on 7 April 1939, re. the deputation from the British Legion, PRO LAB20/6.
146 For an account of the pride associated with the medal, see Ammons, 'Service', 39, CMAC RAMC 1599 Box 337.
147 W. A. Quinton, 'Memoirs', 1929, 11, IWM 79/35/1; John Clarke MacDermott, 'An Enriching Life', 75–6, Liddell Hart Centre for Military Archives. Also see H. T. Bolton, 'Diaries', unpaginated and undated, his first diary, IWM P262.
148 Foot, 'Once a Gunner', 51, IWM 86/57/1.
149 Houghton-Brown, 'Farmer-Soldier', 110, Liddell Hart Centre for Military Archives.
150 James B. Lorimer, 'Letter in War-Time', letter to his mother of 19 April 1915; IWM 96/193/1.
151 Bertie A. Pond, 'Old Soldiers Never Die', 48, IWM 78/27/1.
152 T. A. Bickerton, 'The Wartime Experience of an Ordinary "Tommy"', 1964, 12, IWM 80/43/1; R. H. Bryan, 'My War Diary', 1920, 17, IWM 72/88/1; Ralph H. Covernton, 'Fifty Odd Years of Memoirs', 111, Liddell Hart Centre for Military Archives; Hart, 'Papers', diary for 14 November 1915, Liddell Hart Centre for Military Archives 7/1915/32b; Jones, 'N.C.O.', 87–8, Liddell Hart Centre for Military Archives; Starrett, 'Batman', 39, IWM 79/35/1.
153 Abraham, '1914–1918', 111–12 and 117, IWM P191; Gameson, 'Papers', 6 and 129–30, IWM Con Shelf; Kemp, 'Remembrance', 9, IWM 85/28/1; Albert Joseph Kingston, 'Memoirs', 9 IVM 88/27/1; letter from Arthur Lee, MP, to Lord Kitchener, 8 May 1918, 3, PRO WO159/16; *The Linseed Lance*, 1.2, August 1916, 20, in David William Harwood, 'Papers', Birmingham City Archives MSS 1001; Rowland Myrddyn Luther, 'The Poppies are Blood Red', 23, IWM 87/8/1.
154 Cobb, 'Memories', 4, IWM 73/188/1.
155 Ernest Lye, 'A Worm's Eye View of Suvla Bay', 18, IWM 81/9/1.
156 Harold E. Mellersh, 'Schoolboy into War', 120, IWM Con Shelf.
157 Maurice John Bethell, 'Correspondence and Papers', letter from W. Stephen King-Hall of HMS *Southampton* to Miss Agatha Bethell, 7 June 1916, Liddell

Hart Centre for Military Archives. See also Sheard, 'Manuscript Memoirs', vol. 3, 435–5, IWM P285.

158 Dunham, *The Long Carry*, 182.

159 Begg, *Surgery*, 91.

160 Albert William Andrews' diary for 28 December 1915, in Sue Richardson, *Orders are Orders. A Manchester Pal on the Somme. From the Account of Albert William Andrews of the 19th Manchesters. Written in 1917* (Swinton, 1987), 26. Also see Begg, *Surgery*, 97.

161 Thomas Parkes, 'Diary 1916', 9 April 1916, Liddell Hart Centre for Military Archives.

162 A. C. Warsop, 'One Man's War', 1965, 12, IWM 86/2/1. See also Macmillan, 'The War to End War', 27, IWM Con Shelf, and William Charles Sims, 'Diary 1 August 1916–2 September 1918', 17, Bristol Record Ofice 40340.

163 H. M. Butterworth, *Letters Written in the Trenches Near Ypres Between May and September 1915* (Wellington, New Zealand, 1916), 10 July 1915, 31; Bere, 'Papers', letters to his wife, 19 and 25 November 1916 and 10 February 1917, IWM 66/96/1; A Caseby, 'Jottings from the Spiritual Side of the Army', *c.*1920, unpaginated, IWM 78/4/1; Chapman, *A Passionate Prodigality*, 63; Basil Clarke, 'How the Wounded are brought Home', *The Great War*, viii.132, 24 February 1917, 312; Foot, 'Once a Gunner', 61 and 79, IWM 86/57/1; Gervis, *Arms and the Doctor*, 12–13 and 47–8; Hare, 'War Diary', 6, 4 May 1914, CMAC RAMC 1327 Box 288; Lye, 'A Worm's Eye View', 24, IWM 81/9/1; Mrs D. M. Richards, 'Blues and Reds. Memoir of her First World War Nursing Experiences', chapters 1 and 5, IWM P328; Arthur Sardens, 'Diary of a Manchester Medical Attendant on the Hospital Ship No. 1 Soudan, 8 February-30 August [1915]', 3 May 1915, Manchester County Council Local Studies Unit Misc. 780; R. S. Smylie, 'Papers', copy of a poem, 'Nightmare. In N. 10 C. C. S. P – - e', IWM 86/9/1.

164 'Memorandum from Sir Alfred Fripp, Sir Alexander Ogston, Sir E. Cooper Perry and Dr. T. J. Harder criticising the RAMC', 1916, 1–2, in papers of Sir Charles Burtschaell, 'Papers and Reports', CMAC RAMC 446/13.

165 Guy Buckeridge, 'Memoirs of my Army Service in the Great War', *c.*1920, 38, IWM P273, and Gameson, 'Papers', 50, diary for 13 August 1916, IWM Con Shelf. This fear continued in the 'astral plane' according to spiritualists' accounts of the words of dead servicemen in J. S. M. Ward, *A Subaltern in Spirit Land* (London, 1920), 71. This can be exaggerated: for instance, see Jones, 'N.C.O.', 248–9, Liddell Hart Centre for Military Archives.

166 Walter J. Shewry, 'My Life with the Post Office Rifles', 3, IWM 88/52/1.

167 *Manchester Guardian*, 24 October 1914, quoted in Mrs W. A. Albright, *Stories of Heroism and Kindliness* (Manchester, n.d.), 7.

168 Oswin Creighton, *With the Twenty-Ninth Division in Gallipoli: A Chaplain's Experiences* (London, 1916), 127; Shewry, 'My Life'; Herbert Thompson (a blinded veteran), in James McMillan, *The Way It Was, 1914–1934* (London, 1979), 108.

169 George Horton, *A Brief Outline of My Travels and Doings whilst serving in the Army from 1884 to 1918* (Belfast, 1982), 83 and 69.

170 Macmillan, 'The War to End War', 60, IWM Con Shelf. For a similar description, see Buckeridge, 'Memoirs', 59, IWM P273; letter from Raymond Lodge to his family, 16 June 1915, in Lodge, *Raymond*, 47; Niall MacFhionnghaile, *Donegal, Ireland, and the First World War* (Leitrim, 1987), 66. The love/hate relationship between British and German soldiers was understood in a variety of ways. For example, in a spiritualist letter from a dead man, the following story is related: 'Two soldiers went forth to war, and the bullet of each pierced the heart of the other. Their hate was hot as love. Then

in the sudden darkness of death, they reached for each other's hand; their hate had found its other pole and they melted together in love': Elsa Barker, *War Letters from the Living Dead Man* (London, 1918), 69.

171 Tom B. Butt, letter to John Pollard, 24 May 1968 reminiscing about the battle of Le Cateau, IWM 90/18/1.

172 May, 'Diaries', 25 February 1916, IWM 91/23/1.

173 Letter from Raymond Lodge to his family, 16 June 1915, in Lodge, *Raymond*, 47.

174 Revd Charles Ivor Sinclair Hood, 'Papers', diary for 9 October 1915, IWM 90/7/1.

175 Macmillan, 'The War to End War, 66, IWM Con Shelf.

176 For descriptions of fraternization, see Clements, 'Diaries', 4 May 1915, IWM 86/76/1; 'Diary of an Unidentified Soldier in the Border Regiment', 25 and 16 December 1914, IWM Misc. 550; Richard Lintott, letter to his mother, 27 December 1914, IWM 86/66/1; Quinton, 'Memoirs', 24–5, IWM 79/35/1; For an historical discussion, see Tony Ashworth, *Trench Warfare 1914–1918: The Live and Let Live System* (London, 1980), 24–47.

177 These organizations changed their names and amalgamated with other groups a number of times. For instance, the British Legion was formed out of the National Federation of Discharged and Demobilized Sailors and Soldiers, the National Association of Discharged Sailors and Soldiers, the Comrades of the Great War, and the Officers' Association.

178 See the papers of the Old Contemptibles' Association, IWM Misc. 727 Item 42.

179 Hugh Wansey Bayly, *Triple Challenge, or War, Whirligigs and Windmills. A Doctor's Memoirs of the Years 1914 to 1929* (London, 1930), 246.

180 See W. H. Barnes's membership card, Royal British Legion, 'Miscellaneous Papers: Burnley Branch', Lancashire Record Office, DDX. 1302, acc. 4401, Box 1.

181 *Kriegsgefangener. The Association of Ex-Prisoners of War*, no. 2, 1933, 1.

182 Letter from P. H. Henderson, to 'My Dear Jordan', 18 January 1965, IWM Misc. 83 Item 1273. They were both members of the 8th Field Ambulance Old Comrades' Association.

183 For instance, see *The Campaigner. In the Interests of the United Association of Ex-Naval and Military Civil Servants*, 'General Secretary's Notes', 25 January 1920, 1, MRC MSS 148/5; 'Minutes of the Birmingham No. 2 Branch of the British Legion', minutes for 13 January 1932 and 15 January 1936, Birmingham City Archive MSS 1696/1; *News Chronicle*, 21 April 1938; *The Times*, 20 March 1918.

184 Ralph I. Smith, 'The Somme', unpaginated, IWM 86/36/1.

185 Letter to the editor, from 'Equality' of Bedale, North Yorkshire, *Northern Echo*, 25 June 1936. Also see minute from T. S. Owen, 13 September 1929 to Mr Reid, regarding a deputation from the Limbless Ex-Service Men's Association reminding him that limblessness was only one of many service disabilities, PRO LAB2/1201/ED33763/1929.

186 Letter from E. Howard, general secretary of the Ex-Services' Welfare Society, to Dr Cunningham-Brown of the Medical Services Department, Ministry of Pensions, on 23 April 1923, PRO PIN15/2498.

187 One woman whose intentions were misunderstood by a soldier 'hissed, almost biting his head off', screaming, 'This bitch 'as no milk!': Lawrence Gameson, 'Papers', 160, IWM Con Shelf.

188 Mrs Ethel Cox, 'Letters and Other Papers', letter from 'Jim' in France, undated, Birmingham City Archive MSS 1546/1/18.

189 R. Graham Dixon, 'The Wheels of Darkness', 58, IWM 92/36/1.

190 Leslie Hall, *Hidden Anxieties. Male Sexuality 1900–1950* (Cambridge, 1991), 37.

191 Richard Davenport-Hines, *Sex, Death and Punishment. Attitudes to Sex and Sexuality in Britain since the Renaissance* (London, 1990), 228. Roger Davidson, 'Measuring "The Social Evil": The incidence of Venereal Disease in Inter-war Scotland', *Medical History*, xxxvii (1993), 167–86, argues that the 'problem' of venereal disease was exaggerated.

192 For a discussion, see Helen Ruth Elizabeth Ware, 'The Recruitment, Regulation and Role of Prostitution in Britain from the Middle of the Nineteenth Century to the Present Day', Ph.D. thesis, Bedford College, University of London, 1969, 501.

193 For instance, Ralph Smith recalled that, when he was camped near Amiens, his colonel had only twenty passes to allocate among four companies: Smith, 'Enlistment', unpaginated, IWM 86/36/1. Also see Courtney, 'Letters', letter to his sister Linda, 14 December 1916, Birmingham University Library no. 8/152.

194 Cox, 'Letters and Other Papers', letter from 'Jim' in France, undated, Birmingham City Archive MSS 1546/1/1.

195 Will H. Bowyer, 'Letters', letter to his girlfriend Dorothy, from Egypt, 5 December 1917, IWM 87/51/1. Also see the letter to Marie Stopes from 'A.B.', second lieutenant, 6th Battalion, The Welsh Regiment, 16 February 1919, in which he says that he is twenty-eight-years-old and has been married one year, and yet the marriage has not been consummated because of the war: CMAC PP/MCS/A31.

196 Murray, 'To Passchendaele and Back', 83, IWM P457.

197 Kemp, 'Remembrance', 8, IWM 85/28/1.

198 'Royal British Legion, Miscellaneous Papers, (Burnley Branch)', letter from Will to his brother Jack, 16 January 1914, Lancashire Record Office, DDX1302, Acc. 4401, Box 2.

199 Eardley Davidson, 'Half a Life', 213, Liddle Collection, Leeds.

200 James Williamson, 'Memoirs', 1948, 45, IWM P443.

201 *Report of an Enquiry by Mrs Tennant regarding the Conditions of Marriage Off the Strength* [Cd. 7441], H. C. 1914, LI.

202 'Love and the Sergeant', *Evening Express*, 2 September 1926, in 'West Lancs. Territorial and Auxiliary Forces' Association, Newspaper Cuttings', Liverpool Record Office Acc. 2074.

203 Frank Percy Crozier, *Brass Hat in No-Man's-Land* (London, 1930), 57–8. See also the discussion by Graham, *A Private in the Guards*, 256–7.

204 For instance, see Revd John Sellars, '1917–1919. The War Diary', 7 February 1918, IWM 87/10/1.

205 Mellersh, 'Schoolboy into War', 64, IWM Con Shelf.

206 Davidson, 'Half a Life', 237–40, Liddle Collection, Leeds.

207 Colin C. Stanley, 'Letters', letter to his wife, no date, 1916, from Aldershot, IWM 84/52/1.

208 Rowarth, 'The Misfit Soldier', 9–10, 16, 17, 18, 19, 20, 49, IWM 80/40/1.

209 Garth Smithies Taylor, 'Letters to his Family, 1914–1916', 10 April 1916, Liddle Collection, Leeds.

210 Mellersh, 'Schoolboy into War', 184a, IWM Con Shelf. For descriptions of the disgust felt towards prostitutes by some men, see Sims, 'Diary', 14–15, Bristol Record Office 40340.

211 Pond, 'Old Soldiers Never Die', unpaginated (p. 22), IWM 78/27/1.

212 Karl Engler, 'Dual Nationality', 42, IWM 87/48/1.

213 G. A. Cook, 'Two Letters to D. Norah Schuster', letter dated 8 March 1917, Liddle Collection, Leeds.

214 Luther, 'The Poppies are Blood Red', 21, IWM 87/8/1.

215 Cordy, 'My Memories', 26–7, IWM 86/30/1. Other servicemen were not so fastidious: see Esler, 'Memoirs', 62, IWM 74/102/1, and Luther, 'The Poppies are Blood Red', 34, IWM 87/8/1.

216 Sheard, 'Manuscript Memoirs', vol. 4, 524, IWM P285.

217 McKechnie, 'Reminiscences', 39, IWM 88/27/1.

218 Rowarth, 'The Misfit Soldier', 10, IWM 80/40/1.

219 Jones, 'N.C.O.', 226–7, Liddell Hart Centre for Military Archives.

220 Gameson, 'Papers', 88, diary for 6 November 1916, IWM Con Shelf.

221 Mudd, 'Letters', letter to his wife, 22 October 1917, IWM 82/3/1. Also see the letter from 'R.A.', 8 September 1922, in Stopes, 'Papers', CMCS PP/MCS/A10, and L. H. Stringer, 'Letters', letter to his fiancée, 20 January 1917, IWM 90/21/1.

222 Gameson, 'Papers', 313, IWM Con Shelf, and Pond, 'Old Soldiers Never Die', unpaginated (p. 12), IWM 78/27/1. For the argument that the 'crisis' of venereal infection between the wars was exaggerated, see Davidson, 'Measuring "The Social Evil": The Incidence of Veneral Disease in inter-war Scotland', *Medical History*, XXXVII (1993). Davidson's statistics on the high level of defaulters at treatment centres do not suggest a panic-stricken population of diseased men. Indeed, medical officers were concerned to eliminate the 'casual attitude' to the disease.

223 Sir W. G. MacPherson, Sir W. P. Herrington, T. R. Elliott and A. Balfour, *Medical Services. Diseases of the War. Volume II* (London, 1923), 118, and Ralph I. Smith, 'Enlistment', unpaginated, IWM 86/36/1. For example, see 'Checking of Venereal Disease – D.O.R.A. 40D', memorandum by the deputy Secretary of State for War, 26 August 1918, which includes the following: 'If he [the soldier] contracts this disease and conceals the fact, he is court martialled, and the penalty upon proof that he has done so is imprisonment with hard labour for two years. If he does not conceal it, but reports it in the ordinary way, he goes to hospital and loses all his pay and emoluments, and his wife loses his separation allowance during the time that he is there': PRO WO32/4745.

224 R. H. Bryan, 'My War Diary', 1920, 21, IWM 72/88/1.

225 *Pearson's Weekly*, 29 January 1916, PRO MEPO2/1698. Also reported in the *Morning Adviser*, 15 January 1916. For more on the scandal concerning drugging soldiers, see PRO MEPO2/1698.

226 For instance, see Mapp, 'Memories', 23, Liddle Collection, Leeds.

227 Bacon, 'Letters', letter to Bacon from his nephew Ralph Creyke, 20 December 1914, IWM P391.

228 Starrett, 'Batman', 120, IWM 79/35/1. Also see the promise by Stringer, 'Letters', letter to his fiancée, 20 January 1917, IWM 90/21/1.

229 Reg J. Bailey, 'Letters', letter to his father from Salonica, 24 July 1916, IWM 92/36/1.

230 Miss D. Williams, 'Letters', letter from 'Jack' who was in Palestine, 23 November 1917, IWM 85/4/1.

231 J. A. Banks, *Prosperity and Parenthood* (London, 1954), 3.

232 For a detailed examination, see my *Working-Class Cultures in Britain, 1890–1960. Gender, Class and Ethnicity* (London, 1994), chapter 3.

233 D. Laurie Rowlands, 'Letter to Sweetheart Mine', 5 February 1918, IWM 93/20/1. Also see Sir Walter Kirke, 'Papers', speech on 27 July 1939, Liddell Hart Centre for Military Archives KIRKE 11/10; Thomas Parkes, 'Diary 1916', 4 March 1916, Liddell Hart Centre for Military Archives; two First World War postcards entitled 'When the War is Over, Maggie', nos 1 and 2 in J. W. Norton, 'Family Papers', Birmingham MSS 1410/11/1 and 2.

234 Begg, *Surgery on Trestle* 16–17.

235 Shipway, 'My Memories', 38, IWM 90/37/1.

236 Hughes, 'The Forgotten Army', 168, IWM 82/25/1.

237 Edward King, 'Papers', letter to 'Libbie', no date, IWM 90/7/1.

238 For examples, see Peter Thomason, 'A Instrument-al-Trio', in B. A. Redfern and F. Butterworth, eds, 'Odds and Ends. A Manuscript Magazine issued annually. Vol. LXIV' (Manchester, 1918), 199, Manchester City Archives M38/4/2/64; May, 'Diaries', 15 February 1916, IWM 91/23/1; Hughes, 'The Forgotten Army', 168, IWM 82/25/1; Bickerton, 'The Wartime Experience', 12, IWM 80/43/1.

239 Gameson, 'Papers', 12, diary for 20 May 1916, written at 1:20 a.m., IWM Con Shelf. Also see his comments on p. 104.

240 Siepmann, 'Rising with the Guns', 68, IWM 85/43/1.

241 Letter from Peter McGregor to his wife, 24 August 1916, in Michael Moynihan, ed., *Greater Love. Letters Home 1914–1918* (London, 1980), 26. For more anger concerning the lies in newspapers, see King, 'Papers', letter to 'Libbie' from France, no date, IWM 90/7/1.

242 Sheard, 'Manuscript Memoirs', vol. 4, 522, IWM P285.

243 Cockburn, 'Diary and Memoirs', 43, IWM P258; 'Silence on Leave', *The Times*, 31 March 1915; Jim Wolveridge, *Ain't It Grand (Or This Was Stepney)* (London, 1976), 19.

244 Letter from JCA, no date but probably 1920, in Marie C. Stopes, 'Papers', CMCS PP/MCS/A10, and letter from Stopes to 'O.B. 21 November 1918, in Marie C. Stopes, 'Papers', CMCS PP/MCS/A31.

245 Alistair L. Crerar, 'Letters and Papers', letter to his sister Dots, 18 January 1916, when he was recovering from a gunshot wound, IWM Con Shelf.

246 Venables, 'The Great War', undated entry for 1918, 77–8, IWM 76/225/1.

247 Arthur H. Hubbard, 'Letters Written May–November 1916', undated letter in 1916 to 'Mother and All', no. 38, IWM Con Shelf.

248 Ralph Scott, *A Soldier's Diary* (London, 1923), 99–100, 18 August 1918.

249 For a detailed account of similar images, see Jay Winter, *Sites of Memory, Sites of Mourning. The Place of the Great War in European Cultural History*, (Cambridge, 1995).

250 Crosse, 'Papers', 19, IWM 80/22/1. Also see Abraham, '1914–1918', 109, IWM P191, and W. Evans, 'Diary', 2 November 1916, IWM Con Shelf.

251 Bere, 'Papers', letter to his wife, 17 March 1917, IWM 66/96/1. Also see Brennan, 'Diary', July–September 1916, 16, IWM P262, and Gameson, 'Papers', 100–1, IWM Con Shelf.

252 David William Jabez Andrews, 'Diary', 13–18 October 1915, 20, CMAC RAMC 2021 Box 424; Begg, *Surgery on Trestle*, 91 and 114–15; Clarke, 'How the Wounded are brought Home', 24 February 1917, 319; E. M. Spearing, *From Cambridge to Camiers under the Red Cross* (Cambridge, 1917), 40.

253 Parkes, 'Diary 1916', 10 May 1916, Liddell Hart Centre for Military Archives. Also see Dixon, 'The Wheels of Darkness', 12 and 141–2, IWM 92/36/1, and D. Laurie Rowlands, 'Letter to Sweetheart Mine', 5 February 1918, IWM 93/20/1.

254 Mudd, 'Letters', letter to his wife, 22 October 1917, written four days before he went missing, IWM 82/3/1.

255 May, 'Diaries', 2 and 7 December 1915, IWM 91/23/1.

256 Revd Fred Wilcox, 'Letters to Dorothy Walker, His Wife, from June 1916', 3 May 1916, Bristol Record Office 32955/173.

257 Quoting Major Mitchell, director of training for the Ministry of Pensions, in Edward T. Devine, *Disabled Soldiers and Sailors. Pensions and Training* (New York, 1919), 187.

258 Letter to the editor from Amy Baker of Burley, Hants., in *The Times*, 2

February 1917. Also see the report of a speech by G. N. Barnes, Minister of Pensions, in 'Crippled Heroes', *Liverpool Chronicle*, 4 May 1917, and minute from Matthew Nathan to the Minister of Pensions, 18 April 1917, PRO PIN15/1147.

259 Respondent MAS4 in Mass Observation. 'Some Psychological Factors in Home-Building', 3 March 1943, Mass Observation Archives FR 1616, 2.

260 Respondent ABb1, in ibid., 2.

261 May, 'Diaries', 28 February 1916, IWM 91/23/1.

262 Royal British Legion, 'Miscellaneous Papers: Burnley Branch', letter to 'My Dear Old Pal' from 'your old pal, Jim' of Douglas, 31 December 1920, Lancashire Record Office, DDX. 1302 Acc. 4401 Box 1.

263 Christopher, letter from Ray Christopher to his mother, 7 May 1917, IWM 88/11/1.

264 Guy Thorne, 'Lovers Home From the War', *Health and Efficiency*, August 1919, 170.

265 May, 'Diaries', 9 November 1915, IWM 91/23/1.

266 Harry J. Thwaites, 'Papers', letter to his wife, 5 May 1915, IWM 87/33/1.

267 Letter from James H. Kaye to the Ministry of Pensions, 24 September 1936, PRO PIN15/38. The greater domestication of disabled men is also argued in 'Resolutions from the British Limbless Ex-Service Men's Association, 1938', 1 PRO PIN15/1414.

268 H. Lennard, 'Autograph Book', 1918, signed by J. McCarthy, IWM 86/86/1.

269 See my *Working-Class Cultures in Britain, 1890–1960*, chapter 3.

270 Simpkins, *Kitchener's Army*, 317. For the limits even within the Pals' Battalion, see p. 88.

Chapter Four: Inspecting

1 Alan T. Peacock and Jack Wiseman, *The Growth of Public Expenditure in the United Kingdom* (London, 1961), xxiv.

2 Cited in Donald Read, ed., *Edwardian England* (London, 1979), 363.

3 For historical analyses, see Anna Davin, 'Imperialism and Motherhood', *History Workshop Journal*, 1978; Greta Jones, *Social Hygiene in Twentieth-Century Britain* (London, 1986); Geoffrey Russell Searle, *The Quest for National Efficiency* (Oxford, 1971); idem, *Eugenics and Politics in Britain 1900–1914* (Leyden, 1976); B. Semmel, *Imperialism and Social Reform* (Cambridge, 1960); Richard Allen Soloway, *Birth Control and the Population Question in England, 1877–1930* (Chapel Hill, 1982); idem, *Democracy and Degeneration* (Chapel Hill, 1990).

4 For contemporary discussion, see Sir John Frederick Maurice, 'National Health A Soldier's Study', *Contemporary Review*, LXXXIII (1903), 41–56; Sir John Frederick Maurice, 'Where to Get Men', *Contemporary Review*, 81 (1902), 78–86; B. S. Rowntree, *Poverty: A Study of Town Life* (London, 1902), 216–17; E. Noble Smith, *Growing Children. Their Clothes – and Deformity* (London, 1899), 6; Arnold White, 'The Cult of Infirmity', *National Review*, XXXIV (1899), 236–45; idem, *Efficiency and Empire* (London, 1901), 101–2; *Inter-Departmental Committee on Physical Deterioration, Report and Appendix* [Cd. 2175], H. C. 1904, XXXII.

5 Jay M. Winter, 'Military Fitness and Civilian Health in Britain during the First World War', *Journal of Contemporary History*, XV (1980), 212.

6 *Ministry of National Service 1917–1919. Report. Volume I. Upon the Physical Examination of Men of Military Age by National Service Medical Boards from November 1st, 1917–October 31st, 1918* [Cmd. 504], H. C. 1919, XXVI, 6. See also *Board of Education. Annual Report for 1914 of the Chief Medical Officer of the Board of Education* [Cd. 8055], H. C. 1914–16, XVIII, 187.

7 Thus, when poaching recruits, Charles Drage merely went down the lines of men feeling their biceps: Drage, *Chindwin to Criccieth: The Life of Godfred Drage* (Caenarvon, 1954), 100.

8 J. Lawson Dicks, *Rickets* (London, 1922), 387.

9 Arthur Clendon, 'Letters to Arthur Clendon from Old Boys and Masters', letter to him from Edgar Hayland, 12 February 1917, Birmingham City Archive no. S256/15/2/3.

10 Ministry of National Service, *Report Vol. 1 Upon the Physical Examination of Men of Military Age by National Service Boards from November 1st. 1917–October 31st, 1918* [Cmd. 504], H. C. 1919, XXVI, 13. For a detailed examination of the statistics, see Jay Winter, *The Great War and the British People* (London, 1987).

11 Nobel Smith, *Growing Children*, 7.

12 Cited by Edward M. Spiers, *The Army and Society, 1815–1914*, (London, 1980). Also see issues of *Nation in Arms*.

13 Winter, 'Military Fitness', 218.

14 Charles E. Carrington, *Soldier from the Wars Returning* (London, 1965), 229–30.

15 This belief was shared by men of all social classes: Clendon, 'Letters to Arthur Clendon from Old Boys and Masters', letter from W. H. Jacobs, dated 'Monday', Birmingham City Archive no. S256/15/1/104; Henry Gother Courtney, 'Letters', letter to his mother, 18 October 1916, Birmingham University Library no. 8/140; Sir Henry C. Darlington, 'Letters from Helles', 1936, 22, Liddell Hart Centre for Military Archives 14/5/15; R. Graham Dixon, 'The Wheels of Darkness', 92/36/1, 58; Sir Basil Liddell Hart, 'Papers', undated letter to his parents in 1914, Liddell Hart Centre for Military Archives 7/1914/4; C. B. Stokes, 'Papers', 93/23/6, file CBS 4/5, letters on 30 April and 28 June 1915; George F. Tizard, 'Letters', letter to Mrs Barclay, his former employer, 3 October 1917, IWM 93/20/1.

16 W. Cecil Christopher, 'Letters', letter to his sister Val, 1 May 1917, IWM 88/11/1.

17 Robert Roberts, *The Classic Slum: Salford Life in the First Quarter of the Century* (London, 1973), 189.

18 Reginald S. Cockburn, 'A Series of Poems and Essays. Compiled and Collected by Officers of the 10th (S) Bn, KRRO during the Latter Months of 1915', unpaginated, IWM P258.

19 For an example, see the lines prefacing Ian Hay's *The First Hundred Thousand* (Edinburgh, 1915), 1.

20 Paraphrased by C. Addison in his preface to F. W. Mott, *War Neuroses and Shell Shock* (London, 1919), ix.

21 Undated letter from 'Jim' of Glasgow, to Marie C. Stopes in her 'Papers', CAMC PP/MCS/A1.

22 For other examples, see *Devonian Association for Cripples' Aid. Fifth Annual Report for the Year ending 31st December, 1932* (Exeter, 1932), 13.

23 This was not unique to the First World War: see O. Anderson, *A Liberal State at War: English Politics and Economies during the Crimean War* (London, 1967), 179.

24 *Board of Education. Annual Report for 1914 of the Chief Medical Officer of the Board of Education* [Cd. 8055], H. C. 1914–16, XVIII, 197–8. See also *Board of Education. Annual Report for 1916 of the Chief Medical Officer of the Board of Education* [Cd. 8746], H. C. 1918, XI, 125; *Board of Education. Annual Report of the Chief Medical Officer of the Board of Education 1919* [Cmd. 995], H. C. 1920, XV, 172.

25 This was not new to the First World War. For a pre-war example, see Revd J. P. Way, 'Military Training', in *The Public School from Within. A Collection of*

Essays on Public School Education written chiefly by Schoolmasters (London, 1906), 213.

26 Frederick William Stevens, *The New Era Handbook of Physical Exercises. The Art of Blending Science, Interest and Harmony in Physical Training* (London, 1922), 7.

27 Thomas Inch, 'Physical Culture and the Great War. What of the Future?', *Health and Strength*, 14 February 1920, 102, and W. Bruce Sutherland, *Physical Culture. The Bruce Sutherland System* (London, 1917), 63. Also see Revd Andrew Clark, *Echoes of the Great War. The Diary of the Reverend Andrew Clark 1914–1919*, ed. James Munson (Oxford, 1985), 17, 9 September 1914, re. Harry Sergeant, employee at Marconi Works in Chelmsford, for an example of a man who began lifting dumb-bells in order to increase his chest measurements and enter the army during the First World War.

28 'Be Healthy and Fit', *Health and Efficiency*, January 1919, 5.

29 John Hargrave, *The Great War Brings it Home. The Natural Reconstruction of an Unnatural Existence* (London, 1919), 5; Dean Inge, *Wit and Wisdom of Dean Inge* (London, 1927), 75; J. Keay, 'War and the Burden of Insanity', *Journal of Mental Science*, LXIV (1918), 325–44; Vernon L. Kellogg, Gaston Bodart and H. W. Westergaard, *Losses of Life in Modern War* (Oxford, 1916); E. B. Poulton, 'Eugenic Problems after the Great War', *Eugenics Review*, VIII (1916), 36. For analysis of the idea that war is dysgenic, see D. P. Crook, 'Peter Chambers Mitchell and Anti-war Evolutionism in Britain during the Great War', *Journal of the History of Biology*, XXII.2 (summer 1989), 325–56, and Jay M. Winter, 'Britain's "Lost Generation" of the First World War', *Population Studies*, XXXI.3 (1977), 449–66.

30 Caleb Williams Saleeby, 'Longest Price of War', *Transactions of the Manchester Statistical Society. Session 1914–15* (Manchester, 1915), 5, paper read on 11 November 1914.

31 *Eugenics Review*, VI.3 (October 1914), 197–8.

32 Eustace Miles, *Quickness and how to increase it* (London, 1919), vi. F. A. Hornibrook, *Physical Fitness in Middle Life* (London, 1925), 16–17, compared the 'British' body unfavourably with that of a 'Polynesian native warrior'.

33 For a civilian example, see Henry A. Cole, *The Part which Technical Colleges can play in the National Campaign for Physical Fitness* (London, 1938), 7. For a military example, see W. Cecil Christopher, 'Letters', letter to his sister Val, 1 May 1917, IWM 88/11/1.

34 *Health and Strength Annual*, 1908, 3.

35 M. B. Davies, *Physical Training, Games and Athletics in Schools. A Text-Book for Training College Students* (London, 1933), 15; Health and Strength, *Correct Breathing for Health. Chest and Lung Development* (London, 1908), 38; M. L. Holbrook, *The Hygienic Treatment of Consumption and Consumptive Tendencies* (London, 1892), v.

36 George Hackenschmidt, *Fitness and Your Self* (London, 1937), 47, and H. E. R. Stephens, 'Physical Education Committee. Education Sub-Committee. Notes on Methods of Physical Training adopted in the Royal Navy', 26 March 1935, 1, PRO ED24/2097.

37 For discussions of the particular benefits of Swedish drill to the blind, see letter from the treasurer of the Liverpool Hardman Street Blind Evening School, to the secretary of the Board of Education, 24 October 1902, PRO ED62/2, and 'The London School for Teaching the Blind. Swiss Cottage, South Hampstead, London N. W., Report for the Year 1909', 8–9, PRO ED62/4.

38 Central Council of Physical Recreation, 'Papers', letter from the general secretary of the TUC to Sir Kinsley Wood of the Ministry of Health, 8 December 1937, re. the malnutrition of unemployed men, MRC MSS. 292/808.4/1.

39 H. G. Mayes, *Keeping Fit. How to be Healthy and Graceful* (London, 1926), 10–11. Also see Hystogen Institute, *Perfect Features and a Beautiful Skin* (London, *c.* 1920), 2, CMAC SA/BMA/C405.

40 F. J. C. Marshall and W. Russell Rees, *Physical Education in Boys' Schools. A Text-Book for Training College Students and Teachers* (London, 1933), 2.

41 Edward Leech, *A Description of the Work of the Central Fund on Behalf of the Wounded in the King's Lancashire Military Convalescent Hospital* (Blackpool, 1917), 12 and 30. Emphasis in original.

42 *Inter-departmental Committee on Physical Deterioration. Minutes of Evidence Taken Before the Inter-Departmental Committee on Physical Deterioration. Vol. II – List of Witnesses and Minutes of Evidence* [Cd. 2210], H. C. 1904, XXXII, 279, evidence by T. C. Horsfall of the Manchester and Salford Sanitary Association.

43 For this debate, see PRO HO45/10631/200605.

44 For two discussions, see 'The Man in the Street', 'The Boy Marauder', *Daily Sketch*, 6 October 1916, and 'General Conference of Chief Constables', 18 January 1936, PRO MEPO2/4231.

45 Edith Neild, *Suggestions for the Preparation of Children for the Years of Adolescence* (London, 1924), 19. For nearly identical statements, see 'Amicus', 'Some Results of True Physical Culture', *Health and Vim*, July 1913, 258, and Eustace Miles, *Ten Rules of Health* (London, 1908), 81.

46 Edward Aston, *How to develop a Powerful Grip* (London, 1946), 3.

47 M. B. Davies, *Physical Training, Games and Athletics in Schools. A Text-Book for Training College Students* (London, 1933), 15, and Board of Education, *Memorandum on Physical Training in Secondary Schools, 1911* (London, 1911), 4. See also minute from 'G. N.' 15 April 1924, PRO ED50/249.

48 This belief can be seen throughout the period examined in this book: for instance, see Board of Education, *Memorandum on Physical Training in Secondary Schools, 1911* (London, 1911), 4; Hare Duke, 'Physical Education Committee. Training of Teachers Sub-Committee. Memorandum on Physical Education. Its Meaning, Purpose and Application', 1 April 1935, 1, PRO ED24/2097; *The Monthly Leaflet of the Ling Association*, XXXIII. 8 (August 1935), 109–10, in the 'Papers of the Ling Physical Education Association', Liverpool University Archive D529; 'Physician and Surgeon', *Youth and Truth. Manhood in the Highest and Best Sense* (London, 1895), 9; Frederick William Stevens, *The New Era Handbook of Physical Exercises. The Art of Blending Science, Interest and Harmony in Physical Training* (London, 1922), 9.

49 *Board of Education. Annual Report of the Chief Medical Officer of the Board of Education 1920* [Cmd. 1522], H. C. 1921, XI, 107.

50 Wilfrid Northfield, *Conquest of Nerves. The Inspiring Record of a Personal Triumph over Neurasthenia* (London, 1933), 21–2. Also see Health and Strength, *The Muscles of the Body. Their Uses and Development* (London, 1910), 6.

51 Eustace Miles, *The Eustace Miles System of Physical Culture. With Hints as to Diet* (London, 1907), 6.

52 This chapter does not look at the arguments for the introduction of dance or swimming as systems of physical training. In terms of training in dance, the most important promoter was Hornibrook, *Physical Fitness*, 36–8. For information on swimming, see Alfred P. Graves and E. C. Streatfield, 'Report on Swimming in the London Elementary Schools', 1908, PRO ED14/19. This chapter also does not examine local authority provisions for physical training. They followed the Board of Education closely but lagged a few years behind. There was one exception: in public gymnasia, 'Swedish' gymnastics predominated while in the evening institutions, 'German' gymnastics predominated. By the late 1920s, this was changing: see 'Physical Education in Evening Institutes', *London Schoolmaster*, v. 39 (September 1927), 6.

53 'Swedish' drill derived from the exercises of Per Henrik Ling in the early nineteenth century. The 'table' was arranged so that more severe movements were followed by easier movements, yet with the amount of exertion gradually increasing until near the end when movements again became simple: see A. D. Munrow, *Pure and Applied Gymnastics* (London, 1955).

54 'Swedish' drill aimed at building up the average of the class rather than producing special skill in one individual, thus no movement was left until correctly executed by all: 'F.C.S.', 'A Review of Physical Education', *School Hygiene. A Monthly Review for Educationalists and Doctors*, I.1 (January 1910), 52.

55 G. Ranger Gull, 'The Great Sport Revival', *Health and Efficiency* (July 1919), 146. Also see *Board of Education. Annual Report for 1917 of the Chief Medical Officer of the Board of Education* [Cd. 9206], H. C. 1918, IX, 113.

56 'Physical Education Committee. "Organisations" Sub-Committee. Relation of the Number of Persons for Whom Faculties for Physical Training are Provided to the Total Population', 14 November 1935, 2, PRO ED24/2097.

57 For the history of the term 'militarist', see Lawrence Radway, 'Militarism', *International Encyclopedia of Social Sciences*, X (New York, 1972), 300–5; Volker R. Berghahn, *Militarism: The History of an International Debate, 1861–1979* (Leamington Spa, 1981); Alfred Vagts, *A History of Militarism: Romance and Reality of a Profession* (London, 1938). The extent to which Britain was a 'militaristic' society in this period is hotly debated: Guy Arnold, *Hold Fast for England: G. A. Henty, Imperialist Boy's Writer* (London, 1980); Correlli Barnett, *Britain and Her Army 1509–1970* (London, 1970); Michael D. Blanch, 'Imperialism, Nationalism and Organised Youth', in John Clarke, Chas Critcher and Richard Johnson, eds, *Working-Class Culture – Studies in History and Theory* (London 1979), 103–20; Michael D. Blanch, 'Nation, Empire and the Birmingham Working Class, 1899–1914', Ph.D. thesis, University of Birmingham, 1975, 375–90; idem, 'British Society and the War', in Peter Warwick, ed., *The South African War: The Anglo-Boer War 1899–1903* (Harlow, 1980), 210–38; Valerie Chancellor, *History of their Masters – Opinion in the English History Textbooks, 1800–1914* (Bath, 1970); Patrick Dunae, 'Boys' Literature and the Idea of the Empire, 1870–1914', *Victorian Studies*, XXIV.1 (Autumn 1980), 105–21; John Gooch, 'Attitudes to War in late Victorian and Edwardian England', in Brian Bond and Ian Roy, eds, *War and Society. A Yearbook of Military History*, 1 (London, 1975), 88–102; Stephen Humphries, '"Hurrah for England": Schooling and the Working Class in Bristol 1870–1914', *Southern History*, 1 (1979), 171–207; Caroline E. Playne, *The Pre-War Mind in Britain: An Historical Overview* (London, 1928); John O. Springhall, 'The Boy Scouts, Class and Militarism in Relation to British Young Movements 1908–1930', *International Review of Social History*, XVI (1971), 125–58; John O. Springhall, 'Lord Meath, Youth and Scouts', *Journal of Contemporary History*, V.4 (1970), 97–111; Anne Summers, 'Militarism in Britain before the Great War', *History Workshop*, II (Autumn 1976), 104–23.

58 'F.C.S.', 'A Review of Physical Education', 52. 'German' drill also made use of track and field work, marching and free exercises.

59 Herbert E. Naylor and Mollie Temple, *Modern Physical Education including Exercises with and without Apparatus, Marching, Games, Etc.* (London, 1920), 2.

60 This is contrary to the argument of David Kirk and Karen Twigg, 'The Militarization of School Physical Training in Australia: The Rise and Demise of the Junior Cadet Training Scheme, 1911–31', *History of Education*, XXII.4 (1993), 400.

61 'Report of the Physical Training Committee', 28 October 1901, 2 PRO ED24/37.

62 Board of Education, *Model Course of Physical Training for use in Upper Departments of Public Elementary Schools* (London, 1901).

63 *Board of Education. Annual Report for 1909 of the Chief Medical Officer of the Board of Education* [Cd. 5426], H. C. 1910, XXIII, 174.

64 J. C. Robertson, 'The Introduction of Military Drill into Schools', *Monthly Leaflet of the Ling Assocation*, 1.4 (April 1904), 2–5.

65 The 'Swedish' system was adopted by the Board of Education in the 1909 syllabus. This syllabus also instituted a uniform system of physical training throughout all the public elementary schools. The navy had adopted 'Swedish' drill three years before the army.

66 *Inter-Departmental Committee on Physical Deterioration. Minutes of Evidence Taken Before the Inter-Departmental Committee on Physical Deterioration, Vol. II – List of Witnesses and Minutes of Evidence* [Cd. 2210], H. C. 1904, XXXII, 126, evidence by J. B. Atkins, London editor of the *Manchester Guardian*. This debate can be seen throughout *Report of the Royal Commission on Physical Training (Scotland). Volume II. Minutes of Evidence and Index* [Cd. 1508], H. C. 1903, XXX.

67 Blanch, 'Imperialism, Nationalism and Organised Youth', 111.

68 *Board of Education. Annual Report for 1909 of the Chief Medical Officer of the Board of Education* [Cd. 5426], H. C. 1910, XXIII, 184–5.

69 Ibid., 181–3.

70 Mott, *War Neuroses*, ix, and Alfred A. Mumford, 'School Cadet Corps', *School Hygiene. A Quarterly Review for Educationalists and Doctors*, IX.1 (April 1918), 17.

71 For the unpopularity of the pre-war army, see Peter Simpkins, *Kitchener's Army. The Raising of the New Armies, 1914–16* (Manchester, 1988), 18–19.

72 Harry Chapman, 'Physical Culture and the War', *Health and Vim* (January 1915), 9.

73 See the comment by the chief medical officer in *Board of Education. Annual Report for 1914 of the Chief Medical Officer of the Board of Education* [Cd. 8055], H. C. 1914–16, XVIII, 188.

74 *Board of Education. Annual Report for 1914 of the Chief Medical Officer of the Board of Education* [Cd. 8055], H. C. 1914–16, XVIII, 188.

75 'F.H.S.', 'Physical Training in Boys' Schools in England', 13 August 1923, 12, PRO ED12/233.

76 Ibid., 12.

77 *Board of Education. Annual Report for 1918 of the Chief Medical Officer of the Board of Education* [Cmd. 420], H. C. 1919, XXI, 164.

78 'F.H.S.', 'Physical Training', 13 August 1923, 12, PRO ED12/233.

79 'Physical Education Committee. Education Sub-Committee. Summary of Replies to Questionnaire Sent to Preparatory Schools', 26 November 1935, 2, PRO ED24/2097. Also see 'Physical Education Committee. Education Sub-Committee. Memorandum by A. G. A. Street on Physical Education in Preparatory Schools', 26 November 1935, 2, PRO ED24/2097.

80 'Qualifications of Physical Training Inspectors', 1938–9, PRO ED23/710.

81 *Board of Education. Annual Report for 1914 of the Chief Medical Officer of the Board of Education* [Cd. 8055], H. C. 1914–16, XVIII, 187.

82 *Board of Education. Report of the Board of Education for the Year 1910–1911* [Cd. 6116], H. C. 1912–13, XXI, 39.

83 *Board of Education. Annual Report for 1914 of the Chief Medical Officer of the Board of Education* [Cd. 8055], H. C. 1914–16, XVIII, 198.

84 *Board of Education. Annual Report for 1917 of the Chief Medical Officer of the Board of Education* [Cd. 9206], H. C. 1918, IX, 117.

85 Ibid., 118.

86 'F.H.S.', 'Physical Training', 13 August 1923, 2, PRO ED12/233; 'Physical Education Committee. Report of the Games Sub-Committee', 10 July 1935, 1,

PRO ED24/2097; Eugen Sandow, *Body-Building, or Man in the Making: How to become Healthy and Strong* (London, 1919), 63; A. G. A. Street, *Physical Training and Exercises for Boys* (London, 1936), 45–7.

87 *Board of Education for the Year 1923–24* [Cmd. 2443], H. C. 1924–25, XII, 136. Even as late as 1927, only ninety-four authorities were employing organisers: *Education in England and Wales. Being the Report of the Board of Education and the Statistics of Public Education for the Year 1926–27* [Cmd. 3091], H. C. 1928, IX, 65.

88 'F.H.S.', 'Physical Training', 13 August 1923, 5 and 7, PRO ED12/233.

89 For further elaboration, see the papers of the National Playing Fields' Association at MRC MSS 292/808.4/2.

90 For the early history of 'British' drill, see B. A. Furlong, 'Alexander Alexander 1849–1928: Building the Foundations of Health and Strength in Liverpool and Southport', *History of Education*, XXI.2 (1992), 179–87. 'British' drill promoted free movements, breathing exercises, military and musical drill, gymnastics, outdoor games and swimming.

91 This was a common accusation: for example, see the minute from George Newman, to the president of the Board of Education, 19 June 1917, PRO ED50/242.

92 M. F. Cahill, 'Letter to Sir George Newman, Board of Education, re. National Physical Training Assocation', 5 September 1916, 1, PRO ED50/242.

93 Letter to the Duchess of Atholl, 6 October 1927, PRO ED50/243; 'Blue Books on Keeping Fit', *Daily Telegraph*, 16 September 1937, PRO ED50/244; 'F.C.S.', 'A Review of Physical Education', *School Hygiene. A Monthly Review for Educationalists and Doctors*, I.1 (January 1910), 53; George Hackenschmidt, *Fitness and Your Self* (London, 1937), 13 and 45–6.

94 *Memorial on Physical Training Presented by the Incorporated British College of Physical Education, the Incorporated Gymnastic Teachers' Institute, and the National Society of Physical Education, to the Board of Education and the Departmental Committee on the Education and Instruction of Children and Young Persons After the War* (January 1919), PRO ED50/242, 9. See also Marshall and Rees, *Physical Education*, 6, and Street, *Physical Training*, 47.

95 M. F. Cahill, 'Letter to Sir George Newman, Board of Education, re. National Physical Training Association', 5 September 1916, 6, PRO ED50/242.

96 Minute from Captain Francis Henry Grenfell, 25 October 1927, PRO ED50/243.

97 Minute from George Newman to the president of the Board of Education, 19 June 1917. PRO ED50/242.

98 'The Board of Education Deputation re. National Physical Training. Minutes of Proceedings', 25 June 1917, 7–8, PRO ED50/242.

99 W. Mortlake Mann, *Respiratory Exercises* (London, 1919), 38.

100 Minute to Sir George Newman, 31 August 1917, PRO ED50/242.

101 Letter from G. L. Abbot, superintendent of the Campden Technical Institute, London, to the Board of Education, undated but 1917, PRO ED50/242.

102 John Lucy, *Keep Fit and Cheerful for Young and Old of Both Sexes* (London, 1937), 53; Marshall and Rees, *Physical Education*, 6; Alfred A. Mumford, 'School Cadet Corps', *School Hygiene. A Quarterly Review for Educationalists and Doctors*, IX.1 (April 1918), 19; Street, *Physical Training*, 47.

103 George Cummings, *The Cummings Road to Health* (London, 1923), 12; Hornibrook, *Physical Fitness in Middle Life* 4–5; Lucy, *Keep Fit*, 11; Bernard McFadden, *Making Old Bodies Young. Thirty-Eight Lessons in Building Vitality and Nerve Force and in the Art of Postponing Old Age* (New York, 1919); Sutherland, *Physical Culture*, 68; Chas T. Trevor, *How to develop a Powerful*

Abdomen (London, 1943), 2; F. A. M. Webster and J. A. Heys, *Keeping Fit at Forty. Simple Exercises for Men of Middle Age* (London, 1931), 10–11.

104 Minute from Captain Francis Henry Grenfell to A. H. Wood, 21 January 1925, PRO ED50/243, and M. B. Davies, *Physical Training, Games and Athletics in Schools. A Text-Book for Training College Students* (London, 1933), 14.

105 Dorothy Wood and M. C. Bywaters, 'An Enquiry Into the Posture of Children attending Public Elementary Schools', 9 November 1932, 6, PRO ED50/61.

106 Boy Scouts' Association, *Report of a Conference of Schoolmasters held at the Imperial Headquarters on Thursday, April 10th, 1924* (London, 1924), 6, speech by Robert Baden-Powell (he was citing Mr Badley of Bedales). Also see Boy Scouts' Association, *Boy Scouts and Citizenship. The Handbook of the Great International Jamboree. Olympia, July 30th to August 7th, 1920* (London, 1920), 54, and Hargrave, *The Great War*, 283.

107 Marshall and Rees, *Physical Education*, 4–5.

108 Mumford, 'School Cadet Corps,' 20. Also see *Manual of Drill for Boy Scouts. Contains every form of Drill* (Glasgow, 1924), preface.

109 Inch, 'Physical Culture', 102. Also see Lieutenant-Colonel Barron, 'Physical Training, with Especial Reference to the Training of Convalescents', *Journal of the Royal Army Medical Corps*, XXVII.4 (October 1916), 460; Clark, *Echoes of the Great War*, 178, 21 January 1917; Lucy, *Keep Fit*, 11; Street, *Physical Training*, 45.

110 PRO ED24/1472. Also see PRO ED12/194.

111 Jack Houghton-Brown, 'Farmer-Soldier', 1945, 101, Liddell Hart Centre for Military Archives.

112 Minute to the president, 17 October 1918, PRO ED23/112; 'Some Notes on the Board's Attitude towards Officers' Training Corps', 15 May 1934, PRO WO32/195; Street, *Physical Training*, 46.

113 For the historiographical debate, see Geoffrey Best, 'Militarism and the Victorian Public School', in Brian Simon and Ian Bradley, eds, *The Victorian Public School* (London, 1975); Peter Parker, *The Old Lie: the Great War and the Public School Ethos* (London, 1987); Edward M. Spiers, *The Army and Society, 1815–1914* (London, 1980).

114 'F.H.S.', 'Physical Training', 13 August 1923, 6, PRO ED12/233.

115 Ibid., 13.

116 Minute to the secretary of the Board of Education, 9 July 1937, PRO ED50/244.

117 Term used in a letter from 'H.' of the War Office to the Right Hon. Viscount Halifax, 11 May 1934, PRO WO32/195.

118 Boy Scouts' Association, *Report of a Conference of Schoolmasters*, 23; 'Future of the Cadets', unknown location, *c.*1920, PRO ED12/194; letter from Granborne of the War Office to H. H. Oates of the Board of Education, 20 March 1917, PRO ED12/26; 'School Cadet Training in Some Midland Counties', 17 January 1917, PRO ED12/321. The statistics refer to the number of corps in September 1915 and September 1919: Peter C. McIntosh, *Physical Education in England since 1800* (London, 1968), 181.

119 Clendon, 'Letters', letter from R. Leslie Duffield, 6 October 1918, and letter from W. H. Jacobs, dated 'Monday', Birmingham City Archive nos S256/15/1/39 and S256/15/1/104.

120 For an interesting example of some of the objections by anti-militarist groups, see the letter from Phyllis Bing, honorary secretary of the Youth Section of the No More War Movement, Croydon, to the president of the Board of Education, Charles Trevelyan, 21 February 1924, PRO WO32/195.

121 'From a London Master's Scrapbook', *London Schoolmaster*, VIII.70 (September 1930), 3.

122 'Training of Cadets', *North Mail*, 27 May 1919, PRO ED12/194.

123 Boy Scouts' Association, *Report of a Conference of Schoolmasters*, 18.

124 Letter to the editor from J. A. Evans, 'Boys and Militarism', *Liverpool Post*, 24 November 1926, in 'West Lancs. Territorial and Auxiliary Force Association, Newspaper Cuttings', Liverpool Record Officer Acc. 2074.

125 The chronology is slightly different for the Officer Training Corps. For instance, their War Office grant was not curtailed until 1930.

126 Minute to George Fletcher, 21 December 1921, PRO ED12/194.

127 'Memorandum on Cadet Work in Secondary Schools – Its Aims and Values', 22 December 1922, 1–2, PRO ED12/195.

128 'Cadet Corps', *The Times*, 12 May 1930, PRO WO32/195.

129 Minute for 1 April 1932, 1–2, PRO WO50/243.

130 'Physical Education Committee. Training of Teachers Sub-Committee, Minutes', 28 November 1935, 1, PRO ED24/2097. Also see 'Minutes of the First Meeting of the Informal Standing Committee on Physical Education, Held at the Offices of the Board of Education on Wednesday, 1st December 1937', 3, PRO ED50/253.

131 *Monthly Leaflet of the Ling Physical Education Association*, XXXV.5 (May 1937), 85.

132 Proposal by R. J. Colson of Ifield, North Crowley, Sussex, 'Notes of Basis for Suggested Scheme to Stimulate Recruits for Voluntary. Service with Brief Amplification', 11 May 1936, and minutes of 29 and 30 June and 1 August 1936, PRO ED50/244.

133 For further elaboration, see the papers of the Central Council of Recreative Physical Training at MRC MSS 292/808.4/1.

134 National Fitness Council, *Report of the Grants Committee to the President of the Board of Education* (London, 1939), 8.

135 'Memorandum of Interview. National Campaign for Physical Fitness', 2 February 1938, Central Council of Physical Recreation, 'Papers', MRC MSS 292/808.4/1.

136 'Lad o' London', 'Tense and Worse', *London Schoolmaster*, XII.111 (November 1934), 11.

137 Walter M. Gallichan, *How to Love. The Art of Courtship and Marriage* (London, 1915), 103.

138 W. L. Marsland, 'Notes on the Early Years of the N. A. S. in Manchester', no date, 1, MRC MSS 38C/3/HIS/4/3, and 'Minutes of a Meeting of the Leicester C. [*sic*] Schoolmasters' Association. Held in Ald. Newton's Schools. June 11th 1920', MRC MSS 38A/LE/1/1. The NAS were preoccupied with two things: equal pay and women teachers for boys. This chapter focuses only on the second aspect.

139 'Man Consciousness', *New Schoolmaster*, IV.20 (May 1923), 10.

140 Ibid., 10.

141 'Town Talk', *New Schoolmaster*, IV.24 (October 1923), 15.

142 John Kay, 'Pioneer Days on Merseyside', undated, 1, MRC MSS 38C/3/HIS/6.

143 F. W. Ordish, 'In Reminiscent Mood. Pioneers of the N.A.S.', *The National Association of Schoolmasters. Fourteenth Annual Conference. Easter 1933. Southampton* (Southampton, 1933), 15.

144 'Minutes of Mass Meeting held at Kingsway Hall, Aldwych, W. C. Saturday 31st May 1919', speech by W. H. Thodag, MRC MSS 38A/LSA/1/1.

145 *National Association of Schoolmasters. Tenth Annual Conference – Easter 1929* (London, 1929), unpaginated, and *The Why and Wherefore of the National Association of Schoolmasters* (London, n.d.), 1.

146 *National Association of Schoolmasters. Tenth Annual Conference – Easter 1929* (London, 1929), unpaginated.

147 *The Why and Wherefore of the National Association of Schoolmasters*, 3.

148 William George Cove, *Equal Pay in the Teaching Profession. A Review* (unpaginated, 1938), 6, and *National Association of Schoolmasters, 1928–1929* (London, 1929), 9, in the NAS Papers, MRC MSS 38A/6/ME/4/3.

149 NAS, *Sex as a Fundamental Factor in Education* (London, n.d.), 9.

150 Letter from Eustace to Mr Hannon, 29 January 1925, PRO ED50/243.

151 Unidentified notice from a newspaper, 'The Fight for the British Boy and the Schoolmaster', MRC MSS 38C/4/3/2.

152 Quoting from the *Sunday Chronicle*, 19 April 1925, the *Brighton Argus*, 10 April 1925 and the *Sussex Courier*, 23 April 1925, in *Opinions of Others. Extracts from Press Comments on the Annual Conference of the National Association of Schoolmasters, 1925* (London, 1925), 3 and 7. Also see 'Board of Education. Secondary Schools and Pupil Training Centres. Inspector's Report. Hunts. Huntingdon Grammar School', 3 November 1927, 1, PRO ED109/2171; NAS, *Sex as a Fundamental Factor*, 14; 'Physical Training of Boys', *New Schoolmaster*, VIII.68 (November 1927), 20; 'W.E.C.', 'Men Teachers for Boys', *New Schoolmaster*, V.35 (October 1924), 9. For the situation in Wales, see minute of 18 October 1934, PRO ED50/248.

153 For protests against women inspecting male physical training instructors (and the responses of the female organizers) between 1925 and 1929, see PRO ED50/243.

154 'I do not regret', *London Schoolmaster*, XIII.1 16 (May 1935), 15. Also see the unidentified newspaper cutting, 'Support for Rebel Schoolmaster', April 1935, MRC MSS 38A/7/1, and NAS, *National Association of Schoolmasters 1935–36* (London, 1936), MRC MSS 38C/4/1/4, 10.

155 'Of General Interest', *London Schoolmaster*, XIV.128 (July 1936), 15. See also Vernon Blunt, *Our Education System must be overhauled. More Male Teachers needed* (London, c.1933), 1, and NAS, *National Association of Schoolmasters 1935–36* (London, 1936), MRC MSS. 38C/4/1/4, 10.

156 Unidentified newspaper cutting, 'Can Women Teachers teach Boys Manliness?', speech by R. Anderson, president of the NAS, MRC MSS. 38A/7/1.

157 'Terse and Worse', by Lad o' London, *London Schoolmaster*, VII.59 (September 1929), 14.

158 Andrew Soutar in the *Sunday Chronicle*, 19 April 1925, quoted in *Opinions of Others*, 4, and 'Of General Interest', *London Schoolmaster*, XIV.128 (July 1936), 15. Also see M. B. Davies, *Physical Training, Games and Athletics in Schools. A Text-Book for Training College Students* (London, 1933), 117; Jack Houghton-Brown, 'Farmer-Soldier', 1945, 9, Liddell Hart Centre for Military Archives; 'Minutes of Mass Meeting held at Kingway Hall, Aldwych, W. C., Saturday 31st May 1919', MRC MSS. 38A/LSA/1/1; 'P. T. Leadership', *The Brigade*, XLVI.1 (March 1939), 9; unidentified newspaper cutting, 'Men Protest against Women Teachers for Boys', February 1930, MRC MSS 38A/7/3; *Yorkshire Post*, 7 August 1924, quoted in 'N. A. S. Notes and Jottings', *New Schoolmaster*, V.34 (September 1924), 10.

159 'The Schoolboy feels insulted', *Recorder*, 15 November 1934, MRC MSS 38A/7/1.

160 Letter from Miss Mary Hankinson, honorary secretary of the Ling Association, to H. G. Maurice, of the Board of Education, 11 April 1908, PRO ED24/285.

161 M. F. Cahill, 'Letter to Sir George Newman, Board of Education, re. National Physical Training Association', 5 September 1916, 2, PRO ED50/242.

162 'Carnegie Hall. Physical Training College for Men, Beckett Park, Leeds', 29 January 1932, PRO ED78/68; Glamorgan County Council Summer School in Physical Training at Berry, 1922, PRO ED82/167; 'The London Central Institute for Swedish Gymnastics', PRO ED50/251; minute on 6 December

1916, PRO ED50/242; minute from A. H. Wood to Captain Francis Henry Grenfell, 24 February 1925, PRO ED50/243; 'Physical Education Committee. Training of Teachers Sub-Committee. Minutes', 17 June 1935, 5, PRO ED24/2097; Scarborough Summer School in Physical Training, 1922, PRO ED82/110.

163 'Physical Education Committee. "Organisations" Sub-Committee. Minutes', 9 December 1935, 3, PRO ED24/2097.

164 NAS, *National Association of Schoolmasters 1924-25* (n.p., 1925), 27-8, MRC 38C/4/1/2.

165 Blunt, *Our Education System must be overhauled*, 2. Also see p. 1.

166 'Terse and Worse', by Lad o' London, *London Schoolmaster*, X.87 (May 1932), 12. This article ended with the statement: 'Others have said that the "talkies" are the cause of the increase in crime, which is, according to brothers, another way of saying what Miss Cowdray said.'

167 'Fundamental Demands', *London Schoolmaster*, XI.100 (October 1933), 1. Also see unidentified newspaper cutting, 'The N.A.S. of Newcastle', MRC MSS. 38A/7/1.

168 'Current Comment – Good Husbands', *New Schoolmaster*, VIII.59 (January 1927), 16.

169 Marjorie Bowen, *Making our Boys Effeminate* (London, 1927), 2, reprinted by the NAS from the London *Evening News*, 25 February 1927.

170 Walter Heape, *Preparation for Marriage* (London, 1914), quoted in London Schoolmasters' Association, *Equal Pay and the Teaching Profession. An Enquiry into, and the Case against, the Demand for Equal Pay for Men and Women Teachers of the same Professional Status* (London, 1921), 56-8.

171 London Schoolmasters' Association, *Equal Pay and the Teaching Profession*, 60-2.

172 Meyrick Booth, *Youth and Sex. A Psychological Study* (London, 1932), 132-3.

173 Quoted in ibid., 134.

174 NAS, *Men Teachers for Boys. Some Views* (London, n.d.), 5.

175 Unidentified address by Dr Crichton Miller, MRC MSS 38A/7/1. Also see unidentified newspaper cutting, 'The N. A. S. of Newcastle', MRC MSS 38A/7/1.

176 John Carl Flugel, *Men and their Motives: Psycho-Analytical Studies* (London, 1934), 65, and idem, *The Psychology of Clothes* (London, 1930), 111.

177 Marshall and Rees, *Physical Education*, 5.

178 They were not the only group concerned with men's dress reform. Earlier movements included the Health and Artistic Press Union, the Sensible Dress Society, and the Hygienic Dress League. Groups active at same time include the Society for Sensible Clothes (for a brief discussion, see 'Notes and News', *Tailor and Cutter*, 8 April 1932, 363).

179 *The Times*, 18 November 1929, 9.

180 *Health and Strength Annual*, 1930, 65, and *The Times*, 18 November 1929, 9.

181 Flugel, *The Psychology of Clothes*, 111.

182 William Kaye, *When Married Life gets Dull* (London, 1911), 83-4; David Adams, 'The Psychological Effects of Atmospheric Pollution', in National Smoke Abatement Society, *Proceedings of the National Smoke Abatement Society of 1932.* 38.

183 J. Bruce Glasier, *Militarism* (London, 1915), 1.

184 'E.R.P.', 'Brighter Clothes for Men', *Punch*, 6 April 1927, and Dr A. C. Jordan, 'Mere Man in Uniform', *New Health*, November 1932, 24.

185 Michael MacDonagh, *In London during the Great War. The Diary of a Journalist* (London, 1935), 31 December 1914, 47.

186 Dean Inge, 'A Distinctive Dress for every Profession', *Evening Standard*, 19 June 1929.

187 H. Denis Bradley, *The Eternal Masquerade* (London, 1922), 240.

188 They were to become 'as beautiful as women' *as well as* like 'Greek Gods'! See Eric Gill, *Clothes. An Essay on the Nature and Significance of the Natural and Artificial Integuments worn by Men and Women* (London, 1931), 196–7, and Graham Seton [G. S. Hutchinson], 'Dress Reform and All That', *New Health*, July 1935, 26.

189 John Hargrave, *The Confession of the Kibbo Kift. A Declaration and General Exposition of the Work of the Kindred* (London, 1927), 99.

190 'Lad o' London', 'Quizzical Culture', *London Schoolmaster*, VI.44 (March 1928), 9. It was noted, however, that there was a danger in imitating women too much: 'If a man tried to dress as women do he would get into an early grave. He would die of consumption. Women has about 25 per cent more resisting power to cold than man has. And he would look rather funny going about with his shoulders and back showing through a thin gauze veil': Kaye, *When Married Life gets Dull*, 83.

191 Edgar J. Saxon, 'First Steps to Fitness', *Health and Life*, September 1934, 280–1, and Dr Leonard Williams, 'A Straight Talk to Men of the Tyranny of Clothes', *New Health*, July 1929, 33.

192 G. R. Brandle, *A Treatise on Premature Baldness. Its Cause, Prevention and Cure* (London, 1897), 11–12; Dr Caleb Williams Saleeby, 'Change Men's Clothes', *New Health*, n.d., c.1929, British Library 1883.c.13; *The Times*, 6 September 1934; letter from Edward Wood of the Borrowood Syndicate to Sir Edward Bradford of New Scotland Yard, 22 January 1901, PRO MEPO2/543 re. a helmet that would reduce the occurrence of baldness amongst policemen.

193 Smith, *Growing Children*, 10–11.

194 '*Men*, Don't Tight Lace!', *Health and Vim*, July 1915.

195 Kaye, *When Married Life gets Dull* 124–5, and 'Lad o' London', 'Quizzical Culture', *London Schoolmaster*, VI.44 (March 1928), 9.

196 John Haddon, *Clothing and its Relation to Health and Disease* (Manchester, 1893), 174–6.

197 Albert Edward Garrett and H. F. Tomalin, *Purpose and Efficiency of Clothing* (unpaginated, c.1912), 2.

198 Haddon, *Clothing and its Relation to Health and Disease*, 174 and 187. Also see G. Richeart, *Health and Beauty* (unpaginated, c.1890), 2.

199 Health and Strength, *Correct Breathing for Health. Chest and Lung Development* (London, 1908), 34–5, and Miles, *Ten Rules of Health*, 56.

200 John S. Taylor, assistant medical officer of health, Manchester, 'Smoke and Health', in National Smoke Abatement Society, *The Smoke Abatement Handbook* (Manchester, 1931), 13.

201 *Sunlight. Journal of the Sunlight League* (Summer 1943), 4.

202 David Adams, 'The Psychological Effects of Atmospheric Pollution', in National Smoke Abatement Society, *Proceedings of the National Smoke Abatement Society of 1932*, 37, and William Graham, *On Smoke Abatement* (Manchester, c.1896), 4.

203 David Adams, 'The Psychological Effects of Atmospheric Pollution', in National Smoke Abatement Society, *Proceedings of the National Smoke Abatement Society of 1932*, 37.

204 Metropolitan Police minute, shorthand notes of speech in Hyde Park, by A. S. Sopley, 22 May 1927, PRO MEPO3/946.

205 Graham, *On Smoke Abatement* 3.

206 Lewis D. Cruickshank and Ernest Watt. *Scottish Board of Health. Interim Report on Artificial Light and X-Ray Therapy* (London, 1925); Edward Jas. Deck, *The*

Sun and How to Use It (London, 1926), 14; 'Evidence from the Newton Committee Report', 1921, PRO HLG55/39; Graham, *On Smoke Abatement*, 4; Dr Hans L. Heusner, *Light Therapy and Pulmonary Tuberculosis* (Slough, 1926), 5.

207 Letter to the editor from W. Bruce Sutherland, president of the Sunlight League, *The Times*, 9 September 1930, 8. See also 'Sunlight and Health', *The Times*, 24 August 1922, 9; William Welby, *It's Only Natural. The Philosophy of Nudism* (London, 1937), 71–2.

208 Deck, *The Sun*, 12–13.

209 Linda Bryder, 'Wonderlands of Buttercup, Clover and Daisies. Tuberculosis and the Open-Air School Movement of Britain, 1907–1939', in Roger Cooter, ed., *In the Name of the Child. Health and Welfare, 1880–1940* (London, 1992), 72–95; Marjorie Cruikshank, 'The Open-Air School Movement in English Education', *Paedogogica Historica*, XVII (1977), 62–74; R. Lowe, 'The Early Twentieth-Century Open Air Movement: Origins and Implications', in N. Parry and D. McNair, eds, *The Fitness of the Nation: Physical and Health Education in the Nineteenth and Twentieth Centuries* (Leicester, 1983), 86–99; D. Turner, 'The Open-Air School Movement in Sheffield', *History of Education*, I (1972), 58–80.

210 William R. Lucas, *Physical Culture Simplified* (London, 1931), 65 and 75. Also see *Man's Own Medical Adviser. A Complete Guide for Men. Dealing with the Prevention and Treatment of their Diseases and the Obligations of Manhood* (London, 1912), which claims that their 'oxygen Cure' will cure venereal diseases, nervousness and impotence, in addition to many other diseases of people living in sedentary occupations in the city where there is an oxygen shortage, and Health and Strength, *Correct Breathing for Health*, 34–5.

211 Deck, *The Sun*, 11.

212 J. P. Muller, *The Fresh-Air Book* (London, 1911), 112.

213 John Langdon-Davies, *The Future of Nakedness* (London, 1939), 71, and Dr Caleb Williams Saleeby, 'Change Men's Clothes', *New Health*, c.1929, British Library 1883.c.13.

214 *'Sunlight' Treatment. A Concise Guide for the Use of Ultra-Violet Irradiation on Actino-Therapy* (London, 1927).

215 Dr Caleb Williams Saleeby, 'Change Men's Clothes', *New Health*, c.1929, British Library 1883.c.13.

216 Liverpool Council of Social Services, *Smoke Abatement* (Liverpool, 1941), 8, quoting Dr. H. E. Wallin, director of the Psychological Clinic at the University of Pittsburgh.

217 Herbert N. Casson, *The Story of Artificial Silk* (London, 1928), 101.

218 Ibid., 92–3.

219 'Sun-Bathing in Hyde Park', unlabelled and undated press cutting, 1927, PRO MEPO3/946.

220 Letter from 'H.S.L.', in *New Health*, September 1927, 74.

221 *The Times*, 8 July 1937.

222 Comment by the editor to the photographs accompanying R. S. Watson, 'A Pioneer in Dress Reform', *New Health*, November 1932, 25. For similar advice, see Miles, *The Eustace Miles System*, 103; *The Times*, 4 July 1929, 14; Leonard Williams, letter to the editor, *New Health*, August 1929, 56.

223 Guy Kendall, letter to the editor, *The Times*, 4 July 1931, 8. He was headmaster of University College School, Frognal, Hampstead.

224 Thomas Macmillan, 'The War to End War: 1914–1918', 1935, 5, IWM Con Shelf.

225 'Shall Trousers Go?', *Tailor and Cutter*, 27 November 1931, 933.

226 'Slips or Costumes', *Tailor and Cutter*, 26 August 1932, 833.

227 'Clothes', *Health and Life*, July 1935, 23.
228 Anne Porter, letter to the editor, *The Times*, 4 August 1932, 11.
229 Revd C. E. Norwood, *Nudism in England* (London, 1933), 26.
230 George Ryley Scott, *The Common Sense of Nudism. Including a Survey of Sun-Bathing and 'Light Treatment'* (London, 1934), 236.
231 'Clothes', *Health and Life*, July 1935, 23.
232 Langdon-Davies, *The Future of Nakedness*, 29.
233 'An Eye Witness', *In a Nudist Camp! (Somewhere in England) or the Naked Truth* (Glasgow, 1933), 20.
234 'Tinkering with Tradition', *Tailor and Cutter*, 8 November 1929, 895.
235 'New Army Dress', *Tailor and Cutter*, 9 December 1932, 1163.
236 'Slackness and Fitness', *Tailor and Cutter*, 25 December 1931, 1021.
237 'The King's Bodyguard', *Tailor and Cutter*, 5 June 1931, 447. Also see 'Dress Reform Debate', *Tailor and Cutter*, 8 July 1932, 647, speech by George Dines.
238 'The Dress Reform', *Tailor and Cutter*, 8 July 1932, 642.
239 'Army Dress Reform', *Tailor and Cutter*, 29 January 1932, 89.
240 'Shall Trousers Go?', *Tailor and Cutter*, 27 November 1931, 933. See also 'Following in Father's Footsteps', *Tailor and Cutter*, 8 November 1929, 895, and 'Flashlight on Fashion', *Tailor and Cutter*, 29 April 1932, 421.
241 'Altered Functions of Special Garb', *Tailor and Cutter*, 3 July 1931, 519.
242 'Dress Reform Debated', *Tailor and Cutter*, 8 July 1932, 647, speech by D. Anthony Bradley.
243 R. S. Watson, 'A Pioneer in Dress Reform', *New Health*, November 1932, 24; unsigned letter to the editor from a man in the clothing trade, *New Health* September 1932, 16–17.
244 'This Dress Reform', *Tailor and Cutter*, 8 July 1932, 642, and 'An Eye Witness', *In a Nudist Camp! (Somewhere in England) or the Naked Truth* (Glasgow, 1933), 19.
245 'Tailors and Dress Reform', *The Times*, 5 September 1929, 7.
246 Diana De Marly, *Fashion for Men: An Illustrated History* (London, 1985). 108.
247 For a fascinating (and erotic) series of letters about male corsets, see Peter Farrer, ed., *Men in Petticoats. A Selection of Letters from Victorian Newspapers* (Liverpool, 1987).
248 For a comment of this, see W. M. Rumsey, 'Approaching the Nude', *Health and Vim*, September 1915, 262.
249 W. Cecil Christopher, 'Letters', letter to his sister Val, 22 May 1916, IWM 88/11/1, and Begg, *Surgery on Trestle*, 50.
250 A. Jack Abraham, '1914–1918: Memoirs of a Non-Hero', c.1973, 22, IWM P191.
251 Hutchinson, 'Dress Reform and All That', 26–7.
252 Dr Alfred C. Jordan, 'Dr C. W. Saleeby', *Sunlight*, v.i (summer 1943), 6; Dr Alfred C. Jordan, letter in *The Times*, 20 August 1929, 8; idem, 'New Dress for Sports and Pastimes', *Tailor and Cutter*, 3 February 1933, 89; 'Letter to the Editor', *New Health*, September 1932, 16–17.
253 Avril Lansdell, *Seaside Fashions 1860–1939* (Dyfed, 1990), 63, and Richard Rutt, 'The Englishman's Swimwear', *Costume. The Journal of the Costume Society*, XXIV (1990), 73–5.
254 Dr A. C. Jordan, 'Mere Man in Uniform', *New Health*, November 1932, 23.
255 The increased popularity of swimming can be seen in the annual report of the Glasgow Corporation Baths and Washhouses. In 1902, the pools were used 78 times for every 100 people in the city: by 1938, the figure was 239. The vast majority of bathers in the swimming pools was men (i.e. 1,339,390 men and 478,763 women). This last statistic refers only to swimming pools (excluding

hot water baths and turkish baths). Quoted in George Ryley Scott, *The Story of Baths and Bathers* (London, 1939), 172.

256 'Dress Reform Debate', *Tailor and Cutter*, 8 July 1932, 647, speech by Francis Wigglesworth, a wool merchant.

257 E. M. Wyche, 'Open-Air Education for Ailing Children', *Child*, VII (1916), 511. He was the senior medical officer of the Education Committee, city of Nottingham.

258 Percy Brentnall, 'Letters', letter to his mother, 17 April 1917, IWM 88/27/1. Also see H. P. Bantin, 'Letters and Postcards, May–November 1917', letter to his wife, 3 June 1917, IWM Con Shelf; Charles Callender, 'Memoirs', 1972, 5, IWM 73/186/1; Robert W. F. Johnston, 'Some Experiences in the Great War of 1914–1918', 49, IWM 82/38/1; G. B. Manwaring, *If We Return. Letters of a Soldier of Kitchener's Army* (London, 1918), 9, letter from a soldier in Kitchener's Army in 1917; C. B. Stokes, 'Papers', 93/23/6, file CBS 4/5, letters of 30 April and 28 June 1915.

259 'Mental Factors in Illness', *The Times*, 22 July 1938, 11, speech by Dr W. R. G. Atkins at a meeting of the British Medical Association.

260 Dr Charles Corfield, 'Letter to the Editor. Sun-Bathing', *The Times*, 10 July 1935, 10, and 'Sun-Bathing for Children', *The Times*, 19 August 1931, 7.

261 For instance, see 'Sunbathing at Keston Common', *The Times*, 14 May 1934, 16.

262 Scott, *The Story of Baths*, 237.

263 Caleb Williams Saleeby, 'Letter to the Editor. Recording of Sunlight', *The Times*, 10 April 1931, 8.

264 F. A. Wright, 'Greek Athletics and Military Training', *Edinburgh Review*, CCXXII.454 (October 1915), 405.

Chapter Five: Re-Membering

1 *To My Unknown Warrior* (London, 1920), 25–6.

2 The best discussion may be found in Paul Johnson, *Saving and Spending. The Working-Class Economy in Britain 1870–1939* (Oxford, 1985), 11–47.

3 Sidney Rogerson, *Twelve Days* (Norwich, 1930), 22.

4 T. W. Pym and Geoffrey Gordon, *Papers from Picardy by Two Chaplains* (London, 1917), 175–6.

5 Oscar P. Eckhard, 'Diary and Letters', diary for 2 September 1915, IWM 78/42/1.

6 'Ex-Private X', *War is War* (London, 1930), 46.

7 Arthur Graeme West, *The Diary of a Dead Officer. Being the Posthumous Papers of Arthur Graeme West* (London, 1918), 20 September 1918, 67.

8 John Hargrave, *At Suvla Bay* (London, 1916), 63.

9 Bertie A. Pond, 'Memoirs', unpaginated (p. 27), IWM 78/27/1.

10 Sir Herbert Babington (Robin) Rowell, 'Memories of Service in the Royal Flying Corps 1915 & 1916', 25, Liddell Hart Centre for Military Archives.

11 R. Graham Dixon, 'The Wheels of Darkness', IWM 92/36/1, 79; letter from John Hodgson to his parents, 29 April 1916, from Mesopotamia, in John S. Riddell Hodgson, 'Letters of a Young Soldier', Birmingham University Library Special Collection MSS 6/i/7; Ralph Smith, 'Diary, April 1915–May 1917', 15 September 1916, Liddell Hart Centre for Military Archives; C. L. Spencer, 'Some Private Recollections of a Base Wallah, 1914–1919', 1933, 24, in the papers of Sir Arthur Mitchell Stuart, Liddell Hart Centre for Military Archives; Wilfred Watkins, 'Reminiscences of Wilfred Watkins (1897–1979) of Treharris, South Wales', recorded 1970, 6, IWM 91/3/1.

12 Ralph Scott, *A Soldier's Diary* (London, 1923), 64. Also see Harold Clegg,

'Memoirs', 55–6, IWM 88/18/1, and Royal British Legion, 'Miscellaneous Papers: Burnley Branch', letter to Will and Gertie from their brother Tom in France, 20 December 1914, Lancashire Record Office, DDX. 1302, Acc. 4401, Box 2.

13 James William Hensher, 'Diary', unpaginated, IWM 91/11/1.

14 John Clarke MacDermott, 'An Enriching Life', 106, Liddell Hart Centre for Military Archives.

15 Miss M. G. Foster, 'Letters', letter to her sister, 14 February 1917, IWM 84/34/1; John Francis Jones, 'N. C. O.', 1934, 68, Liddell Hart Centre for Military Archives; Revd Canon C. Lomax, 'Illustrated Letters', letter to a friend, 1916, IWM 87/13/1.

16 For instance, see Edward Walter Bethell, 'Papers', letter to Lady Bethell from P. C. Ladaire after Bethell's death, Liddell Hart Centre for Military Archives.

17 Official order of the 47th Division, from M. Alexander, 22 May 1917, IWM Misc. 111 Item 1766.

18 Hiram Sturdy, 'Illustrated Account of his Service on the Western Front with the Royal Regiment of Artillery', 80, IWM Con Shelf.

19 Hans Zisser, 'The Sanitation of a Field Army', *Journal of the Royal Army Medical Corps*, XXXII.5 (May 1919), 346. For more on the need to get rid of the mutilated dead before servicemen from the same corps saw them, see MacDermott, 'An Enriching Life', 108, Liddell Hart Centre for Military Archives.

20 Owen Spencer Watkins, *With French in France and Flanders. Being the Experience of a Chaplain attached to a Field Ambulance* (London, 1915), 53–4.

21 The war diary of Revd David Railton, no date, in Michael Moynihan, ed., *God on our Side* (London, 1983), 53.

22 William Clarke, 'Random Recollections of "14/"18', 8, Liddle Collection, Leeds. Also see Walter J. Shewry, 'My Life with the Post Office Rifles', 4, IWM 88/52/1.

23 H. J. Knee, 'A Burial Party Fatigue: An Incident which happened near the Menin Road, Ypres, 1917', 1976, IWM 77/8/1.

24 Albert William Andrews' diary for 3 July 1916, in Sue Richardson, *Orders are Orders. A Manchester Pal on the Somme. From the Account of Albert William Andrews of the 19th Manchesters. Written in 1917* (Swinton, 1987), 52.

25 A. R. Brennan, 'Diary', 14 July 1916, IWM P262; Sir Henry C. Darlington, 'Letters from Helles', 1936, 32, Liddell Hart Centre 22/5/15; Arthur C. L. D. Lees, 'Diary and Letters', letter to his wife, 11 June 1919, IWM 91/22/1; MackDermott, 'An Enriching Life', 93, Liddell Hart Centre for Military Archives; W. A. Quinton, 'Memoirs', 1929, 55, IWM 79/35/1.

26 Elsa Barker in *War Letters from the Living Dead Man* (London, 1918), 143.

27 E. D. Ridley, 'Diary and Letters', diary for 10 January 1915, Cambridge University Library, Manuscripts Department, Add. 7066.

28 F. M. Peckham, 'Memories of An Old Contemptible 1912–1912', 15–6, IWM P316.

29 Lees, 'Diary and Letters', letter to his wife, 11 September 1919, IWM 91/22/1.

30 Knee, 'A Burial Party Fatigue', IWM 77/8/1, and Peckham, 'Memories', 22, IWM P316.

31 Revd John M. Connor, 'Diary', 14 October 1914, IWM 87/10/1.

32 Revd Ernest Courtenay Crosse, 'The History of the Chaplain's Department in the War 1914–1918. Section I. With an Infantry Battalion at the Front', 1919, 26–8, IWM 80/22/1. Also see R. Campbell Begg, *Surgery on Trestle* (Norwich, 1967), 223, and Revd Montague A. Bere, 'Papers', letter to his wife, 16 November 1916, IWM 66/96/1.

33 Anonymous diary entry for 23 February 1916, 'Mesopotamian Diary. With the 5th Buffs along the Tigris 1915–1916', *The Great War. The Illustrated Journal of First World War History*, II.3, part 6 (February 1990), 65.

34 Bere, 'Papers', letter to his family, 30 June 1916, IWM 66/96/1.

35 Scott, *A Soldier's Diary*, 18 August 1922, 99–100. Almost identical words were used by Lawrence Gameson, 'Papers', diary for 24 May 1916, 14, IWM Con Shelf. To be buried wrapped in a blanket was regarded as acceptable practice for men killed in war, but not for women. For instance, Les J. Matthews ('A Sapper Recalls 1914–1919. Egypt, Gallipoli, Palestine', 37, IWM 85/32/1) described how dead men were buried in long communal graves wrapped in blankets but dead nurses were placed in coffins and buried in individual graves.

36 For instance, see Mary Lakeman, *Early Tide. A Mevagissey Childhood* (London, 1978), 107–8, and Alice Linton, *Not Expecting Miracles* (London, 1982), 55.

37 *Report of the Royal Commission on the Poor Laws and Relief of Distress* [Cd. 4499], H. C. 1909, XXXVII, 51, and *Pauperism (England and Wales) Monthly Statistics* [119], H. C. 1914–16, LIV 2. Data for 1901–5.

38 *Judicial Statistics, England and Wales, 1913, Part I – Criminal Statistics. Statistics Relating to Criminal Proceedings, Police, Coroners, Prisons, Reformatory and Industrial Schools, and Criminal Lunatics, for the Year 1913* [Cd. 7767], H. C. 1914–16, LXXXII, 18. For the procedures followed, see PRO MEPO3/796.

39 For a large file of such cases in the 1930s, see PRO MEPO3/725. In the case of war, see Crosse, 'The History of the Chaplain's Department', 20, IWM 80/22/1.

40 'Disturbance of Human Remains at Newcastle on Tyne', March 1910, PRO HO45/10602/190178; 'Dukinfield Roman Catholic Burial Ground', September 1910, PRO HO45/10207/B33616; *Daily Chronicle*, 12 February 1902.

41 PRO MEPO2/1363.

42 For the best discussion of these earlier debates, see Ruth Richardson, *Death, Dissection and the Destitute* (London, 1989).

43 The proportion was lowest in Northumberland and Durham (10 per cent), and highest in Wales (21 per cent) and London (18 per cent): 'Anatomy Acts', no author or date but probably 1919, 1, PRO MH74/42.

44 This need was often misunderstood by the Guardians. For instance, in 1925, the chairwoman of the Nottingham Union argued against the union donating bodies for dissection on the grounds that her husband (a Cambridge graduate of medicine) had warned her that 'anatomy was of no use whatever to a medical man except for the passing of examinations': Alexander Macphail, 'Report of the Anatomy Office for the Quarter Ending 30th September 1925', 6, PRO MH74/33.

45 See the letter to Sir Arthur S. MacNalty of the Ministry of Health from C. Wallace, president of the Royal College of Surgeons, 30 January 1937, PRO MH74/44, and *Surrey Comet*, 25 October 1924, speech at the Kingston Board of Guardians, PRO MH74/30. The dates have been based on the estimate by medical schools that supply was inadequate when the ratio of bodies to every 100 students fell below thirty. The ratios for 1935–8 were added in pencil later by an unnamed person.

46 The sensitivity of many people to the mutilation of the dead was heightened when the peacetime corpse was an ex-serviceman: see the 'veteran scandal' of 1921 in *Essex Times*, 15 October 1921.

47 Letter from S. B. Lowry to the General Inspector of Workhouses and Poor Law Infirmaries, 26 July 1919, PRO MH58/3.

48 Alexander Macphail, 'Report of the Anatomy Office for the Quarter ending 31st March, 1927', 405, PRO MH74/33.

49 Untitled report by Alexander Macphail, 4 March 1911, 4–5, PRO MH74/40; *Anatomical Supply Committee of Great Britain and Ireland, Memorandum of Proceedings in relation to the present Deficiency of Anatomical Supply in the United Kingdom 1919* (London, 1919), 10–11, PRO MH74/42; 'Anatomy – Ireland. Memorandum', 7 December 1912, 1–2, PRO MH74/39; letter to Sir Robert Morant of the Ministry of Health, from Duncombe Mann of the Metropolitan Asylums Board, 4 November 1919, PRO MH74/43.

50 See especially Alexander Macphail's third report for 31 March 1921, 10, PRO MH73/31.

51 *Anatomical Supply Committee of Great Britain and Ireland*, 10–11, PRO MH74/42.

52 Debate amongst the Bermondsey Board of Guardians: *Evening Standard*, 17 September 1921. The debates have been simplified in this chapter since it is not central to the argument of the present book: the complexity of the debates may be seen by examining PRO MH74.

53 Letter from Edward Knight, licensed trader at Cook's School of Anatomy, 4 September 1905, PRO HO45/10062/B2694.

54 Letter from John Wheatley to Boards of Guardians, undated but probably 1924, PRO MH58/2.

55 Alexander Macphail, 'Report of the Anatomy Office for the Quarter ending 31st December, 1929', 511–12, PRO MH74/33.

56 Letter to the secretary to the Ministry of Health from the clerk to the Guardians of the parish of Hammersmith, 11 July 1923, PRO MH74/30.

57 Sir Arnold Wilson and H. J. Levy, *Burial Reform* (Oxford, 1938), 28.

58 'Evidence brought forward by the British Undertakers' Association', 13 March 1917, 2, PRO NATS1/1154.

59 Memorandum to Mr Collins from 'A.N.C.S.', 15 January 1917, PRO NATS1/1154.

60 Letter from H. C. Ambler, undertaker in Birmingham, 30 January 1918, to the deputy commissioner for Trade Exemptions, PRO NATS1/1189 and memorandum to Mr Collins from 'A.N.C.S.', 15 January 1917, regarding a deputation from the British Undertakers' Association, PRO NATS1/1154.

61 Unidentified press clipping, PRO NATS1/1154.

62 This is also the argument of David Cannadine, 'War and Death, Grief and Mourning in Modern Britain', in Joachim Whalley, ed., *Mirrors of Mortality. Studies in the Social History of Death* (London, 1981), 218, and John Morley, *Death, Heaven and the Victorians* (Pittsburgh, 1971), 79.

63 *Health and Wealth. The Organ of the Church Society for the Promotion of Kindness to Animals, the Church Sanitary Association, and the Funeral Reform Association*, part 1, December 1894, 24; *England regenerated through Justice to Ireland, or A Programme of Reforms, proposed to a Reformed Parliament* (London, 1888), 47–8; A. Emrys-Jones, *Disposal of the Dead* (Manchester, 1888), 77–8.

64 Letter from A. C. Altman to the Ministry of Health, Burial Department, 5 October 1936, PRO HLG45/78.

65 Geoffrey Gorer, *Death, Grief and Mourning in Contemporary Britain* (London, 1965), 5.

66 Michael MacDonagh, *In London during the Great War. The Diary of a Journalist* (London, 1935), 28 September 1914, 32. Also see F. Parkes Weber, *Aspects of Death and Correlated Aspects of Life in Art, Epigram and Poetry* (London, 1918), 427.

67 'Easter Sermons', *The Times*, 1 April 1918, 8.

68 'A Soldier Doctor' *A Soldier Gone West*, (London, 1920), 61.

69 J. F. Rutherford, *Talking with the Dead?* (London, 1920), 24, 33, 36, and 39.

70 J. S. M. Ward, *A Subaltern in Spirit Land* (London, 1920), 2.

71 Sir H. Thompson, *Modern Cremation* (London, 1899), 25.
72 *Cremation Committee. Report of the Inter-departmental Committee appointed by the Secretary of State for the Home Department* (London, 1950), 4, and Arthur E. Piggott, *Cremation and the Manchester Crematorium* (Manchester, 1922), 53.
73 *Cremation Society. Cremation Conference. Report of Proceedings* (London, 1947), 11. By the 1930s, even the 'industrial classes' were being passed through the fire: Alfred Hill, *Cremation* (London, 1902), 15–6, and 'Cremation for the Industrial Class', *Pharos*, 1.1 (October 1934), 16–17. In 1934, at the Manchester Crematoria, twenty per cent of the total number of cremations were carried out at the reduced rate for people insured under the National Health Scheme: *Pharos*, 1.2 (January 1935), 20. For a history of the movement, see Peter Creffield Jupp, 'The Development of Cremation in England 1820–1990: A Sociological Analysis', Ph.D. thesis, London School of Economics, 1992.
74 J. Page Hopps, *The Etherealisation of the Body* (London, 1894), 2.
75 Lord Ronald Sutherland-Gower, *Cleanliness versus Corruption* (London, 1910), 3. Also see Thompson, *Modern Cremation*, 75, and *Brighton and Hove Herald*, 15 December 1934, quoted in *Pharos*, 1.3 (April 1934), 14.
76 Piggott, *Cremation*, 74.
77 Florence G. Fidler, *Cremation* (London, 1930), 65–6.
78 William Holder, *Cremation versus Burial: An Appeal to Reason against Prejudice* (Hull, 1891), 21 and 24.
79 Dr Stenson Hooker and E. P. Vollum, *Premature Burial and its Prevention*, 2nd edn (London, 1911); Sutherland-Gower, *Cleanliness versus Corruption*, 3; Franz Hartmann, *Premature Burial* (London, 1896).
80 Guy Chapman, *A Passionate Prodigality. Fragments of an Autobiography* (London, 1933), 252.
81 The theme 'cremation equals purity' can be found prior to the war, but it became more common after 1914. The putrefaction theme became less common. For earlier examples of the purity theme, see Hopps, *The Etherealisation of the Body*, 2; Holder, *Cremation Versus Burial*, 39–40; *England regenerated through Justice to Ireland*, 49–51.
82 George A. Noble, *Cremation. Its History and Modern Practice*, 2nd edn (London, 1914), 14.
83 Cremation Society of England, *About Cremation* (London, 1923), 4, and Noble, *Cremation*, 14.
84 Fidler, *Cremation*, 30.
85 Hopps, *The Etherealisation of the Body*, 4.
86 See Alun Howkins, 'The Discovery of Rural England', in Robert Colls and Philip Dodd, eds, *Englishness. Politics and Culture 1880–1920* (London, 1986), 62–88, and Martin J. Wiener, *English Culture and the Decline of the Industrial Spirit* (Cambridge, 1981).
87 Cremation Society of England, *About Cremation*, 4. By 1930, in two out of every five cremations the ashes were scattered in gardens of rest: Fidler, *Cremation*, 30–1.
88 Fidler, *Cremation*, 30–1.
89 *Brighton and Hove Herald*, 15 December 1934, quoted in *Pharos*, 1.3 (April 1934), 14.
90 Albert C. Freeman, 'Designing a Crematorium', in P. Herbert Jones and George A. Noble, eds, *Cremation in Great Britain* (London, 1931), 115.
91 H. T. Herring, 'Foreword. The Ideal Crematorium', in Jones and Noble, eds, *Cremation*, 9–10.
92 Frank Dunham, *The Long Carry. The Journal of Stretcher Bearer Frank Dunham 1916–18*, ed. R. H. Haigh and P. W. Turner (Oxford, 1970), 18 February 1917, 31.

93 Oscar P. Eckhard, 'Diary and Letters', diary for 2 September 1915, IWM 78/42/1, and Henry Williamson, *The Wet Flanders Plain* (London, 1929), 130–1. The American bodies were shipped back to the United States.

94 'House of Commons Debate', CXXVIII, 1920, col. 1930, speech by Sir James Remnant.

95 *The Times*, 18 December 1919, 18.

96 Ibid., 15, comment by Lord Cecil.

97 'House of Commons Debate', CXXVIII, 1920, col. 1944, speech by Viscount Wolmer.

98 *The Clan Macrae. Unveiling Ceremony of the Clan Macrae War Memorial. Cnoc-a-Clachan, Kintail* (Cnoc-a-Clachan, 1922), 8.

99 'House of Commons Debate', CXXVIII, 1920, col. 1941, speech by Viscount Wolmer.

100 'House of Commons Debate', CXXVIII, 1920, col. 1941, speech by Viscount Wolmer.

101 'House of Commons Debate', CXXVIII, 1920, col. 1931, speech by Sir James Remnant.

102 Hugo Beaumont Burnaby, 'Papers', undated letter from [June] 1931, to Mrs Burnaby from A. C. Clinch, Liddell Hart Centre for Military Archives.

103 Ibid., letter to Mrs Burnaby from the honorary secretary of the Queen's Royal Regiment, 11th (S.) Lambeth Battalion, H. C. Burberry, 12 June 1931.

104 The best discussion may be found in Jay Winter, *Sites of Memory, Sites of Mourning. The Place of the Great War in European Cultural History*, Cambridge, 1996.

105 For instance see the discussion on the Irish conflicts in Keith Jeffery, 'The Great War in Modern Irish Memory', in T. G. Fraser and Keith Jeffery, eds, *Men, Women and War* (Dublin, 1993).

106 *Llandudno War Memorial Unveiling Ceremony and Dedication. 11th November, 1922* (Llandudno, 1922), 3.

107 *Book of Remembrance. Colwyn Bay War Memorial 1914–18* (Colwyn Bay, 1922), 2.

108 Catherine Moriarty, 'Christian Iconography and First World War Memorials', *Imperial War Museum Review*, VI, n.d., 63–75.

109 Edgar Oswald Gale, 'Letters to Family', IWM P331.

110 Crosse, 'The History of the Chaplain's Department', 30, IWM 80/22/1.

111 Ridley, 'Diary and Letters', letter to his mother on New Year's Eve, Cambridge University Library, Manuscripts Department Add.7066.

112 Letter to Clendon from Molly C. Thompson, 17 December 1916, in Arthur Clendon, 'Letters to Arthur Clendon from Old Boys and Masters', Birmingham City Archive S256/15/2/86.

113 Colin Robert Ballard, 'Letters mainly to his Family, 1874–1916', letter to his mother of 1 March 1915, Liddell Hart Centre for Military Archives.

114 Crosse, 'The History of the Chaplain's Department', 71–2, IWM 80/22/1.

115 Arthur Schuman, 'Memoirs', 8, IWM 82/1/1. For a similar response, see the letter from John Hodgson to his parents, 21 June 1916, from Mesopotamia, in Hodgson, 'Letters of a Young Soldier', Birmingham University Library Special Collection MSS 6/i/7.

116 'The Watchers', *Daily Express*, 20 April 1918.

117 Mary MacLeod Moore, 'Missing', *Sunday Times*, 8 July 1917. See also Gameson, 'Papers', 149, letter from Alice M. Petty, 15 April 1917, IWM Con Shelf; William G. Marlborough, 'Papers', IWM 86/48/1; letter to Mrs Masser, May 1918, IWM Misc. 163 Item 2512.

118 'Among the Missing', in John Cotton, *Gleanings. Some Gathered Verses and Wildings from my Field of Thought* (Bromsgrove, 1922), 12.

119 See the letters in IWM Misc. 126 Item 1964; Misc. 100 Item 1556; William G. Marlborough, 'Papers', IWM 86/48/1.

120 Sir Sydney Frank Markham, 'Papers', letter to his parents, 23 August 1916, IWM P46. He was a member of the Graves Registration Committee 1915–17.

121 Mrs D. M. Richards, 'Blues and Reds. Memoir of her First World War Nursing Experiences', chapter 2, 5, IWM P328. Also see 'Mystery Soldiers', *News of the World*, 9 January 1927, and Edward Paton, 'The Missing Do Not Return', *The Star*, 27 February 1928.

122 Some were not even injured and were shocked to discover that they had been reported killed: for instance, Revd John M. Connor, 'Diary', 23 November 1914, IWM 87/10/1. Examples of this confusion may be found in Bere, 'Papers', letter to his wife, 8 June 1917, IWM 66/96/1; H. J. Dickenson, letter to the War Office, 14 June 1918, IWM 85/15/1; Arthur H. Hubbard, 'Letters written May–November 1916', letter to 'Mother and All', 5 August 1916, IWM Con Shelf; H. M. Prince, 'Papers', CMAC RAMC 1924 Box 403; Spencer, 'Some Private Recollections', 62, in the papers of Sir Arthur Mitchell, Liddell Hart Centre for Military Archives.

123 Letter from Margaret Jarvis of Surrey, to Mrs Masseur, 22 October 1918, IWM Misc. Item 163 (2512). Such sentiments were restricted to women. See the heartrending letter from M. J. Berk, 12 May 1914, to Arthur Clendon, in Clendon, 'Letters', Birmingham City Archive S256/15/1/11a: 'I had not tell you that I cannot get reconciled to the loss of my dear son. it comes over me like a flood & I feel completely overwhelmed especially when the war news is not good. I feel he has given his life in vain, I do not know how to shape mine without him' (spelling and punctuation as in original).

124 John William Rowarth, 'The Misfit Soldier', 55, IWM 80/40/1.

125 Revd Charles Ivor Sinclair Hood, 'Papers', diary for 23 October 1915, IWM 90/7/1.

126 Sturdy, 'Illustrated Account', 56, IWM Con Shelf. For a discussion of the problems faced by religious institutions, see Thomas Macmillan, 'The War to End War: 1914–1918', 1935, 149, IWM Con Shelf; Niall MacFhionnghaile, *Donegal, Ireland and the First World War* (Leitrim, 1987), 70; *War Office Statistics of the Military Effort of the British Empire during the Great War 1914–20* (London, 1922). For the failure of religious institutions, see the letter from Henry Courtney to his mother, 4 November 1916, from Salonica, in Henry Gother Courtney, 'Letters', Birmingham University Library Archives, no. 8/143; 'Ricardo' [pseud. Richard Louis-Bertrand Moore], *The Warblings of a Windy Warrior* (Birimingham, 1923); D. Laurie Rowlands, 'Letters', letter to 'Sweetheart Mine', 5 February 1918, IWM 93/20/1; J. S. M. Ward, *A Subaltern in Spirit Land* (London, 1920), ix. For sympathetic accounts that also look at how the religious hierarchy responded to the criticisms, see J. Smyth, *In this Sign Conquer: the Story of the Army Chaplains* (London, 1968); A. Wilkinson, *The Church of England and the First World War* (London, 1978); Laurinda S. Stryker, 'Languages of Sacrifice and Suffering in England in the First World War', Ph.D. thesis, University of Cambridge, 1992.

127 For instance, see Chapman, *A Passionate Prodigality*, 71; MacFhionnghaile, *Donegal*, 80; 'Mark VII' [pseud. Mark Plowman], *A Subaltern on the Somme in 1916* (London, 1927), 16.

128 James Williamson, 'Memoirs', 1948, 19, IWM P443. For discussion of this phenomenon, see Aidan Reynolds and William Charlton, *Arthur Machen. A Short Account of his Life and Work* (London, 1963), 118, and Wilkinson, *The Church of England*, 194–5. The original rumour was invented by Arthur Machen, 'The Bowmen', *Evening News*, 29 November 1914. For the debunking

of the Angel of Mons, see John Terraine, *The Smoke and the Fire. Myths and Anti-Myths of War 1861–1945* (London, 1980), 17–21.

129 Rutherford, *Talking With the Dead?*, 40. Also see p. 132.

130 Bere, 'Papers', letters to his wife, 29 and 30 March 1917, IWM 66/96/1.

131 A. Wyatt Tilby, 'The Riddle of After-Life', *Edinburgh Review*, 227.464 (April 1918), 253.

132 Winter, *Sites of Memory, Sites of Mourning*. Also see Logie Barrow, *Independent Spirits. Spiritualism and English Plebians 1850–1910* (London, 1986); Ruth Brandon, *The Spiritualists. The Passion for the Occult in the Nineteenth and Twentieth Centuries* (London, 1983); Janet Oppenheim, *The Other World. Spiritualism and Psychical Research in England, 1850–1914* (Cambridge, 1985); Alex Owen, *The Darkened Room. Women, Power and Spiritualism in Late Victorian England* (London, 1989). For contemporary comment on the impact of the war on spiritualism, see James H. Hyslop, *Contact with the Other World. The Latest Evidence as to Communication with the Dead* (London, 1919), 445, and Hester Travers Smith, *Voices from the Void. Six Years' Experience in Automatic Communications* (London, 1919), xiii.

133 'Archbishop's Committee on Spiritualism. Report of the Committee to the Archbishop of Canterbury', 1937, 5, in the Harry Price Collection, University of London Library 15,331.

134 M. J. Petty, 'Streatham War Memorials', 1983, 7, Cambridge Central Library (Cambridgeshire Collection) C.62. Also see Clive Chapman and 'G. A. W.', *The Blue Room. Being the Absorbing Story of the Development of Voice-to-Voice Communication in Broad Light with Souls who have passed into the Great Beyond* (Auckland, 1927), 110.

135 R. Feilding-Ould, *An Address on 'The Cult of the Spirit'* (St Albans, 1930), 3–4.

136 'A Business Man', *Common Sense View of Religion*, (London, 1927), 17; 'A Soldier Doctor', *A Soldier Gone West* (London, 1920), preface (pp. 7–8); Basil Wilberforce, *After Death What?* (London, 1916), 24.

137 Winifred Graham, *My Letters from Heaven. Being Messages from the Unseen World given in Automatic Writing to Winifred Graham by her Father, Robert George Graham* (London, n.d.), 27, and F. Heslop, *Speaking across a Borderline. Being Letters from a Husband in Spirit Life to his Wife on Earth* (London, c. 1915), 12–13.

138 Sir Oliver J. Lodge, *Raymond or Life After Death* (London, 1918), 83. Also see Elsa Barker in *War Letters from the Living Dead Man* (London, 1918), 61–5; L. Margery Bazett, *The Broken Silence* (London, 1931), 26; Percyvall Hart Dyke, *Seeing through Another's Eyes* (Huntingdon, c.1922), 9, 28, 38; Heslop, *Speaking across a Borderline*, xi, 14–17; Petty, 'Streatham War Memorials', 7, Cambridge Central Library (Cambridgeshire Collection) C.62; Estelle W. Stead, *Faces of the Living Dead. Remembrance Day Messages and Photographs* (Manchester, 1925), 10–13.

139 L. Kelway-Bamber, *Claude's Book* (London, 1918), 1–2; Rutherford, *Talking with the Dead?*, 38; Stead, *Faces of the Living Dead*, 15.

140 Rutherford, *Talking with the Dead?*, 28, and automatic writing from a 'New Correspondent', on 25 June 1916, in 'Recorder', *Do Thoughts Perish? Or The Survival after Death of Human Personalities* (London, 1915), 45–6. See also 'A Business Man', *Common Sense View of Religion*, 16, and 'M. A.', *From Worlds Unseen* (London, 1930), 15.

141 Private Dowding, *Private Dowding. A Plain Record of the After-Life Experiences of a Soldier killed in Battle* (London, 1917), 6–8.

142 Automatic writing on 4 June 1916, from 'H****', a soldier killed at Neuve Chapelle in 1915, in 'Recorder', *Do Thoughts Perish?*, 26. The question about what happens to dead Germans preoccupies Barker in *War Letters*. Her hatred

of what she described as raping and pillaging Germans makes this question especially pertinent for her.

143 See 'M. A.', *From Worlds Unseen*, 13 and 15.

144 Lodge, *Raymond*, 194–6. Also see Chapman and 'G. A. W.', *The Blue Room*, 64; Kelway-Bamber, *Claude's Book*, 11; 'Recorder', *Do Thoughts Perish?*, 37; Revd Charles Dayton Thomas, *Life beyond Death with Evidence* (London, 1928), 107; Ward, *A Subaltern in Spirit Land*, 185 and 225.

145 Miss D. Joan Thompson, 'Papers', 1920, 24, IWM 73/35/1.

146 Philip Longworth, *The Unending Vigil. A History of the Commonwealth War Graves Commission 1917–1967* (London, 1967).

147 Arthur C. L. D. Lees, 'Diary and Letters', letter to his wife, 8 June 1919, IWM 91/22/1, and *Reports by the Joint War Committee and the Joint War Finance Committee of the British Red Cross Society and the Order of St John of Jerusalem* (London, 1921), 360.

148 Longworth, *The Unending Vigil*, 9.

149 Lees, 'Diary and Letters', letter to his wife, 28 June 1919, IWM 91/22/1.

150 For some examples, see Max Pemberton, 'Missing!', *Weekly Dispatch*, partially dated, October 1917, in Miss D. Joan Thompson, 'Papers', 1920, 24, IWM 73/35/1. This was also true if the body was found: for instance, generals and senior officers were buried separately from other servicemen: Sir Maurice Holt, 'Papers', 'Clearing a Battlefield', 1, instructions on how to clear a battlefield, CAMC RAMC 380/2/4 Box 40.

151 Miss D. Joan Thompson, 'Papers', letter to her from Lucan, director of the British Red Cross and Order of St John March 1919, 'Papers', IWM 73/35/1.

152 Herbert Jeans, 'In Death's Cathedral Palace', *British Legion Journal*, IX.5 (November 1929), and E. E. Tisdall, 'How They Chose the Unknown Warrior', *British Legion Journal*, XIX.5 (November 1939), 141.

153 Stuart Sillars, *Art and Survival in the First World War*, Basingstoke, 1987, 155. For a comparison between the popularity of Kitchener and Sir John French, see Richard Holmes, 'Sir John French and Lord Kitchener', in Brian Bond, ed., *The First World War and British History* (Oxford, 1991).

154 Victor Wallace Germains, *The Truth about Kitchener* (London, 1925), 318.

155 Henry D. Duvray, *Lord Kitchener. His Works and His Prestige* (London, 1917); E. S. Grew, *Field Marshal Lord Kitchener. His Life and Work for the Empire*, 3 vols (London, 1916); Horace G. Groser, *Lord Kitchener. The Story of His Life* (London, 1916); Nandkunverba, *Field-Marshal Earl Kitchener of Khartoum* (London, 1916); J. B. Rye and Horace G. Groser, *Kitchener. In His Own Words* (London, 1917); Harold F. B. Wheeler, *The Story of Lord Kitchener* (London, 1916).

156 For instance, in 1926, statues of Lord Kitchener were unveiled on Horse Guards Parade (9 June) and off Marwick Head on Orkney (2 July). For a first-hand report of the unveiling of this second memorial, see Rear Admiral J. Howson, 'Midshipman's Journal', IWM PP/MCR/375.

157 Reginald Baliol Brett (Reginald, Viscount Esher), *The Tragedy of Lord Kitchener* (London, 1921); Victor Wallace Germains, *The Truth About Kitchener* (London, 1925); S. Stuart Starritt, *Kitchener: Soldier and Statesman* (London, 1928).

158 For instance, see Anita Dudley, *Valediction: Sonnets to Kitchener* (London, 1916); the poem by G. G. Napier, 'Kitchener Drowned', undated, in the British Library; Robert J. C. Stead, *Kitchener and Other Poems* (Toronto, 1917).

159 Ernst Carl ('Germany's Master-Spy in England'), *One against England. The Death of Lord Kitchener and the Plot against the British Fleet* (London, 1935); Donald MacCormick, *The Mystery of Lord Kitchener's Death* (London, 1959); Clement Woods, *The Man Who Killed Kitchener* (London, 1932).

160 *The Times*, 20 July 1926, 9; 27 July 1926; 7; 4 August 1926, 12.

161 Franklyn Morris, 'The Kitchener Myth', *Illustrated Sunday Herald*, 22 August 1926. Also see 'The Loss of the Hampshire', *The Times*, 10 August 1926, 13, and 'Ten Years Ago', *The Times*, 5 June 1926, 15.

162 Frank Power, *Is Kitchener Dead?* (London, 1926), 4–6.

163 Philip Magnus, *Kitchener. Portrait of an Imperialist* (London, 1915), 379.

164 Letter from Mrs J. Carrley of Elmwood, Winnipeg, 28 September 1926, PRO MEPO2/2469; Ala Mana [pseud. Margaret Mabel O'Brien], *The Message: Lord Kitchener Lives* (Vancouver, 1922); Mabel Nixon Robertson, 'The Other Side of God's Door': Messages from Lord Kitchener, Mary Baker Eddy, and Others* (London, 1920); Power, *Is Kitchener Dead?*, 4–6.

165 Power, *Is Kitchener Dead?* In this booklet, Power claimed to have received this story from one of the twelve survivors – at least one survivor wrote a pamphlet denouncing the journalist: W. S. Phillips ('A Survivor'), *The Loss of H.M.S. 'Hampshire' and the Death of Lord Kitchener* (London, c.1930).

166 Power, *Is Kitchener Dead?*, 18.

167 Frank Power, *The Kitchener Mystery* (London, 1926), 91 and 96.

168 'New Moves in the "Kitchener's Body" Hoax', *World's Pictorial News*, 22 August 1926.

169 'The Kitchener Myth and An Empty Coffin', *Daily Chronicle*, 17 August 1926.

170 PRO MEPO2/2469.

171 James Douglas, 'The Kitchener Outrage', *Sunday Express*, 22 August 1926.

172 Ibid. When Peter Gates (the man who broke the story to the press) sued the *Referee* for not paying him the agreed amount, the judge sided with the newspaper, stating that Gates had rights to payment 'neither in the law, fact, or morals': *The Times*, 16 November 1926, 8.

173 Douglas, 'The Kitchener Outrage'.

174 Ibid.

175 Ibid.

176 Power, *The Kitchener Mystery*, 71.

177 There was a difference between being entitled to military honours or a military funeral party, and to be entitled to a military funeral. The first was allowed to have troops at the funeral while at the second the deceased was entitled to financial concessions up to a total maximum expenditure of £7 (this might include provision of a coffin, burial and the attendance of troops): see minute of 30 September 1920, PRO WO32/4849.

178 Minutes of 14 March 1920 and 23 September 1921, and protests from various organizations and committees, PRO WO32/4849.

179 Preston, 'The Empty Coffin', and an unidentified press clipping by Sir Sidney Low, 'Can the Ghouls be Suppressed?', PRO MEPO2/2469.

180 Preston, 'The Empty Coffin', and 'Ten Years Ago', *The Times*, 5 June 1926, 15.

181 Preston, 'The Empty Coffin'.

182 John Murray, 'The Secret People', 5 IWM P328.

183 Frank Power, 'Kitchener's Grave Found', *Referee*, 8 August 1926.

184 Ibid.

185 Ibid. See also reports in files in PRO MEPO2/2469 and Power, *The Kitchener Mystery*, 25 and 89–90.

186 'Memorial to Lord Kitchener', *The Times*, 3 July 1926, 17.

187 Reg J. Bailey, 'Letters', letter to his father from Salonica, 28 June 1916, IWM 92/36/1.

188 'F.A.P.', 'K. of K.', *R.A.M.C. Magazine*, I, 11 May 1917, 3, CMAC RAMC 945/5 Box 199.

189 'Lord Kitchener', *The Times*, 8 June 1926, 12; *The Times*, 10 June 1926, 11; 'Memorial to Lord Kitchener', *The Times*, 3 July 1926, 17.

190 'Ten Years Ago', *The Times*, 5 June 1926, 15.

191 Ibid., 15.
192 Frank Power, 'Kitchener's Grave Found', *Referee*, 8 August 1926.
193 'John Brown's Body', *Star*, 14 August 1926.
194 Frank Power, 'Kitchener', *Referee*, in PRO MEPO2/2469. Also see 'The Kitchener Myth and An Empty Coffin', *Daily Chronicle*, 17 August 1926.
195 *Manchester Guardian*, 12 November 1920.
196 *To My Unknown Warrior*, 14.
197 Ibid., 14–17.
198 Ibid., 7–8. Also see Power, *The Kitchener Mystery*, 1 and 89–90, and idem, *Is Kitchener Dead?*, 18.
199 Power, 'Kitchener's Grave Found'.
200 *To My Unknown Warrior*, 7–8. For other tragic stories of families searching for their loved ones, see Henry Augustine Buckmaster, 'Letters', 1914–1918, letters between Revd Charles John Buckmaster and Revd J. O. Coops, 28 September 1918, 31 December 1920, and one undated, Wigan Archive Service, and Royal British Legion, 'Miscellaneous Papers: Burnley Branch', Lancashire Record Office, DDX. 1302, acc. 4401, Box 2.
201 *The Times*, 13 January 1917. The resentment of the bereaved about their treatment by the wartime officials was discussed in 'House of Commons Debates', CXXVIII, 1920, cols 1943–5.
202 Statement of Norton Gardner, a cinematographic operator from Surrey, 17 August 1926, PRO MEPO2/2469, and *Daily Sketch*, 19 August 1926.
203 W. H. Abbott, *The Unknown Warrior and Other Poems* (London, 1929), 29.
204 Power, 'Kitchener's Grave Found'.
205 E. H. Carrier, *The Unknown Warrior and Other Poems* (London, 1926), 2–3.
206 Richard Hayes McCartney, *Our Kitchener* (New York, 1917), 1.
207 G. G. Napier, *Kitchener Drowned* (unpaginated, 1930), 1.
208 Reginald S. Cockburn, 'Diary and Memoirs', 25–6, IWM P258; Albert V. Conn, 'Memoirs', 1974, 22, IWM 81/41/1; Sir Henry C. Darlington, 'Army Book 152. Correspondence Book (Field Service)', copy of a letter to brigade major, 17 September 1915, Liddell Hart Centre for Military Archives 14/5/15; Dixon, 'The Wheels of Darkness', IWM 92/36/1, 77; Eckhard, 'Diary and Letters', diary for 4 September 1915, IWM 78/42/1; Pond, 'Memoirs', unpaginated (p. 42), IWM 78/27/1; A. Reeve, 'Diary', 10 September 1914, IWM 90/20/1; Schuman, 'Memoirs', 6, IWM 82/1/1; T. A. Silver, 'Stapenhill Darby and Joan Club. Minute Book', unpaginated, IWM 74/108/1; Sturdy, 'Illustrated Account', 6, IWM Con Shelf. Sometimes shooting a serviceman on one's 'own side' was not a mistake: William Charles Sims, 'Diary 1 August 1916–2 September 1918', 17 October 1917, 21, Bristol Record Office 40340, described the shooting of wounded men caught in the mud.
209 Georgette Agnew, *Songs of Love and Grief* (London, 1922), 5.
210 Mrs W. A. Albright (collected by), *Stories of Heroism and Kindliness* (Manchester, n.d.), 7, from the *Manchester Guardian*, 24 October 1914. This collection contains many more examples.
211 John A. Boullier, *Jottings by a Gunner and Chaplain* (London, 1917), 56.
212 Dixon Scott, 'The Letters of Dixon Scott', letter from Dixon Scott to A. N. Monkhouse, May 1915, Manchester City Council Local Studies Unit.
213 Pym and Gordon, *Papers*, 51–2.
214 Albert William Andrews' diary for 24 June 1916, in Richardson, *Orders are Orders*, 44.
215 Thus, a soldier bitten by a dog in Salonica was heralded as a 'wounded hero, our first "wounded" casualty!': letter to his mother, 13 November 1916, from Salonica, in Courtney, 'Letters', Birmingham University Library Archives, no.

8/145. Also see Courtney's comments about the 'hero' in fiction published during the war: letter no. 8/155.

216 Eckhard, 'Diary and Letters', diary for 25 August 1915, IWM 78/42/1.

217 Buckmaster, 'Letters', 61, Wigan Archive Service.

218 Garth Smithies Taylor, 'Letters to his Family, 1914–1916', letter from his mother to her sister, 25 October 1916, Liddell Hart Centre for Military Archives.

219 George Higgins of the 17th King's Liverpool Regiment, 'Correspondence', letter of condolence to Mr and Mrs Higginson on the death of their son, from Arnold I. Draper, 18 July 1916, Liverpool Records Office Acc. 2641.

220 'The Common Man', *Manchester Guardian*, 12 November 1920.

221 Preston, 'The Empty Coffin'.

222 Boullier, *Jottings*, 56. For a contrary view, see David Cairnes, *The Army and Religion: An Enquiry and its Bearing upon the Religious Life of the Nation* (London, 1919), 44–5.

223 Douglas, 'The Kitchener Outrage'.

224 *To My Unknown Warrior*, 25–6.

225 For an excellent discussion of these issues, see Adrian M. Gregory, *The Silence of Memory: Armistice Day, 1919–1946* (Oxford, 1994).

226 'The Unknown Warrior', *The Times*, 11 November 1920, 15, and 'In the Abbey', *The Times*, 12 November 1920, ii (Supplement).

227 'The Editorial', *The Times*, 11 November 1920, 15.

228 David Railton, 'The Origin of the Unknown Warrior's Grave', *Our Empire*, VII (November 1931), 36, and John Hundevad, 'The Unknown Warrior', *The Legionary*, XXX.3 (August 1955), 20–1.

Photographic Acknowledgements

The author and publishers wish to express their thanks to the following sources of illustrative material and/or permission to reproduce it: Fotek, Bath: no. 54; Bristol Records Office: no. 8; Whybrow, Birmingham: no. 9; British Library, London: nos 3, 4, 7, 13, 17, 27, 35, 36, 43, 45, 52, 57, 59, 60 and 61; Imperial War Museum, London: nos 5, 11, 12, 14, 15, 16, 20, 28, 29, 30, 31, 32, 34, 35, 36, 37, 38, 39, 40, 41, 42, 44, 46, 50, 55, 62, 63, 65 and 66; The Wellcome Institute Library, London: nos 1, 2, 6, 10, 19, 25, 26, 33, 47, 48, 58 and 64; Manchester City Archives: no. 21; Stearn: no. 58.

Index